THE MEMOIRS OF
SIR SIDNEY SMITH

THE MEMOIRS OF
SIR SIDNEY SMITH

by

EDWARD HOWARD

VOLUMES I & II

Fireship Press
www.FireshipPress.com

The Memoirs of Sir Sidney Smith

Copyright © 2008 by Fireship Press

ISBN-13: 978-1-934757-10-9
ISBN-10: 1-934757-10-1

BISAC Subject Headings:

BIO008000	BIOGRAPHY & AUTOBIOGRAPHY / Military
HIS027150	HISTORY / Military / Naval
HIS015000	HISTORY / Europe / Great Britain

This work is based on the 1839 edition of the *Memoirs of Sir Sidney Smith* by Edward Howard and published originally by Richard Bentley, London.

1.0

CONTENTS OF VOLUME ONE

CONTENTS OF VOLUME TWO

VOLUME ONE

CHAPTER I

INTRODUCTORY REMARKS • THE CHIVALRIC CHARACTER OF SIR SIDNEY SMITH BRIEFLY NOTICED • A SUCCINCT ACCOUNT OF HIS FAMILY • AN ANECDOTE INDICATIVE OF HIS FUTURE CHARACTER.

IT has always been the heaviest calamity attendant upon mankind, that war has supplied the world with its great men and its heroes. History has afforded us a record of ten conquerors, and men strong in battle, for one just and good man. Such is our natural depravity, that the same remark may be applied, up to the recorded advent of our Saviour, to the Holy Scriptures themselves. It is true that Christianity has pointed out to us other and better glories than those obtained by the waste of human blood, and the woe and wail of war. But this God-born revelation has been too often heard only to be scoffed at and disregarded. Still worse, it has many times been made the plea for slaughter and the defence of atrocities, in unlimited murder, the most revolting. Men have ever looked upon carnage as the royal road and the short cut to glory.

This being the case, it necessarily follows that the pursuits of war will hold out the most temptation to the ambitious and those conscious of much talent. The competition for military pre-eminence will always be great, and those who may be so fortunate as to obtain that pre-eminence must consequently be found to possess some great superiority over the rest of those who are striving in the same race, though this superiority seldom amounts to real greatness, even in the false worldly sense—in the true, philosophical, and Christian, scarcely ever.

Let it not be thought that we undervalue the great natural talents and the high and extensive acquirements that are necessary to form the successful and accomplished commander. They certainly are of the broad, the open, and the palpable order. Though they are not veiled in the highest heaven of philosophic contemplation, or require to be brought from the deepest mines of thought and mental abstraction, yet must they be of that sound, sterling, and well working nature that a strong mind alone can master a clear one employ them. We detest war—yet, with the general feeling, we admire the warrior.

We have commenced with this somewhat deprecatory introduction, lest hereafter, being carried away by our admiration of the military character of the subject of these Memoirs, we should be thought, in our enthusiasm, to wish to place him in a rank too elevated among those who have achieved for themselves the title of "Great." All our panegyric must be listened to with a reference to classes of greatness far beyond the reach of the mere warrior.

And, beyond the laurels of the mere warrior, Sir Sidney Smith has won for himself a meed of which no vast desolator or wholesale conqueror can boast. With the prominent heroes, of whatever time, ancient or modern, a well-regulated mind hardly can be brought to sympathise. We admire and shudder. We look upon them as sublime calamities. These fiery scourges in the hands of Providence seem to be so far above or beyond our human affinities, that we can barely entertain with them one feeling in unison. Were they, or any one of them, living, and within the reach of our every-day communion, were it not for the impulse of vanity, we should never think of offering them our friendship, exposing to them our amiable weaknesses, or of seeking from them an interchange of familiar thoughts. Of their countenance we might be proud, and their approbation we might covet, but of their affection we should never dream.

With this class, neither in the multitude of his victories, nor in vastness of any one conquest, can Sir Sidney Smith be associated. But a higher degree of praise, a more lofty because a better honour, is due to him. In his person, though he has not revived the age of chivalry, he has shown what is the real splendour of the chivalric character. All his public actions seem to have been less the offspring of mere military calculation and naval science, than of the intuition of the most romantic courage and the highest moral feeling, always controlled by a prudence and intrepidity that no danger, however sudden, could surprise, and no difficulty, however menacing, vanquish. That such is the principal feature of his character the following pages will fully exemplify.

The prepossession in favour of good blood should not be regarded as a prejudice. We should not deny to the human what is conceded to the other animal races. This is less a moral than a mere physical question, though the results are most conspicuously and best shown in moral action. Revelation teaches us, and we devoutly conform to the lesson, that, in the eye of the Omnipotent, all men are equal. This is in a religious sense. But we know that, in a worldly view, not only are all men the one differing from the other, but the races of men show a distinction still more marked. William Sidney Smith possesses the advantage of good blood in a very high degree.

Sir Sidney Smith is a collateral and no very remote relative to the late Lord Chief Baron Sir Sidney Stafford Smithe, and of the SMYTHE Lord Viscount Strangford. These are descendants from Customer Smith, who flourished in the reign of Queen Elizabeth. Consequently, the ancient and genuine orthography of the name is Smythe; but as the subject of this biography has always in his official documents spelt his name SMITH, and as in that spelling the augmentation to his family arms has been granted, to it we shall consequently adhere. Unfortunately, we have no means of ascertaining for what reason or at what time this orthography was changed. It is of but small moment in itself, though, to the antiquarian and the genealogist, it may appear of paramount importance.

That the change is of some antiquity, is evident by the following inscription upon a large gravestone among the pavement in the nave of the church of New Shoreham. It is an epitaph to the memory of Sir Sidney's grandfather, and runs thus:

Here lieth
The Body of CORNELIUS SMITH,
Who served his King, Country, and Friend.
Faithful and honourable, he was an indulgent Husband,
A kind Father, and friendly to his Acquaintance:
Who died, much lamented, the 28th of October, 1727,
Aged 66 Years.

This Cornelius Smith was the father of Captain Edward Smith, of the Burford, who was mortally wounded at the attack of La Guira, Feb. 19th, 1743, and grandfather of General Edward Smith, colonel of the 43rd Regiment, and governor of Fort Charles, Jamaica. This gentleman served with the hero Wolfe at the reduction of Quebec, and died at Bath on the 19th of January 1809.

Sir Sidney Smith is a nephew of this General Smith, and a son of this general's younger brother. Sir Sidney's father served in the early part of the war of 1756, as aide-de-camp to the Right Honourable Lord George Sackville, and afterwards held an office in the royal household. Sir Sidney's mother was a Miss Mary Wilkinson, daughter of Pinkney Wilkinson, Esq., a very opulent merchant.

From the riches of his maternal grandfather Sir Sidney Smith derived but little benefit, as his father having married in opposition to the wishes of Mr. Wilkinson, and for other reasons that will be afterwards alluded to, the vast property left by that gentleman was devised to his other daughter, Lady Camelford.

There seem to have been great causes of mutual dissatisfaction between Sir Sidney's father and maternal grandfather, as, the former having withdrawn his sons from the protection of the latter, the old gentleman, some little time previous to his death, cancelled a codicil to his will, by which, notwithstanding the little harmony that subsisted between him and his son-in-law, he had made some provision for his grandchildren.

By this daughter of Mr. Wilkinson the father of Sir William Sidney Smith had three sons and no daughter whatever. The eldest of these sons, now Colonel Charles Douglas Smith, is still living, enjoying his well-earned honours and great affluence, acquired by long and meritorious services in the East Indies. Colonel Smith first entered the army in a regiment raised by Lord Suffield. This gentleman has a son in the Exchequer Office.

The second son, William Sidney Smith, who was born in Park Lane, Westminster, we believe towards the close of the year 1764, is the subject of these Memoirs.

John Spencer Smith, the third and youngest son, procured the appointment of page to Queen Charlotte, and so well recommended himself in that capacity, and so highly were his general talents appreciated, that he was sent on a mission of great importance to the court of Wurtemberg. He afterwards travelled to Constantinople, and it is confidently believed that he there converted to Christianity and subsequently married, a Turkish lady of high rank and of great wealth. As will be seen in the course of these pages, he was ultimately of the greatest service to Sir Sidney Smith in all his operations in Egypt, and as our minister at the Ottoman court preserved and increased the good understanding that then subsisted between a government so fastidious and inconstant and ourselves. He is now in the enjoyment of a well-earned pension.

We have already briefly adverted to the loss to William Sidney and his brothers of their fair proportion of the grandfather's vast fortune. That this loss has been to them a blessing rather than an injury, the success in life of them all, and the splendid career of one of them, most fully prove. It appears to us that Sir Sidney's father was treated rather harshly throughout the course of these unhappy disagreements. It is a most invidious task to attach anything approaching to censure on any of the progenitors of this distinguished family. We will hastily pass over these occurrences, as they do not appear to have greatly influenced the fortunes of Sir Sidney Smith. Let it be sufficient to mention, that the angry grandfather, owing to some representations made to him by his daughter, removed his three sons from under the care and fostering protection of the father, when they were receiving the first rudiments of their education under the celebrated Mr. Knox of Tunbridge, and caused them to be placed at a boarding-school in Bath, kept by a Mr. Morgan. That Mr. Wilkinson possessed the power thus cruelly to divide the sons from their father, arose out of the circumstances of his being able to withhold from his son-in-law a very great proportion of his not too abundant income. That he could do this neither justly nor legally, a verdict of an English jury subsequently determined:—that he did it with impunity, for some years, is certain.

When William Sidney Smith was between the age of eleven and twelve, Captain Smith, no longer able to bear this unnatural separation, and his yearning to have them under his own care and protection, took away, clandestinely we believe, his three sons from the school at which they had been placed, to his house at Midgham. This commendable and parental act was visited upon him by an attempt to straiten him in his pecuniary resources. The indignant father appealed to the laws of his country, and his conduct was vindicated by obtaining the costs, and heavy damages against his persecutors.

We do not lay much stress upon the opinion that the future man may be indicated by the predilections of the infant; indeed, experience, would rather teach us another doctrine; but as many very sensible persons like to reduce everything to a system, we will, for their satisfaction, and for the amusement of others, relate a puerile anecdote that strongly displayed young Smith's predilection for aquatic exploits; indeed, that at that unjudging age he loved them better than praying—a very singular depravity, but which, we trust, will be forgiven to him in consideration of his extreme youth.

When William Sidney's father had abducted (for it was in reality an abduction) his children from their boarding-school at Bath, he removed with them to his seat at Midgham in Berkshire. The mansion had been built by Captain Smith's father, and the extensive grounds surrounding it were laid out with great taste. Among the other accessories to the beauty of the place was a large piece of deep water, which immediately attracted the almost undivided attention of the embryo admiral—almost, we say, for even then he showed symptoms of that refined and graceful gallantry to the softer sex that has always marked his character. In fact, he divided his attention with a tolerable impartiality between a young lady of his own age, (eleven years,) this piece of water, and a large washing-tub.

It was the custom of Captain Smith to summon all his household to prayer every evening, and they were called together, in a kind of patriarchal fashion, by the sounding of a horn. One summer's evening the horn was blown the usual number of times; but to the customary blast no William Sidney appeared. The father grew alarmed, and, as his fears arose, so did the echoes of the horn upon the evening breeze. The young absentee heard the holy summons plainly enough, but he did not obey it, solely because he could not.

His non-appearance had caused great alarm, and the evening devotions were postponed in order that the household might search for the lost and beloved son. He was at length found in a situation extremely nautical, but agreeable only to himself. He had embarked in the large washing-tub his youthful protegée, and taking a long pole, he had contrived, by its means, to place his circular ship, with himself and passenger, in the very centre of the large and deep water. We know very well, upon the best authority, which is that of the nursery, that, when seven wise men went to sea in a bowl, they made a very foolish expedition of it; we must not, therefore, greatly blame young Smith when we relate that by some inadvertence, probably a slight attention to the young lady, the companion of his dangers, he lost his pole.

Unfortunately, just as his alarmed father arrived, it fell calm, and the only motion the tub had was that unpleasant one of the pillory, going slowly round and round. There stood the future hero of many fights, with his arms folded in a manner that reminds one now of the prints of Napoleon on the Island of St. Helena.

Those on shore were totally at a loss how safely to bring the frail vessel with its precious charge on shore, for a very little shifting or tottering would have overturned it. None of the spectators could swim, and night was drawing on apace, when, to add to the dismal nature of the scene, William Sidney's companion began to wail most bitterly. Indeed, the situation of the children became critical, if not dangerous. It fell, however, to the lot of him who had created, to unravel the difficulty. Having sufficiently enjoyed the glory of his situation, (he was always a little fond of display,) he hailed those on shore, and told them to fasten the string of his kite to a favourite dog that belonged to him. This being done, he called him to the tub, and thus conveyed a towing line on board the first craft that he had the honour of commanding.

When the tub was brought to the bank of the lake, so nicely fitted was the cargo to the tonnage of the tub, that the children were nearly drowned, because the one was attempted to be taken out a little before the other. The father and one of the servants at length snatched them both out simultaneously, and flung them on the grass. Captain Smith was so much affected that he could not, at first, speak.

"Now, father, we will go to prayers," said the young desperado.

"We had better," he replied, with feelings that a father only can appreciate.

Though this anecdote may be, by some, deemed puerile, we think that it strongly marks the two principal traits of character that Sir Sidney displayed through the whole course of his life—a recklessness in running into danger, and great resources of mind in getting out of it with credit.

It was at Midgham that William Sidney formed some of his most useful and distinguished friendships; among others, the Duke of St. Albans, the Lords Rivers and Delaware, and Lord Rodney, who was a constant visitor, and with whom he first went to sea.

William Sidney Smith did not long remain under the paternal roof, and, during the small time that he enjoyed that advantage and happiness, he was deprived of the soothing attention of one who, on account of those differences so much to be deplored, with her family, was unfortunately living separate from her husband. She did not survive to witness the renown of her sprightly and favourite son, as she passed into a happier state of existence before he returned from his second trip to sea. She died and was interred at Bath.

Those who knew well Sir Sidney Smith in his boyhood, describe him as then being a most vivacious specimen of juvenility—quick, daring, and mercurial, and not far removed from a little Pickle. In his person, though of small size, he was eminently handsome, with clustering and curling black hair, dark clear complexion, and with a high colour. At the earliest age he evinced an utter contempt of danger, and a decision of character, that, under proper training, warranted the most sanguine hopes of future excellence. Among his other qualities, an aptitude for invention, and a power of adaptation of his then limited capabilities, both in the prosecution of his studies and amusements, early displayed themselves. He was a boy for whom you might fear a little, whom you could not help loving much, arid whom you must admire entirely.

CHAPTER II

Sir Sidney's first entrance into the Navy • Some reflections on the early appointments of that period • His various juvenile services until he was made Post Captain.

WE have now to introduce our young subject upon that arena that was afterwards to prove the scene of exploits that elevated the already-exalted naval fame of his country to a still loftier glory, and where he entwined the military with the naval laurel in the triumphal crown that he threw at the feet of England's Genius of Victory.

Long before his little feet had mimicked the officer-stride on the deck of a man-of-war, he had, in his infant imagination, commanded, fought, and conquered. His thoughts, his dreams, his short moments of seriousness, and his long hours of playfulness, were all devoted to fighting the French. He seemed to have been born with, and nurtured in, an antipathy to that nation, with which fate had ordained that he should pass the greatest portion of his life, either as their battling enemy, their impatient prisoner, or their welcome guest. He appears, in his earliest youth, to have been a merry and graceful parody of one of the young Hannibals. The French—the French—he would annihilate them! His puerile antipathies ripened into a very disastrous though gallant and no longer prejudiced opposition to that nation, which he commenced by hating, and finished by beating and respecting.

His father being gentleman usher to Queen Charlotte, and enjoying much of her personal favour, the reader must not be surprised, considering how naval matters were managed at that period, to learn that little Smith strutted a midshipman on board of the Sandwich, under Lord Rodney, before he was twelve years of age.

It would be a difficult matter successfully to defend appointments of this description by argument—or rather, that which we might produce as arguments, would no longer be considered as such in these march-of-mind-boasted days. All that we can do, is to imitate that shrewd person, who, when a very learned philosopher was strenuously arguing that there could not, by possibility, be any such thing as motion, merely got up and walked across the room. To those who condemn these boyish appointments as contrary to justice and subversive of the service, we shall perhaps admit their reasonings to be unanswerable without being in the least convincing, and content ourselves with mentioning the glory of, in this respect, the unreformed navy, and pointing to such names as those of Duncan, Jervis, Nelson, and, last though not least among them, Sir Sidney Smith, who all entered the service about the same age.

Improper, perhaps, as at heart we acknowledge these appointments to be, we must now introduce him, stiff in his uniforms, with his shrill treble pipe imitating the hoarse tones of command, and shaking off the schoolboy a little before he could gracefully creep into the seemliness and importance of the officer and the man. However, he showed an astonishing precocity in his metamorphosis; and, long before other lads had divested themselves of the fear and the tyranny of the ferula and the rod, he had already become respectable as a friend, and something to be dreaded as an enemy among men.

From reports to which we can safely give credit, we find that he was universally beloved on board the Sandwich, and almost immediately drew upon himself the favourable notice of his superior officers.

In the very subordinate capacity of a midshipman—and he was a very young midshipman in his first ship—it cannot be expected that he could perform any feat worthy of record. In this situation he had to learn the first and the most distasteful duty—to obey. Comparatively speaking, his post was a private, and certainly an obscure one, and hardly any naval combination of circumstances, however stirring they might have been, could then have put him prominently forward.

From the Sandwich he passed into the Greyhound in the same rank, gaining thus experience in two very different classes of vessels. During the period of his service in this latter ship, nothing occurred to him that demands a place in this biography.

Immediately that he had served the time allotted by the rules of the navy, he obtained his commission as lieutenant on the 22nd of May, 1781, and was, what is technically called, "made" into the Alcide 74, at that time commanded by Captain C. Thompson.

In this last-mentioned line-of-battle ship he shared in the action of Admiral Graves off the Chesapeake; and though no opportunity was offered to him in that affair eminently to distinguish himself in the limited sphere in which he was compelled to act, he did that which English seamen have ever done—his duty.

Those conversant with the naval history of the country, must well remember the many indecisive skirmishes that took place between Lord Howe and the Count de Grasse, in the seas near the island of St. Christopher's, in the West Indies. At this period, the weather-gage was considered almost as a gage of victory, and hostile fleets would consume days in endeavouring to gain it. The French count took advantage of this prejudice; and when the English admiral bore down upon the French fleet, the line of the latter would discharge its raking broadside, bear up, and run to leeward, and again forming the line, have recourse to the same tactics. By means of this slippery manoeuvre, this particular action consisted of nothing but numerous and indecisive skirmishes. It gave Sir Sidney a lesson that he remembered in his after life, and it was one by which English commanders profited in succeeding encounters.

It does not fall within the scope of our undertaking to record the victories of the naval chiefs under whom our officer had the good fortune to act in a subordinate capacity. We have merely to mention them to show that the extent of his services justified his very rapid promotion, notwithstanding his very early youth.

He participated in the gallant Sir George B. Rodney's glorious victory of the 1st of April, 1782, and, immediately subsequent to this splendid event, he obtained his commission, bearing date 2nd of May, 1782, as commander, and was appointed to the Fury sloop of war, having served as a lieutenant less than one year.

In the next year, 1783, he was made post captain, an exceedingly rapid, and a not strictly regular, promotion—a rapidity of advancement that can only be accounted for by his father's interest at court, and justified by Sir Sidney's great merit. He was a post captain at the juvenile age of nineteen, having served as a commander only one year and five days.

With this promotion he obtained the command of the Alcmene, a small class frigate of twenty eight guns; and as a short and deceitful though a profound peace had appeared to have hushed up the angry feelings of the European powers, he returned to England, and on his arrival his ship was immediately paid off.

Now, with the certainty of life, was the certainty of the highest honours of his noble profession assured to him. Without meaning the imbecility of a pun, before he had reached his majority as a civilian, as a naval officer he ranked with a full colonel in the army. The minor man was a full post. He had passed, when in the eye of the law he was only considered as an infant, as a warrior entitled to the command of hundreds of men, those difficult, and too often impassable portals which open to that path, which requires only time to guide the fortunate traveller to the high station of admiral of the red. Truly may it be said of Sir Sidney, that he possessed, in an eminent degree, that (by the Romans) much venerated attribute in a commander, good luck; and it was happy for his country, and glorious to our hero, that he possessed merits equal only to his brilliancy of accident.

On his return to England he found his worthy parent residing at Carrington-street, May Fair; and though, as yet, he had not graven his name deeply on the tablets of fame, he had signalised himself sufficiently to make all connected with him proud to own him as an acquaintance, friend, or relation. His father, at this period, seemed to exist but for his favourite son; every indulgence was his that he could bestow, and much more excellent advice was at his son's service than he chose to receive. It must be confessed that at this time he fell in with the gaieties of his station, and the opportunities that were offered him in the best metropolitan society, but in a manner neither vicious nor outrageous. With the exception of some few passages of love, with which our biography has nothing to do, he might be pronounced at this period of his life a rather staid young man.

CHAPTER III

WITH increasing ardour for a profession in which he had already given
so great a promise of future excellence, and impatient of a life of inactivity, our officer, in 1788, upon a prospect of a rupture between Sweden
and Russia, with a generous sympathy for the party which appeared to be
the weaker, entered into the naval service of the former.

His distinguished bravery and very superior naval science drew upon
him the general attention, and purchased for him the gratitude of the
Swedish nation. It was a severe service in stormy regions, and an inclem-
ent climate. Captain Smith had first to discipline before he fought his
crews. In the several severe encounters which proved the more bloody
and disastrous in wreck, on account of the ignorance of the belligerents,
the fleets of the Empress Catherine had bitterly to deplore the assistance
that was brought to their opponents in the person of our officer.

The digression can hardly be thought to be unwarrantable, when it
gives an abstract of some of the encounters between the naval armament
of these rival northern powers. It was in those that Captain Sidney Smith
saw some most severe service, and gained great knowledge and experience in the desperate school of actual fight. We will select from among
these transactions a short account of the battle of the Galleys, which may
not be unacceptable to the admirers of our hero's character.

Just as the stormy April of 1790 was terminating, the grand fleet of
Sweden—for Sweden then had a grand fleet, and was a considerable naval power—under the command of the Duke of Sudermania, consisting of
twenty-three ships of the line and eighteen frigates, sailed from
Carlscrona, in the province of Smaland.

This expedition was well planned. Its pretended object was that of preventing the junction of two divisions of the Russian fleet, one of which was then riding at anchor in the port of Revel, the other in the port of Cronstadt. The real views, however, were much more extensive, being to attack in detail, by first capturing the port of Revel, and destroying the fleet there, when the other division, it was confidently believed, would fall an easy sacrifice.

This design was bravely attempted, but it was not attended with that success that might have been hoped from the strength of the armament, the bravery of the seamen, and the skill and intrepidity of the native and foreign officers employed. The result of the attack brought no tarnish to the glory of those who conducted it.

In most maritime expeditions, and more especially those which are destined to act against fortresses and batteries on shore, the elements may prove the most potential allies, or the most formidable enemies. The truth of this was fully exemplified in this attack upon Revel and the Russian fleet. This fleet, then lying at anchor, consisted of eleven sail of the line, three of which were three-decked ships, and four large frigates. Independently of their own guns, this powerful fleet was defended in a very advantageous manner by numerous batteries in the harbour, and by the fortifications about the town, all of which were mounted with heavy cannon.

The Swedes approached boldly, receiving and returning a tremendous fire. Under all these disadvantages, which became the more apparent as they were the more closely encountered, the Duke continued this desperate attack with unabating intrepidity, and when he was, to all appearance, on the very threshold of success, the wind suddenly changed, and so violent a storm ensued, that his vessels were obliged to close their lower-deck ports, thus rendering the tiers of his heaviest metal useless, and reducing his attacking power by one half.

The adverse hurricane also prevented many of his ships from taking any share in the action whatever, so that, after proving courage, conduct, and good seamanship, he was obliged to return with his fleet, at the moment when the enemy appeared all but defeated.

This was not the extent of his disasters. The wind setting dead in upon the shore, the fury of the elements drove the Prince Charles, of sixty guns, after being dismasted, into the hands of the Russians. The Ricket Stander, of the same force, was wrecked, abandoned, and set fire to by orders of the Duke; and the Valeur, another line-of-battle ship, was drifted on shore, but was afterwards enabled to escape, and get to sea again, by throwing overboard a part of her guns.

Amidst all these misfortunes, it was soon discovered that English officers were on board, and

Captain Sidney Smith in personal command in this discomfited fleet, by the rapidity with which its damages were repaired. On the very next day, such were the zeal and diligence of the Duke of Sudermania, and the commanders under his direction, that the fleet was again under sail a league and a half from Norglon, and so completely repaired from its recent damages, that it waited with impatience to make a second attack. On the 3rd and 4th of June, 1790, two more desperate battles were fought in the Gulf of Wilbourg, in which the party that our hero espoused was again defeated; the Swedes losing seven ships, three frigates, six galleys, and about sixty armed small craft. The Russians also suffered severely. The slaughter, as might reasonably be expected, was particularly fatal to the English officers in the Russian service. In these affairs the point of the utmost danger was the point of honour. Captains Dawson and Trevenor were slain, and Captain Marshall also lost his life on the same occasion. Being mortally wounded, he had the agony, in the bitterness of the hour of death, to see the ship that he had commanded, and the crew that he had disciplined, sink with him, his colours still flying in melancholy defiance. Captains Aikin and Miller were also grievously wounded.

We must premise, that an unsuccessful attempt had been made by the King of Sweden, who commanded in person, to destroy the Russian squadron in Viborg. The approach of the Prince of Nassau, with the Cronstadt division, had already made the position of the Swedes at the entrance of Viborg Bay extremely critical, the more especially as their scarcity of ammunition, and their want of provisions, made their return to their own ports a measure of first necessity.

In this situation of affairs, the king resolved to avail himself of a strong easterly wind, which set in on the 3rd of June, to gain Swerksund and Sweaborg. It was necessary for the fleet to penetrate through a narrow pass, and, in so doing, to sustain the fire of four Russian ships of the line, two of which were placed on each side of the strait; and, after this, to engage the whole of Admiral Tschitcshakoff's line, which, at a small distance, was drawn up along the coast, while his frigates were ranged and judiciously placed among the islands which lie nearer the shore.

Unappalled by this display of superior force, the Swedish van, led on by Admiral Modée, passed the Narrows without suffering any material loss, firing with great spirit both broadsides at the same time against the enemy on either side, The cannonade from the four Russian line-of-battle ships was, however, so powerful, and so well supported, that it was resolved by the Duke of Sudermania to attempt their destruction by fireships; but this operation proved so unsuccessful, that they were driven back upon two of his own fleet, a ship of the line and a frigate, both of which were blown up.

The Swedish admiral, instead of having recourse to so uncertain an experiment as fireships, should have placed a vessel of equal force alongside each of these Russian vessels, and having thus masked their fire, the smaller vessels could have passed up the centre of the strait in absolute safety, and then the protecting ships could have followed, forming an excellent protective rear-guard. The unfair means of war by fire-vessels was then much in vogue, but now we are happy to say that among civilised nations their employment is generally condemned, and their utility disallowed.

The Swedes being confused in a considerable degree, by this peculiarly distressful accident, the ships that were to follow were unable to proceed with the requisite order and circumspection; four of them struck upon the rocks, and were thus left at the mercy of the enemy.

During the further course, along the coast, of this bewildered navy, already so diminished in force, three more vessels of the line surrendered to the Russian flag. This engagement, so ill fought as to nautical manoeuvring, yet so well contested as to personal bravery, continued all night and a part of the next day, and it was not until the evening that the duke, with the shattered remains of his fleet, found safety in the port of Sweaborg, leaving three line-of-battle ships and one frigate in the hands of the Russians, the same number of line-of-battle ships and one frigate stranded on the Russian shores, and witnessing the destruction of another ship of the line and another frigate by fire, besides losing a schooner and a cutter, supposed to have been sunk.

The small craft taken or sunk were supposed to amount to sixty, and with the galleys eight hundred men of the Swedes were captured. The whole loss of the Swedes in this affair was above seven thousand men. To add to these disasters, all the baggage of the fleet, amounting in value to several millions of dollars, fell into the hands of the Russians.

In this protracted encounter, our young officer, whilst he shared in the danger, must have gained an admirable lesson in naval warfare. Every possible variety of circumstance must have been presented to him, and from the alternate success and discomfiture of the belligerents he must have acquired a deep insight into all the strategy of maritime war. The lesson was deeply traced and largely written in blood, and after-exploits proved that it had not been studied in vain.

Captain Sidney Smith had at that period but little respite: he was soon to witness a repetition of the same scene, but with happier results to the cause in which he had engaged.

Though the events of the actions of the 3rd and 4th of June were thus unfortunate to the Swedes, his Majesty was in a short time able to reappear at sea in so effective a condition as not only again to contend for victory, but also to obtain ample compensation for his former losses.

Having supplied his armament with provisions and ammunition, and being joined by the division under Lieutenant-Colonel Cronstadt, which had not been able to reach the Bay of Viborg, so as to participate in the late engagement, the king sailed immediately, with a view to prevent the Prince of Russia, who was advancing with the Russian Cronstadt and Viborg squadrons, from getting into the port of Frederickham. This he was so fortunate as to accomplish.

In consequence of this proceeding, an action took place on the 9th of July, in which the king commanded in person nominally—Sidney Smith actually, who was at the royal elbow during the whole of the engagement. It began at half-past nine in the morning, and lasted twenty-four hours.

On the preceding day, several vessels of the Russian in-shore squadron were discovered at Aspo; on which the king, attended by M. de Armstadt, went to reconnoitre. On the 9th, the Prince of Nassau advanced towards the Swedish shore, and the signal was made for the Swedish fleet to arrange itself in order of battle. By nine in the morning, the enemy had formed his line, and made sail towards Cape Musalo. The right wing of the Swedes advanced to meet them, and the firing commenced briskly on both sides.

Immediately after, the king, on board the Seraphim galley, made the signal for a general attack. The enemy still approached with a spirited fire, which was so warmly returned by both the Swedish wings, that at noon the left of the enemy began to give way. Both the right and left of the Swedes being reinforced by several divisions which had been previously placed in the Sound, they were enabled to continue the action with increased vigour. At the same time, the Russian line having received some reinforcements, the eastward wing again advanced and returned to the conflict.

But their renewed endeavours were in vain. About four o'clock in the afternoon some of their larger galleys were beaten from the land, and struck their colours. Of those, several afterwards foundered, and several were taken possession of by the Swedes.

Gustavus was not absolutely without loss himself. One of his best galleys, the Udema, caught fire about six o'clock and sank; but happily the whole of her crew was saved. The same fate befel one of the Russian xebecs, and after this the smaller vessels began to sheer off.

Many of the enemy's heavy galleys continued firing till the evening, and then made sail with a view of effecting their escape. Some ran on the shoals and struck their flags. At eleven, darkness compelled a cessation of hostilities. The conquered vessels were taken possession of, and the prisoners removed.

As early as three next morning the cannonade was renewed, and shortly after, one of the Russian frigates surrendered, and several of the smaller craft were taken. The enemy then commenced retreating in every direction, and to set fire to their stranded ships. They were pursued till ten at night, arid forty-five captured. Out of the Russian vessels that were sunk, one officer and one surgeon only were saved. Six of the stranded vessels were burned by the Swedes. The victors computed the number of their prisoners at four thousand five hundred, including two hundred and ten officers.

Thus, in this action, after having for so long a period trembled upon an equality, whilst thousands on both sides were passing to judgment, the scales of victory inclined towards Gustavus. The Russians, in their turn, suffered a defeat, with the loss of five frigates, fifteen galleys, two floating batteries, with twenty other vessels, and, a great quantity of naval and military stores; and, as before mentioned, four thousand five hundred prisoners were also captured.

On this memorable occasion, an English officer of the name of Dennison commanded the Russian frigate Venus, and, by his presence of mind and gallantry, very nearly effected the capture of the King of Sweden's sacred person, as he gained possession of the galley in which that monarch had embarked.

Captain Smith, who was with the sovereign, observing the gallant and seaman-like style in which the Venus was bearing down upon the galley, became assured that she must be under the command of an Englishman, and suggested to the king that it was high time for them to look out for their mutual safety; an advice not at all to be disregarded under the pressing nature of the contingency. The king, being fully conscious of his imminent danger, shuffling off his royal dignity for the nonce, like a very prudent j and private individual, conveyed himself and his adviser into a small boat that was lying alongside, and pulled off to another and a safer vessel.

The non-nautical reader may suppose, that, in this instance, the future hero of Acre showed abundantly that better part of valour named "discretion." So he did; and without at all impugning his valour in the abstract, it must be understood that the galley was nothing more than a sort of great row-boat, as little able to contend, vessel to vessel, with a frigate, as a minnow with a pike. The gallantry and seaman-like conduct of Dennison were not displayed in the taking of this galley, but in his making his way to her, by breaking through the greatly superior obstructing force.

This noble fellow was killed on the same day.

Let us pause, for a moment, in the course of our narrative, and attempt an apology for Sir Sidney Smith, and those of his brave countrymen who degraded themselves to mercenaries in a quarrel, on opposite sides, in which they could have had no patriotic, and hardly a public interest. Humanity requires one, and the enlightenment of the present day will let nothing pass as a justification that will not bear the test of a sound morality.

If biography be something only to extol that which is commendable, and to gloze over faults, and palliate that which is discreditable, it is a species of writing that cannot too soon become extinct. That, lately, memoirs have partaken of this nature, is lamentably true. When written in this manner, they become to the rising generation false guides and lying finger-posts. They are painted all white, on which dark letters of instruction are nowhere to be seen.

We have just described Englishman opposed to Englishman, fellow-subject to fellow-subject; and in this almost suicidal contest we see the country deprived of some of its most gallant defenders, the king of some of the best supporters of his crown, families of their fathers, and the ornaments and the nourishers of social circles ruthlessly destroyed. The picture is true, and, the more nearly examined, as it is true so is it re-volting.

For acts like these, the fervour of youth cannot be pleaded; youth, far more prone to act than to reflect, yet, in numerous cases, as well as age, must deliberate. The drawing the sword for a foreign potentate, even in the youngest, must be an act of deliberate calculation. The responsibility, therefore, must remain upon the mercenary's conscience.

In the case before us, neither party of the English belligerents could have been influenced to shed the blood of each other on the score of phi-lanthropy, or in advocacy of the cause of the human race. Liberty was not then fully appreciated anywhere, and nowhere so little as among the people of the two nations that were opposed to each other.

We will not suppose, for a moment, that these gentlemen embarked in this quarrel, on different sides, for their private emolument. Hired gladiatorship, however highly it may have been estimated on the conti-nent, has never yet been the naturalised occupation of the English. It would therefore appear that, the more we examine this question, the greater, we find, are the difficulties that surround it, and the more spe-cious are the fallacies by which a justification must be attempted. In fact there is no justification, in the broad and general point of view, for either party of the English officers that were thus unnaturally opposed to each other. On this point we insist, for the sake of religion, for the sake of hu-manity, for the sake of patriotism. We speak thus decidedly, in order that our feeble voice may impress upon the youth of the present and of the future day, that it is a crime against God and against man to draw the sword of the slayer in any other save their country's cause.

As to the apology of our hero at finding him in the predicament that we have thus strongly condemned, the one that we are going to produce will be thought weak upon the general merits, but powerful as applicable to Sir Sidney's individual case. Let the reader always remember that we offer an apology, not a defence. This apology consists in his thirst for dis-tinction, in his passionate love of glory, merging in and displaying them-selves in an unquenchable zeal for the honour of his country. It was this that led him into the error, not an error of the heart but of calcula-tion—an error to which people of chivalrous characters are peculiarly liable.

Sir Sidney Smith continued to serve the King of Sweden with great advantage to that prince, and reputation to himself, until the peace of Riechenback, and, for his eminent services, was rewarded with the grand cross of the order of the Sword.

That his splendid, yet we think misplaced services, were not regarded with the stern view of the moralist by our own government of that period, is evident, by his own sovereign conferring upon him the additional hon-our of an English knighthood, at St. James's.

CHAPTER IV

ENTERS THE TURKISH SERVICE • FITS OUT A MAN-OF-WAR AT HIS OWN
RISK • GETS A REINFORCEMENT OF SEAMEN AT SMYRNA • JOINS LORD
HOOD AT TOULON • SOME ACCOUNT OF THE TRANSACTIONS AT THAT
PLACE.

IMPATIENT of the inactivity of peace, and despising the blandishments
and dissipation of fashionable society, his mind could find sustenance
and satisfaction only in the bustle and excitement of actual service. We
find him, therefore, in 1793, serving as a volunteer in the Turkish marine,
and, when thus employed, he happened to be at Smyrna when the war
broke out with France. This intelligence was to him like the sound of the
trumpet to the war-horse. Whether he had received the usual notice from
the Admiralty, issued on similar occasions, we know not—to Sir Sidney it
would have been of little moment. Nothing now occupied his thoughts
but the best and most advantageous method of repairing to his post
among the defenders of his country. His thirst now for the "pomp and
circumstance of war" was a virtue.

In this emergency, his mind always teeming with resources, he determined to repair to England with some advantage to his country. He
came not single-handed. At this time there were several valuable seamen
out of employ at Smyrna. He was resolved that they should not be lost to
his sovereign. Accordingly, at his own risk, he purchased one of the
latteen-rigged, fast-sailing craft of the Archipelago, and with equal humanity and patriotism manned it with these men, who would otherwise
have been, at this critical juncture, lost to the service.

Without the protection of a letter of marque, he shipped himself,
with about forty truculent fellows, in this diminutive man-of-war, and
hoisting the English flag and pennant, he named it the Swallow Tender,
and sailed down the Mediterranean in search of the English fleet, which
he found at Toulon, a short time before the evacuation of that sea-port,
and the destruction of its magazines, dockyard, and arsenals.

It was at this memorable epoch, and on this fatal spot, that Bonaparte first signalised himself. Many and sufficiently accurate are the accounts extant of the siege of this strongly fortified place by the French, when it was temporally held by the combined British and Spanish forces, for the partisans of the Bourbons. It is not our office to enter fully into the operations, or to give a minute detail of the events that led to the calamitous results; but we must give some account of them, the better to understand the position in which Lord Howe found himself, and the English and allied forces co-operating with him. Oppressed, irritated, and almost driven to despair by the multiplied and still multiplying atrocities of the democrats who were then devastating France under the direction of the ferocious Robespierre, the southern sections of that distracted kingdom openly displayed a monarchical feeling. They ardently longed for the peaceful and mild tyranny of the Bourbons.

On the 23rd of August, 1793, commissioners representing the sections of the department of the Rhone went on board the Victory, the flagship of Lord Howe, then lying off Marseilles, expecting to meet commissioners from Toulon, deputed by the sections of the department of Var, for the same purpose—that of recalling Louis XVIII., and re-establishing a monarchical government.

With this view, on the 26th of August, the deputies of all the sections agreed to proposals made by Lord Howe, and signed a declaration which consisted of eighteen articles, investing him, at the same time, personally with the command of the harbour, the forts, and the fleet at Toulon. Lord Howe, having received assurances of the good disposition of the principal part of the officers and seamen of the French ships, resolved to land fifteen hundred men, and take possession of the forts which commanded the ships in the road.

Acting up to this intention, notwithstanding a display of opposition by their Admiral St. Julian, a stanch republican and withal a most turbulent spirit, the honourable Captain Elphinstone, afterwards Lord Keith, at midday on the 28th of August, took possession of the fort of La Malgue.

In pursuance of Lord Hood's directions, he took the command as governor, and sent a flag of truce, with a preparatory notice to St. Julian, that such French ships as did not proceed without delay into the inner harbour, and put their powder on shore, would be treated as enemies. St. Julian, however, was found to have escaped during the night, with the greater part of the crews of seven line-of-battle ships, which were principally attached to him; all but these seven ships removed into the inner harbour in the course of the evening.

The Spanish fleet, under the command of Don Juan de Langaras, appeared in sight as the British troops were in the act of landing to take possession of Fort la Malgue.

Having thus made himself master of Toulon and the adjacent forts, Lord Hood issued, on the same evening, another proclamation which greatly soothed the minds of the inhabitants. The English troops received, on the 29th of August, a reinforcement of one thousand men, who were disembarked from the Spanish fleet on the same day the British fleet worked into the outer roads of Toulon, followed by the Spanish, and anchored at noon without the smallest obstruction.

The junction of two such powerful fleets, that had often met in fierce contention, but which now rode peacefully in one of the finest harbours in the world, formed a singular and cheerful sight, inspiriting to the loyal inhabitants, and proving to the republicans that they owed their late supremacy more to terror than to affection.

On the 30th of August, Lord Hood judged it expedient, for the more effectual preservation of good order and discipline in the town, to appoint Rear-Admiral Goodall governor of Toulon and its dependencies. This was the more necessary, as a detachment of the republican army, commanded by Casteaux, consisting of seven hundred and fifty men, with some cavalry and ten pieces of cannon, approached the village of Ollioulle, near Toulon.

On this being ascertained, Captain Elphinstone immediately marched out of Fort Malgue at the head of six hundred troops, English and Spanish, and attacking the enemy with great spirit, soon made them abandon their posts, took four of their pieces of cannon with their equipments, many horses, and much ammunition.

Our loss was immaterial. In this attack Captain Elphinstone displayed a knowledge of military tactics which was hardly expected from an officer in the British navy.

On the 6th of September Lord Mulgrave arrived at Toulon, and, at the request of Lord Hood, accepted the command of the British troops, with the rank of brigadier-general, until his Majesty's pleasure should be known. In consequence of the report made by his lordship of the forces that would be requisite to defend the several ports in the vicinity of Toulon, Lord Hood despatched a pressing letter to Sir Robert Boyd, the governor of Gibraltar, requesting fifteen hundred soldiers, with a number of artillery-men, and an able engineer.

By the middle of September our post began to be kept in a constant state of alarm by the continually increasing numbers of Casteaux's army on the west, and that of Italy on the east; each of them consisting of nearly six thousand men. At the same time, Lord Hood had apprehensions that some desperate attempt would be made from within the town by upwards of five thousand disaffected seamen. The committee-general of the sections, and the French royalist Rear-Admiral Trogroffe, represented that to get rid of them was absolutely necessary to the safety of the loyalists. This was the more especially evident, as, previously to Lord Hood taking possession of Toulon, they had agreed that those men should be sent home, provided that they did not take any active part in obstructing the operations of the British fleets. These conditions not yet having been fulfilled, they, in consequence, began to be very clamorous and unruly. All these causes pressing upon the mind of Lord Hood, he judged it expedient to embark them in four of the most unserviceable of the French ships, Le Patriote, L'Apollon, L'Orion, and L'Entreprenant, to each of which a passport was given.

These ships were dismantled of their guns, excepting two on the forecastles of each, to be used as signals in case of distress. They had no small arms, and only twenty ordnance cartridges on board of each ship. They sailed under flags of truce; two for Brest, one for Rochefort, and one for L' Orient.

In addition to the motives just related, which induced Lord Hood thus to act, and strictly adhere to the convention previously formed with the civil and military government of Toulon, there were also others that had a powerful influence on his conduct. Amidst this mass of five thousand seamen, who were reported turbulent and disaffected, many were devoted to the cause of the inhabitants of Toulon, and were ready to make every exertion in favour of monarchy; therefore, as it was confidently rumoured that Brest, Rochefort, and the other seaports of France, would take an active part in the same cause, there was good reason to hope that the arrival of these seamen would accelerate, at the several ports, similar exertions in behalf of Louis XVIII. His Majesty's ships Leviathan and Bedford arrived at Toulon, on the 28th of September, with eight hundred Sardinian troops, and also Marshal Forteguerri, commodore of the Sicilian squadron, with two thousand troops from Naples. This served considerably to cheer the spirits of the garrison, as well as of the Toulonnese, as, for the last fortnight, scarcely a day had passed without an attack upon the town from one quarter or another. Casteaux's army now amounted to eight thousand men on the west, and that on the east, under Le Poype, to seven thousand, with reinforcements continually pouring into both.

The enemy had also opened a battery of twenty twenty-four pounders upon our gunboats, and the ships that covered them; and though they were soon dismounted by the vessels under Rear-Admiral Gell, and the works totally destroyed with very great slaughter, yet the enemy renewed them three successive times, and, to the last moment, persevered in their attacks upon our gunboats and advanced ships.

During the night of the 21st of September, the French, availing themselves of a fog, very unexpectedly surprised a post occupied by the Spaniards, and thus got possession of the height of Pharon, immediately over Toulon; but at noon, on the 1st of October, when in the very act of establishing themselves with about two thousand men, they were attacked by the troops under Lord Mulgrave, and, after a short but spirited action, driven from the height with great slaughter. Many of the flying parties were forced headlong, at the point of the bayonet, over the rocks.

The loss of the allied forces amounted to only seven killed and seventy-two wounded, whilst the French had one thousand four hundred and fifty put *hors de combat*, [Ed. Out of the fight] and forty-one taken prisoners.

The batteries of the French on the Hautier de Ranier were also destroyed in the night of the 8th of October, with a considerable quantity of artillery and ammunition. The ensuing night, Captain Smith, assisted by Lieutenant Scrofield, of the royal navy, and the seamen under their command, made a successful sortie on some batteries recently erected by the enemy, which they completely destroyed. The French, notwithstanding these defeats, obtained possession of Cape le Brun on the 11th, but were again overcome and driven from thence with considerable loss.

Major-General O'Hara and Major-General Dundas arrived on the 22d of October—the former with a commission to be governor of Toulon, with its dependencies. Lord Hood had the mortification to find, at this critical juncture, that Sir Robert Boyd was so sparing of succours for the defence of Toulon, that he had sent from Gibraltar only half the force which had been earnestly requested early in September.

Lord Hood, perceiving his fleet much weakened by the number of the seamen who were sent on shore to defend the forts, found it expedient to despatch a ship to the Grand Master of Malta, requesting that one thousand five hundred Maltese seamen might be sent to serve in the British fleet during its continuance in the Mediterranean, who should have the same rations, treatment, and the same monthly wages, as the British. The Grand Master, in the most handsome manner, furnished the desired reinforcement.

CHAPTER V

ON the evening of the 11th of November, the French, with a large force, vigorously attacked our post upon the heights de Grasse, called Fort Mulgrave, and one of the most essential positions that covered the shipping in the harbour of Toulon. The attack was principally directed on that part of the place which was occupied by the Spaniards on the right. General O'Hara, who was dining on board the Victory, hastened on shore. When he reached the height, he found that the French were close to the works, and the Spaniards in full retreat, firing their muskets in the air. The general instantly directed a company of Royals to advance, who immediately leaped upon the works and put the enemy to flight, after leaving six hundred men dead and wounded upon the field. The loss of the English amounted to sixty-one only.

The British admiral, in addition to what he had already experienced since his taking possession of Toulon, had to undergo a fresh vexation at the end of November, and one, too, of the most serious and alarming nature, considering the augmented force of the surrounding enemy, and the critical situation of the posts to be defended. After having been flattered with the most positive hopes of receiving, towards the middle of this month, five thousand Austrian troops, and when he had actually despatched Vice-Admiral Cosby with a squadron of ships and transports to Vado Bay to convey them, as previously concerted between Mr. Trevor, his Majesty's minister at Tunis, and himself, by letters received from Mr. Trevor on the 18th of November, his lordship's hopes were at once destroyed, and with them all expectation of the arrival of a single Austrian soldier at Toulon.

The enemy, at the close of November, having opened a battery against the fort of Malbosquet near the arsenal, and from which battery shot and shells could reach the town, it was resolved to destroy it, and to bring off the enemy's guns.

For this purpose, General O'Hara digested a distinct and masterly plan of attack, which he communicated, on the evening of the 29th of November, to the commanding officers of the troops of each nation. Accordingly, on the morning of the 30th, this plan was so far executed as to surprise the enemy's redoubt most effectually. The British troops having obtained full possession of the height and battery, their ardour and impetuosity were not to be restrained in this moment of success; but continuing to pursue the flying enemy, in a scattered manner, a full mile beyond the works, the consequence was, that the latter, collecting in great force, in their turn obliged our troops to retreat, and to relinquish the advantages they had at first obtained.

General O'Hara arrived at the battery at the moment it was retaken, and, perceiving the disorder of the troops thus driven back, was hastening to rally them, when, most unfortunately, he received a wound in the arm, which bled so much as to render him incapable of avoiding the enemy, by whom he was made prisoner as he sat down under the shelter of a wall.

Let us see the account that, in his own words, Bonaparte gave of this transaction. "I made General O'Hara prisoner, I may say, with my own hand. I had constructed a masked battery of eight twenty-four pounders and four mortars, in order to open upon the Fort Malbosquet, which was in possession of the English. It was finished in the evening, and it was my intention to have opened upon the English in the morning. While I was giving directions to another part of the army, some of the deputies from the Convention came down. In those days they sometimes took upon themselves to direct the operations of the armies, arid those imbeciles ordered the batteries to commence, which order was obeyed.

"As soon as I saw this premature fire, I immediately conceived that the English general would attack this battery, and most probably carry it, as another had not yet been arranged to support it. In fact, O'Hara, seeing the shot from that battery would dislodge his troops from Malbosquet, from which last I would have taken the fort that commanded the harbour, determined upon attacking it. Accordingly, early in the morning, he put himself at the head of his troops, and actually carried the battery and the lines which I had formed—(Napoleon here drew upon a piece of paper a plan of the situation of the batteries)—to the left, and those to the right were taken by the Neapolitans. While O'Hara was busy in spiking the guns, I advanced with three or four hundred grenadiers, unperceived, through a bog, and covered with olive trees, which communicated with the batteries, and commenced a terrible fire upon his troops. The English, astonished, at first supposed that the Neapolitans, who had the lines upon the right, had mistaken them for French, and said it is those *canaglie* of Neapolitans who are firing upon us; for even, at that time, your troops despised the Neapolitans. O'Hara ran out of the battery and advanced towards us. In advancing, he was wounded in the arm by the fire of a sergeant; and I, who stood at the mouth of the *boyau*, seized him by the coat, and drew him back among my own men, thinking he was a colonel, as he had two epaulets on.

"While they were taking him to the rear, he cried out that he was commander-in-chief of the English. He thought that they were going to massacre him, as there existed a horrible order at that time from the Convention, that no quarter was to be given to the English. I ran up, and prevented the soldiers from ill-treating him. He spoke very bad French, and as I saw he imagined that they intended to butcher him, I did everything in my power to console him, and gave directions that his wound should be immediately dressed, and that every attention should be paid to him. He afterwards begged that I would give him a statement of how he had been taken, in order that he might forward it to his government in his justification."

Though we are not among those who give more implicit credence to all the conversational statements of Bonaparte than we do to his state documents, we believe his version of the transaction to be the right one. The previous description of this misfortune is compiled from the documents furnished to our government. We do not think them rigidly, though they may be essentially, correct. For the glory of the English army, we would rather place Bonaparte's account upon the records of our history. We will not suppose that the English troops were so undisciplined as to pursue a flying enemy in a disorderly manner for more than a mile, not only without orders, but against the will of their officers. It is very *ad captandum* to the misjudging public to represent the French flying before the English, even though it ended in the discomfiture of the latter. Still less can we credit that the commander-in-chief would join in so wild a sally, and upon so trifling an occasion. The real facts were, that the English had surprised their enemies, and were, in their turn, themselves surprised.

We dwell thus long upon these affairs, firstly, because Sir Sidney certainly bore in them the most conspicuous, and performed the most useful part. Without his exertions, it will be immediately seen, that from this fierce contest we should not have plucked a single laurel wherewith to console us for our defeat; and secondly, we wish to place the odium of this cruel, momentous, and disastrous defeat, upon those who were, undoubtedly, its cause.

At this time the French army before Toulon amounted to forty thousand men, and after the surrender of Lyons, considerable as it already was, it became augmented daily. The army of the coalesced powers never exceeded twelve thousand, and even these were composed of five different nations, speaking five different languages; consequently not well formed to co-operate the one with the other. Of the actual British, there were never more than two thousand three hundred and sixty. The circumference necessary to be occupied for the complete defence of the town extended fifteen miles, with eight principal posts, and several immediate dependencies. It will naturally excite astonishment that the place could be held for so long a time as seven weeks,

Early on the 17th of December, Fort Mulgrave, on the height La Grasse, was stormed by an immense body of the enemy, after having kept up an incessant fire upon it, with shot and shells, for four-and-twenty hours. As usual, the right, occupied by the Spaniards, soon gave way, by which means the French entered the works, and got entire possession of the height. At the same time they attacked and carried the heights of Pharon, immediately over Toulon.

Things were now growing to a crisis. A council of war, that sure herald of discomfiture, was summoned, and it was determined to evacuate a place that could be no longer held.

The Spanish admiral, Langara, undertook to destroy the ships in the inner harbour or basin, and to scuttle and sink the two powder-vessels, which contained all the powder belonging to the French ships, as well as that belonging to the distant magazines within the enemy's reach.

The disarray had already begun. The Neapolitans deserted their posts, and stole on board their ships in confusion and disorder; and the next morning, December 18th, the Neapolitan commanding officer at the post of Sepel sent word that there he would no longer remain. The retreat of the British troops and the evacuation, could not therefore be deferred. Accordingly, in the night, the whole of the troops embarked without the loss of a single man, and fourteen thousand eight hundred and seventy-seven men, women, and children, of the royalists of Toulon, were sheltered in the British ships.

It was now Sir Sidney's turn to come into action. By this time, the Republican forces pressed so energetically upon the place, that its final occupation by them seemed to rest entirely with themselves. It therefore became necessary to decide upon the disposition of the French ships in the harbour and on the stocks, and the arsenal then full of military and naval muniments of war; and this too at the very critical moment, when the extrication of the allied army from their dangerous position was the paramount object of solicitude, and just then occupied nearly all the attention, and absorbed all the naval capabilities, of the combined squadrons.

CHAPTER VI

AT the crisis mentioned in the last chapter, Sir William Sidney Smith, having delivered up his troublesome charge to the commander-in-chief Lord Hood, was, as his guest on board of the Victory, then waiting for a passage to England. At this anxious moment he volunteered his services to burn the French fleet, magazines, and everything that could at all be of service to the naval or military equipments of the enemy. This was deemed almost visionary, certainly impracticable with the slender means that could then be afforded to our hero. It was, however, one of those possible impracticabilities in which his genius rejoiced. Against the almost universal opinion, he accomplished the undertaking in a manner that justified his appointment to so forlorn an enterprise—ten ships of the line, and several frigates, in the arsenal and inner harbour, with the mast-house, great storehouse, and other buildings, being completely destroyed.

It is well understood and confessed by all impartial men, that the fortifications surrounding Toulon were, owing to the treachery and imbecility of our allies; ill defended, and the evacuation of the place too long deferred. Had neither of these contingencies happened, the immense naval force, with all its appointments, would have passed over quietly into the possession of the English, and thousands of the royalist Frenchmen saved, who were slain on the republicans taking the place, or who afterwards fell victims to the ruthless guillotine, or the still more ruthless noyades. This was at the acme of the reign of terror.

The proximate cause of this disaster, which spread confusion and almost terror throughout the English fleet, was, as before related, the permitting the enemy to gain possession of an elevated battery, on a point of land that laid open the British naval force to a destructive can-nonade. This post, so commanding, so all-important, was strangely ne-glected by the military; hence all the confusion, disarray, and misery that ensued.

It was the high destiny of Sir Sidney Smith gallantly to remedy some of the consequences of this mistake. Already was a large portion of the enemy in the town; plunder and murder had commenced their savage orgies, and, to increase this infliction upon the distracted inhabitants, the galley-slaves had obtained their liberty, when, with his officers and the few men under his command, and surrounded by a tremendous confla-gration, he found that he had nearly completed his dangerous service.

But little more remained to be done, when the loud shouts and the republican songs of the enemy announced their approach to the spot where Sir Sidney and his small band were spreading around them de-struction. The scene became terrible; for the screams of the wounded, and the roaring and the hissing of the voluminous flames, were drowned, at rapid intervals, by the rattling volleys of musketry, the terrific explo-sion of shells, and the thunder-emulating booming of the artillery. War revelled in rapine, and whilst his feet were saturated with human blood, his many-toned and hideous voice seemed to shake the smoke-obscured firmament.

Whilst all these horrors were enacting, and which seemed even so terrible to the vindictive and exasperated enemy that their progress was, for a space, arrested, a most overwhelming explosion of many thousand barrels of gunpowder, on board of the Iris frigate, lying in the inner road, stunned at once the pursuing and the flying, and inflicted a transient stu-por upon everything then and there living. The solid ground reeled under the unstable foot, and the waves of the sea undulated menacingly as if they would overwhelm the trembling land. The scene could have been likened only to the horrors of an earthquake, combined with a volcanic eruption.

Below were the tottering and falling houses, the crash of glass, and the cries of the maimed and crushed; above was one vast canopy of lurid fire, from which were descending bursting bombs, fragments of burning timber, arid every description of fiery-pointed missiles—the whole inter-spersed with flashes of intense and variously coloured light. Every one near the spot seemed to be threatened with instant destruction.

Fortunately, however, only three of Sir Sidney's party lost their lives on this terrible occasion.

It is a lamentable thing, and history will confirm the assertion, that in all combined movements, where men of different nations have to carry them into effect, the most egregious blunders will ensue. The Spaniards have always been reckoned to be a gallant and brave people—but with more than their share of that parent of all mistakes and misfortunes, ob-stinacy. A party of these self-willed Spaniards, who were too proud fully to consider the purport of their positive and distinct orders, or too treacherous to obey them, were the cause of all this terror and calamity. They were commanded to go and scuttle and sink the powder-laden frigate they went and set fire to her.

Now the reader must understand that, up to this period, Sir Sidney went first into the inner harbour, where he destroyed all the shipping he found there, and afterwards repaired on a similar service on shore to the arsenal. When he had completed the destruction of everything in his reach, to his astonishment he first discovered that our fear-paralysed or perfidious allies had not set fire to any one of the ships then lying in the basin before the town; he therefore hastened thither with his boat, to counteract the treachery or the cowardice of the Spaniards. But he was too late. Already had the republicans gained possession of these vessels; already had the boom been laid across the entrance to the basin; already he found that those but just now defenceless hulks were converted into formidable batteries. He was forced to desist from his endeavours to cut the boom, from the incessant volleys of musketry directed upon his boats from the French flagship and the wall of the royal battery.

Much of the proceedings that followed, and the causes that produced them, must for ever remain enveloped in mystery. Recriminations and charges, many and bitter, have taken place between the English and Spanish, concerning these atrocities. Perfidy and treachery have been openly alleged against our allies. For ourselves, we are rather inclined to suppose that the Spaniards and Italians were so confounded at the novel situation in which they found themselves, that, in doing they knew not what, they left undone that which it was their imperative duty to do, and thus, through their fear-impelled commissions and omissions, they seemed to be treacherous when they were only cowardly.

The grounds of affixing the black stigma of treachery upon the Spaniards are principally these. Early in the occupation of the place, the Spanish admiral communicated to Lord Hood the very bold intelligence that his Catholic Majesty had appointed him, Langara, to be sole commander-in-chief. This, of course, Lord Hood resisted; but whether the treason (if any) sprang from this quarrel, or this quarrel was but the arranged commencement of the treason, we will not pretend to determine. However, the Don took up a very menacing attitude, for he placed his twenty-one ships of the line so that he completely enclosed the British fleet, consisting only of ten, placing his own ship alongside the Victory, and one three-decker on her bow, and another on her quarter.

The next indication of treachery was an insidious proposal to Lord Hood that the combined fleets should depart from Toulon, and make a diversion in favour of Paoli in Corsica, thus leaving the place at the mercy of the Republicans. He then wished to tempt the English admiral away on an expedition against Tunis; and finally endeavoured to raise a quarrel, because some Corsican men-of-war were riding in the roads with their national flag at their mastheads.

Now, when we look at the supineness of the Spaniards, and consider it in reference to the whole course of their proceedings, though we may not fully condemn, yet we certainly must hesitate to acquit them. Unfortunately the spirit of the two antagonist principles of monarchy and democracy ran so high at this time, that the evidence of the writers of that day, even as to the simplest facts, cannot be relied on. A work was published in France, and translated into English, which distinctly stated that Robespierre said, in one of his official despatches, "Arguments of weight, and especially golden arguments, seldom fail of having some effect. The Spanish admirals and generals in the Mediterranean had instructions rather to watch than to act with the English." And also, "It was at one time determined to withdraw the army from before Toulon, and retire on the other side of the Durance; when, fortunately, the Spanish courier arrived, and everything was settled between my brother on our part, and Major S. on the other, with respect to Toulon." This brother was one of the commissioners attached to the army of Toulon. It is still further stated that Robespierre asserted, "The Spaniards, in consequence of this agreement, fled on all sides, (being attacked at an appointed time,) and left the English everywhere to bite the dust; but particularly at a stronghold called by them Fort Mulgrave. The ships which the Spaniards had to burn, they did not set fire to. The British ships had more than one escape at this period. Conformably to the agreement, the Spaniards were to attempt the destruction of some others, by cutting the cables, and by blowing up some old French men-of-war, laden with powder, in the harbour. This, indeed, they did, but too late to cause any damage to the English; and in this instance alone have we any reason to complain of the Spaniards."

Speaking of the conflagration of the ships, Bonaparte himself says, "Sir Sidney Smith set them on fire, and they would have been all burned, if the Spaniards had behaved well. It was the prettiest *feu d' artifice* [Ed. Fireworks] possible."

This dictum certainly goes no farther than a corroboration as to the incapacity of these allies, to assist whom has caused, and is still causing, the loss of so much money, anxiety, and blood.

To return to Sir Sidney Smith's proceedings. Our officer, finding affairs in this critical situation, immediately proceeded to burn, after having liberated the prisoners, the two prison-ships, Le Héros and Thémistocle, which he completely effected. Hardly was this service performed, when he and his gallant little party were astonished by the explosion of the Montreal, another powder-ship, by means equally unexpected and base, and with a shock even greater than that of the former disaster; but the lives of Sir Sidney Smith and the gallant men who were then serving under him were again providentially saved from the imminent danger in which they were so suddenly placed.

Threading a thousand perils, and literally pulling through showers of grape and musketry, the brave band which had thus so much damaged the enemy and served their country, at length reached the Victory in safety. This exploit was the most striking and the most glorious feature of these ill-conducted proceedings. The fame of our officer was commensurately increased. Men began to look up to him as one destined, hereafter, to extend the conquests and uphold the honour of the British empire. From the kindness of his natural disposition, and the amenity of his manners, his successes, great and dazzling as they were, created for him less envy than usually attends transcendent merit. Men of all classes and of all ranks spoke well of him. By the seamen he was all but idolised.

We present our readers with Sir Sidney's despatch on this momentous occasion:

Toulon, Dec. 18. 1793

MY LORD, Agreeably to your lordship's order, I proceeded with the Swallow tender, three English and three Spanish gunboats, to the arsenal, and immediately began making the necessary preparations for burning the French ships and stores therein. We found the dock-gates well secured by the judicious arrangements of the governor, although the dockyard people had already substituted the three-coloured cockade for the white one. I did not think it safe to attempt the securing any of them, considering the small force I had with me, and considering that a contest of any kind would occupy our whole attention, and prevent us from accomplishing our purpose.

The galley-slaves, to the number of at least six hundred, showed themselves jealous spectators of our operations: their disposition to oppose us was evident; and being unchained, which was unusual, rendered it necessary to keep a watchful eye on them on board the galleys, by pointing the guns of the Swallow tender and one of the gunboats on them in such a manner as to enfilade the quay on which they must have landed to come to us, and assuring them, at the same time, that no harm should happen to them if they remained quiet. The enemy kept up a cross fire of shot and shells on the spot, from Malbosquet and the neighbouring hills, which contributed to keep the galley-slaves in subjection, and operated in every respect favourably for us, by keeping the republican party in the town within their houses, while it occasioned little interruption to our work of preparing and placing combustible matter in the different storehouses, and on board the ships; such was the steadiness of the few brave seamen I had under my command. A great multitude of the enemy continued to draw down the hill towards the dockyard wall; and as the night closed in, they came near enough to pour in an irregular though quick fire of musketry on us from the Boulangerie, and of cannon from the height which overlooks it. We kept them at bay by discharges of grapeshot from time to time, which prevented their coming so near as to discover the insufficiency of our force to repel a closer attack. A gunboat was stationed to flank the wall on the outside, and two field-pieces were placed within against the wicket usually frequented by the workmen, of whom we were particularly apprehensive. About eight o'clock I had the satisfaction of seeing Lieutenant Gore towing in the Vulcan fireship. Captain Hare, her commander, placed her, agreeably to my directions, in a most masterly manner across the tier of men-of-war, and the additional force of her guns and men diminished my apprehensions of the galley-slaves rising on us, as their manner and occasional tumultuous debates ceased entirely on her appearance. The only noise heard among them was the hammer knocking off their fetters, which humanity forbade my opposing, as they might thereby be more at liberty to save themselves on the conflagration taking place around them. In this situation we continued to wait most anxiously for the hour concerted with the governor for the inflammation of the trains. The moment the signal was made, we had the satisfaction to see the flames rise in every quarter. Lieutenant Tupper was charged with the burning of the general magazine, the pitch, tar, tallow, and oil storehouses, and succeeded most perfectly; the hemp magazine was included in this blaze: its being nearly calm was unfortunate to the spreading of the flames, but two hundred and fifty barrels of tar, divided among the deals and other timber, insured the rapid ignition of that whole quarter which Lieutenant Tupper had undertaken.

The masthouse was equally set on fire by Lieutenant Middleton of the Britannia. Lieutenant Porter, of the Britannia, continued in a most daring manner to brave the flames, in order to complete the work where the fire seemed to have caught imperfectly. I was obliged to call him off, lest his retreat should become impracticable: his situation was the more perilous, as the enemy's fire redoubled as soon as the amazing blaze of light rendered us distinct objects of their aim. Lieutenant Ironmonger, of the Royals, remained with the guard at the gate till the last, long after the Spanish guard was withdrawn, and was brought safely off by captain Edge of the Alert, to whom I had confided the important service of closing our retreat, and bringing off our detached parties, which were saved to a man. I was sorry to find myself deprived of the further services of Captain Hare: he had performed that of placing his fireship to admiration, but was blown into the water, and much scorched, by the explosion of her priming, when in the act of putting the match to it. Lieutenant Gore was also much burnt, and I was consequently deprived of him also, which I regretted the more, from the recollection of his bravery and activity in the warm service of Fort Mulgrave. Mr. Bales, midshipman, who was also with him on this occasion, deserves my praise for his conduct throughout this service. The guns of the fireship going off on both sides as they heated, in the direction that was given them, towards those quarters from whence we were most apprehensive of the enemy forcing their way in upon us, checked their career. Their shouts and republican songs, which we could hear distinctly, continued till they, as well as ourselves, were in a manner thunderstruck by the explosion of some thousand barrels of powder on board the Iris frigate, lying in the inner road, without us, and which had been injudiciously set on fire by the Spanish boats in going off, instead of being sunk as ordered. The concussion of air, and the shower of falling timber on fire, was such as nearly to destroy the whole of us. Lieutenant Patey, of the Terrible, with his whole boat's crew, nearly perished: the boat was blown to pieces, but the men were picked up alive. The Union gunboat, which was nearest to the Iris, suffered considerably, Mr. Young being killed, with three men, and the vessel shaken to pieces. I had given it in charge to the Spanish officers to fire the ship in the basin before the town, but they returned, and reported that various obstacles had prevented their entering it. We attempted it together as soon as we had completed the business in the arsenal, but were repulsed, in our attempt to cut the boom, by repeated volleys of musketry from the flagship and the wall of the Battery Royal. The cannon of this battery had been spiked by the judicious precautions taken by the governor previously to the evacuation of the town.

The failure of our attempt on the ships in the basin before the town, owing to the insufficiency of our force, made me regret that the Spanish gunboats had been withdrawn from me to perform other service. The adjutant Don Pedro Cotiella, Don Francisco Riguielme, and Don Francisco Truxillo, remained with me to the last; and I feel bound to bear testimony to the zeal and activity with which they performed the most essential services during the whole of this business, as far as the insufficiency of their force allowed it, being reduced, by the retreat of the gunboats, to a single felucca, and a mortar-boat which had expended its ammunition, but contained thirty men with cutlasses.

We now proceeded to burn the Héro and Thémistocle, two seventy-four gun ships, lying in the inner road. Our approach to them had hitherto been impracticable in boats, as the French prisoners, who had been left in the latter ship, were still in possession of her, and had shown a determination to resist our attempt to come on board. The scene of conflagration around them, heightened by the late tremendous explosion, had, however, awakened their fears for their lives. Thinking this to be the case, I addressed them, expressing my readiness to land them in a place of safety, if they would submit; and they thankfully accepted the offer, showing themselves to be completely intimidated, and very grateful for our humane intentions towards them, in not attempting to burn them with the ship. It was necessary to proceed with precaution, as they were more numerous than ourselves. We at length completed their disembarkation, and then set her on fire. On this occasion I had nearly lost my valuable friend and assistant, Lieutenant Miller of the Windsor Castle, who had staid so long on board, to insure the fire taking, that it gained on him suddenly, and it was not without being very much scorched, and at the risk of being suffocated, that we could approach the ship to take him in. The loss to the service would have been very great, had we not succeeded in our endeavours to save him. Mr. Knight, midshipman of the Windsor Castle, who was in the boat with me, showed much activity and address on the occasion, as well as firmness throughout the day.

The explosion of a second powder-vessel equally unexpected, and with a shock even greater than the first, again put us in the most imminent danger of perishing; and when it is considered that we were within the sphere of the falling timber, it is next to miraculous that no one piece, of the many which made the water foam around us, happened to touch either the Swallow or the three boats with me.

Having now set fire to everything within our reach, exhausted our combustible preparations and our strength to such a degree that the men absolutely dropped on the oars, we directed our course to join the fleet, running the gauntlet under a few ill-directed shot from the forts of Balaguier and Aiguillette, now occupied by the enemy; but, fortunately, without loss of any kind, we proceeded to the place appointed for the embarkation of the troops, and took off as many as we could carry. It would be injustice to those officers whom I have omitted to name, from their not having been so immediately under my eye, if I did not acknowledge myself indebted to them all for their extraordinary exertions in the execution of this great national object. The quickness with which the inflammation took effect on my signal, its extent and duration, are the best evidences that every officer and man was ready at his post, and firm under most perilous circumstances.

We can ascertain that the fire extended to at least ten sail of the line; how much farther we cannot say. The loss of the general magazine, and of the quantity of pitch, tar, rosin, hemp, timber, cordage, and gunpowder, must considerably impede the equipment of the few ships that remain. I am sorry to have been obliged to leave any, but I hope your lordship will be satisfied that we did as much as our circumscribed means enabled us to do in limited time, pressed as we were by a force so much superior to us. I have the honour to be, &c.

W. SIDNEY SMITH

Right hon. Lord Hood, &c. &c. &c. *

* Here follows a list of the officers employed, and of the killed and wounded:

Lord Hood showed at once his judgment and his sense of the value of Sir Sidney's services, by appointing him to be the bearer of the despatches to England, containing an account of these stirring events. He was favourably—indeed, without incurring the blame of exaggeration, we may say, was enthusiastically received in London. He was caressed at the Admiralty, and distinguished at the court of his sovereign.

As it is our office to record the events of Sir Sidney's life more as a public than as a private character, we shall not inflate these volumes with anecdotes, which, however pleasing in themselves, have nothing to do with the official career of his usefulness and of his glory. It will be sufficient to say, that, during his short cessation from actual service, he was sought for and cherished in the best and most distinguished circles.

LIST OF SHIPS OF THE LINE, FRIGATES, AND SLOOPS,
OF THE DEPARTMENT OF TOULON.

In the road where the English
fleet entered Toulon:

SHIPS OF THE LINE

Now with the English fleet	*Guns*
Le Commerce de Marseilles	120
Le Pompée	74

Burnt at Toulon

Le Tonnant	80
L'Heureux	74
Le Centaur	74
Le Commerce de Bordeaux	74
Le Destin	74
LeLys	74
Le Héros	74
Le Thémistocle	74
Le Dugay Trouin	74

Sent into the French ports on the Atlantic, with French seamen, etc.

Le Patriote	74
L'Apollon	74
L'Orion	74
L'Entreprenant	74

Burnt at Leghorn.

Le Scipion	74

Remaining at Toulon.

Le Genereux	74

FRIGATES
Now with the English fleet.

Le Perle	40
L'Aréthuse	40

Fitted out by the English.

L'Aurora	32

Put into commission by order of Lord Hood.

La Topaze	32

Remaining in the power of the Sardinians.

L'Alceste	32

SLOOPS
Now with the English fleet.

La Poulette	26
Le Tarleston	14

Burnt at Toulon.

La Caroline	20
L'Auguste	20

Fitted out by the English.

La Belette	26
La Proselyte	24
La Sincere	20
Le Mulct	20
La Moselle	20

Fitted out by the Neapolitans.

L'Employe	20

Fitted out by the Spaniards.

La Petite Aurore	18

Sent to Bordeaux.

Le Pluvier	20

Fitting out when the English fleet entered Toulon
SHIPS OF THE LINE.
Burnt at Toulon.

Le Triomphant	80
Le Suffisant	74

Now with the English fleet.

Le Puissant	74

Remaining at Toulon.

Le Dauphin Royal	120

FRIGATE

Burnt at Toulon.

Le Serieuse	32

In the harbour, in want of repair:

SHIPS.

Burnt at Toulon.

Le Mercure	74
La Couronne	80
Le Conquerant	74
Le Dictateur	74

Remaining at Toulon.

Le Languedoc	80
Le Censeur	74
Le Guerrier	74
Le Souverain	74

Unfit for Service.

L'Alcide	74

FRIGATES

Burnt at Toulon.

Le Courageux	32
L'Iphigenie	32
L'Alerte	16

Having on board the powder magazines, burnt at Toulon.

L'Iris	32
Le Montreal	32

Fitted out by the English as a bomb-ketch.

La Lutine	32

Remaining at Toulon.

La Bretonne

In commission before the English
fleet entered Toulon:

SHIP

In the Levant.

La Duquesne   74

FRIGATES AND SLOOPS

In the Levant.

La Sibylle	40
La Sensible	32
La Melpomène	40
La Minerve	40
La Fortunee	32
La Flèche	24
La Fauvette	24

Taken by the English.

L'Imperieuse	40
La Modeste	32
L'Eclair	20

At Ville Franche

La Vestale	36
La Badine	24
Le Hazard	30

At Corsica

La Mignon	32

At Cette

La Brune	24

In ordinary at Toulon.

La Junon	*40*

Building

One ship of 74 guns
Two frigates of 40 guns

CHAPTER VII

HAVING, by the late splendid though incomplete operations, given earnest to his superior officers, and to the country at large, that he was possessed of abilities of the highest order, Sir Wm. Sidney Smith was appointed by the Lords of the Admiralty, in the commencement of the year
1794, to the command of the Diamond frigate, on the station of the British Channel.

The officers and the crew of the Diamond soon experienced the beneficial effects of his enlightened and energetic command. At this period
very many and very hurtful prejudices existed in the service. A mixture of
firmness and conciliation in the carrying out of improvements soon removed most of the anomalies that interfered with the due efficiency of
the force under Captain Sir Sidney Smith's command. The Diamond became one of the most perfect specimens of a vessel of war in the British
navy. Next to the conquest or destruction of the enemy, the greatest glory
that can be achieved by the commander is the ennobling of the force under his government by judicious expedients, and the employing an enlightened discipline to enable him to do so.

It would be tedious to enumerate all the minutiae of a blockading
cruise in the Channel—the chase by day, and the dangerous approximation to the enemy's harbour by night—the interchange of shot with the
batteries, and the verifying of the charts, under the very guns of the enemy, by soundings in the boats. Though each of these operations may
seem to be but a little matter of itself, the whole makes a service no less
arduous than it is necessary. Insignificant as this may appear to be, it
affords an ample field in which the abilities of the officer in command
can be fairly and almost fully tested.

No sooner had the year 1795 been ushered in by the din of a war soon to become almost universal, than the government at home received what was considered to be authentic information that the French fleet, under Admiral Villare de Joyeuse, had ventured from the protection of the harbour of Brest, and was actually upon the open seas, on a cruise. On the 2nd of January, Sir John Borlase Warren, an officer who had already distinguished himself, sailed from Falmouth, with a squadron of frigates, to reconnoitre Brest and the contiguous line of French coast. To penetrate into the mouth of this harbour was the hazardous commission that devolved on Captain Smith. The Diamond, in an incredibly short space of time, was so completely Frenchified in appearance—but in appearance only—that her gallant captain was enabled completely to deceive the enemy. With the utmost coolness he sailed into the harbour in the evening, remained there the whole of the night, and departed early on the following morning, without, for a moment, having his disguise suspected. In returning from this bold undertaking, he actually passed within hail of a French line-of-battle ship.

Having, by this manoeuvre, satisfactorily ascertained that the French fleet had really ventured to put to sea, he returned in safety with the important intelligence to his anxious commodore.

Nothing particularly worth narrating occurred to our officer until the month of May following, when he assisted at the capture of a convoy of transports. His untiring vigilance was next exhibited on the 4th of July following, when he made a brave but ineffectual attempt to capture two French ships of war, having under their protection a large convoy of merchant vessels. In this gallant affair the batteries of La Hogue proved too strong for the attacking force. Even this failure had more than its compensating advantages, in the terror that it occasioned to the enemy, and the paralysing opinion that it gave them of British daring. In this attempt the Diamond had the misfortune to have one man killed and two wounded.

Sir Sidney's official despatch was as follows:

Diamond at anchor off the Island of St. Marcou,

July 5, 1795

Sir, In pursuance of the orders of the Lords Commissioners of the Admiralty, I sailed from St. Helen's on the evening of the 1st instant, and stretched across the Channel towards Cherbourg, his Majesty's ships Syren and Sybille, also four gunboats, in company. On looking into that port, we found that one of the three frigates which had been seen there the last time we were off, was missing: the master of a neutral vessel, just come out, informed me that she had sailed to the eastward, and I accordingly proceeded in quest of her. Going round Cape Barfleur, we saw two ships, one of them having the appearance of the frigate in question, at anchor under the sand, and immediately made sail towards them; we soon after saw a convoy coming along-shore within the islands of Marcou. The wind dying away, and the ebb-tide making against me, I was obliged to anchor, and had the mortification of seeing the enemy's vessels drift with the tide under the batteries of La Hogue, without being able to approach them. At four o'clock in the morning of yesterday, the breeze springing up with the first of the flood, I made the signal to the squadron, and weighed and worked up towards the enemy's ships, which we observed warping closer inshore under the battery on La Hogue Point.

As we approached, I made the signal for each ship to engage as she came up with the enemy, and at nine o'clock began the action in the Diamond. The other frigates, having been sent in chase in different quarters the day before, had not been able to anchor so near as we did, and were consequently to leeward, as were two of the gunboats. The Fearless arid the Attack were with me, and their commanders conducted them in a manner to merit my approbation, by drawing off the attention of the enemy's gunboats, of which they had also two. The small vessels of the convoy ran into the pier before the town; the largest, a corvette, continued warping into shoal water; we followed, engaging her arid the batteries for three quarters of an hour, when, finding that the enemy's ship had attained a situation where it was impossible to get fairly alongside of her without grounding likewise, and the pilots being positive as to the necessity of hauling off from the shore, where the water had already begun to ebb, I acquiesced under their representations, and wore ship. The Syren and Sibylle were come up by this time, and the zeal and ability of their commanders would, I am persuaded, have carried them into action with some effect, if I had not annulled the signal to engage, which I did, to prevent them getting disabled, as we were, when we had no longer a prospect of making ourselves masters of the enemy's ship. She had suffered in proportion, and we now see her lying on her broadside with her yards and topmasts struck, but, I am sorry to say, so much sheltered by the reef which runs off from La Hogue Point, that I cannot indulge a hope of her being destroyed.

In justice to my officers and ship's company, I must add, that their conduct was such as gave me satisfaction. I received the most able assistance from the first lieutenant, Mr. Pine, and Mr. Wilkie, the master, in working the ship, on the precision of which everything depended, circumstanced as we were with respect to the shoals and the enemy. The guns of the main-deck were well served under the direction of Lieutenants Pearson and Sandsbury, and the men were cool and collected.

No officer was hurt; but I am sorry to say that I have lost one of the best quartermasters in the ship, Thomas Gullen, killed, and two seamen wounded; the enemy fired high, or we should have suffered more materially from their red-hot shot, the marks of which were visible in the rigging. We have shifted our fore and main topmasts, which, with two topsail-yards, were shot through; and having repaired our other more trifling damages, I shall proceed in the attainment of the objects of the cruise. Fishing boats, with which we have had an intercourse, confirm all other accounts of distress for want of provisions, and the consequent discontent in this distracted country.

I have the honour, &c.

W. SIDNEY SMITH

Evan Nepean, Esq.

There is but little in this despatch worthy of notice, but as a sample of this sort of composition. The skirmish was itself trifling, and the service it rendered to the country but small. It evinces, however, an indomitable purpose of effecting everything within the reach of human power, and is, to our eyes, very valuable on account of the mention of his quartermaster. It is usual, in these chronicles of slaughter, to record the deaths of the petty officers and seamen, in the mass only. The exemption to this rule is very honourable to Sir Sidney Smith—even on so slight an occasion as was afforded to him by this letter of service. Honours, rewards, and distinctions should be scattered more liberally among the foremast men.

Very shortly after, as the accuracy of the English charts of parts of the coasts of Normandy was much doubted, Captain Sir Sidney Smith made very numerous soundings, and minute observations on the nature of the ground over which the tides of this part of the Channel so impetuously rush. By these laudable exertions, the Admiralty charts were brought very nearly into a state of perfection. He also, about this time, by the means of his boats, took possession of the small islands of St. Marcou, situate about four miles distance from the same coast. Though there was nothing apparently very splendid in this conquest, and the surface of territory added to the British dominions not very extensive, yet it proved a very useful acquisition, as it afforded a point from whence, a little time afterwards, a regular communication was established with the French royalists.

In this year nothing of moment occurred until the latter end of August, when Captain Sidney Smith fell in with and gave chase to the French corvette La Nationale, of two-and-twenty guns, which, in endeavouring to elude the pursuit of the Diamond amid the labyrinth of rocks before Treguier, found the fate that she endeavoured to avoid. In hugging the reefs too closely, she struck on the Roanna. The breeze was fresh, and the eddying and foaming waters toiled among the crags, and flung its waves completely over the rock-fettered vessel. She was a beautiful craft, and for some time seemed to brave, with impunity, the endless assaults of the angry seas. But her doom had gone forth, and, straining and groaning terribly, gave unequivocal signs of approaching dissolution. It was then that repentance came too late upon the unhappy crew, for having preferred the insidious and treacherous asylum of rocks and crags to the generosity of a brave enemy.

In this situation, and whilst she was getting out her boats, the devoted corvette filled and fell over. Had national law and the usages of war been strictly adhered to, Sidney Smith would have been justified in leaving the enemy to their fate, who had thus, to avoid capture, all but wantonly destroyed their ship: at least, upon the mildest construction, he had sufficient cause not to risk the lives of his own seamen in a hazardous attempt to save those of his enemies. But these considerations weighed but lightly with his chivalrous feeling of humanity. The boats of the Diamond were soon amidst the boiling surf, and alongside of the separating vessel. Her own boats had already taken on board a considerable part of her crew; and those of Captain Smith's frigate were only able to save nine.

The French captain was washed from the wreck, and perished but a few seconds before the British boats were alongside his vessel. More than twenty of the French experienced a similar fate. The swell was tremendous, and in a very short time not a vestige of the wreck was to be seen. The sea was so much agitated that the Diamond, in waiting for her boats, was forced to come to single anchor in the offing.

On the 17th of March, 1796, (the following year,) this enterprising commander having received intelligence that a small squadron of armed vessels, consisting of one corvette, four brigs, two sloops, and three luggers, had taken shelter in the small fort of Herqui, near Cape Trehel, he immediately, with his own frigate, the Diamond, the Liberty man-of-war brig, and the Aristocrat cutter, repaired to this place. The channel leading to this small port is narrow and intricate, and strongly defended by all the art of fortification. However, this formidable array of defence was seen only to be despised. The ships under the command of Sir Sidney Smith stood boldly in, and commenced cannonading the batteries, whilst Lieutenant Pine of the Diamond, with a party of seamen, and Lieutenant Carter of the same ship, with a party of marines, under the cover of the fire, stormed and most gallantly carried these defences. In this desperate service Lieutenant Pine was seriously, and Lieutenant Carter mortally, wounded. The French vessels were all burned, with the exception of one of the luggers, which kept up its fire to the last. The corvette was a vessel of some force, mounting sixteen guns, and was named L'Etourdie. The loss of the English in this attack was two sea men killed and five wounded, exclusive of the officers of whom we have before spoken a loss wonderfully small, considering the arduous nature of the service performed, and the strength of the obstacles to be overcome. We subjoin Sir Sidney's despatch on the occasion.

Diamond, off Cape Trehel, March 18, 1796

Sir, Having received information that the armed vessels detached by the Prince of Bouillon had chased a convoy, consisting of a corvette, three luggers, four brigs, and two sloops, into Herqui, I proceeded off that port to reconnoitre their 'position and sound the channel, which I found very narrow and intricate. I succeeded, however, in gaining a knowledge of these points sufficient to determine me to attack them in the Diamond without loss of time, and without waiting for the junction of any part of the squadron, lest the enemy should fortify themselves still farther on our appearance. Lieutenant M'Kinley of the Liberty brig, and Lieutenant Gosset of the Aristocrat lugger, joined me off the Cape, and, though not under my orders, very handsomely offered their services, which I accepted, as small vessels were essentially necessary in such an operation. The permanent fortifications for the defence of the bay are two batteries on a high rocky promontory. We observed the enemy to be very busily employed in mounting a detached gun on a very commanding point of the entrance. At one o'clock yesterday afternoon this gun opened upon us as we passed; the Diamond's fire, however, silenced it in eleven minutes. The others opened on us as we came round the point, and their commanding situation giving them a decided advantage over a ship in our position, I judged it necessary to adopt another mode of attack, and accordingly detached the marines and boarders to land behind the point, and take the batteries in the rear. As the boats approached the beach, they met with a warm reception, and a temporary check, from a body of troops drawn up to oppose their landing; the situation was critical. The ship being exposed to a most galling fire, and in intricate pilotage, with a considerable portion of her men thus detached, I pointed out to Lieutenant Pine the apparent practicability of climbing the precipice in front of the batteries, which he readily perceived, and with an alacrity and bravery of which I have had many proofs in the course of our service together, he undertook and executed this hazardous service, landed immediately under the guns, and rendered himself master of them before the column of troops could regain the heights. The fire from the ship was directed to cover our men in this operation; it checked the enemy in their advancement, and the re-embarkation was effected, as soon as the guns were spiked, without the loss of a man, though we have to regret Lieutenant Carter, of the marines, being dangerously wounded on this occasion. The enemy's guns, three twenty-four pounders, being silenced and rendered useless for the time, we proceeded to attack the corvette and the other armed vessels, which had, by this time, opened their fire on us to cover the operation of hauling themselves on shore. The Diamond had anchored as close to the corvette as her draught of water would allow. The Liberty brig was able to approach near, and on this occasion I cannot omit to mention the very gallant and judicious manner in which Lieutenant M'Kinley, her commander, brought this vessel into action, profiting by her light draught of water to follow the corvette close. The enemy's fire soon slackened, and the crew being observed to be making for the shore on the English colours being hoisted on the hill, I made the signal for the boats, manned and armed, to board, directing Lieutenant Gosset in the lugger to cover them. This service was executed by the party from the shore, under the direction of Lieutenant Pine, in a manner that does them infinite credit, and him every honour as a brave man and an able officer. The enemy's troops occupied the high projecting rocks all round the vessels, whence they kept up an incessant fire of musketry, and the utmost that could be effected at the moment was to set fire to the corvette (named L'Etourdie, of sixteen guns, twelve-pounders, on the main-deck), and one of the merchant brigs, since, as the tide fell, the enemy pressed down on the sands close to the vessels; Lieutenant Pine therefore returned on board, having received a severe contusion on the breast from a musket ball. As the tide rose again, it became practicable to make a second attempt to burn the remaining vessels; Lieutenant Pearson was accordingly detached for that purpose with the boats, and I am happy to add, his gallant exertions succeeded to the utmost of my hopes, notwithstanding the renewed and heavy fire of musketry from the shore. This fire was returned with great spirit and evident good effect; and I was much pleased with the conduct of Lieutenant Gosset in the hired lugger, and Mr. Knight in the Diamond's launch, who covered the approach and retreat of the boats. The vessels were all burnt, except an armed lugger which kept up her fire to the last. The wind and tide suiting at ten at night to come out of the harbour again, we weighed and repassed the Point of Herqui, from which we received a few shot, the enemy having found means to restore one of the guns to activity. Our loss, as appears by the enclosed return, is trifling, considering the nature of the enterprise, and the length of time we were exposed to the enemy's fire. Theirs, I am persuaded, must have been very great, from the numbers within the range of the shot and shells. The conduct of every officer and man under my command meets with my warmest approbation. It would be superfluous to particularise any others than those I have named: suffice it to say, the characteristic bravery and activity of British seamen never were more conspicuous. Lieutenant Pine will have the honour to present their Lordships with the colours which he struck on the battery, and I beg leave to recommend him particularly to their Lordships, as a most meritorious officer.

I have the honour to be, &c.

W. SIDNEY SMITH

Evan Nepean, Esq. Secretary to the Admiralty

A return of the killed and wounded belonging to his Majesty's Ship Diamond, in the three Attacks of the Enemy's Batteries and Shipping in Herqui, the 7th of March, 1796.

Killed—two seamen. Wounded—First Lieutenant Horace Pine, Lieutenant Carter of the Marines, and five seamen.

W. S. SMITH

This feat is one of those acts of daring, almost peculiar to the British navy, that success only seems to justify. The actual gain to the English cause, and the positive detriment to the enemy, seem almost trifling when compared with the risk. As glory is generally great as to the magnitude of the act, and a defeat in this case would have been inglorious in the extreme, we must examine more deeply into the question before we can properly appreciate small but heroical acts like the above. It is in their moral effect on the enemy on the one hand, and on our national character on the other, that we must look for their excellence. If a nation supposes that its foe will dare everything, that foe will prove little short of what it has the credit for. As far as regards the nation in whose favour is the presentiment, that nation will be in general victorious, although the force opposed to it be reckoned superior; and should this over-confidence produce a rashness of action that entails defeat, the victory will be so dearly sold, that victors will be cautious not again to reap such another victory.

This line of argument more forcibly applies to the naval than to the military service. The latter depends more upon combination, strategy, and previous arrangement, and the calculation of chances enters much less into the plan of operations. But, in a naval engagement, how much depends upon accident! A flaw of wind, a stray shot, one person deficient in his duty, and all is lost, save honour. Be it remembered always, that seamen fight over, and almost in contact with, their magazines. Truly it is a mighty game of chance, but a game that is sure to be lost for want of skill, and yet, with the greatest skill, may be gloriously lost for the want of fortune. It seems, then, most wise to dare all, but dare wisely; and few, nay none, have been more wise in their daring than Sir Sidney Smith.

CHAPTER VIII

AT this period, when the Diamond came into harbour to refit for service after her various cruises, Sir Sidney Smith used frequently to come up to London, and mingle with the abounding festivities of the metropolis. Though he had his peculiarities, yet, with many and strong temptations, he might justly be denominated "a steady man." At this time he was decidedly handsome, and, though not tall, of a compact, well-built, symmetrical frame, with a dark and somewhat Hebraical countenance, and a profusion of jet-black curling hair. Notwithstanding the fierce bravery of his character, his features were always remarkable for a degree of refinement, not often found either in the pale student or the silken courtier. In his character, mind predominated.

He had his singularities, and where is the thorough-bred seaman who has not? He had himself trained a beautiful and docile horse into an amusing playmate, as well as a valuable servant. When told to give a prance for "King George," he would rear on his hind legs, and dance like a well-educated dog. When requested to pay the like compliment to Bonaparte, he would take the request as an insult; stiffen out his limbs into an attitude of defiance, and snort indignantly. When mounting his favourite Bucephalus at the door of his hotel, Captain Smith would do it in the most approved style of the fashionable equestrians of the day, and preserve all the proprieties of equitation, until he was fairly clear of the suburbs. Then would he fling the stirrups across the back of his horse, settle himself sailor-fashion in his saddle, and ride as if he were chasing the wind, and the wind-chasing promises of amendment.

We are now approaching one of the principal events of our hero's life; but our friends must not suppose that we use the term hero in the novel, but in the historical, acceptation of the word. This act, which terminated so unfortunately for him, seems to have been of a nature much less hazardous than that which we have just narrated, which took place off Herqui, and to have been planned with scientific foresight; yet the results were not only disastrous to our gallant commander, but also highly detrimental to the interests of his country, in depriving it, for a length of time, of his invaluable services. On the 8th of March, being near the shore off Havre, with his boats, on a reconnoissance, he fell in with and took possession of a French lugger privateer, which, by the strong influx of the tide, was, with its captors and their boats, carried a considerable way up the Seine, and far beyond the numerous forts. Thus unpleasantly situated, it may be fairly said, in the interior of the country, he found himself in a situation not very dissimilar from that of the renowned nephew of Gil Perez.

Thus entrapped, Sir Sidney Smith remained during the whole night. The first breaking of the morning presented to the French a very curious and unaccustomed picture. There lay in the middle of their own river the long black hull of the lugger, lately theirs, in tow by a string of English boats, the crews of which were pulling with a strength and energy that British seamen only can display. Great was the Gallic commotion. Amid the incessant crowing of their national cocks, which were doing their matutinal duty this fine spring morning, in announcing the commencement of another day, was heard the clamour of the national guard, the shouting of the peasantry on the river, and the shriller cries of the females, mingled with the baying of innumerable dogs, and the calling of the canonniers to each other, as they rushed into their various forts and unlimbered the guns.

In this crisis, the enemy seems to have wanted neither courage nor conduct; for in addition to the fire from the batteries, which played upon the boats and the prize, several gunboats and other armed vessels attacked this little party, and, in less than an hour, another lugger, of force superior to the one captured, was warped out and made to engage her late consort. This unequal fight lasted a considerable time, although Sir Sidney Smith was exposed to the fire of much heavier metal, and had, at the same time, to guard the captive Frenchmen. Never was a combat more unequal, or an unequal combat more obstinately sustained. At this period our officer seems to have been gifted with a charmed life, for the grape-shot was poured into his vessel literally in showers. After having, of his little force, seen eleven men put *hors de combat*, that is to say, four killed and seven badly wounded, he had to undergo that severest of mortifications, to haul down the English colours that had been floating over the French, and to render up himself, his boats, his prize, and his companions prisoners of war, to the number of somewhere about twenty.

As all this passed fully in the view of the remaining officers and seamen of the Diamond, they were extremely mortified at not being able to render their captain and their companions the least assistance. They did, however, all that they could. They sent in a flag of truce to Havre, re-

questing to know if their highly-valued captain was unwounded, and en-
treating for him every indulgence compatible with his present unfortunate situation. The reply was courteous, and full of promise; but the courtesy was hollow, and the promise shamefully broken, as a detail of the
indignities to which Sir Sidney was subsequently exposed will fully exemplify.

So daring was this act, and so little were the apparent advantages to
be gained by the risk, that the French could not well understand it, and
assigned a thousand contradictory motives for this conduct, not one of
them, probably, the true one. We have stated the facts as given to the
world officially by Sir Sidney. There may have been some deep political
design in thus venturing into "the bowels of the land "—some occult manoeuvre that it would be treachery to reveal.

Among other vague surmises of the French, was one, that he himself,
or in the person of Monsieur T., was on an extensive, and to the French
dangerous espionage, and under this impression the French at first confined him in the Temple as a spy. How they could have come to this conclusion is somewhat difficult to determine, seeing that he came into
Havre, though on a small scale, attended with all "the pomp and circumstance of war."

So serious, however, did Sir Sidney find this conviction on the minds
of those who then ruled the destinies of the French, that our hero thought
it necessary to appeal to the good sense and generosity of Bonaparte, on
his return from Italy; but even he, who, when not crossed in his ambitious views, had no deficiency of generosity and compassion, found the
circumstances, as they were generally represented, so strong against him,
and the manner of his capture so ambiguous, that he would not interfere
in the prisoner's favour.

Others, who knew that he was actually taken in open war, with the
command of men with arms in their hands, and in actual possession of a
capture, became ingenious in other explanations, which appear to us
equally ridiculous and remote from the truth. Some said that it was to
win a foolish bet, others that it was a female attraction; and not a few, for
an overwhelming desire to go to the theatre at Havre. That he was taken
in a very singular position is certain, but we believe ours to be the true
account of the matter.

His justly deserved fame: his unceasing vigilance, and his courage
bordering on rashness, had rendered him peculiarly obnoxious to the
revolutionised nation, and the French Directors showed the respect they
felt for his heroism by departing from the established system, consecrated by the law of nations, which humanely prescribes an exchange of
prisoners during the continuance of war. Captain Sir Sidney Smith was
not to be exchanged. He was conveyed to Paris, and confined in the Temple for the space of two years—a time truly dreadful when spent in rigid
incarceration.

It would not be foreign to the subject, were we to pour out the vials of our indignation upon such unworthy and dastardly conduct as was then exhibited by these *soi-disant* renovators of human institutions, the republican French authorities. But abhorrent as were their proceedings towards

Sir Sidney Smith and several other distinguished captives, it was mercy and beneficence compared with that which they displayed to the best and bravest of their own countrymen. Truly the regeneration of the human race was attempted in the brazen furnace of cruelty, and fed with the flames of democratic and dastardly revenge.

The above-mentioned little skirmish, so awkward in its results to Sir Sidney Smith, furnishes us with an example of that which we have just advanced, that in naval operations the best conduct is often controlled and baffled by chance. When the privateer lugger was at first taken possession of, there was a steady breeze blowing from off the land, but before things could be well arranged on board of her by the captors, there fell a dead calm, and she began to drift rapidly up the Seine. It may be urged that she ought to have been abandoned after having been scuttled. But Sir Sidney had a right also to 'depend upon the chapter of chances. The night before him was long, and the tide would certainly turn, and the wind probably change. We do not think that there is a British officer in the service who would not have acted in a similar manner.

CHAPTER IX

WE are now to consider our subject as a captive, and view him in the
struggle against the oppression and tyranny of the French authorities.
We see him no longer controlling and directing the energies of hundreds
of seamen warriors, with the boundless ocean for the scene of action the
freest of the free, and with none other restraint, either upon deed or will,
than the prudential dictates of his own magnanimous mind. No, for a
space, we must view him no more in this glorious light, but consider him
as concentrating all his mental energies within the walls of a strongly
guarded prison, waging with unlimited power the war only of the mind,
yet still glorious, still unshaken and unconquered. How many gallant
men who are heroes on the field and on the wave, are less than women in
the cell! If these spirits be not fed with the atmosphere of liberty, they
pine and dwindle away until the light of their lives expires, and they go
mad or die. After all, the dungeon is the true test place for greatness of
soul. Infinitely more easy is it to be heroic on the scaffold or in the
breach, for these are but the efforts of the moment, than to remain for
years in a prison unsubdued. How Sir Sidney Smith bore this terrible or-
deal will be shortly seen. Were we writing a romance instead of a biography, the two years of Sir Sidney Smith's confinement would amply supply
us with exciting materials sufficient for two volumes. Fears, hopes, de-
spondency, even love, were all in their turn brought into play. When Sir
Sidney was captured, he was accompanied by his secretary and a gentleman of the name of T——, who had emigrated, and was in constant attendance on Sir Sidney in the hope of serving the royalist cause. Thus
suddenly and unexpectedly finding himself a captive in a country where
he would be looked upon as a traitor and executed as a spy, the commo-

dore arranged with him that he should assume the character of his servant; and so well did he act up to the disguise, that he was never suspected for a moment. He was called John, by his supposititious master, and Mr. T.'s assimilation of the menial proved to be perfect.

At Havre, Sir Sidney was treated with the most unjustifiable rigour, subjected to insult, taunted with being a spy, and threatened with a trial by a military commission. So obnoxious had he become by his activity, and the detriment he had been to his enemies, that they would have gladly hung him, had not the fear of retaliation prevented this mean vengeance. He was, however, a prisoner much too valuable to be permitted to remain so near the seacoast, and the French government accordingly ordered his removal to Paris. In that metropolis, he was at first confined to the prison called the Abbaye, and, with his two companions in adversity, kept under the most rigorous surveillance as well as the closest confinement.

But no external circumstances could paralyse the activity of a mind such as Sir Sidney's. Escape formed the constant object of his thoughts. He did not confine himself to idle wishes, but set about deeds. His consultations with his fellow sufferers were incessant, but such was the rigour of his custodiers that, for a length of time, nothing feasible could be suggested. The window of their common sitting-room looked into the street, and thus brought liberty, though not within their reach, in a most tantalising proximity. Looking out thus continually upon the general thoroughfare of their fellow men held out to them, without cessation, illusive hopes. Indeed, they felt certain that, sooner or later, this circumstance would aid them in their escape.

Whenever there is anything remarkably dangerous and remarkably chivalrous to perform, (the usual deeds of war excepted,) we are sure to find woman the principal agent. Three ladies, who could see the prisoners from the windows of their apartment, by the blessed feminine intuition immediately took a lively interest in their fate. Their ingenuity kept pace with their generous sympathy. They rapidly learned to exchange intelligence with the objects of their solicitude by the means of signals, arid a regular correspondence immediately ensued.

So unceasing and lynx-eyed was the vigilance to which every action of Sir Sidney Smith was subjected, that he was forced to adopt a very novel sort of telegraph, wherewith to communicate with his fair correspondents. It was the catching and destroying flies upon the different squares of glass that admitted light to his apartment. Thus several minute lives were sacrificed, before the imprisoned hero could well rid himself of a single idea. We have read of the great waste of fly-life for the amusement of a Roman emperor, but the necessity of this wholesale slaughter on the part of the gallant Sir Sidney must form his apology.

These ladies made the proposition themselves, to do all that lay in their power to aid them in their escape; an offer, we may be sure, that Sir Sidney accepted with an eager gratitude, and they instantly began operations in his behalf.

Before the stern moralist condemns these womanly exertions in favour of the unfortunate on the score of the want of patriotism, it must be remembered that the dominant party in France was not then the most numerous, and that there was virtue in a cherished, though secret, loyalty to the vanquished royal cause. They had not, however, the reward of success for their ceaseless exertions, and the enormous expenses to which they freely subjected themselves. They continually contrived to elude the vigilance of Sir Sidney's keepers. On both sides borrowed names were used, taken from the Grecian Mythology, so that the three prisoners were in direct correspondence with three of the Muses, Thalia, Melpomene, and Clio.

But all their exertions were unavailing, all their little plans frustrated. The only good that they were able to effect, was feeding and supporting the minds of their *protegés* with that most delicious of nutriments, hope. Scheme after scheme failed, and in the midst of a very plausible one, Sir Sidney and his companions were suddenly removed into the Temple.

But the walls of the Temple were not more impervious to them than had been those of the Abbaye. They soon contrived to renew their correspondence, and not a day passed that did not find them provided with some new plan for escape. The captive commodore, at first, accepted them all with eagerness, but mature reflection soon convinced him that they were as visionary as they were generous. In the first place, he was resolved not to leave his secretary behind him, and his resolution was still stronger in favour of the *soi-disant* John. The discovery of the real character of the latter would have been to him an instant and ignominious death, and his safety was much dearer to his master than his own emancipation.

Now this John was a very likely, pleasant, and clever fellow, and for his facetious qualities, and his general pleasing deportment, was allowed a considerable degree of liberty in the Temple.

He was highly, almost extravagantly, dressed as an English jockey, and well knew how to assume the manners befitting the character. But we cannot forbear remarking, in this place, on the stolidity of the French Directory, who took a personal interest in the retention of Sir Sidney Smith, and on the stupidity of the officials whom they had selected to enforce their views. Indeed, we can only account for it on the supposition of their profound ignorance of English manners. That a buck-skinned, booted, and spurred jockey should accompany Sir Sidney Smith, and be made prisoner with him in a cutting-out expedition under the batteries of Havre, must exhibit a very singular specimen of the genus, sailor; and might well make Messeurs les Concernès, in viewing such an article, exclaim with the miserly father, in Moliere's excellent comedy,

Que le diable fait-il dans cette galère?
[ED. Why the devil is he getting mixed up in this bad situation?]

But, however, not only was John so inexplicably in *cette galère*, but he was taken out of it, and, as we have seen, put in prison, and in prison

he was soon completely at home. Every one was fond of him. He frater-
nised with the turnkeys, and made love to the governor's daughter. As the
little English jockey was not supposed to have received an education the
most profound, he was compelled to study how sufficiently to mutilate
and Anglicise his own mother tongue. He soon accomplished this like a
clever farce-player. Indeed, he acted so well, that he almost overdid his
part; for, in fraternising with the turnkeys he would sometimes get drunk
with them, and in making love to the governor's daughter he promised
her marriage, in which promise her faith was strong, which was very
naughty in John, as he had long been a married man.

It may be said that, at this time, all the prisoners seemed as if they
were acting a comedy; for John appeared very eager and attentive to his
fictitious master, and always spoke to him in the most respectful manner.
In return for this, Sir Sidney repeatedly scolded this jockeyfied emigrant
with great unction and gravity; and so well did they both play their parts,
that Sir Sidney confesses that he sometimes ceased to simulate, and
found himself forgetting the friend in the master, and most seriously rat-
ing his valet soundly.

At length John's wife, Madame de T. arrived at Paris, and immediately commenced making the most uncommon exertions for the liberation of the three prisoners. She is represented to have been a most interesting lady, with a considerable share of personal beauty. She dared not,
however, fearing discovery, come herself to the Temple, but from a
neighbouring house she had the satisfaction of daily beholding her husband, as he paced to and fro in the courts of the Temple—a feeling in
which her captive partner fully participated.

In the attempts for Sir Sidney's liberation, it appears that the ladies
always took the initiative. Madame de T. devised and communicated a
plan to a sensible and courageous young person of her acquaintance, who
acceded immediately to it without hesitation. This convert to the cause of
our hero was also influenced, like the three Muse-named ladies, by sentiments of what he conceived to be the true patriotism, for, in giving his
adhesion to the cause of the prisoners, he said to Madame de T. "I will
serve Sir Sidney Smith with pleasure, because I believe that the English
government intend to restore Louis XVIII. to the throne. But if the commodore is to fight against France, and not for the King of France, Heaven
forbid that I should assist."

At this time, there were several agents of the emigrant king who were
confined in the Temple, and to effect whose liberation a M. l'Oiseau was
assiduously labouring. It was therefore proposed that all should go off
together, that is to say, Sir Sidney's party and the royalist agents. One of
these, a M. la Vilheurnois, being condemned to only one year's confinement, was resolved not to entail upon himself any more evils, but quietly
to remain until he should be relieved by the due course of his sentence;
but the two others, Brothien and Duverne de Presle, had agreed to join in
the attempt.

For some unexplained reasons, this plan completely failed, not improbably owing to the treachery or the misconduct of M. Le Presle; but of this we speak doubtingly. However, it is in these words that Sir Sidney Smith himself inculpates him: "Had our scheme succeeded, this Duverne would not, perhaps, have ceased to be an honest man; for, till then, he had conducted himself as such. His condition must now be truly deplorable, for I do not think him formed by nature for the commission of crimes."

CHAPTER X

AS M. C. l'Oiseau was indefatigable in making his preparations, they were soon in such a state of forwardness, that it was immediately resolved the attempt should be made. As all the arrangements seemed the best that could be adopted under existing circumstances, our gallant officer and his companions determined to follow them up to the best of their abilities.

In the cellar that adjoined the prison, it was purposed to make an excavation sufficiently wide to admit freely the passage of one person, but which it would be necessary to make twelve feet long. A Mademoiselle D——, who generously abetted these attempts, in order to mask their operations, nobly rejecting every prudential consideration, carne and resided in the apartments over this cellar, of which premises the prisoners' confederates had contrived to possess themselves, and they were consequently completely at their disposal.

As Mademoiselle D—— was young and attractive, the other lodgers in the mansion attributed to her alone the frequent visits of Charles l'Oiseau. The lovers of romantic adventure will perceive that here is plot involved within plot, and sufficient elements of confusion to form a Spanish comedy.

Everything for some time seemed to proceed favourably, and the hopes of the incarcerated rose correspondingly. No one unconnected with the scheme, residing in the house, had any suspicions of the undermining that was thus actively going forward. Miss D—— also brought with her an amiable little child, only seven years of age, who was so well tutored that, instead of betraying the secret, she was in the habit of continually beating a little drum, with which she drowned the noise made by the work of excavation.

Hitherto M. l'Oiseau had alone worked upon this hole, and, as he had now laboured a considerable time, he began to fear, very naturally, that he had commenced and driven forward his operations much too deeply in the earth; it was therefore necessary that the wall should be sounded, and, for this purpose, an experienced mason was requisite. Madame de T. who seems, after all, to have acted as the tutelary genius of this escapade, undertook to procure one—an office as delicate as it was dangerous, in times when suspicion was so active, and death so closely attendant on suspicion. She succeeded, and not only brought him, but engaged to detain him in the cellar until all the prisoners had effected their liberation, which was to take place on that very day. No sooner was this worthy artificer conveyed into the cellar, and instructed as to the nature of his services, than he immediately perceived that he was to be made the instrument to assist some of the victims of the government. However, he proceeded without hesitation, and he only stipulated with the parties employing him in this hazardous business, that, if he were arrested, care should be taken of his poor children.

All this must strike every one, that the disaffection to the then government must have been though secret from terror, as general, we may add, as just. Multitudes were willing to thwart its projects, or deal out to it some blow, providing there was the probability only of impunity.

It was the concealed labours of the many against the despotism of the few. In this view we cannot look upon the exertions of those thus aiding persons who had so recently been in arms against their country to escape, in the light either of traitors or unpatriotic conspirators.

The mason laboured, and found that the excavation had reached from the cellar to the wall of the garden of the Temple; but instead of finding it to be too low, it proved to be too high. The perforation of this wall commenced, and every stone was removed with the greatest precaution—but in vain! The hopes of months were frustrated in a moment! The last stones rolled outwards into the garden of the Temple, and fell at the feet of the sentinel. The alarm was sounded, the guard arrived, and, in a moment, all was discovered. Very fortunately, the friends of the prisoners had just time to escape, and not one of them was taken.

They had provided for all conjunctures, and had so well arranged their measures, that, when the commissaries of the Bureau Central came to examine the cellar and the rooms above them, they found only a few pieces of furniture, trunks filled with logs of wood and hay, and some hats decorated with the tricoloured cockade, for the use of those who had intended their escape, as they had in their possession only black ones.

After this tantalising failure, when everything seemed so auspicious, and everything had been so admirably conducted, Sir Sidney Smith wrote to Madame de T. to console both her and her young friend. Indeed, the latter needed every sympathy, for his misery was nearly insupportable at this bitter frustration of his well devised scheme.

Sir Sidney and his companions were in no manner depressed in spirits by this defeat, but were continually contriving some new scheme for their freedom. Defeat will only discourage weak minds; and the reader must have already discovered that there was very little of weakness in the mind of our hero. These manifold machinations did not escape the notice of the keeper; but his principal prisoner cared so little about his suspicions, that he was frequently so frank as to acknowledge that there was good cause for them.

This prince of jailers seems to have met this frankness with a corresponding openness, for he often said, "Commodore, your friends are desirous of liberating you, and they only do their duty; I also am doing mine in watching you more narrowly."

Though this keeper was a man of the sternest severity in act, yet, in manner, he never departed from the rules of civility and politeness. He was the *preux chevalier* [ED. - Literally: brave and noble knight] of jailers. He treated all his captives with as much kindness as his sense of duty permitted him to show them, and even piqued himself upon his generosity. Various and very tempting proposals were made to him, but he indignantly rejected them all, and merely responded to them by watching his charge the more closely. He had very nice notions of honour, and though he thought himself too humble himself to boast of them, he expected and respected them in others.

One day, as Sir Sidney was dining with him, this keeper perceived that his guest regarded an open window in the room with all the wistful attention of one long imprisoned. Now this window opened on the street, and the gaze gave the keeper so much uneasiness, that it highly amused the commodore. However, not wishing to give the good man who behaved so well to him too long a probation, he said to him, laughing, "I know what you are thinking of; but fear not. It is now three o'clock. I will make a truce with you till midnight; and I give you my word of honour, until that time, even were the doors open, I would not escape. When that hour is passed, my promise is at an end, and we are enemies again."

"Sir," said he, "your word is a safer bond than my bars or bolts: till midnight, therefore, I am perfectly easy."

This tells highly for both parties—nor is this all. When they arose from table, the keeper took Sir Sidney aside, and said to him, "Commodore, the Boulevard is not far off. If you are inclined to take the air, I will conduct you thither." This proposition struck the prisoner with the utmost astonishment, as he could not conceive how this man, who, but lately, appeared so severe and so uneasy, should thus suddenly come to the resolution of making such a proposal. Me accepted it, however, and, in the evening, they went out. From that time forward, this mutual confidence always continued. Whenever the distinguished prisoner was desirous to enjoy perfect liberty, a suspension of hostilities was offered until a certain time, and this was never refused by his generous enemy; but, immediately the armistice terminated, his vigilance was unremitting. Every post was scrupulously examined, and every fitful order of the Directory that, at times, he should be kept more closely, was enforced with a rigid scrupulosity.

CHAPTER XI

UNDER these circumstances of restraint, Sir Sidney again found himself free only to contrive and prepare for freedom, and the jailer again to treat him with the utmost rigour. Sir Sidney did not lack amusement. We are sadly afraid that this exquisite race of jailers is extinct. Sir Sidney Smith has himself placed upon record this man's creed of honour; we rather think that he gave his superiors too much credit. He would not have found all prisoners of rank like Sir Sidney. It was thus that he frequently addressed his captive: "If you were under sentence of death, I would permit you to go out on your parole, because I should be certain of your return. Many very honest prisoners, and I myself among the rest, would not return in the like case; but an officer, and especially an officer of distinction, holds his honour dearer than his life. I know this to be a fact, commodore, therefore I should be less uneasy if you desired the gates always to be open."

This was just, so far as regarded his chivalrous prisoner, but how prudent as a general maxim, let the list of parole-breakers testify. This amiable trustiness has called forth the following remark from our officer, in the accuracy of which we implicitly trust. "My keeper was right. Whilst I enjoyed my liberty, I endeavoured to lose sight of the idea of my escape; and I should have been averse to employ, for that object, means that occurred to my imagination during my hours of liberty. One day I received a letter containing matters of great importance, which I had the strongest desire immediately to read; but as the contents related to my intended deliverance, I asked leave to return to my room, and break off the truce. The keeper, however, refused, saying, with a laugh, that he wanted to take some sleep, and I accordingly postponed the perusal of my letter till the evening."

In the midst of these exchanges of courtesy and confidence, the Directory again thought proper to have Sir Sidney treated with the utmost rigour. No opportunity of flight now occurred, and the keeper punctually obeyed his orders; and he who, on the previous evening had granted him the greatest liberty, now doubled the guards in order to exercise the greatest vigilance. Cessations of hostilities were at end, promenades on the Boulevards to be enjoyed only in the imagination .

Among the prisoners was a man condemned for certain political offences to ten years' confinement, and who was suspected by the other prisoners of acting in the detestable character of a spy on his companions. These suspicions Sir Sidney thought well founded, and therefore experienced the greatest anxiety on account of his disguised friend, John the jockey. From these fears he was relieved, for he was so fortunate as, soon after, to obtain John's liberty. An exchange of prisoners being about to take place, our officer was able to obtain for him that which was pertinaciously and unjustly refused to himself, getting his supposed servant included in the cartel: had the shadow of a suspicion existed of his real character, he would have been most assuredly detained; yet, luckily, no difficulty arose, and he was liberated. When the day of his departure arrived, this kind and affectionate friend could scarcely be prevailed upon to leave his benefactor and protector, and it was long before he yielded to the most urgent entreaties. They parted with tears, which were those of unfeigned pleasure on the part of Sir Sidney, seeing that his friend was leaving a situation of the greatest danger.

In the whole of this part of the transaction there is much that is truly comic. The amiable jockey was regretted by every one. The turnkeys' hearts softened, and their lips opened, for they heartily and piously drank a good journey to him. The girl he had been courting wept bitterly for his departure, whilst her good mother, who thought John a very hopeful youth, felt fully assured that, one day, she should call him her son-in-law. In the midst of all these ludicrous ambiguities, we must say that there was a little dash of needless cruelty in the deception practised on the confiding girl; but we must wait for the march of improvement extending still farther, before the softer sex are fully included in man's laws of honour.

Sir Sidney had soon the extreme satisfaction to learn that his friend had safely arrived in London, and the knowledge of his safety made his own captivity the more endurable.

The commodore would also willingly have effected the exchange of his secretary, but that estimable gentleman was opposed to all mention of it, as he would have looked upon it as an infraction of that friendship of which he had given so many proofs. His principal did not very forcibly press the matter, as he, unlike Mr. De T., had no other dangers to apprehend than those that were common to all prisoners of war.

On the 18th Fructidor of republican France, the 4th of September of Christianity, for some reasons never fully understood, the rigour of Sir Sidney's confinement was still further increased. That paragon of jailers, with whom we have become so well acquainted, and whose name, which ought to be immortalised, was Lasne, was suddenly displaced, and his successor immediately made the commodore actually a close prisoner. Thus were Sir Sidney's hopes of a peace, which had just then been much talked of, and of his own release, crushed together. He now saw in this wanton severity a demonstration in the Directory of the most hostile character to the English nation, and a new barrier to future accommodation thrown up by this cruel treatment of distinguished English subjects.

But, amidst all these present adversities and gloomy apprehensions for the future, another proposal was made to the gallant captive, which, as a last resource, he was resolved to accept. The plan was simple, and could not but be effective, if wisely conducted. It was merely, by properly forged official documents, to order the removal of the prisoner to another place of confinement, and, in the supposititious transit, to convey him first to a place of safety, from whence he might ultimately make his escape. A French gentleman, enthusiastically attached to the royal cause, a M. de Phèlypeaux, whom the reader will again meet in these Memoirs, was the author of this scheme. As he was a gentleman not only distinguished by generosity, but by acumen in judgment and activity in conduct, the execution of the project was cheerfully confided to him. The order for removal having been accurately imitated, and, by means of a bribe, the real stamp of the minister's signature having been procured, nothing remained but to find men bold and trustworthy enough to simulate the necessary characters that should be employed to effect the removal. Mr. Phèlypeaux and Charles l'Oiseau would have eagerly undertaken this part of the stratagem also, but both being well known, and even notorious at the Temple, it was absolutely necessary to employ others. Messrs B—— and L—— therefore, both persons of tried courage, accepted the office with pleasure and alacrity.

With this forged order they boldly came to the Temple, M. B—— in the disguise of an adjutant, and M. L—— as an officer. They presented their order, which the keeper having perused, and of which he carefully examined the seal and the minister's signature, he went into another room, leaving the two gentlemen in the most cruel suspense. After a considerable time, which anxiety increased into hours, he returned, accompanied by the gréffier or register of the prison, and ordered Sir Sidney to be sent for. When the gréffier informed the prisoner of the order of the Directory, Sir Sidney pretended to be much concerned at it, as it appeared to him to argue further persecutions on their part. Hearing this, the adjutant assured him in the most serious manner, that "the government were very far from intending to aggravate his misfortunes, and that he would be very comfortable in the place to which he was ordered to conduct him." After this farcical exhibition, the commodore expressed his gratitude to all the servants employed about the prison, and then, with a very commendable despatch, he commenced packing up his clothes.

On his return, all ready for the approaching liberty, the gréffier remarked that, at least six men from the guard must accompany the prisoner; with which precaution the *soi-disant* adjutant coincided, and, without the least appearance of confusion, ordered them immediately to be called out. No sooner, however, had he given these orders, than he seemed, on a sudden, to have called to his mind the law of chivalry and of honour; so turning abruptly to Sir Sidney, he thus addressed him: "Commodore, you are an officer—I am an officer also. Your parole will be sufficient. Give me but that, and I have no need of an escort."

"Sir," replied the prisoner, "if that is sufficient, I swear on the faith of an officer to accompany you wherever you choose to conduct me."

Every one applauded these noble sentiments; and the only hardship that Sir Sidney felt in doing them sufficient justice, was in the difficulty that he found in suppressing his laughter. The keeper now asked for a discharge, and the gréffier, handing the book to M. B——, he boldly signed it, with an imposing flourish, "L'Oger, adjutant-general."

During these proceedings, Sir Sidney occupied the attention of the turnkeys with praises for their politeness and urbanity, and loaded them with favours, in order that they might have no leisure for reflection. The precaution seemed to be wholly needless, as they appeared to be thinking of nothing but their own advantage.

At last these tedious ceremonies were ended, and the gréffier and the governor accompanied the party as far as the second court; arid their suspense was nearly at an end when they found the external gate opened to them, through which, after a tantalising exchange of punctilio and politeness, they finally and joyfully passed, and had the extreme consolation of hearing it bolted behind them.

They instantly entered a hackney coach, and the adjutant ordered the coachman to drive to the suburb of St. Germain. But this fellow, either from his natural stupidity, or from some little plot of extortion, drove his vehicle, before he had proceeded one hundred yards, against a post, broke his wheel, and injured an unfortunate passenger. This *contre-tems* immediately collected a demonstration of the sovereign people in the shape of an angry crowd, who were exasperated at the injury the poor fellow had sustained from the misconduct of the coachman. The mob, at this time, was not to be despised; so Sir Sidney and his friends, taking their portmanteaus in their hands, went off in an instant.

Though they were much noticed by the people, the mob, for once, acted justly, confining themselves to the office of abusing the coachman. Notwithstanding this fracas, before the party could make off, the driver became clamorous for his fare, when W——, through an inadvertency that might have compromised the safety of them all, gave the fellow a double *louis d'or*. Luckily this had no ill effects.

Directly that they quitted the carriage, they separated, and Sir Sidney Smith arrived at the rendezvous, accompanied only by his secretary and M. Phèlypeaux, the last-mentioned gentleman having joined them near the prison. Though our officer was most anxious to wait for his two friends, in order to thank and to take his leave of them, M. de Phèlypeaux maintained that there was not a moment to be lost. He was, therefore, obliged to defer the expression of his gratitude until fortune should offer him a better opportunity, and they immediately departed for Rouen, at which place a gentleman had made every preparation for their reception.

At Rouen, they were obliged to remain several days; but as their passports were perfectly regular, they did not take much care to conceal themselves, for in the evenings they walked about the town, or took the air on the banks of the Seine. Finally, everything having been prepared for their crossing the Channel, they quitted Rouen and reached Havre, from whence they embarked in an open boat, and were picked up by the Argo, 44, Captain Bower, and landed at Portsmouth; and, without encountering any further danger, Sir Sidney arrived in London with his secretary, as well as with M. de Phèlypeaux, who could not prevail on himself to leave them.

During our hero's captivity in the Temple, Mrs. Cosway, a well-known artist of the day, and who afterwards published a poem in four cantos, entitled "the Siege of Acre," contrived to obtain a sight of Sir Sidney from a window or by some other means, and made a sketch of him as he sat by the bars of his prison. The head was in profile, and bore some resemblance to the original, but the features are of too haggard a contour to be acknowledged as an accurate likeness. The extraordinary thinness of the figure may be accounted for, by the effect of two years' confinement, during which he was overwhelmed with every indignity that oppression could lay upon the subject of its displeasure.

The above is the substance of a quotation from a very valuable publication, but it says too much. It appears, by the foregoing narrative, that Sir Sidney had, during the greater part of his imprisonment, free intercourse with his friends, an unrestricted correspondence, and, at intervals, much personal liberty. That he suffered, at times, most of the miseries of captivity, is certain, but never to the extent of bringing upon him the extreme incarceration for which the author of this paragraph would solicit our pity. Mrs. Cosway, her picture and her poem, are almost totally forgotten, though her subject is so worthy of immortality; and we have only mentioned this fact, in order to show the intense interest which everything connected with Sir Sidney Smith excited at the time.

It was in May, 1798, that Sir Sidney so unexpectedly arrived in London, where he was welcomed by the universal congratulations of the people. So rigid had been the care with which he had been confined, and knowing the value that the French Directory placed upon the boast of having the most active commodore in the English service in their prison, his arrival was looked upon, in some measure, as a miracle, which, at first, but few could prevail upon themselves to believe. We need not state, that he immediately became the first lion of the day.

His sovereign took the lead in these demonstrations of interest, and received him with the warmest affection, and showed in what estimation he held him, not only by his behaviour on his public presentation, but by honouring him with an immediate and private interview at Buckingham-house.

That these demonstrations were more than the offspring of policy, may be proved by the interest that his Majesty took for his officer's liberation, before he effected it so cleverly for himself. He had permitted M. Bergeret, the captain of the Virginia French frigate, which had been captured by Sir Edward Pellew, to go to France and endeavour to negotiate an exchange between Sir Sidney and himself; but, as we have before seen, being unable to succeed, he very honourably returned to England. The King, to give the French Directory a lesson in generosity, commanded his Secretary of State to write to M. Bergeret, to inform him, that, as the object of his mission to his own country was now obtained, his Majesty was graciously pleased, seeing the trouble to which he had been put, and as a mark of satisfaction which his conduct had afforded him, to restore him to liberty, and permitted him to return to his country without any restriction whatever.

CHAPTER XII

WE are now approaching the most brilliant epoch of Sir Sidney's martial career. It was necessary on the part of the English government to do all that lay in their power to oppose the aggrandising principles and the propaganding spirit of the French republic. That republic would fain have had but one nation in Europe, and that nation the French, but with many thrones and many kings at Paris. Had these visionary schemes succeeded, the civilised world might have been excellently ruled by the departmental demagogues assembled in the French metropolis; but every man out of France, who prized his nationality, and felt an honest glow at the simple words, "My country!" was ready to arm and to die in opposing this generalising and regenerating system.

After much diplomacy and infinite trouble, the obtuse Turk was made to see that if the republican power were not efficiently opposed, shortly everything within its scope would be French in name, and the subject and the slave to democrat France in reality. With all his faults, the Turk is obstinately national. He prepared to fight for what the new philosophy deemed a foolish prejudice.

In the September of 1798, the Sublime Porte began to show unequivocal symptoms of having awakened to a proper sense of his own position, and to the interests of the nation entrusted to his government. His new political feelings were energetically developed by a vigorous measure of reprisal against all the persons and property of the French that could be discovered in his dominions, and by fulminating a manifesto of extraordinary bitterness against the self-constituted government established in Paris.

This welcome display on the part of the Ottoman Porte caused the most active preparations in London for the speedy conclusion of a treaty of alliance, offensive and defensive, between Great Britain and Turkey. The more effectually to bring this measure to a happy maturity, the British government resolved to bestow a ministerial character upon the English officer destined to the difficult task of associating and co-operating with the Turkish fleets and armies. The choice of the person to fulfil this character, at once so delicate and so arduous, naturally and very justly fell upon Sir William Sidney Smith; and he was accordingly included in the especial full powers as joint plenipotentiary with, and despatched to, the British minister then residing at Constantinople. Sir Sidney had been appointed, on the 2nd of July, 1798, to the command of the Tigre of eighty guns; and in that ship he sailed on his honourable mission from Portsmouth, on the 29th of October of the same year. This service was peculiarly grateful to our officer, as his brother was, at that time, the English envoy to the Ottoman Porte.

On the 5th of January, 1799, he had a conference with the Reis Effendi, at which was present Mr. Spencer Smith, the English ambassador. Among the presents destined for the Grand Seignior, and which Sir Sidney Smith was charged to present, were a perfect model of the Royal George, and twelve brass field-pieces, three-pounders with their caissons so constructed as to be portable on camels.

On the 11th he took up his residence at the beautiful palace of Bailes, in which the ambassadors of the Venetian republic formerly lived. He was accompanied by several military and naval officers, some French emigrants, and a guard of marines. He was received by the Ottoman court with all the distinction due to a foreigner in a public character.

The expediency of appointing naval and military officers to diplomatic functions has been often called into question. We not only think it often expedient, but also highly beneficial. In all negotiations, the principal staple should be a singleness of purpose and an unswerving honesty. In all matters of treaty, the parties must have some definite object. To carry out this object, determination, good sense, and honesty are alone necessary. These are always acquired in the naval and military services; they are too seldom found, and if once possessed, too often lost, amidst the suppleness and chicanery of a court, and the amusing tortuosities of diplomacy. Special pleading is not natural to the English character; but an Englishman knows both what is due to him, and what he wants; and he has invariably found that the worst method for him to obtain these, is by the negociation of those educated to negociate, who have generally finessed away all their notions of integrity, and protocolled themselves out of their powers of perception of right and wrong. Need we cite instances, now going on before our eyes, of this melancholy truth? Whatever may have been the faults of the Tory administration, they evinced both good sense and vigour in the frequent employment of naval and military characters in diplomatic offices, and never more so than in the nomination of Sir William Sidney Smith to be joint plenipotentiary to the Ottoman Porte.

This appointment of Sir Sidney's gave, however, great umbrage in several eminent and influential quarters. There is but little doubt but that the already justly-acquired celebrity and the increasing renown of Sir Sidney had that influence upon human feeling which signal success will always have upon even the best of us. We have it upon an authority that it would be treason in literature to doubt, that Sir Sidney's appointment to a separate command in the Mediterranean was more than distasteful, even an annoyance, to Earl St. Vincent, and more especially so to Lord Nelson.

"The Quarterly Review," for October 1838, states distinctly that, owing to a little ambiguity in the orders of the Admiralty in appointing Sir Sidney Smith to serve under Lord Nelson entirely, Lord St. Vincent was overlooked; but lie too well knew the rules of the service to let Sir Sidney slip through his hands. All his anxiety was respecting the feelings of Nelson. On this subject he thus wrote to Lord Spencer from Gibraltar.

"An arrogant letter, written by Sir Sidney Smith to Sir William Hamilton, when he joined the squadron forming the blockade off Malta, has wounded Rear-Admiral Nelson to the quick, (as per enclosed,) which compels me to put this strange man immediately under his lordship's orders, as the King may be deprived of his (Lord Nelson's) valuable services, as superior to Sir Sidney Smith at all times as he is to ordinary men. I experienced a trait of the presumptuous character of this young man during his short stay at Gibraltar, which I passed over, that it might not appear that I was governed by prejudice in my conduct towards him."

This is a severe sentence passed upon our hero; but we really cannot help thinking that the disclaimer of prejudice, so energetically put forward, was rather premature. The bitterness with which he styled the hero of Acre this young man does not speak highly of the gallant old Earl's utter freedom from prejudice. We wish, for the sake of his own reputation, that he had not made use of this waspish expression; but it must not be too much dwelt upon, considering the vast merits and the eminent services of the veteran commander.

There was always something peculiar in the manner of Sir Sidney Smith—a peculiarity that, with the malevolent, would admit of a very wide construction—that it often found a very ungenerous one, is lamentably but too true. Without meaning anything that approaches to disparagement in reference to the manners of Sir Sidney's cotemporary brother officers, we are bound to state that, from his infancy, he had much of the deportment of the courtier in his carriage, and a little of the *petit-maître* [ED. young fop] in his appearance. He had had already, at a very early age, great success—he was ardent in his imagination, and fluent in his speech. These are sometimes dangerous gifts. They are too often great betrayers—leading to a promptitude of action, and a recklessness of expression, that the very sober-minded may often deem an approximation to incipient insanity. We thus find Earl St. Vincent, in his well-disciplined mind, suspicious of Sir Sidney Smith's conduct, and designating him as "a strange man." That he appeared, at times, strange, is as undoubtedly true as that he sometimes did strange things—but this strangeness led to very glorious consequences.

The good old admiral goes on to remark:

"I even, in fact, had good reason to be dissatisfied with Sir Sidney Smith, who is stated 'to have commenced his command before Alexandria by counteracting the system laid down by his lordship,' and which always," says Earl St. Vincent, "appeared to me fraught with the most consummate wisdom;" and he adds, "my only apprehension is, that Sidney Smith, enveloped in the importance of his ambassadorial character, will not attend to the practical part of his military profession."

May we be permitted to remark, that this borders nearly upon the ungenerous? Why found an imputation so injurious upon a mere *ex parte* and unproved statement? But the sequel is the best refutation to this attack. Sir Sidney did not, "enveloped in the importance of his ambassadorial character" omit "to attend to the practical part of his military profession" Lord Nelson's system must, undoubtedly, have been good, because it was Lord Nelson's; but that Sir Sidney Smith's could not have been bad, we have the best and most popular of all testimonies to prove—success.

Again, Earl St. Vincent, in the following abstract of a letter to Nelson, complains, for the first time, of his health, and cause of dissatisfaction from home.

"I am not well, and have great cause for dissatisfaction from higher quarters. He (Sir Sidney Smith) has no authority whatever to wear a distinguishing pennant, unless you authorise him, for *I* certainly shall not. Your lordship will therefore exercise your discretion on this subject, and every other within the limits of your command. I have sent a copy of the orders you have judged expedient to give Sir Sidney Smith (which I highly approve of) to Lord Spencer, with my remarks; for I foresee that both you and I shall be drawn into a tracasserie about this gentleman, who, having the ear of ministers, and telling his story better than we can, will be more attended to."

We do not like this. It is petulant and womanly. Down with the miserable stripe of bunting in an open and seaman-like manner; if it be an assumption on the part of Sir Sidney, down with it—but let us have no pining at or whining about it.

But this, we are sorry to say, appears to us to be of a piece with the sneer upon his being the gentleman. Do those, who really are gentlemen, ever attempt to convey a taunt by imputing to another the fact that he is a gentleman? If this be used by the Earl as a term of reproach, what then must he himself have been? If it was meant as a sarcasm, it is a sarcasm of a most villanous taste, and decidedly as wanting in point as it is in good-nature.

But then Sir Sidney had "the ear of the minister," and could tell his own story better than either Earl St. Vincent or Lord Nelson. It is distressing to see two renowned leaders drivelling about this. He could not tell his story better than either the hero of the Nile or of the Cape. When he had a good tale, it told itself well; but, in his despatches, we do not find any very alarming bursts of eloquence. They are decidedly less forcible and elegant than we should expect from such a man.

And shortly after, in another letter, he says:

"I fancy ministers at home disapprove of Sir Sidney Smith's conduct at Constantinople; for, in a confidential letter to me, a remark is made, that our new allies have not much reason to be satisfied with it. The man's head is completely turned with vanity and self-importance."

The "Quarterly Review" thus makes the "*amende*" for what we think something too severe in its remarks upon the bearing of our officer.

"With all Sir Sidney's faults, however, the memorable defence of Acre, with small means, against the overwhelming force of Bonaparte, entitles him to the gratitude of the British nation, and will, if our annals speak true, immortalise his name.

"Of this we are assured, whether the annals of our country be true or false, (for not on their veracity but on their duration the matter depends,) his fame will be equally lasting with that of the proudest of our heroes. So intimately is Sir Sidney Smith's name associated with the glory of the country, that, among naval men, whenever the names of Howe, Duncan, or Nelson, have been mentioned with enthusiasm, the peroration has always been the praise of our officer. We may safely say that in the cockpit he is idolised, an especial favourite in the gunroom, and in the cabin deeply respected. The very chivalry of his character, which makes him, in the eyes of the young and ardent, the object of their deep admiration, will always be a matter of suspicion to the old, the wily, and the shrewd politician.

"For ourselves, highly as he stands in our estimation, we do not think that it ever was advisable to have entrusted him with the sole command of armaments so extensive, that a failure would turn the tide of success of a whole war against us, or place the nation in peril. His character was formed for the detached and the brilliant. It appears that success or failure was always, to him, an object secondary to that of exciting astonishment, or gaining glory."

Sir Sidney was already most favourably known to the Turks; for, when he was with them before, he had brought out with him a clever architect, a Mr. Spurnham, and fifteen able shipwrights. These superintended and assisted at the building of several fine Turkish vessels; and in one year, that of 1798, they were thus enabled, with many smaller vessels, to construct a three-decker and another line-of-battle ship of eighty-four guns, which, in Sir Sidney Smith's official mission, by the assistance of the crew of the Tigre, they were enabled to launch and fully equip for service. These vessels afterwards formed a part of Sir Sidney's squadron.

During the whole time that the Turkish ships were serving with the English, there were placed on board the former, petty officers and some experienced seamen to instruct the Osmanlie crew how to work them; and thus assisted, they did no discredit to their generous allies in their various maritime manoeuvres.

Now, during the interval of Nelson's glorious victory of the Nile, and the arrival of Sir Sidney Smith on the Syrian coast, Bonaparte had almost entirely subjugated Egypt, and had already commenced a well-conceived plan of colonisation and organisation of his own important conquest. His promptitude and talent for the administration of the internal affairs of a kingdom, so extraordinary as that of Egypt, cannot be too highly eulogised. Already had he established so much order and regularity among these new subjects to the French, arid established in these dominions so many military resources, that he conceived himself enabled to lead on his army, and to endeavour to subdue the contiguous provinces to the East. His troops were fully prepared for the expedition. By this demonstration he threatened the subjugation of the remaining Turkish provinces in that quarter, and was even enabled to give us some alarm, though completely unfounded, for our invaluable British establishments in India. Though much of the apprehensions excited by the brilliant success and rapid movements of the French leader were totally baseless, yet the policy would have been a very weak one, had the confederated powers not sought means to check his progress, and to destroy the moral effect produced upon the inhabitants of the East by his victorious career. Very great exertions were accordingly made on the part of the Sublime Porte, and their new allies, the English, to arrest the course and counteract the designs of the future Emperor of the French.

Deeply impressed with this community of interests, preparations were made throughout Syria for military resistance to the march of the French by the Ghezzar Pasha, who was to be still further supported by an army which was to form a junction with him, by traversing Asia Minor. It was supposed that this force would be sufficiently strong to warrant the experiment of an attack on the frontier of Egypt, without waiting for the advance of the French. This demonstration was to have been supported by a powerful diversion towards the mouths of the Nile, and made still more effective by the operations of a strong corps under Murad Bey.

CHAPTER XIII

THIS plan of operations was well arranged, but the Turks had not sufficiently advanced in military science to act upon extensive combinations. All these preparations, for a time, proved futile when opposed to the well-considered tactics of Bonaparte. That consummate general, having obtained intelligence that the arrival at the Ottoman court of Commodore Sir William Sidney Smith would be the signal for the commencement of these too widely diffused operations, determined not to wait for the combined movement, but to act, at once, against a part of the force to be employed against him. He therefore determined to commence offensive operations against the Pasha. The French forces destined for this expedition amounted to about thirteen thousand men. The face of the country being entirely impracticable for artillery, the republican general had no other means of conveying it to the destined scene of operations but by sea. He therefore shipped his train at Alexandria. Rear-Admiral Perrée was sent with three frigates to convoy the flotilla, having orders afterwards to cruise off Jaffa. It may not be here out of place to state that this town, Jaffa, had been stormed and taken by the French on the preceding 7th March, on which occasion the whole of the Turkish garrison was put to the sword. The conquest was not worth the cost. In the assault the French lost above twelve hundred of the élite of their army. To show also the desperate policy and the extraordinary lengths to which Bonaparte would sometimes proceed, he announced that in this expedition to Palestine he purposed to take possession of Jerusalem, rebuild the Temple, restore the Jews, and thus disprove the prophecies of the divine Founder of the Christian religion. But it must be remembered, in order to vindicate such boasting from the imputation of insanity, that, at that time, infidelity was the road to Gallic power, and the revilement of Christianity not unpleasing to his newly-acquired subjects.

After this digression, we must hasten to return to our commodore, and narrate the progress of the operations in which he was so materially concerned. Being apprised of the enemy's intentions, he left the Turkish capital, in the Tigre, on 19th February, 1799, and after making several needful arrangements with Hassan Bey, the Ottoman governor of Rhodes, who happened to be an old sea-captain, he sailed from that island, and arrived off Alexandria on the 3d of March. He here found in command Captain Trowbridge, whom he immediately relieved, and then despatched his friend and second lieutenant, Lieutenant Wright, to St. Jean d'Acre, to decide, with its commander, upon the necessary measures for the obstinate defence of that fortress.

We will take this opportunity of mentioning, that this brave officer, Wright, who honoured and was honoured with the friendship of Sir Sidney, was as unfortunate as he was brave. In the subsequent gallant and glorious defence of Acre, to which we shall shortly refer, he received a severe and dangerous wound, and was afterwards promoted to the rank of commander. Just as the great prizes of his profession seemed to be soliciting his grasp, he had the mortification of being made prisoner by the French, and died in that situation after a protracted, rigorous, and cruel confinement. For these harsh measures the French authorities have some palliation in the very suspicious service on which he was employed when captured. At one time, it was generally supposed that he was assassinated, whilst in prison, by the orders of Bonaparte. This, however, turns out to be a malicious calumny. It proves, however, the value that public opinion placed upon Wright; for to be thought the object of personal fear to a man like Bonaparte is no mean commendation. His old friend and commander has given proof of his esteem, for he has, since the peace, caused a handsome monument to be erected to his memory at that Paris which was so long the scene of their mutual sufferings.

This gives us occasion to relate an anecdote of a very humble individual, connected with the fate of poor Wright, and alike elucidatory of the character of Sir Sidney. This anecdote, trivial as it may appear to the superciliously grave, ought not to be undervalued, since it affords us the enviable opportunity of placing upon record a single effort of our enterprising commodore to conciliate the Muses—an effort that possesses one most excellent quality, not usually met with in the poetical effusions of the day, yet no less to be desired—it is brevity.

When Wright received his severe wound, it was reported to Sir Sidney that he was actually killed. The commodore's grief was excessive, and when, immediately after, Colonel Douglas, of the royal marines, reported the successful springing of a mine that had destroyed a vast number of the enemy, Sir Sidney's principal thought was about his old companion and tried friend, Wright. "Let the French," &c. &c., was Sir Sidney's reply; "but if you love me, and it be possible, bring in the body of poor Wright."

The colonel immediately called to one of his men, a gigantic, red-haired, Irish marine, who, by some singular means, had contrived to get himself named James Close. Pointing to the mass of carnage that lay sweltering in the ditch below, where the slightly wounded and the actually dying were fast hastening into mutual corruption under the burning sun, "the colonel said, "Close, dare you go there, and bring us the body of poor Wright?"

"What darn't I do, yer honour?" was the immediate reply, and exposed to the musketry of the enemy, wading through blood, and stumbling over dead bodies and scattered limbs, he, unhurt, at length found Wright, not killed, but only wounded, and he brought him away safely from these shambles of death and the plague. The French spared him for the sake of the heroism of the act.

The rescue was complete, for Close conveyed him to the hospital, where he soon completely recovered, to find, not long after, a less honoured death.

This intrepid conduct brought the marine into especial favour with Sir Sidney, and had his education but have warranted promotion, his advancement would have been rapid. The commodore did for him all that he could; he exempted him from the wearying routine of a private's duty, and made him his orderly, thus limiting his services to a mere personal attendance on Sir Sidney.

It would seem that James Close was not so great a hero in resisting the temptation of a naval life, grog, and the illegal means of obtaining it, as he was fearless of the enemy, and great in the field. Indeed, it requires a most amiable believer in the intuitive integrity of our species, not to pronounce that, for a little peccadillo or so, he deserved to be hung; but of this we cannot judge, as the truth of the matter will ever remain in the deepest mystery.

Our gallant hero—not James Close, but his commander-in-chief had received from the King of Sweden a beautiful and very valuable diamond ring, and which, amongst other jewellery, and with his orders, he always wore on state occasions. At a grand dinner given at the monastery at Acre, and at which all the superior officers of both the English and Turkish service were present, with every other civilian of note, that part of the ornaments that consisted of Sir Sidney Smith's rings was lost. He was in the habit, just before he washed his hands after dining, to take from off his hands his *bijouterie*, and place the trinkets under the tablecloth—a very provident plan, when the guests happen to be numerous and miscellaneous. This custom he put in practice on this day, but unfortunately, when he rose from the table, he totally forgot the treasure that he had left beneath the tablecloth, and retired as happy as if his fingers had displayed their wonted effulgence.

It was usual, on these high occasions, for Sir Sidney Smith's body-guard, consisting of a party of the royal marines, to place themselves at the vacated table, when the guests had withdrawn, and finish the fare provided for their superiors—a munificent regulation, highly creditable to Sir Sidney.

On this day, the custom was honoured, not by the breach, but the observance; for not only did the fragments of the feast disappear, but the rings also, as, shortly after the viands were consumed, Sir Sidney missed his ornaments, and a strict but ineffectual search ensued.

The Greeks have a bad character, and on this occasion they received the full benefit of it, as it was supposed that the attending descendants of Homer's heroes had made to themselves the lucky appropriation; and being Greeks, the English very wisely deemed that search would be fruitless, and recovery hopeless.

For two years the stigma lay with the Athenians, when, in 1801, the marines disembarked from the Tigre to assist Abercromby in his operations. After the action of the 13th of March, it fell to the duty of these marines narrowly to invest the Castle of Aboukir. One day, four of these marines, (we do not know why posterity should not be acquainted with their names,) Clark, Stanton, West, and James Close, were taking their ease in their hut, which an envious shot from the castle disturbed, by killing Clark and Stanton, and thus naturally causing the two survivors narrowly to search, as is the laudable custom on such occasions, the dead bodies of their comrades. Among other good things that they possessed, there were found in Stanton's pockets (at least Close said so) two rings, of which the said Close took particular care.

Some little time after, Close was again ordered on shore on military duty, and he then entrusted these rings to the care of another of his comrades, named Connor—Close, thinking this Connor to be a particularly steady man, and consequently that they would be more safe in his keeping, on board, than in his own, on shore.

In order to do full justice to this opinion, Connor goes on board on the same day, and very carefully gets gloriously drunk, and "appetite increasing by what it fed on," that is to say, the act of drinking making him much athirst for more, he sells the heaviest of the rings, the veritable King of Sweden, for a mere thimbleful of the poison, to his messmate, who, having the spirit of barter strongly upon him, sells it again to Sir Sidney Smith's steward for the enormous value of half a gallon of bad wine. The steward immediately recognised it as the great diamond, "the right royal Gustavus," as Sir Sidney was wont to call it, and of whose majesty no tidings had been heard for two years.

Investigation immediately followed discovery, and it was speedily traced up to James Close, who was sent on board and interrogated strictly. Of course, he laid the primal theft at the door of the departed, well knowing and acting upon the proverb, that "dead men tell no tales," at least on this side of the grave. It was never known exactly what degree of credence Sir Sidney gave to this account; but as it was certain that even dead men ought not to be robbed, James Close stood within the terrors of the law, and, consequently, Close found himself immediately in close custody. The officers of the Tigre endeavoured to prevail upon their commander to bring the prisoner to a trial by court-martial, but his heroic conduct towards Captain Wright operated strongly in his favour; so after a few days' confinement Sir Sidney sent for him on deck, and ordering him to be released, thus addressed him:

> You're Close by name, and Close in every thing,
> And Close you've kept, O Close, my diamond ring.

It was very fortunate for the culprit that his captain was more in the rhyming than the flogging vein, for we think it not unlikely that the fecundity of Sir Sidney's head saved the marine's back. However, the lines were looked upon as a monument of poetical genius, and the distich stuck as closely to poor Close as any punster of a reasonable good-nature could have wished.

As faithful chroniclers of the events connected with these Memoirs, we feel bound to state the general impression among the officers and seamen of the English squadron respecting the real character of Wright. Before Sir Sidney commenced his renowned defence of Acre, Wright was the second lieutenant of the Tigre. It is well known that he was landed by Sir Sidney Smith, in his own barge, at a short distance from Alexandria, in the night-time, not openly as a British naval officer, but bearded, moustachioed, and shawled *á la Turque*, and for the express purpose of obtaining valuable information. Conscious of the dubiety of his mission, on stepping on shore he thus addressed the boat's crew: "Men, beware of your words! I am going to serve my king and country, if, by the help of God, I can." Then turning to his commander, he exclaimed, "Sir Sidney, do not forget the boat's crew."

The vulgar belief may have been erroneous, but it was asserted that he was constantly employed by Sir Sidney as a spy, and the fact was neither concealed nor denied on board the Tigre.

But to resume. Sir Sidney, after bombarding Alexandria in the vain hope of arresting the march of Bonaparte towards Acre, which was not then sufficiently strengthened to stand a siege, sailed for that devoted place, off which he anchored on the 15th of March. He immediately landed, and proceeded to inspect the fortifications. These he found in a dilapidated and most ruinous state, and almost destitute of artillery. Making the best arrangements that the shortness of the time until the attack would be expected, and the paucity of the materials for a defence permitted, on the 17th of March the commodore again put to sea in the Tigre's boats, and proceeded to the anchorage of Khaiffa, in order to intercept that portion of the French expedition which would take its route along the sea-coast, and which Sir Sidney was convinced must necessarily soon make its appearance. His anticipations were correct, for, at ten o'clock on the same night, he discovered the approach of the enemy's advanced guard, moving leisurely forward by the sea-side. They were mounted upon asses and dromedaries, and offered a novel and somewhat grotesque spectacle. Having thus satisfied himself as to their actual approach, the commodore, with all haste, returned on board the Tigre, from which ship he immediately despatched Lieutenant Bushby, in a gunboat, to the mouth of a small river (the brook Kishon of the Scriptures) that flows into the bay of Acre. He had strict orders to defend the ford across this little stream to the utmost, and by no means to suffer the French to advance by this way on the town.

At the break of day, this intelligent officer admirably worked out his commander's intentions. This curiously mounted advanced guard had, unexpectedly, so vigorous and so destructive a fire opened upon them, that they were driven, in great confusion, both from the shore and the ford, and great was the overthrow of men, as well as of dromedaries and asses. Indeed, a tumultuous dispersion of the whole force ensued, and was scattered on the skirts of Mount Carmel.

Taught by this repulse, the main body of the French army avoided carefully this pernicious and gunboat-guarded ford, and, to escape a similar attack, were obliged to make a large circuit, and advance upon Acre by the road of Nazareth. This they did without much difficulty, for they soon drove in the Turkish outposts, and encamped upon an insulated eminence skirting the sea, upon a parallel direction with the town, and about one thousand toises* distant from it. As this elevation extended to the northward as far as Cape Blanc, it commanded a plain to the westward of seven miles in length, and which plain is terminated by the mountains that lie between St. Jean d'Acre and the river Jordan. This position of the republican forces was as commanding and as good as could be well desired. Favoured by the shelter afforded them by the outlying gardens, the unfilled ditches of the old town, and an aqueduct that adjoined to the glacis, they opened their trenches against the crumbling works of the town on the 20th, and at no greater distance than one hundred and fifty toises.

We have here again to make a cursory mention of a very brave and clever loyalist, M. Phèlypeaux, who had been in the service of Louis XVI. as an engineer. He was skilful in his profession, and in his private capacity a very worthy man. Though, at this time, still young, he had been involved in many extraordinary adventures, having served in all the campaigns of the army of Condé. He commanded at Berri, and was taken, and only escaped an ignominious death by breaking out from a state-prison. As we have before narrated, he accompanied Sir Sidney to England, at the time the latter made his escape from the custody of the French Directory. The strictest friendship, founded upon mutual esteem, subsisted between M. Phèlypeaux and our hero, and he accompanied him as a volunteer in this Syrian expedition, and proved of infinite service by materially strengthening the works of this miserable place, which was so

---

* [ED. - A toise was six feet (i.e. about 1.949 meters) in France before 10 December 1799. Between 10 December 1799 and 1 January 1840 (when this book was written) it was exactly 2 meters.]

shortly afterwards to prove his tomb, as he died there on the 2nd of May following.

This experienced engineer officer was materially assisted by Captain Miller[+] of the Theseus, who furnished guns and ammunition to the utmost of his power.

But it seems that all this display of skill and activity would have proved inefficient against the skill and bravery that supported the attacks of the French, had not their vessels, having on board the greater part of their battering-train and ammunition, fallen into our hands. We have before mentioned that this artillery had been ordered round by sea by Bonaparte, from Alexandria, under the command of Rear-Admiral Perée. This flotilla was just rounding Cape Carmel, when it was discovered by the Tigre, pursued, and overtaken.

The capture was not so complete as could have been wished. The protecting force consisted of a corvette and nine gunboats. Two of these and the corvette, containing Bonaparte's personal property, escaped. Seven gun-vessels, mounting altogether thirty-four guns, and containing two hundred and thirty-eight men, were captured, together with the train of artillery. The cannon, platforms, and ammunition, were immediately landed at Acre, and used for its defence, and the gunboats manned and employed in molesting the enemy's posts established on the sea-coast, harassing their communications, and intercepting their convoys. The sea has always been fatal to the French, and, notwithstanding the difficulty of the country, we are inclined to think every obstacle should have been encountered by them in this transport of their artillery, rather than have trusted it to that element, which, as an arena of contention with the English, has always been to them so disastrous.

[+] Captain Ralph Willet Miller was made post-captain in 1796, and commanded the Captain seventy-four, bearing the broad pennant of Commodore Nelson, in the action off Cape St. Vincent, 14th February, 1797. He was afterwards appointed to the Theseus seventy-four, which ship he commanded at the battle of the Nile. After having been three days off Jaffa, whither he was despatched by Sir William Sidney Smith, the Turkish blue flag was confided to him, an honour never before conferred upon a Christian. It imparts the power of a pasha over the subjects of the grand seignior. The premature death of this meritorious officer was occasioned by the blowing up of the afterpart of the Theseus, while lying off Jaffa.

CHAPTER XIV

THIS year the equinoctial gales had been unusually severe, and the commodore, with the Tigre and the naval force under his command, had been compelled to take shelter under the lee of Mount Carmel. On his return to the roadstead off Acre, he found that the French had taken advantage of his unwilling and enforced absence to push their attacks vigorously. Their approaches had reached the counterscarp, and had penetrated even into the ditch of the north-east angle of the town wall. This angle was defended by a tower which they were rapidly undermining, in order to increase a breach they had already made in it, but which breach they had found to be impracticable when they endeavoured to storm it on the 1st of April.

In this mining operation they were greatly impeded by the fire of the guns that had been lately captured from the French, and which had been quickly mounted and judiciously placed by Captain Wilmot of the Alliance, who was unfortunately shot by a French rifleman a few days afterwards, the 8th of April, as he was mounting a howitzer on the breach. These guns played so actively and destructively under the direction of Colonel Phèlypeaux, that the enemy's fire slackened considerably, and the widening of the breach was but slow in progress.

Yet this successful opposition had no effect upon the mine, and the most serious apprehensions were entertained that its firing would be fatal to the defence of the town. To counteract this, a sortie was resolved upon. It was finally arranged that a body of British seamen and marines was to endeavour to possess the mine, whilst the Turkish troops were to attack the French in their trenches on both sides. As this decisive operation was intended to be a surprise, the sally was made before daylight on the 7th of April. Owing to the impetuosity and noise of the Turks, this plan entirely failed, and the dreaded mine remained in all its terrors.

In no military effort upon record did the French display greater perseverance or more desperate bravery. In every one of their attacks they seemed to understand beforehand that destruction was to be the rule, and escape the exception. With this predestination strong upon them, they went up to the breach coolly and regularly, and with as much nonchalance as if death were an unimportant part of their military evolutions. Indeed, repeated attempts were made to mount the breach under such circumstances of desperation as to excite the pity of their British foes to see such vain and bloody sacrifices of energy and courage.

Though hostilities were carried on with such vigour and apparent rancour in the trenches and on the breach, yet there were frequent suspensions of operations, and the distinguished French generals, on such occasions, derived much pleasure from visiting Sir Sidney on board the Tigre. On one of these occasions, and after the besieging party had made some progress, Generals Kleber and Junot were, with Sir Sidney Smith, walking the quarter-deck of the Tigre in a very amiable mood of amicability, one on each side the English commander-in-chief.

After a few turns in silence, Junot, regarding the battered fortifications that lay before him, and they being dwindled by distance into much insignificancy, thus broke out in the spirit of false prophecy—

"Commodore, mark my words! three days hence, by this very hour, the French tricolor shall be flying on the remains of that miserable town."

Sir Sidney very quickly replied, "My good general, before you shall have that town, I will blow it and you to Jericho."

"*Bien obligé*! Very much obliged," Kleber observed; "much obliged indeed—it will be all in our way to India."

"With all my heart," rejoined Sir Sidney, "I shall be most happy to assist you, Bonaparte, and your whole army, forward in that style; and we will commence as soon as you please."

The offer, though very kindly made, was neither accepted nor replied to.

Nine times had the enemy attempted to storm the trench, and on each occasion had been beaten back with profuse slaughter, such was the determined bravery opposed to their desperate assaults, when, on the fifty-first day of the siege, the long-expected and anxiously looked for reinforcements, under Hassan Bey, appeared in the distance. Before its junction could be effected, and relief thrown into the town, Bonaparte was resolved to do the utmost that his genius and the bravery of his army could achieve. His efforts were, therefore, renewed with the most impetuous vigour, whilst, on the part of the besieged, they were met with a corresponding spirit. All that skill and bravery could perform was mutually displayed. Under all disadvantages, the enemy, however, continued to advance, and at length got possession of the long-disputed north-east tower. This they accomplished, not by the explosion of the mine, but, having battered down the upper part of the structure, they ascended over the ruins, and, at daylight on the fifty-second morning of the siege, the tricolored flag was seen floating on the outer angle of the tower.

This display damped, considerably, the enterprise of the Turkish soldiers, and the fire of the besieged on the French lines was sensibly slackened. The enemy had also, during the night, obtained another important advantage, having been enabled to construct two traverses that completely screened them from the flanking fire of the Tigre and the Theseus, which, till then, had taken deadly effect upon every advance towards the breach. These two traverses were thrown up directly across the ditch, and were constructed with dead bodies intermingled with sandbags.

Such, as we have above described, was the critical position of the Turkish garrison and their brave allies when Hassan Bey's reinforcement arrived. The reader will of course understand that they came along the sea-coast in transports. These troops, before the vessels anchored, were hurried into the boats, but they were still distant from the shore, whilst the French were rallying the last and their best energies to carry the town. Such being the critical position of affairs, a strenuous and sudden effort on the part of the British was indispensable to preserve the place for a short time, until the landing and receiving the reinforcements into the fortress.

This effort, at once gallant, wise, and successful, with its subsequent operations, we shall give in Sir William Sidney Smith's own words, in his animated and graphic official report to Lord Nelson.

Tigre, Acre, May 9.

My Lord, I had the honour to inform your lordship, by my letter of the 2d instant, that we were busily employed completing two ravelins for the reception of cannon to flank the enemy's nearest approaches, distant only ten yards from them. They were attacked that very night, and almost every night since, but the enemy have each time been repulsed with very considerable loss. The enemy continued to batter in breach with progressive success, and have nine several times attempted to storm, but have as often been beaten back with immense slaughter. Our best mode of defence has been frequent sorties to keep them on the defensive, and impede the progress of their covering works. We have thus been in one continued battle ever since the beginning of the siege, interrupted only at short intervals by the excessive fatigue of every individual on both sides. We have been long anxiously looking for a reinforcement, without which we could not expect to be able to keep the place so long as we have. The delay in its arrival being occasioned by Hassan Bey's having originally had orders to join me in Egypt, I was obliged to be very peremptory in the repetition of my orders for him to join me here: it was not, however, till the evening of the day before yesterday, the fifty-first day of the siege, that his fleet of corvettes and transports made its appearance. The approach of this additional strength was the signal to Bonaparte for a most vigorous and persevering assault, in hopes to get possession of the town before the reinforcement to the garrison could disembark.

The constant fire of the besiegers was suddenly increased tenfold; our flanking fire afloat was, as usual, plied to the utmost, but with less effect than heretofore, as the enemy had thrown up epaulments and traverses of sufficient thickness to protect him from it. The guns that could be worked to the greatest advantage were a French brass eighteen-pounder in the light-house castle, manned from the Theseus, under the direction of Mr. Scroder, master's mate, and the last mounted twenty-four-pounder in the north ravelin, manned from the Tigre, under the direction of Mr. Jones, midshipman. These guns being within grape distance of the head of the attacking column, added to the Turkish musketry, did great execution; and I take this opportunity of recommending these two petty officers, whose indefatigable vigilance and zeal merit my warmest praise. The Tigre's two sixty-eight pound carronades, mounted in two dgermes, lying in the Mole, and worked under the direction of Mr. Bray, carpenter of the Tigre, (one of the bravest and most intelligent men I ever served with,) threw shells into the centre of this column with evident effect, and checked it considerably. Still, however, the enemy gained ground, and made a lodgment in the second story of the northeast tower; the upper part being entirely battered down, and the ruins in the ditch forming the ascent by which they mounted. Daylight showed us the French standard on the outer angle of the tower. The fire of the besieged was much slackened, in comparison to that of the besiegers, and our flanking fire was become of less effect, the enemy having covered themselves in this lodgment and the approach to it by two traverses across the ditch, which they had constructed under the fire that had been opposed to them during the whole night, and which were now seen, composed of sandbags, and the bodies of their dead built in with them, their bayonets only being visible above them. Hassan Bey's troops were in the boats, though as yet but half way on shore. This was a most critical point of the contest, and an effort was necessary to preserve the place for a short time till their arrival.

I accordingly landed the boats at the Mole, and took the crews up to the breach, armed with pikes. The enthusiastic gratitude of the Turks, men, women, and children, at the sight of such a reinforcement, at such a time, is not to be described.

Many fugitives returned with us to the breach, which we found defended by a few brave Turks, whose most destructive missile weapons were heavy stones, which, striking the assailants on the head, overthrew the foremost down the slope, and impeded the progress of the rest. A succession, however, ascended to the assault, the heap of ruins between the two parties serving as a breastwork to both; the muzzles of their muskets touching, and the spear-heads of their standards locked. Dgezzar Pasha, hearing the English were on the breach, quitted his station, where, according to the ancient Turkish custom, he was sitting to reward such as should bring him the heads of the enemy, and distributing musket cartridges with his own hands. The energetic old man, coming behind us, pulled us down with violence; saying, if any harm happened to his English friends, all was lost. This amicable contest, as to who should defend the breach, occasioned a rush of Turks to the spot; and thus time was gained for the arrival of the first body of Hassan Bey's troops. I had now to combat the Pasha's repugnance to admitting any troops but his Albanians into the garden of his seraglio, which had become a very important post, as occupying the terreplein of the rampart. There were about two hundred of the original one thousand Albanians left alive. This was no time for debate, and I overruled his objections by introducing the Chifflick regiment, of one thousand men, armed with bayonets, disciplined after the European method under Sultan Selim's own eye, and placed, by his Imperial Majesty's express command, at my disposal. The garrison, animated by the appearance of such a reinforcement, was now all on foot; and there being consequently enough to defend the breach, I proposed to the Pasha to get rid of the object of his jealousy, by opening his gates to let them make a sally, and take the assailants in flank: he readily complied, and I gave directions to the colonel to get possession of the enemy's third parallel or nearest trench, and there fortify himself by shifting the parapet outwards. This order being clearly understood, the gates were opened, and the Turks rushed out; but they were not equal to such a movement, and were driven back to the town with loss. Mr. Bray,* however, as usual, protected the town-gate efficaciously with grape from the sixty-eight pounders. The sortie had this good effect, that it obliged the enemy to expose themselves above their parapets, so that our flanking fires brought down numbers of them, and drew their force from the breach, so that the small number remaining on the lodgment were killed or dispersed by our few remaining hand grenades thrown by Mr. Savage, midshipman of the Theseus. The enemy began a new breach by an incessant fire directed to the southward of the lodgment, every shot knocking down whole sheets of a wall, much less solid than that of the tower, on which they had expended so much time and ammunition. The group of generals and aides-de-camp, which the shells from the sixty-eight pounders had frequently

---

* Mr. Bray was carpenter of the Tigre, and appears to have been a very superior man in every respect to the generality of warrant officers.

dispersed, was now re-assembled on Richard Coeur de Lion's Mount. Bonaparte was distinguishable in the centre of a semicircle: his gesticulations indicated a renewal of attack, and his despatching an aide-de-camp showed that he waited only for a reinforcement. I gave directions for Hassan Bey's ships to take their station in the shoal water to the southward, and made the Tigre's signal to weigh, and join the Theseus to the northward. A little before sunset, a massive column appeared advancing to the breach with a solemn step. The Pasha's idea was not to defend the breach this time, but rather to let a certain number of the enemy in, and then close with them according to the Turkish mode of war. The column thus mounted the breach unmolested, and descended from the rampart into the Pasha's garden, where, in a very few minutes, the bravest and most advanced among them lay headless corpses; the sabre, with the addition of a dagger in the other hand, proving more than a match for the bayonet. The rest retreated precipitately; and the commanding officer, who was seen manfully encouraging his men to mount the breach, and who we had since learnt to be General Lannes, was carried off, wounded by a musket-shot. General Rombaud was killed. Much confusion arose in the town from the actual entry of the enemy, it having been impossible, nay impolitic, to give* previous information to every body of the mode of defence adopted, lest the enemy should come to a knowledge of it by means of their numerous emissaries.

The English uniform, which had served as a rallying point for the old garrison, wherever it appeared, was now in the dusk mistaken for French, the newly-arrived Turks not distinguishing between one hat and another in the crowd, and thus many a severe blow of a sabre was parried by our officers, among which Colonel Douglas,* Mr. Ives, and Mr. Jones, had nearly lost their lives, as they were forcing their way through a torrent of fugitives. Calm was restored by the Pasha's exertions, aided by Mr. Trotte, just arrived with Hassan Bey; and thus the contest of twenty-five hours ended, both parties being so fatigued as to be unable to move.

Bonaparte will, no doubt, renew the attack, the breach being, as above described, perfectly practicable for fifty men abreast; indeed the town is not, nor ever has been defensible, according to the rules of art, but according to every other rule it must and shall be defended: not that it is in itself worth defending, but we feel that it is by this breach Bonaparte means to march to farther conquests. It is on the issue of this conflict that depends the opinion of the multitude of spectators on the surrounding hills, who wait only to see how it ends, to join the victors; and with

---

* The late Sir John Douglas, of the Royal Marines.

such a reinforcement for the execution of his known projects, Constantinople, and even Vienna, must feel the shock.

Be assured, my lord, the magnitude of our obligations does but increase the energy of our efforts in the attempt to discharge our duty; and though we may, and probably shall be overpowered, I can venture to say that the French army will be so much farther weakened before it prevails, as to be little able to profit by its dear-bought victory.

I have the honour to be, &c.

W. SIDNEY SMITH

Rear-Admiral Lord Nelson

This despatch is exceedingly well written, and is made singularly graceful by the air of modesty which pervades it. Sir Sidney well understood the nature of the contest, and that to the moral effect of victory or defeat, the loss or the salvation of the miserable heap of ruins called Acre was but as dust in the balance.

Already had the Syrians been so prepossessed with the irresistibility of the French forces—an idea by no means preposterous when the invariable success of these invaders was considered—that all efforts of resistance had been paralysed. Had it not been for the stimulating influence of British courage, Bonaparte would have met with no opposition, and he and his generals, there is every reason to suppose, would have been wholly unimpeded in whatever plans of conquest, personal aggrandisement, or political vengeance, they might have concerted.

This British opposition in defence of Acre fell with peculiar and exasperating force upon the commander-in-chief of the republican army. This was displayed by the increased irritability of his temper; and, in the fervour of this very natural vexation, he called for the most cruel sacrifices on the part of his brave followers, and evinced a determination to extend them to the utmost limits of human endurance. We are no depredators of the extraordinary genius of Bonaparte, nor do we think that, placed in the situation he was, he could, or that he ought to have acted differently. The obstacle before him must, he well knew, be surmounted, or, sooner or later, defeat and universal discomfiture awaited him. It might, perhaps, have been well for the destiny of nations and the tranquillity of Europe, had he met with a less sturdy opponent than Sir Sidney. Had he succeeded before St. Jean d'Acre, another and a less disastrous course might have been opened to his ambition.

But we must return to this singular siege and still more singular defence. The gallant antagonist of the future first consul was fully aware of the advantage he had gained, and well knew how to improve it to the utmost. Rightly judging that the prejudice in favour of Gallic invincibility must be considerably shaken by the late events, and by the fatal check that was given to the advancement of their arms, Sir Sidney wrote a circular letter to the princes and chiefs of Mount Lebanon, and to the shieks of the Druses, by which he exhorted them to do their duty to their sovereign by intercepting the supplies of the enemy on their way to the French camp. This sagacious proceeding had all the good consequences that might have been expected from it. Two ambassadors were sent to the commodore, informing him that, in consequence of his mandates, measures had been taken to cut off the supplies hitherto furnished to the invaders; and, as a proof of the accuracy of this assertion, eighty French prisoners, who had been captured in the defence of their convoys, were placed at the disposal of the British.

Thus baffled in front, and straitened on all sides, the paramount object of the French was to mount the breach. To this every other consideration must give way. Accordingly, General Kleber's division was ordered from the fords of the river Jordan, where it had been successfully opposed to the army of Damascus, to take its turn in an attempt that had already occasioned the loss of the flower of the French troops of the besieging division, with more than two-thirds of its officers. But on the arrival of General Kleber and his army, there was other employment found for them.

In the sally before mentioned, made by the Turkish Chifflick regiment, it had shown a want of steadiness in the presence of the enemy, and was in consequence censured. The commandant of that corps, Soliman Aga, having received orders from Sir Sidney Smith to obtain possession of the enemy's third parallel, availed himself of this opportunity to retrieve the lost honour of his regiment; and, the next night, carried his orders into execution with that ardour and resolution, which not only completely effected the service upon which he was sent, but also highly benefited the public cause by the gallant display of his men. The third parallel was gained; but the gallant Turk, wishing to do more, and thus to elevate his regiment to a position still more honourable than that which they had forfeited, attacked the second trench, but without the same success that attended his first attempt, as he lost some standards. However, he retained possession of the works long enough to spike four of the enemy's guns, and do them other material damage.

On the arrival, therefore, of Kleber's division, its original destination of mounting the breach was changed into that of recovering these works, which, after a furious contest of three hours, arid much loss of life, was accomplished. Notwithstanding this very limited success, the advantage evidently remained on the side of the besieged. Indeed the resistance displayed, though unsuccessfully, was decisive, as it so far damped the zeal of the French troops that they could not be again brought to the breach.

CHAPTER XV

FROM this moment all the efforts of the French were feeble and dis-
jointed. Discontent prevailed universally through the ranks, and the officers openly expressed their discontent and disapprobation at the frantic
proceedings of their general. The siege was virtually at an end. Fortunately for posterity, we are enabled to give Sir Sidney Smith's impression
of Bonaparte's conduct during the siege, and after his retreat from Acre.
It is officially stated, and is a most important document.

After this failure, the French grenadiers absolutely refused to
mount the breach any more over the putrid bodies of their unburied companions, sacrificed, in former attacks, by Bonaparte's
impatience and precipitation, which led him to commit such palpable errors as even seamen could take advantage of. He seemed
to have no principle of action but that of pressing forward; and
appeared to stick at nothing to obtain the object of his ambition,
although it must be evident to every body else, that even if he had
succeeded in taking the town, the fire of the shipping must drive
him out of it again in a short time: however, the knowledge the
garrison had of the inhuman massacre at Jaffa, rendered them
desperate in their personal defence. Two attempts to assassinate
me in the town having failed, recourse was had to a most flagrant
breach of every law of honour and of war. A flag of truce was sent
into the town by the hand of an Arab dervise, with a letter to the
Pasha, proposing a cessation of arms for the purpose of burying
the dead bodies, the stench from which became intolerable, and
threatened the existence of every one of us on both sides, many
having died delirious within a few hours after being seized with

the first symptoms of infection. It was natural that we should gladly listen to this proposition, and that we should consequently be off our guard during the conference. While the answer was under consideration, a volley of shot and shells on a sudden announced an assault, which, however, the garrison was ready to receive, and the assailants only contributed to increase the number of the dead bodies in question, to the eternal disgrace of the general, who thus disloyally sacrificed them. I saved the life of the Arab from the effect of the indignation of the Turks, and took him off to the Tigre with me, from whence I sent him back to the general with a message, which made the French army ashamed of having been exposed to such a merited reproof. Subordination was now at an end; and all hopes of success having vanished, the enemy had no alternative left but a precipitate retreat, which was put in execution in the night between the 20th and 21st instant. I had above said that the battering-train of artillery (except the carriages, which were burnt) is now in our hands, amounting to twenty-three pieces. The howitzers and medium twelve-pounders, originally conveyed by land with much difficulty, and successfully employed to make the first breach, were embarked in the country vessels at Jaffa, to be conveyed coastwise, together with the worst among the two thousand wounded, which embarrassed the march of the army. The operation was to be expected; I took care, therefore, to be between Jaffa and Damietta before the French army could get as far as the former place. The vessels being hurried to sea, without seamen to navigate them, and the wounded being in want of every necessary, even water and provisions, they steered straight to his Majesty's ships, in full confidence of receiving the succours of humanity, in which they were not disappointed. I have sent them on to Damietta, where they will receive further aid as their situation requires, and which it was out of my power to give to so many. Their expressions of gratitude to us were mingled with execrations on the name of their general, who had, as they said, thus exposed them to peril, rather than fairly and honourably renew the intercourse with the English, which he had broken off by a false and malicious assertion that I had intentionally exposed the former prisoners to the infection of the plague. To the honour of the French army be it said, this assertion was not believed by them, and it thus recoiled on its author. The intention of it was evidently to do away the effect which the proclamation of the Porte began to make on the soldiers, whose eager hands were held above the parapet of their works to receive them when thrown from the breach. He cannot plead misinformation as his excuse, his aide-de-camp, M. Lalle-mand, having had free intercourse with these prisoners on board the Tigre, when he came to treat about them; and they having been ordered, though too late, not to repeat their expressions of contentment at the prospect of going home. It was evident to both sides, that when a general had recourse to such a shallow, and at the same time to such a mean artifice as a malicious false-hood, all better resources were at an end, and the defection in his army was consequently increased to the highest pitch. The ut-most disorder has been manifested in the retreat; and the whole track between Acre and Gaza is strewed with the dead bodies of those who have sunk under fatigue, or the effect of slight wounds; such as could walk, unfortunately for them, not having been embarked. The rowing gunboats annoyed the van column of the retreating army in its march along the beach, and the Arabs harassed its rear when it turned inland to avoid their fire. We observed the smoke of musketry behind the sand-hills from the attack of a party of them which came down to our boats, and touched our flag with every token of union and respect. Ismael Pasha, governor of Jerusalem, to whom notice was sent of Bona-parte's preparations for retreat, having entered this town by land at the same time that we brought our guns to bear on it by sea, a stop was put to the massacre and pillage already begun by the Naplausians. The English flag rehoisted on the consul's house (under which the Pasha met me) serves as an asylum for all relig-ions, and every description of the surviving inhabitants. The heaps of unburied Frenchmen lying on the bodies of those whom they massacred two months ago, afford another proof of divine justice, which has caused these murderers to perish by the infec-tion arising from their own atrocious act. Seven poor wretches are left alive in the hospital, where they are protected, and shall be taken care of. We have had a most dangerous and painful duty, in disembarking here, to protect the inhabitants; but it has been effectually done; and Ismael Pasha deserves every credit for his humane exertions and cordial co-operation to that effect. Two thousand cavalry are just despatched to harass the French rear, and I am in hopes to overtake their van in time to profit by their disorder; but this will depend on the assembling of sufficient force, and on exertions of which I am not absolutely master, though I do my utmost to give the necessary impulse, and a right direction.

I have every confidence that the officers and men of the three ships under my orders, who, in the face of a most formidable en-emy, have fortified a town that had not a single heavy gun mounted on the land-side, and who have carried on all inter-course by boats, under a constant fire of musketry and grape, will be able efficaciously to assist the army in its future operations. This letter will be delivered to your lordship by Lieutenant Canes, first of the Tigre, whom I have judged worthy to command the Theseus, as captain, ever since the death of my much-lamented friend and coadjutor, Captain Miller. I have taken Lieutenant England, first of that ship, to my assistance in the Tigre, by whose exertions, and those of Lieutenant Summers and Mr. Atkinson, together with the bravery of the rest of the officers and men, that ship was saved, though on fire in five places at once, from a deposit of French shells bursting on board her.

I have the honour to be, &c.

W. SIDNEY SMITH

Right Hon. Lord Nelson, etc.

All who ever knew, either officially or personally, Sir William Sidney Smith, will avouch that he is incapable of willful misrepresentation. With all our respect for Bonaparte's splendid genius, and fully entering into the astounding difficulties with which he was surrounded, we must pronounce that the above-quoted document is damnatory to his fame. We have attentively perused, arid deeply considered, the numerous defences by his adherents and admirers, as well as what the Emperor himself has said upon those charges so abhorrent to humanity, and we have found in those attempted justifications nothing but the palliations of expediency. His conduct at Acre is a great blot upon his fame.

When Barry O'Meara, the English surgeon attached to Bonaparte at St. Helena, conversed with Bonaparte on this subject, he honestly replied, that "Sir Sidney displayed great talent and bravery;" and confessed that he was the chief cause of his failure there, on account of his having taken all his battering-train in the manner we have narrated. He declared that, had it not been for that, he would have taken Acre in spite of him. He acknowledged that he behaved very bravely, and that he was most ably supported by Phèlypeaux, whom Bonaparte called a man of talent, saying that he had studied engineering under him. He also does justice to Major Douglas, remarking that he behaved very gallantly; and proceeds in his remarks, accounting for his defeat, thus: "The acquisition of five or six hundred seamen as canonniers was a great advantage to the Turks, whose spirits they revived, and whom they showed how to defend the fortress. But he committed a great fault in making sorties,"(one of which, by its success, turned the fate of the struggle,) "which cost the lives of two or three hundred brave fellows, without the possibility of success; for it was impossible that he could succeed against the number of French before Acre.

"I would lay a wager that he lost half of his crew in them." (The ex-emperor was wrong there.) "He dispersed proclamations among my troops, which certainly shook some of them; and I, in consequence, published an order, stating that he was mad, and forbidding all communication with him. Some days after, he sent, by a lieutenant or midshipman, a flag of truce, with a challenge to meet me at some place which he pointed out, in order to fight a duel. I laughed at this, and sent back intimation that when he sent Marlborough to fight me, I would meet him. Notwithstanding this, I like the character of the man."

We may be indulged in some observations upon this *fanfarade*, which is altogether highly honourable to Sir Sidney; still more so, seeing it came from the mouth of a renowned and beaten enemy.

In the abstract, we do not think that the dispersing incitements to revolt amongst the soldiery of an enemy is a legitimate—we know it not to be a fair—method of warfare; but, in this case, it was only a very gentle retaliation of a system carried on outrageously by Bonaparte himself. We hold it to be as ungenerous and as treacherous to endeavour to raise to revolt and to poison the minds of the enemy, as it would be morally to drug the wells and springs at which they must drink. But Bonaparte set the example of this moral poisoning, and fought in Egypt almost as much by proclamation as by the ball and bayonet. The taunt, therefore, comes with but an ill grace from the mouth of Napoleon.

He could not help dashing a little cold water into his freewill offering of praise; he was beaten, and therefore he not very wisely undervalues and depreciates the powers which chastised him, which is a foolish sacrifice of pique at the shrine of personal vanity.

As to the account of the duel affair, which we are inclined to believe, we confess that it is rather out of the usual routine of military matters, and, being a bad imitation of two or three examples of antiquity, is in execrable taste. But it is a mistake only of a high and chivalrous mind; and viewing the gasconading answer of the challenged, we think Napoleon gains nothing at all by the story. Sir Sidney, in common with every Englishman of that period, had strong prejudices against Bonaparte, as the very head and heart of the demoralising and irreligious principles that it seemed to be the aim of France to establish throughout the world. To annihilate, at a single blow, this moral pest, seemed to be well worth the risk of one life to say nothing at all of the purely personal insult that Bonaparte publicly put upon him, in proclaiming him mad.

And a very pleasant thing it is to reflect upon—the making an opponent mad by a general order. If Sir Sidney Smith was affected with madness, there was dreadful method in it—a method that out-manoeuvred and out-generalled the man that discovered the insanity. We gladly take the wheat from this testimony of Bonaparte, and leave to him, and to those who blindly admire him, the chaff.

We think that it may be fairly stated that the retreat of Bonaparte from before Acre was conducted in a spirit of exasperation and cruelty, generated by disappointed pride and baffled ambition. He was great only in success, and a stranger to the greatest of greatness—greatness in adversity. In after life he attempted this grandeur, but could not support the character.

As he wended his miserable and discomfited way from the scene of his defeat, he seems to have been wholly the slave of passion and resentment, and to regret that his powers of showing his anger, mighty as they were, were too little for the magnitude of his will.

It has been urged against him that, in his march the magazines and granaries with which he met were all fired, that desolation and rapine marked his progress, that the cattle were wantonly destroyed, and "that the affrighted inhabitants, with rage in their hearts, beheld, without being able to prevent, the disasters which marked their invader's way." This may be true, but it is the common picture of all retreating armies; and let it be remembered that Bonaparte, as he marched, was continually in hostilities, and that it would not have been the most approved military strategy to have left to his pursuers magazines and well-stored granaries, with herds of fat cattle. Let us confine ourselves, in our condemnation of this great man, to the facts, and to the charges brought against him, in truth and in honesty, by Sir Sidney Smith. As we have before stated, some of his acts have been explained, and some palliated; yet still, the amount of guilt is heavy against him.

In a siege of so long a duration as that which we have just narrated—a siege in which the actual fighting was not only daily and hourly, but almost un-intermitting, acts of individual heroism were numberless, and must remain for ever unrecorded. However, very many of these little Homeric episodes became extremely popular, and obtained their immortality of a day, and some even found their way into print. We believe that we are acquainted with most of them, having repeatedly had the tedium of a middle watch changed into four hours of pleasurable excitement, by a full description of this siege, with all its attendant anecdotes, from a brother officer, an eye-witness. These anecdotes it would be amusing to preserve, and we would willingly give them a place in this biography, were they not foreign to our subject. One, however, we cannot refrain from shortly narrating, as many versions of it have appeared, and we believe that ours only is the true one. It is succinctly this.

The seamen of the squadron took each their turn for the military service on the walls of Acre. One of them, belonging to the Tigre, had observed, in his spell ashore, the body of a French general, splendid in his uniform, that lay exposed in the very centre of the ditch. This dwelt on the mind of the honest, though—the truth must be told—somewhat obtuse-minded tar. Indeed, he had never shown himself remarkable either for intellect or activity, and held no higher office in the ship than a waister. Yet, by some unexplained mental process, the fate and the unburied corpse of the French general had fixed themselves so strongly on his imagination, that he was determined, at all risks, to give his glittering dead opponent the rights of sepulture. The next day, though out of his turn, he asked and obtained permission to take his spell on the walls. Nothing divided the hostile entrenchments but this same ditch, and so closely placed were the foes to each other, that a moderate whisper could be easily heard from one embankment to the other. Nothing appeared above these embankments but a serried line of bayonets, for if a hat or a head, or anything tangible, appeared on either side, it was saluted with a volley of perforating balls. It was about noon, and the respective hostile lines were preserving a dead silence, anxiously watching for the opportunity of a shot at each other. Our seaman—without informing any one of his intention, had provided himself with a spade and pickaxe—suddenly broke the ominous silence by shouting out, in a stentorian voice, "Mounseers, a-hoy! Vast heaving there a bit, will ye? And belay over all with your poppers for a spell." And then he shoved his broad unmeaning face over the lines. Two hundred muskets were immediately pointed at him, but seeing him with only the implements of digging, and not exactly understanding his demand for a parley, the French forbore to fire. Jack very leisurely then scrambled over the entrenchment into the ditch, the muzzle of the enemy's muskets still following his every motion. All this did not in the least disturb his *sang froid*; but going up to the French general, he took his measure in quite a business-like manner, and dug a very decent grave close alongside the defunct in glory. When this was finished, shaking what was so lately a French general very cordially and affectionately by the hand, he reverently placed him in his impromptu grave, then shovelled the earth upon and made all smooth above him. When all was properly completed, he made his best sailor's bow and foot-scrape to the French, shouldered his implements of burial, and climbed over into his own quarters with the same imperturbability that had marked his previous appearance. This he did amidst the cheers of both parties.

Now, our friend the waister seemed to think that he had done nothing extraordinary, and only remarked that he should sleep well. A few days after, another gaudily decorated French general carne on board the Tigre, on some matters of negotiation, which when completed, he anxiously expressed a desire to see the interrer of his late comrade. The meeting took place, and Jack was highly praised for his heroism in a long speech, not one word of which, though interpreted to him, could he comprehend. Money was then offered him, which at first he did not like to take; but he at length satisfied his scruples by telling the French officer he should be happy to do the same thing for him as he had done for his brother general—for nothing. The French general begged to be excused, and thus ended the interview.

Apologising for this somewhat simple digression, we return to our biography; and it is with unfeigned pleasure that we relate that the world was not, at that time, wholly deficient of gratitude, and that splendid services were splendidly rewarded, without distinction of clique, creed, or party. When the Grand Seignior received the news of the horrible carnage in and before Acre, he shed tears. This grief, however, for the slaughter of his subjects did not prevent his rejoicing at the signal defeat Bonaparte sustained, and sustained wretchedly. His Imperial Majesty, to testify his satisfaction, presented the messenger with seven purses, containing altogether three thousand florins, and immediately sent a Tartar to Sir William Sidney Smith, with an aigrette and sable fur (similar to those bestowed upon Lord Nelson) worth twenty-five thousand piastres. He afterwards conferred upon him the insignia of the Ottoman order of the Crescent.

The loss on the part of the British, in this glorious achievement, was comparatively small. The British squadron consisted of the Tigre, the Theseus, and the Alliance; and these ships together had fifty-three killed, thirteen drowned, and eighty-two taken prisoners. We have already mentioned the death of some of the officers.

The English estimation of Sir William Sidney Smith's eminent services nobly kept pace with Turkish gratitude. The enthusiasm of his country in his favour was general, and a reference to the parliamentary reports of the time bear a lasting and unequivocal testimony to the feelings of approbation with which his spirited as well as wise conduct was viewed. George III. himself, on the opening of the parliamentary session, on the 24th of September, 1799, noticed the heroism of Sir Sidney Smith, and the advantage that the nation were deriving from his success before Acre. Not only did the king's ministers and friends, but even their opponents, forgetting the rancours of party feeling in their enthusiasm for a military victory so splendid, when military victories had not yet become the rule of the British arms, joined most heartily in the national applause.

On the 2d of October, when the imperial parliament had met to pay a nation's just tribute of praise to its naval defenders, Lord Spencer thus did himself honour in addressing his brother peers.

He said, that "he had next to take notice of an exploit which had never been surpassed, and scarcely ever equalled, in the annals of history he meant the defence of St. Jean d'Acre by Sir Sidney Smith. He had no occasion to impress upon their Lordships a higher sense than they already entertained of the brilliancy, utility, and distinction of an achievement, in which a general of great celebrity, and a veteran victorious army, were, after a desperate and obstinate engagement, which lasted almost without intermission for sixty days, not only repulsed, but totally defeated, by the gallantry and heroism of this British officer, and the small number of troops under his command.

"He owned it was not customary, nor did he think it had any precedent in the proceedings of parliament, that so high an honour should be conferred on long services, which might be performed by a force so inconsiderable in point of numbers; but the splendour of such an exploit, as defeating a veteran and well-appointed army, commanded by experienced generals, and which had already overrun a great part of Europe, a fine portion of Africa, and attempted also the conquest of Asia, eclipsed all former examples, and could not be subjected to the rules of ordinary usage. He, therefore, in full confidence of universal approbation, moved "the thanks of the House to Captain Sir William Sidney Smith, arid the British seamen under his command, for their gallant and successful defence of St. Jean d'Acre against the desperate attack of the French army, under the command of General Bonaparte."

This speech was received with great and universal cheering; upon which Lord Hood rose and said, "He could not give a vote on the present occasion without bearing his testimony to the skill and valour of Sir Sidney, which had been so conspicuously and brilliantly exerted when he had the honour and benefit of having him under his command. Had that officer been at the head of a more considerable force, there was every probability that not a Frenchman would have escaped. The nation must be sensible of the importance and benefit of the service that had been achieved; and judging from his character and conduct, he made no doubt but even this was only an earnest of his future glory, whenever an opportunity presented itself."

Lord Grenville said, "There never was a motion, since he had had a seat in that House, to which he gave a more hearty concurrence and assent. The circumstance of so eminent a service having been performed with so inconsiderable a force was, with him, an additional reason for affording this testimony of public gratitude, and the highest honour this House had it in its power to confer. By this gallant and unprecedented resistance, we behold the conqueror of Italy, the future Alexander, not only defeated and driven from the situation at which he had arrived, but also obliged to retreat in disorder and confusion to parts where it was not likely that he would find shelter from the pursuit of British skill and intrepidity. How glorious must the whole appear, when they looked to the contrast between the victors and the vanquished! Bonaparte's progress throughout the whole of his military career was marked with every trait of cruelty and treachery. Sir Sidney Smith, in defiance of every principle of humanity, and of all the acknowledged rules of war, had been long, with the most cool and cruel inflexibility, confined in a dungeon of the Temple, from which he only escaped by his own address and intrepidity. But the French, by making him an exception from the general usages of war, had only manifested their sense of his value, and how much they were afraid of him. This hero, in the progress of events, was afterwards destined to oppose the enemy in a distant quarter; and, instead of indulging in any sentiments of revenge or resentment against his former persecutors, indulged the natural feelings of his heart, by interfering and saving the lives of a number of French prisoners. Soon after this, when victorious in an obstinate contest, where he was but indifferently supported by the discipline of the native troops, or means of defence in the fortifications of the fortress, he generously and humanely lent his protecting aid to a body of miserable and wounded Frenchmen, who implored his assistance, when the cruelty and obstinacy of their own general had devoted them to almost ineviable destruction."

The motion was then agreed to *nem. diss.*, with a vote of thanks to the British officers, seamen, and troops under Sir Sidney Smith.

In the House of Commons, on the previous 16th of September, Mr. Dundas, in moving the thanks of the House on a similar occasion to that which we have just related, thus alluded to the services of our gallant officer.

"A twelve-month had not elapsed since this country felt some apprehension on account of the probable destination of the French army in Egypt—an apprehension which was much allayed by the memorable and glorious victory of Lord Nelson. The power of that army had been still much further reduced by the efforts of Sir Sidney Smith, who, with a handful of men, surprised a whole nation, who were his spectators, with the brilliancy of his triumph, contesting for sixty days with an enterprising and intrepid general at the head of his whole army. This conduct of Sir Sidney Smith was so surprising to him, that he hardly knew how to speak of it; he had not recovered from the astonishment which the account of the action had thrown him into. He had looked at it over and over again, and no view that he had been able to take of it had quite recovered him from the surprise and amazement which the account of the matter gave him. However, so it was; and the merit of Sir Sidney Smith was now the object of consideration, to praise or to esteem which too highly was impossible. He had heard that Sir Sidney Smith, who had his difficulties, had been spoken of lightly by some persons; whoever they were, they were inconsiderate, and they might be left now to their inward shame, if they did not recant. Be that as it might, the House, he was confident, agreed with him that the conduct of Sir Sidney Smith, for heroism, and intrepidity, and active exertion, was never surpassed on any occasion. He was glad of the opportunity that he had to say this."

He then moved, that "the thanks of this House be given to Captain Sir Sidney Smith, for the conspicuous skill and heroism by which, with a few seamen under his command, he animated the Turkish troops against the formidable and desperate attack of the French army under the command of General Bonaparte." Passed, *nem. con.*

In this gratifying and distinguished manner were unanimously voted the thanks of both Houses of Parliament to Sir William Sidney Smith, and the officers and seamen under his command. To the commodore these demonstrations were accompanied by a testimonial more substantial, if not more honourable, in the shape of a well-earned pension of one thousand pounds per annum.

Nor did municipal gratitude lag in this generous race of recompensing the brave. The city of London presented our hero with its freedom, accompanied by a sword valued at one hundred guineas. From the Turkey Company he also received a sword valued at thrice the price of the gift of the metropolitan corporation.

CHAPTER XVI

BONAPARTE'S ASSUMPTION OF MAHOMETANISM • HIS VICTORY OVER
THE TURKS • HIS FLIGHT FROM EGYPT • SUCCESSES OF THE ENGLISH
AND THEIR ALLIES • KLEBER'S PROPOSITION TO EVACUATE EGYPT •
THE CONVENTION OF EL-ARISCH

WE are sincerely grieved that it falls to our lot so often to be compelled to mention the delinquencies of our once inveterate and at last conquered foe, the late Emperor of the French. We do this in no spirit of detraction, as we trust that there is sufficient of credit accruing to Sir Sidney Smith, without being compelled to place his conduct in striking contrast with his then infuriated enemy. But some of the unjustifiable acts of Bonaparte we must relate, in order that the measures undertaken by Sir Sidney to counteract their effects may be fully understood.

About a month after the defeated and disorganised republican army reached Cairo, a Turkish Squadron came to an anchor off Aboukir. In announcing this event to the Egyptian Mussulmans Bonaparte had recourse to the following unwarrantable and absurd expressions in his proclamation: "On board that fleet are Russians, who hold in horror all who believe in the unity of God, because, in their lies, they believe in three Gods; but they will soon see that it is riot in the number of gods that strength consists. The true believer who embarks in a ship where the cross is flying, he who hears, every day, the one only God blasphemed, is worse than an infidel."

This assumption of credence in the Mahomedan faith was despicably mean, and wholly unworthy of the talents of a great general. He needed not this paltry deceit, for he conquered this force honourably and fairly in the field.

On the 11th of July, the Turkish army disembarked, at Aboukir, and soon made themselves masters of the fort, the garrison of which they put to the sword, in retaliation of the massacre which disgraced the French at

Jaffa. It is earnestly to be wished that English influence had prevented this last useless atrocity useless to the momentary conquerors, but replete with evil consequences to them in the sequel.

Confident of victory over a rash and undisciplined army, which had thus commenced its inauspicious career by a gratuitous cruelty, Bonaparte immediately commenced his preparations by augmenting his cavalry with a number of fleet Arabian horses, and immediately set forward to meet his enemy.

In the meanwhile, Sir Sidney Smith, after the dispersal of the French army from before Acre, leaving every assistance in his power to the Turkish forces to enable them, with spirit, to follow up their advantages, had repaired to the different islands in the Archipelago, in order to refit the vessels and to recruit the health of the crews of his little squadron, and to Constantinople also, to concert such measures with the Ottoman government that might lead to the final expulsion of the common enemy from Egypt. He returned to Aboukir bay just in time to witness the encounter between the Turks and the French, which proved so disastrous to the former, and which defeat was the more mortifying to him, as he was unable to render any assistance to his rash allies.

At six o'clock on the morning of the 25th, the French made their appearance before the lines of entrenchment that the Turks had thrown up before Aboukir. At the first onset the French, who immediately attempted to storm the works, were repulsed with great loss to themselves. But the Mussulmans, though individually brave, had not yet learned to act in combined masses with success, even against a beaten enemy. Elevated by the partial advantage that their bravery and physical strength had procured, they rushed out tumultuously from their entrenchments, and, according to their custom, began lopping off the heads of the slain and wounded. In the dispersion necessary to this barbarous operation, they exposed themselves to an impetuous attack of the republican generals, Lannes and the afterwards celebrated Murat. A dreadful carnage ensued, which terminated in a total defeat of the Turbans, and the recapture of Aboukir.

In this sanguinary conflict the greatest part of the Turkish army perished, for those who escaped the sword were mostly drowned in their fruitless attempt to get off to the vessels in the bay. As they had so lately refused quarter to the enemy, they expected and they received none.

Disastrous as was this defeat to the common cause, it was productive of one advantage, the freeing of the Egyptian soil from the presence of Bonaparte. This last victory of his forces afforded him the means of making his flight appear the less dishonourable. He immediately sent home a splendid despatch of his victory, and, four days after its receipt by the Directory, he astonished them by his presence, having left Egypt on the 24th August, and landed at Frejus on the following 7th of October, to commence a career of military glory, for long unchecked until the fatal opposition of the English in Spain.

Towards the conclusion of this October, a considerable reinforcement of troops and ships having arrived from Constantinople, Sir William Sidney Smith, accompanied by the Turkish vice-admiral, Seid Ali Bey, resolved to proceed to the Damietta branch of the Nile, and to make an attack on that quarter, which, by thus occupying the attention of the enemy, would leave the Grand Vizier more at liberty to advance on the French, with the grand Egyptian army, on the side of the Desert. This plan of operations had been previously arranged between the commanders of the two forces. The result of this we will give in the commodore's own words, in his despatch to Lord Nelson, dated November 8th, 1799. It is a melancholy recital, and goes completely to prove how inadequate were the Turkish troops to act in masses.

"I lament to have to inform your Lordship of the melancholy death of Patrona Bey, the Turkish vice-admiral, who was assassinated at Cyprus in a mutiny of the Janissaries on the 18th October.

The command devolved on Seid All Bey, who had just joined me with the troops from Constantinople, composing the second maritime expedition for the recovery of Egypt. As soon as our joint exertions had restored order, we proceeded to the mouth of the Damietta branch of the Nile to make an attack thereon, as combined with the Supreme Vizier, in order to draw the attention of the enemy that way, and leave his highness more at liberty to advance with the grand army on the side of the Desert. The attack began by the Tigre's boats taking possession of a ruined castle, situated on the eastern side of the Bogaz, or entrance of the channel, which the inundation of the Nile had insulated from the mainland, leaving a fordable passage. The Turkish flag displayed on the tower of this castle was at once the signal for the Turkish gunboats to advance, and for the enemy to open their fire in order to dislodge us: their nearest post being a redoubt on the mainland, with two thirty-two pounders, and an eight-pounder field-piece mounted thereon, at point-blank shot distance.

"The fire was returned from the launch's carronade, mounted in a breach in the castle, and from field-pieces in the small boats, which soon obliged the enemy to discontinue working at an intrenchment they were making to oppose a landing. Lieutenant Stokes was detached with the boats to check a body of cavalry advancing along the neck of land, in which he succeeded; but, I am sorry to say, with the loss of one man killed and one wounded. This interchange of shot continued with little intermission during the 29th, 30th, and 31st, while the Turkish transports were drawing nearer to the landing-place, our shells from the carronade annoying the enemy in his works and communications; at length the magazine blowing up, and one of their thirty-two pounders being silenced, a favourable moment offered for disembarkation. Orders were given accordingly; but it was not till the morning of the 1st of November that they could effectuate this operation.

"This delay gave time for the enemy to collect a force more than double that of the first division landed, and to be ready to attack it before the return of the boats with the remainder. The French advanced to the charge with bayonets. The Turks completely exculpated themselves from the suspicion of cowardice having been the cause of their delay; for when the enemy were within ten yards of them, they rushed on, sabre in hand, arid in an instant completely routed the first line of the French infantry. The day was ours for the moment; but the impetuosity of Osman Aga and his troops occasioned them to quit the station assigned them as a corps of reserve, and to run forward in pursuit of the fugitives. European tactics were of course advantageously employed by the French at this critical juncture. Their body of reserve came on in perfect order, while a charge of cavalry on the left of the Turks put them completely to the rout in their turn. Our flanking fire from the castle and boats, which had been hitherto plied with evident effect, was now necessarily suspended by the impossibility of pointing clear of the Turks in the confusion. The latter turned a random fire on the boats, to make them take them off, and the sea was in an instant covered with turbans, while the air was filled with piteous moans, calling to us for assistance. It was (as at Aboukir) a duty of some difficulty to afford it them, without being victims to their impatience, or overwhelmed with numbers: we however persevered, and saved all, except those whom the French took prisoners, by wading into the water after them; neither did the enemy interrupt us much in so doing."

Nothing discouraged by this repulse, or at least putting a bold face on these disasters, on the 29th of December ensuing, a detachment of marines, under Colonel Douglas, Lieutenant-Colonel Bromley, Captains Winter and Trotte, and Mr. Thomas Smith, midshipman of the Tigre, accompanied an advanced body of the army of the Grand Vizier from Gaza to El Arish.

The fort El Arish was summoned, and the French refusing to capitulate, the place was reconnoitred by the English, and batteries immediately erected; the whole of which when opened had the most complete success. On the morning of the 29th, the enemy ceased to return the fire of the besiegers, and the fort, without any terms of capitulation being stipulated, was taken possession of. This success was disgraced by the revengeful ferocity of the Turks, whose thirst for blood could not be restrained. Three hundred of the French garrison were put to the sword by the Osmanlis.

The admixture of the British forces with the Turks had taught these barbarians admiration, but not mercy. They were unceasing in their applause of the cheerful manner in which the detachment from the English squadron performed their unusual duties, exposed as they were on the Desert without tents, ill-fed, and with nothing but brackish water to drink. They beheld with astonishment these triumphs of civilised discipline.

The year 1799 was hardly completed, when General Kleber, who had been left in command in Egypt on its abandonment by Bonaparte, had entered into a convention with the Grand Vizier for the total evacuation of Egypt by the French forces. This document was finally signed on the

24th January, 1800, and to which Sir William Sidney Smith, as auxiliary commander on the part of Great Britain, willingly acceded.

Convention for the Evacuation of Egypt, agreed upon by Citizens Desaix, General of Division, and Poussielgue, Administrator-general of Finances, Plenipotentiaries of the Commander-in-Chief Kleber, and their Excellencies Moustafa Raschid Effendi Testerdar, and Moustafa Rassiche Effendi Riessul Knitab, Ministers Plenipotentiaries of his Highness the Supreme Vizier.

The French army in Egypt, wishing to give a proof of its desire to stop the effusion of blood, and to put an end to the unfortunate disagreements which have taken place between the French republic and the sublime Porte, consent to evacuate Egypt on the stipulations of the present convention, hoping that this concession will pave the way for the general pacification of Europe.

I. The French army will retire with its arms, baggage, and effects, to Alexandria, Rosetta, and Aboukir, there to be embarked and transported to France, both in its own vessels and in those which it will be necessary for the Sublime Porte to furnish it with: and in order that the aforesaid vessels may be the more speedily prepared, it is agreed, that a month after the ratification of the present convention, there shall be sent to the fort of Alexandria a commissary, with fifty purses, on the part of the Sublime Porte.

II. There shall be an armistice of three months in Egypt, reckoning from the time of the signature of the present convention; and in case the truce shall expire before the aforesaid vessels to be furnished by the Sublime Porte shall be ready, the said truce shall be prolonged till the embarkation can be completely effected, it being understood on both sides that all possible means will be employed to secure the tranquillity of the armies and of the inhabitants, which is the object of the truce.

III. The transport of the French army shall take place according to the regulations of commissaries appointed for this purpose by the Sublime Porte and General Kleber; and if any difference of opinion shall take place between the aforesaid commissaries respecting the embarkation, one shall be appointed by Commodore Sir Sidney Smith, who shall decide the difference according to the maritime regulations of England.

IV. The forts of Cathie and Salachich shall be evacuated by the French troops on the 8th day, or at the latest on the 10th day after the ratification of this convention. The town of Mansoura shall be evacuated on the 15th day, Damietta and Balbey on the 20th day. Suez shall be evacuated six days before Cairo. The other places on the east bank of the Nile shall be evacuated on the 10th day. The Delta shall be evacuated fifteen days after the evacuation of Cairo. The west banks of the Nile and its dependencies shall remain in the hands of the French till the evacuation of Cairo; and meanwhile, as they must be occupied by the French army till all its troops shall have descended from Upper Egypt, the said western bank and its dependencies will not be evacuated till the expiration of the truce, if it is impossible to evacuate them sooner. The places evacuated shall be given up to the Sublime Porte in the same situation in which they are at present.

V. The city of Cairo shall be evacuated after forty days, if that is possible, or at the latest after forty-five days, reckoning from the ratification of the treaty.

VI. It is expressly agreed, that the Sublime Porte shall use every effort that the French troops may fall back through the different places on the left bank of the Nile, with their arms and baggage, towards the head-quarters, without being disturbed or molested on their march in their persons, property, or honour, either by the inhabitants of Egypt or the troops of the imperial Ottoman army.

VII. In consequence of the former article, and in order to prevent all difference and hostilities, measures shall be taken to keep the Turkish always at a sufficient distance from the French army.

VIII. Immediately after the ratification of the present convention, all the Turks and other nations, without distinction, subjects of the Sublime Porte, imprisoned or retained in France, or in the power of the French in Egypt, shall be set at liberty; and, on the other hand, all the French detained in the cities and seaport towns of the Ottoman empire, as well as every person of whatever nation they may be, attached to French legations and consulates, shall be also set at liberty.

IX. The restitution of the goods and property of the inhabitants and subjects of both sides, or the payment of their value to the proprietors, shall commence immediately after the evacuation of Egypt, and shall be regulated at Constantinople by commissaries appointed respectively for the purpose.

X. No inhabitant of Egypt, of whatever religion he may be, shall be disturbed either in his person or his property, on account of any connexions he may have had with the French during their possession of Egypt.

XI. There shall be delivered to the French army, as well on the part of the Sublime Porte as of the courts of its allies, that is to say, of Russia and of Great Britain, passports, safe conducts, and convoys, necessary to secure its safe return to France.

XII. When the French army of Egypt shall be embarked, the Sublime Porte, as well as its allies, promise that till its return to the continent of France it shall not be disturbed in any manner; and on this side, General-in-Chief Kleber, and the French army in Egypt, promise not to commit any act of hostility during the aforesaid time, either against the fleets or against the territories of the Sublime Porte, and that the vessels which shall transport the said army shall not stop on any other coast than that of France, except from absolute necessity.

XIII. In consequence of the truce of three months stipulated above with the French army for the evacuation of Egypt, the contracting parties agree, that if in the interval of the said truce some vessels from France, unknown to the commanders of the allied fleets, should enter the port of Alexandria, they shall depart from it, after having taken in water and the necessary provisions, and shall return to France with passports from the allied courts; and in case any of the said vessels should require reparation, these alone may remain till the said reparations are finished, and shall depart immediately after, like the preceding, with the first favourable wind.

XIV. The General-in-Chief Kleber may send advices immediately to France, and the vessel that conveys them shall have the safe conduct necessary for securing the communication, by the said advices, to the French government, of the news of the evacuation of Egypt

XV. There being no doubt that the French army will stand in need of daily supplies of provisions during the three months in which it is to evacuate Egypt, and during other three months, reckoning from the day on which it is embarked, it is agreed, that it shall be supplied with the necessary quantities of corn, meat, rice, barley, and straw, according to a statement which shall be immediately given in by the French plenipotentiaries, as well for the stay in the country as for the voyage. Whatever supplies the army shall draw from its magazines, after the ratification of the present convention, shall be deducted from those furnished by the Sublime Porte.

XVI. Counting from the day of the ratification of the present treaty, the French army shall not raise any contribution in Egypt; on the contrary, it shall abandon to the Sublime Porte the ordinary leviable contributions which remain to it, to be levied after its departure, as well as the camels, dromedaries, ammunition, cannon, and other things which it shall not think necessary to carry away. The same shall be the case with the magazines of grain, arising from the contributions already levied, and the magazines of provisions. These objects shall be examined and valued by commissaries sent to Egypt by the Sublime Porte, and by the commander of the British forces, conjointly with those of the General-in-chief Kleber, and paid by the former, at the rate of the valuation so made, to the amount of three thousand purses, which will be necessary to the French army, for accelerating its movements and its embarkation; and if the objects above mentioned do not amount to this sum, the deficit shall be advanced by the Sublime Porte, in the form of a loan, which will be paid by the French government upon the bills of the commissaries appointed by General-in-chief Kleber to receive the said sum.

XVII. The French having expenses to incur in the evacuation of Egypt, it shall receive, after the ratification of the present convention, the sums stipulated, in the following order, viz. the fifteenth day and the twentieth day, five hundred purses; the fortieth day, the fiftieth, sixtieth, the seventieth, and eightieth day, three hundred purses; and finally, the ninetieth day, five hundred purses. All the said purses, of five hundred Turkish piastres each, shall be received in loan from the persons commissioned to this effect by the Sublime Porte; and in order to facilitate the execution of the said disposition, the Sublime Porte, immediately after the ratification of the convention, shall send commissaries to the city of Cairo, and to the other cities occupied by the armies.

XVIII. The contributions which the French shall receive after the date of the ratification and before the notification of the present convention in the different parts of Egypt, shall be deducted from the amount of the three thousand purses above stipulated.

XIX. In order to facilitate and accelerate the evacuation of the places, the navigation of the French transport-vessels which shall be in the ports of Egypt shall be free during the three months' truce, from Damietta and Rosetta to Alexandria, and from Alexandria to Damietta and Rosetta.

XX. The safety of Europe requiring the greatest precautions to prevent the contagion of the plague from being carried thither, no person, either sick, or suspected of being infected by this malady, shall be embarked; but all persons afflicted with the plague, or any other malady, which shall not allow their removal in the time agreed upon for the evacuation, shall remain in the hospitals, where they shall be under the safeguard of his highness the Vizier, and shall be attended by the French officers of health, who shall remain with them until their health shall allow them to set off, which shall be as soon as possible. The eleventh and twelfth Articles of this convention shall be applicable to them as well as to the rest of the army; and the commander-in-chief of the French army engages to give the most strict orders to the different officers commanding the troops embarked, not to allow the troops to disembark in any other ports than those which shall be pointed out by the officers of health as affording the greatest facility for performing the necessary, accustomed, and proper quarantine.

XXI. All the difficulties which may arise, and which shall not be provided for by the present convention, shall be amicably settled between commissioners, appointed for that purpose by his highness the Grand Vizier and the General-in-Chief Kleber, in such a manner as to facilitate the evacuation.

XXII. These presents shall not be effectual until after the respective ratifications, which are to be exchanged in eight days; after which, they shall be religiously observed on both sides.

Done, signed, and sealed with our respective
seals, &c., January 24, 1800.

DESAIX, General of Division,
POUSSIELGUE,
Plenipotentiaries of General Kleber.

MOUSTAFA RASCHID EFFENDI TESTERDAR, MOUSTAFA
RASSTCHE EFFENDI RIESSUL KNITAB
Plenipotentiaries of his Highness the Supreme Vizier.

A true copy, according to the French part transmitted to the Turkish Minister in exchange for their Turkish copy.

(Signed) POUSSIELGUE,
DESAIX.
(Countersigned) KLEBER.

By these documents it will be seen that it was stipulated that the French army, with all its stores, artillery, baggage, &c., with the French ships of war and transports at Alexandria, should be permitted to return to France unmolested by the allied powers.

It is in the following manner that General Kleber justifies his conduct to the French nation. It will be seen, in a moment, how much he overstates the difficulties to which he was opposed.

Kleber, General-in-Chief of the Army of Egypt, to the Executive Directory of the French Republic.

Camp of Salachich, January 30

I have signed, citizens Directors, the treaty relative to the evacuation of Egypt, and I send you a copy of it. That which bears the signature of the Grand Vizier cannot reach this place for a few days, the exchange of signatures being to take place at El-Arisch.

I have given you an account, in my former despatches, of the situation in which this army was placed. I have informed you also of the negotiations which General Bonaparte had commenced with the Grand Vizier, and which I have continued. Though at that time I had little dependence on the success of these negotiations, I hoped that they would so far retard the march, and relax the preparations of the Grand Vizier, as to give you time to send me assistance in men or in arms, or, at least, orders respecting the disagreeable circumstances in which I was placed. I founded this hope of assistance upon my knowledge that the French and Spanish fleets were united at Toulon, and only wanted a favourable wind for sailing: they did indeed sail, but it was only to repass the Straits, and to return to Brest. This news was most distressing to the army, which learned, at the same time, our reverses in Italy, in Germany, in Holland, and even in La Vendée, without its appearing that any proper measure had been taken to arrest the course of the misfortunes which threatened even the existence of the republic.

Meanwhile the Vizier advanced from Damascus. On another quarter, about the middle of October, a fleet appeared before Damietta. It disembarked about four thousand Janizaries, who were to be followed by an equal number, but time was not left for their arrival. The first were attacked, and completely defeated in less than half an hour: the carnage was terrible; more than eight hundred of them were made prisoners.

This event did not render the negotiations more easy. The Vizier manifested the same intentions, and did not suspend his march any longer than was necessary for forming his establishments, and procuring the means of transporting his troops. His army was then estimated at sixty thousand men; but other pashas were following him, and were recruiting his army with new troops from all parts of Asia, as far as Mount Caucasus. The van of this army soon arrived at Jaffa.

Commodore Sir Sidney Smith wrote me about this time, that is to say, some days before the debarkation of Damietta; and as I knew all the influence which he had over the Vizier, I thought it my duty not only to answer him, but even to propose to him, as a place for holding conferences, the ship which he commanded: I was equally repugnant to receiving in Egypt English or Turkish plenipotentiaries, or to sending mine to the camp of the latter. My proposition was accepted, and then the negotiations assumed a more settled aspect. All this, however, did not stop the Ottoman army, which the Grand Vizier conducted towards Gaza.

During all this time the war continued in Upper Egypt, and the Beys, hitherto dispersed, thought of joining themselves to Mourad, who, constantly defeated, alluring to his cause the Arabs and the inhabitants of the province of Bennissoeuf, continued to keep some troops together, and to give disturbance. The plague also threatened us with its ravages, and already was weekly depriving us of several men at Alexandria and other places.

On the 21st of December, General Desaix and citizen Pouisselgue, whom I had appointed plenipotentiaries, opened the conferences with Sir Sidney Smith, on board the Tigre, to whom the Grand Vizier had given power to treat. They were to have kept on the coast between Damietta and Alexandria, but a very violent gale of wind having obliged them to get into the open sea, they remained out at sea for eighteen days: at the end of this time they landed at the camp of the Vizier. He had advanced against El-Arisch, and had possessed himself, on the 30th of December, of that fort. This success was entirely owing to the remarkable cowardice of the garrison, which surrendered, without righting, seven days after the attack. This event was so much the more unfortunate, as General Regnier was on his march to raise the blockade before the great body of the Turkish army had arrived.

From that moment it was impossible to hope to protract the negotiations to any length. It was necessary to examine maturely the danger of breaking them off, to lay aside all motives of personal vanity, and not to expose the lives of all the Frenchmen entrusted to me, to the terrible consequences which farther delay would render inevitable.

The most recent account stated the Turkish army to amount to eighty thousand men, and it must still have increased: there were in it twelve pashas, six of whom were of the first rank. Forty-five thousand men were before El-Arisch, having fifty pieces of cannon, and waggons in proportion: this artillery was drawn by mules. Twenty other pieces of cannon were at the gates of Gaza with the corps of reserve: the remainder of the troops were at Jaffa, and in the neighbourhood of Ramli. Active foraging parties supplied the Vizier's camp with provisions: all the tribes of the Arabs were emulous of assisting this army, and furnished it with more than fifteen thousand camels.* I am assured that the distributions were regularly made. All these forces were directed by European officers, and from five to six thousand Russians were every moment expected.

To this army I had to oppose eight thousand five hundred men, divided on the three points, Katich, Salachich, and Belbeys. This division was necessary, in order to facilitate our communications with Cairo, and in order to enable us to grant assistance speedily to the post which should be first attacked: in fact, it is certain that they all might have been turned or avoided. This is what Elfi Bey has recently done, who, during the negotiations, entered with his Mamalukes into the Charkie, in order to join the Billis Arabs, and to rejoin Mourad in Upper Egypt. The remainder of the army was distributed as follows: one thousand men, under the command of General Verdier, formed the garrison of

Lesbe, and were employed to raise contributions of money and provisions, and to keep in obedience the country between the canal of Achmoun and that of Moes, blindly directed by the sheik Leskam. Eighteen hundred men were under the command of General Lannes, to supply with provisions the garrisons of Alexandria, Aboukir, and Rosetta, to restrain the Delta and the Batrira. Twelve hundred men remained at Cairo and Gaza, and they were obliged to furnish escorts for the convoys of the army; and, finally, two thousand five hundred men were in Upper Egypt, on a chain of more than one hundred and fifty leagues in extent: they had daily to fight the Beys and their partisans. The whole formed fifteen thousand men. Such, in fact, estimating them at the highest, may be reckoned the number of the disposable combatants in the army.

Notwithstanding this disproportion of force, I would have hazarded a battle, if I had had the certainty of the arrival of succours before the season of a debarkation. But this season having once arrived without my receiving reinforcements, I should have been obliged to send five thousand men to the coasts. There would have remained to me three thousand men to defend a country, open on all parts, against an invasion of thirty thousand cavalry, seconded by the Arabs and the inhabitants, without a fortified place, without provisions, money, or ships. It behoved me to foresee this period, and to ask myself what I could then do for the preservation of the army. No means of safety remained; it would be impossible to treat, but with arms in our hands, with undisciplined hordes of barbarous fanatics, who despise all the laws of war: these motives affected every mind; they determined my opinion. I gave orders to my plenipotentiaries not to break off the negotiations, unless the articles proposed tended to the sacrifice of our glory or our security.

I finish this account, citizens Directors, by observing to you, that the circumstances of my situation were riot foreseen in the instructions left me by General Bonaparte. When he promised me speedy succours, he founded his hopes, as well as I did, upon the junction of the French and Spanish fleets in the Mediterranean: we were then far from thinking that these fleets would return into the ocean, and that the expedition of Egypt, entirely abandoned, would become a ground of accusation against those who had planned it. I annex to this letter a copy of my correspondence with the Grand Vizier, and with Sir Sidney Smith and my plenipotentiaries, and all the official notes sent on either side: I annex also a copy of the reports which have been given relative to the capture of El-Arisch.

The French army, during its stay in Egypt, has engraved on the minds of the inhabitants the remembrance of its victories, that of the moderation and equity with which we have governed, and an impression of the strength and power of the nation by whom it was sent. The French name will be long respected, not only in this province of the Ottoman empire, but throughout all the East, and I expect to return to France with the army at the latest by the middle of June.

Health and respect,
KLEBER

Kleber, Commander-in-Chief, to the Divan of Cairo, and to those of the different Provinces of Egypt

Head-quarters Salachich, February 6

You have for a long time known the constant resolution of the French nation to preserve its ancient relations with the Ottoman empire. My illustrious predecessor, General Bonaparte, has often declared it to you since the circumstances of the war have induced us to visit this country. He neglected no measure to dissipate the apprehensions which had been infused into the Porte, led as it was to conclude an alliance equally contrary to its interests and ours. The explanation sent by him to the court of Constantinople failed in re-establishing so desirable an union; and the march of the Grand Vizier against Damascus having opened a more direct mode of communicating, he commenced negotiations, and confided to me the task of terminating them, at the moment when affairs of superior interest obliged him to return to Europe. I have this day concluded them, and restore this country to the possession of our ancient ally. The re-establishment of the commerce of Egypt will be the first effect of the measure. The treaty shall be the first clause of a peace, which is become necessary to the nations of the West.

When Lord Keith, the British commander-in-chief in the Mediterranean, heard of these proceedings, he despatched the following letter to General Kleber:

On board his Majesty's Ship the Queen Charlotte, June 8, 1800

SIR, I inform you that I have received positive orders from his Majesty not to consent to any capitulation with the French troops which you command in Egypt and Syria, at least unless they lay down their arms, surrender themselves prisoners of war, and deliver up all the ships and stores of the port of Alexandria to the allied powers.

In the event of this capitulation, I cannot permit any of the troops to depart for France before they have been exchanged. I think it equally necessary to inform you, that all vessels having French troops on board, and sailing from this, with passports from others than those authorised to grant them, will be forced by the officers of the ships which I command to remain in Alexandria; in short, that ships which shall be met returning to Europe, with passports granted in consequence of a particular capitulation with one of the allied powers, will be retained as prizes, and all individuals on board considered as prisoners of war.

(Signed) KEITH

Many very painful reflections will be suggested by this unfortunate and somewhat Thrasonical letter. It must have been excessively painful to Sir Sidney, and is not a little insulting to the Sublime Porte. It was as unwise as it was discourteous. It proved rife with the most disastrous consequences; and its errors, let them have originated where they might, were only expiated by some of the bravest and noblest of English blood. As it was in direct opposition to that excellent maxim which inculcates the providing of a golden bridge for a flying enemy, its results may be easily anticipated.

This ill-advised letter was given out in public orders to the French, with the following brief but soul-stirring remark from General Kleber.

Soldiers! we know how to reply to such insolence by victories prepare for battle.

KLEBER.

The General of Division, Chief of the Staff,

(Signed) "DAMAS."

This imprudent disavowal of the acts of the allied Turkish and British commanders morally doubled the strength of the enemy. They immediately recommenced hostilities, and rapid and considerable advantages were gained over the Turks.

In the midst of these operations, orders arrived from the British cabinet to accede to the convention of El-Arisch. They were too late. The French had already made themselves masters of the strong posts in the country, and were now fully resolved to persevere in their original object the complete conquest of Egypt, and the making it a French colony.

One of the earliest consequences of this mistaken policy was the defeat of the Turks at El-hanka, on which occasion eight thousand of them were left dead upon the field of battle.

We will briefly dismiss this affair by the insertion of two official letters, both of them explanatory in their way; the one from Sir Sidney Smith, the other from Lord Keith.

Sir Sidney Smith to Citizen Poussielgue,

Administrator-General of the Finances.

On board the Tigre, March 8, 1800

I lost not a moment to repair to Alexandria, as soon as I could complete the provisioning of my ships, in order to inform you in detail of the obstacles which my superiors have opposed to the execution of a convention such as I thought it my duty to agree to, not having received the instructions to the contrary, which reached Cyprus on the 22d of February, bearing date the 10th of January.

As to myself, I should not hesitate to pass over any arrangement of an old date, in order to support what took place on the 24th and 31st of January; but it would be only throwing out a snare to my brave antagonists, were I to encourage them to embark. I owe it to the French army, and to myself, to acquaint them with the state of things, which, however, I am endeavouring to change. At any rate, I stand between them and the false impressions which have dictated a proceeding of this kind; and as I know the liberality of my superiors, I doubt not that I shall produce the same conviction on their minds that I feel myself, respecting the business which we concluded. A conversation with you would enable me to communicate the origin and nature of this restriction; and I propose that you should proceed, on board an English frigate, to the commander-in-chief in the Mediterranean, who has newly arrived, in order to confer with him on the subject.

I depend much on your abilities and conciliatory disposition, which facilitated our former agreement, in order again to support my reasonings respecting the impossibility of revoking what has been formally settled, after a detailed discussion and a mature deliberation. I then propose, sir, that you should come on board, in order to consult on what is to be done in the difficult circumstances in which we are placed. I view with calmness the heavy responsibility to which I am subject; my life is at stake—I know it; but I should prefer an unmerited death to the preservation of my existence, by exposing both my life and my honour.

I have the honour to be, with perfect consideration and high esteem, sir, your very humble servant,

W. SIDNEY SMITH

This is candid, upright, and honourable; and, although a little too much worded for effect in the latter part, is just such an epistle that we might expect from one of Sir Sidney's chivalrous character.

M. Poussielgue went on his philanthropical mission, first writing the following letter.

Letter from Citizen Poussielgue to Lord Keith
On board the Constance, 13 Germinal, (April 19.)

MY LORD, At the moment of quitting Egypt to return to France, in virtue of the convention signed at El-Arisch, I learned at Alexandria the obstacles which your orders had raised to the execution of that convention, although it had already been partly carried into effect, with that good faith which the candour of the contracting parties must have inspired.

I resolved to proceed directly to you, my lord, to request you to revoke your orders, wish to explain to you all the motives that should induce you to adopt this measure; or, if you cannot consent to what I desire to solicit, that you will immediately send me to France, in order that the French government may treat directly with the English government on this affair.

The lives of fifty thousand men are at stake, who may be destroyed without any motive, since, according to the solemn treaty made with the English, Russians, and Turks, all hostilities had terminated.

I have not powers ad hoc for the step I have taken; but there is no necessity for claiming what would be considered as a right between nations the least civilised. The demand appears to me so just and so simple, and besides so urgent, that I have not thought it necessary to wait for the orders of General Kleber, who, I am certain, would not consent to the smallest modification of the treaty, though his fidelity in executing it has rendered his position much less advantageous.

At the moment we concluded the convention at El-Arisch, under the simple pledge of English good faith, we were far from suspecting that obstacles would be started from that same power, the most liberal of those with whom we had to treat.

For the rest, my lord, I am not a military character, and all my functions have ceased. Two years of fatigue and sickness have rendered my return to my country indispensable. I aspire only to repose with my wife and children, happy if I can carry to the families of the French I left in Egypt the news that you have removed the only obstacle to their return.

POUSSIELGUE.

The following is Lord Keith's explanation, dated April 25th.

Lord Keith's Answer

Minotaur, April 25

I have this day received the letter which you have done me the honour to write. I have to inform you, that I have given no orders or authority against the observance of the convention between the Grand Vizier and General Kleber, having received no orders on this head from the king's ministers. Accordingly I was of opinion, that his Majesty should take no part in it; but since the treaty has been concluded, his Majesty, being desirous of showing his respect for his allies, I have received instructions to allow a passage to the French troops, and I lost not a moment in sending to Egypt orders to permit them to return to France without molestation. At the same time I thought it my duty to my king, and those of his allies whose states lie in the seas through which they are to pass, to require that they should not return in a mass, nor in ships of war, nor in armed ships. I wished likewise that the cartel should carry no merchandise, which would be contrary to the law of nations. I have likewise asked of General Kleber his word of honour, that neither he nor his army should commit any hostilities against the coalesced powers; and I doubt not that General Kleber will find the conditions perfectly reasonable.

Captain Hay has received my orders to allow you to proceed to France with the adjutant-general Cambis, as soon as he arrives at Leghorn.

KEITH

This letter contrasts strangely with the former one from his lordship to General Kleber; but we discover by it that he wished it to be understood that he acted on his own notions of his duty to his king, in disavowing the convention of El-Arisch.

Notwithstanding the combined successes of General Kleber and his army, he still found his and their situation so harassing, that he was willing to agree to a renewal of the terms formerly accepted by the Grand Vizier and Sir Sidney Smith, for the evacuation of Egypt; and Lord Keith being now authorised to accede to them, all obstacles seemed to have been satisfactorily removed. But all these good dispositions were rendered of no avail by the assassination of General Kleber on the 15th of June. This event will be best detailed by transcribing General Menou's letter to Sir Sidney Smith.

Letter from General Menou to Sir Sidney Smith, informing
him of the Assassination of General Kleber,
and of his having taken upon himself the chief command.

J. Menou, General in Chief, to Sir Sidney Smith,
Commander of his Britannic Majesty's ship of war the Tigre.

Head-quarters at Cairo, 1 Messidor (June 19), Year 8
of the French Republic, one and indivisible.

SIR, I have received the letter which you did me the honour of writing to me, under date of the 9th of June, from on board the Tigre, off Rhodes. Since the French army is deprived of its leader, by the atrocious assassination of the General-in-chief Kleber, I have taken upon myself the command of it. Your allies the Turks not having been able to conquer the French near Malarich, they have, to be revenged, made use of the dagger, which is only resorted to by cowards. A Janissary, who had quitted Gaza about forty-two days ago, had been sent to perpetrate the horrid deed. The French willingly believe the Turks only to have been guilty. The account of the murder shall be communicated to every nation, for all are equally interested in avenging it. The behaviour which you, sir, observed, with regard to the convention at El-Arisch, points out to me the road which I have to pursue. You demanded the ratification of your court: I must also demand that of the counsels who now govern the French nation, for any treaty that might be concluded with the English and their allies. This is the only legal way, the only one admissible in any negotiations that may ever take place. As well as you, sir, I abhor the flames of war; as well as you, I wish to see an end put to the misery which it has caused. But I shall never, in any point whatever, exempt myself from what the honour of the French republic and of her arms requires. I am fully convinced that these sentiments must also be yours. Good faith and morality must prevail in treaties concluded between nations. The French republicans know not those stratagems which are mentioned in the papers of Mr. Mories. They know not any other behaviour than courage during the combat, magnanimity after the victory, and good faith in their treaties.

One hundred and fifty Englishmen are prisoners of war here;* had I followed only the dictates of republican magnanimity, I would have sent them back, without considering them as prisoners, for they were taken on the coast of Egypt, not with arms in their hands, and I am fully convinced that the consuls would have approved of it; but your allies have detained citizen and chief of brigade Baudet, adjutant of General Kleber, whose person ought to have been held sacred, as he had been sent with a flag of truce. Contrary to my principles and my inclination, I have, therefore, been forced to reprisals against your countrymen; but they shall be set at liberty immediately on the arrival of citizen Baudet at Damietta, who shall there be exchanged against Mustapha Pasha, and several other Turkish commissaries. If, sir, as I have no doubt, you have some influence over your allies, this affair will soon be settled, which interests your honour, and evidently endangers one hundred and fifty of your countrymen. I have the honour to repeat to you, sir, that with enthusiastic pleasure I shall see the termination of a war which has, for so long a period, agitated the whole world. The French and English nations are destined mutually to esteem, not to destroy one another; but when they enter into negotiations with each other, it must only be done on conditions which are equally honourable to both, and promotive of their welfare. Receive, sir, the very sincere assurances of my esteem and high respect.

I have the honour to be, &c.

ABDALLAH BEY, J. MENOU

---

* Alluding to the officers and crew of H. M. ship Centurion, which was wrecked on the cost.

This letter is certainly to the purpose, and just what might have been expected after so unhappy an event. It shows, also, the habitual respect in which our officer was held by his stern and desperate foes. It produced the following conciliatory and amicable answer.

Letter from Sir Sidney Smith to General Menou,
Commander-in-Chief of the French Army in Egypt;
originally written in French; dated Jaffa, June 22, 1800.

GENERAL, I received this evening the letter which you did me the honour of writing to me on the 20th instant. At the instant when I expected to see General Kleber, under the most favourable and satisfactory auspices, I learned, with the liveliest concern and the most heartfelt sorrow, his tragical fate. I immediately communicated the intelligence to the Grand Vizier and the Ottoman ministers, in the terms in which you announced to me that sad event; and nothing less than the certainty and detail with which you communicated it, could have induced their excellencies to credit the information. The Grand Vizier has declared to me, formally and officially, that he had not the slightest knowledge of those who had been guilty of the assassination; and I am persuaded that his declaration is true and sincere. Without entering into the particulars of this unfortunate event, I shall content myself with answering the articles of your letter that relate to our affairs.

If the Grand Vizier has detained in his camp the aide-de-camp Baudet, despatched to him at Jebli-il-Illam, it was because his excellency did not think proper to suffer any person to quit his camp at the moment when he saw himself surrounded by his enemies. Baudet was detained at Jebil-il-Illam in the same manner as the Turkish officers destined to serve reciprocally with him as hostages were detained at Cairo.

This aide-de-camp was sent to the Ottoman squadron to be exchanged, according to your desire; and during that interval, his excellency the Captain Pacha having arrived here, the exchange was postponed in consequence of his absence from the squadron. When his excellency shall have joined the squadron, the exchange may be carried into effect, should you think proper, as the aide-de-camp Baudet is off Alexandria; but I cannot perceive why you make the release of one hundred and fifty English, who were shipwrecked at Cape Brulos, depend upon a transaction relating only to yourself and the Porte. I expect from your good faith and your justice, according to the regulations settled between both nations relative to the reciprocal exchange of our prisoners, which we are authorised to enforce, that you will allow Captain Buttal, his officers and crew, to return.

Your promises expressive of the hope of reciprocity on my part cannot apply to this circumstance, and I think it superfluous to offer you in return the assurance of my good offices in favour of any person who may be reduced to the painful situation which I have myself experienced. I am convinced that the Grand Vizier will sanction with his generous and dignified approbation all the humane proceedings which we may adopt with respect to one another. The tricks of warfare are unknown to us both, and while I shall continue to behave to you with the same candour and the same good faith which I have manifested to the present moment, I shall earnestly employ all my means to prevent any person on whom I may possess influence from pursuing a contrary line of conduct. Be assured that the hostile dispositions which have been recently announced, and which have acquired extent and publicity, may be appeased by the opportunities furnished to both parties by the present circumstances of mutual correspondence and communication, and that we shall at length be united by the ties of sincere friendship. In the mean time we shall prosecute hostilities against you with the means which we have hitherto employed against you, and we shall endeavour to render ourselves worthy of the esteem of your brave troops.

The hostilities which you have committed without waiting for Admiral Keith's answer, who was unacquainted with the convention concluded for the evacuation of Egypt, have furnished us with a rule for our conduct. I had not demanded of my court the ratification of the convention; I merely was desirous to remove some obstacles that might have opposed the return of the French to their country.

As General Kleber did not, in the late preliminaries which were agreed to, give us to understand that it was necessary the treaty which was to have followed them should be ratified by the consuls, this condition now introduced by you in your preliminaries has the appearance of a refusal to evacuate Egypt, and the Grand Vizier has commissioned me to require of you, on that head, a clear and precise answer. You wish, as I do, for a termination of the war which desolates the whole world.

It is in your power to remove one of the obstacles in the way of peace, by evacuating Egypt according to the terms agreed upon with General Kleber; and if you refuse, we shall exert all our means, and those of our allies, in order to compel you to accept conditions which may not prove so advantageous. I cannot suppress my regret at being forced to fulfil that duty; but the evacuation of Egypt being an object of so much interest to the cause of humanity, the mode of accomplishing it by correspondence and conference is still open.

As the admiral, under whose orders I am, is at a considerable distance, I am authorised to agree to such arrangements as the necessity of circumstances may dictate; and although, from the nature of events, I am not warranted in offering any new proposition, I am, however, ready and disposed to receive all those which you may think fit to make. I can declare to you officially that I shall exert all my efforts to prevent any rash proceedings, and to oppose all vexatious measures, from whatever quarter they may arise.

I shall literally adhere to all the instructions of my court. I know its principles to be founded upon the most punctilious equity and the most perfect good faith. My conduct shall be conformable to its principles, and all my exertions shall be directed to the performance of my duty, by promoting its interests.

As it is not yet decided in what direction I am about to act, I beg you will transmit me your answer in two despatches, the one addressed to Alexandria, and the other to Jaffa, at the camp of the Grand Vizier.

SIDNEY SMITH

We now proceed to subjoin another despatch from Menou to Bonaparte, as it goes more into particulars concerning this atrocious transaction.

*Menou, Provisional General-in-Chief, to Citizen
Bonaparte, First Consul of the Republic.*

Head-quarters at Cairo, 14th Messidor, (July 3.)

CITIZEN CONSUL, A horrible event, of which there are few examples in history, has provisionally raised me to the command of the army of the East. General Kleber was assassinated on the 25th of last month (June 14.) A wretch, sent by the Aga of the Janissaries of the Ottoman army, gave the General-in-Chief four stabs with a poniard, while he was walking with citizen Protain, the architect, on the terrace which looks from the garden of the head-quarters into the square of Esbekier. Citizen Protain, in endeavouring to defend the general, received himself six wounds. The first wound which Kleber received was mortal. He fell—Protain still lives. The general, who was giving orders for repairing the head-quarters and the garden,* had no aide-de-camp with him, nor any individual of the corps of guards: he had desired to be alone: he was found expiring. The assassin, who was discovered in the midst of a heap of ruins, being brought to the head-quarters, confessed that he was solicited to commit this crime by the aga of the Janissaries of the Ottoman army, commanded by the Grand Vizier in person. This vizier, unable to vanquish the French in open warfare, has sought to avenge himself by the dagger, a weapon which belongs only to cowards. The assassin is named Soleyman-el-Alepi. He came from Aleppo, and had arrived at Cairo, after crossing the Desert on a dromedary. He took

---

* The head-quarters had been damaged by cannon-shot during the siege.

up his lodging at the grand mosque Eleaser, whence he proceeded every day to watch a favourable opportunity for committing his crime. He had entrusted his secret to four petty cheiks of the law, who wished to dissuade him from his project; but who, not having denounced him, have been arrested, in consequence of the depositions of the assassin, condemned to death, arid executed on the 28th of last month (June 17). I appointed to conduct the trial a commission *ad hoc*. The commission, after conducting the trial with the utmost solemnity, thought it proper to follow the customs of Egypt in the application of the punishment. They condemned the assassin to be impaled, after having his right hand burnt; and three of the guilty cheiks to be beheaded, and their bodies burnt. The fourth, not having been arrested, was outlawed. I annex, citizen consul, the different papers relative to the trial.

At present, citizen consul, it would be proper to make you acquainted with the events, almost incredible, that have occurred in Egypt; but I must first have the honour of informing you, that General Kleber's papers not being yet in order, I can only inform you of those events by a simple reference to the date of the transactions. When circumstances are more favourable, I shall send you the details.

Napoleon thus pays his tribute to the high sense of honour and the right-mindedness of our hero on this very important and delicate business. "He manifested great honour in sending immediately to Kleber the refusal of Lord Keith to ratify the treaty, which saved the French army, If he had kept it secret for seven or eight days longer, Cairo would have been given up to the Turks, and the French army necessarily been obliged to surrender to the English."

There is much of grandeur in this conduct of Sir Sidney. All the temptations lay adversely to his high sense of honour. We believe that his conduct, had he sacrificed the French army, would have met applause and reward from his superiors at home. In the agitated state of the public feeling, it would have wonderfully increased his popularity; and the abstraction of so many thousand well-tried veterans from the force opposed to his country would have been, though dishonourably obtained, a real and substantial good. All the *ad captandum* advantages were on the side, not of a treachery, but merely of the permitting one by others, and that, too, well disguised under diplomatic forms. All these considerations he resisted he saved the French army, but at the same time he saved his country's honour, and advanced his own.

During these momentous concerns, in which Sir Sidney acted so conspicuous, and often the principal part, he found time to exercise his private benevolence. Having been apprized that a young man of the name of Thevenard was among the miserable captives held by the Turks, and knowing that his father was a person of the highest respectability at Toulon, he interested himself successfully for his release. Sir Sidney also provided for his safe conveyance from Rhodes; and, on his arrival, sent him the following* characteristic note of invitation.

On board the Tigre, June 15th, 1800.

Mr. Thevenard is requested to come and dine with Sir Sidney Smith on board the Tigre, this day at three o'clock. Sir Sidney takes the liberty to send some clothes, which he supposes a person just escaped from prison may require. The great-coat is not of the best; but, excepting English naval uniforms, it is the only one on board the Tigre, and the same Sir Sidney Smith wore during his journey from the Temple till he reached the sea. It will have done good service if it again serves a similar purpose, by restoring another son to the arms of his aged father dying with chagrin.

Sir Sidney's kindness did not stop here. He generously completed the good work that he had begun, by supplying him with money and all kind of necessaries, together with a recommendation to his brother, the minister at Constantinople, and to several other persons of respectability in that city.

CHAPTER XVII

THE CONDUCT OF SIR SIDNEY SMITH CONSIDERED RESPECTING HIS
CONCURRENCE WITH THE CONVENTION OF EL-ARISCH • PARLIAMEN-
TARY PROCEEDINGS UPON IT • SHORT SPEECH OF HIS LATE MAJESTY
WILLIAM IV.

HAVING brought down our narrative of these transactions to this epoch, it becomes a duty to us to look at home, and see in what light these transactions were viewed by those who possessed the right and the ability to decide upon them. The question very naturally resolved itself into two distinct interrogatories. Firstly, had Sir Sidney Smith the power to do that which he did? and, secondly, without reference to his authority, was that which he did done well?

It is notorious that the ministry and Mr. Pitt, with a great proportion of the nation, believed that the terms granted to General Kleber were altogether too lenient; and that he and his army must, in the nature of events, have been shortly compelled to surrender at discretion. Men's minds were too rashly led to this conclusion, because, by an accident, a packet of letters, directed from Kleber's army to the French government, was, about this juncture, intercepted, which letters, purporting to describe the actual state of the French army in Egypt and Syria, were of such a nature as to induce the persuasion that the enemy could by no means sustain his post, and that the troops were upon the eve of a complete disorganisation: and also because that Sir Sidney Smith having performed great deeds, impossibilities were expected at his hands, thus being made a martyr to his own superior merits.

Thus prepared to prejudge the question, it was angrily asked, had Sir Sidney the authority to conclude a convention, apparently so unwise, if not altogether treacherous to the best interests of his country?

This momentous subject led to the following proceedings in the House of Commons:

Mr. T. Jones begged the attention of the house to the subject of the evacuation of Egypt; a subject to which he had already called that attention last session, and which had now become, by the incapacity of his Majesty's ministers, the bone of contention between England and France, and the stumbling-block of peace. From the correspondence on the table, it was evident that those counsels which opposed the evacuation of Egypt by the invading army, presented a very serious obstacle to the conclusion, and even to the negotiation of a peace. Of the two points most insisted on by France, and which operated as impediments to peace, one was the demand of sending succours to Egypt; and it remained for the House to inquire, why that difficulty had not been precluded, by accepting the terms of the convention agreed on by General Kleber and the Grand Vizier, and guaranteed by the sanction of a general officer? Mr. Jones, after six motions that he had made on the 23d of July, last session, on the subject of the evacuation of Egypt, were read by the clerk, said, that the object of his motion this day would be, the production of a letter, on the subject of which almost the whole of the voluminous correspondence which he held in his hand turned. Having read a number of extracts from the correspondence, and particularly Lord Grenville's instruction to Mr. Hammond, for holding a conference with Mr. Otto, on the subject of the proposed armistice between Great Britain and France, he asked if Sir Sidney Smith was not joined with his brother Mr. Spencer Smith, as joint plenipotentiary of Great Britain at the court of Constantinople? Had he not power to treat at Acre? Did not ministers know that, in conjunction with the Bashaw Ghezzar, Sir Sidney offered to convey the French out of Egypt, individually or in the aggregate? Did his Majesty's ministers, previous to January 24, 1800, countermand the orders under which, it was presumed, he acted from the beginning of May in the preceding year, as if not warranted in his conduct? Did they, to prevent a repetition of such conduct, express their anger within the eight following months, or even some time after he had acceded to the convention? Did not Lord Elgin, before and since the present year, instruct Sir Sidney Smith to get the French out of Egypt by all possible means? Was not the intention of the court of London, not to ratify the original treaty, sent immediately to General Kleber in the first instance? Ought it not to have been sent to the French general through Sir Sidney Smith? Ought not our ally, the Ottoman Porte, to have had the earliest notice? Arid farther, did not La Constance galley deliver the letter of Lord Keith, first to Kleber at Alexandria, and then proceed with the same instructions to Sir Sidney, who was on duty at Cyprus? What was the consequence? Did not eight or nine thousand of our good allies perish in the field? Was not the very existence of the Ottoman government threatened at its centre? In Mr. Hammond's letter to Lord Grenville, after the conference with Mr. Otto, which letter referred, almost in every line, to Egypt, there was this particular assertion, "Mr. Otto added, that he would not conceal from me, that the reinforcement which France intended to send to Egypt amounted to twelve hundred men, and that the supply of military stores consisted chiefly of ten thousand muskets. The language of Mr. Otto, in this part of our conversation, and of Mr. Talleyrand's letter, appeared to me to be so decisive and peremptory, that I was induced to ask of him, distinctly, whether I was to understand that this stipulation was a point from which the French government would not recede? Mr. Otto replied, that, in his opinion, the French government would not recede from it." Mr. Jones having recapitulated the whole of the correspondence, moved, "That the letter alluded to in General Kleber's letter to the Kaimakan of the Sublime Porte, be now laid on the table of that House."

Mr. Pitt replied, that it would be hardly possible for his Majesty's ministers to comply with the object of the present motion. It would be a very difficult thing for government to undertake for the production of a letter referred to in one from General Kleber to the Kaimakan, even supposing the representation given of it to be true, and the description of it in the motion proper, which it was not. But the answer he had to give to the reasoning of the honourable gentleman was exceedingly short. The motion appeared to be altogether unnecessary. He was not aware of any good end that could be answered, nor of any blame that could be fixed on ministers, in consequence of a French general being referred to a letter, which evidently, on the face of the transaction, must have been written before government was acquainted with the convention alluded to having been signed by any British officer. The letter, therefore, could not state any new fact: nor had Mr. Jones offered anything in addition to what he had urged unsuccessfully in the last session of Parliament. As soon as it was known in England that the French general had the faith of a British officer pledged to him, and was disposed to act upon it, instructions were sent out to have the convention executed, though the officer in question had, in fact, no authority to sign it. The contents of Lord Keith's letter were far from being a secret. It was printed, quoted, and universally known in July last, when Mr. Jones brought forward a question on the same subject, which the House thought proper to negative. The next thing for the House to consider was, in what manner the present subject was connected with the late correspondence between France and this country relative to an armistice. By the observations accompanying the motion, it was shown that, in making the proposal, the French government meant to derive great advantage from the relief it might be enabled to send both to Malta and Egypt; a relief which it could not hope for, while our fleets and armies pursued their operations against them: and thus it was evident that France set great value on reinforcing those places, which we had an equal interest in preventing them from doing. As we had, since the convention of El-Arisch, taken Malta from the enemy, we were, in a degree proportionate to the importance of that island, masters of preventing them from sending any reinforcements to Egypt, the maritime places of which were, besides, blocked by our fleets. So far then it was plain, that, in respect to Egypt, France was not on higher ground, now that we were in possession of Malta, than it was at the time when General Kleber first entered into the capitulation. And he could not conceive what it was that gentlemen thought they could complain of. When Parliament considered the conduct of his Majesty's ministers, in refusing to acquiesce in a convention which they did not know to have had the sanction of a British officer, it should discuss that conduct with a reference to what was the state of Kleber's army at the time; with a reference to the condition of the war in Italy at the beginning of the campaign, when it was extremely doubtful whether the issue might be favourable to one side or the other; and most of all, in this doubtful state of the termination of the contest, with a reference to the effect which such a reinforcement as that of the army of Egypt might be likely, under all the circumstances, to have on the war on the continent.

Mr. Grey, in answer to, these positions, respecting the position of Kleber's army, the state of the belligerent armies in Italy, and the existing circumstances of the war, all together, said, that the present motion did not preclude the consideration of any of these topics, but only asked for such information as would enable the House to judge of Admiral Keith's instructions. It was not to be supposed that the present motion would stand alone, but, if carried, be followed by others of a more comprehensive nature. With respect to Sir Sidney Smith's powers, it was not necessary for him to be specially instructed, either to sanction or to reject a convention. Sir Sidney was the British officer commanding on the spot. And nothing was more undeniable, than that every military commandant had power to accept any stipulations which his prudence might direct him to agree to with the enemy, without having any special authority for the purpose. On such occasions, government were bound, in good faith, to admit what their officers stipulated: and, if it were otherwise, the consequences would be subversive of those principles on which war was now conducted between civilised nations. On these and other grounds, Mr. Grey defended the propriety and the necessity of the motion: which he considered as a preliminary step to further inquiry into the conduct of ministers on this important and interesting subject. Mr. Grey's observations on the powers of Sir Sidney Smith were supported by Mr. Sheridan, Mr. Tierney, and Mr. Hobhouse. Mr. Sheridan observed, that the House of Commons could not, without a neglect of its duty, omit entering into an inquiry into the matter before them: for he held it as a principle, which should never be lost sight of, that when an officer, either general or admiral, was employed, to take it for granted, that whatever such an officer did in name and on the behalf of the country he served, was done according to his instructions, until the contrary was proved; otherwise nations could never confide in any proposal. Mr. Tierney said, that it was a part of the national compact to regard officers under government, abroad upon service in time of war, as having a certain portion of power, to be exercised according to their discretion, for the purpose of alleviating, or perhaps putting an end to, the horrors of war. What was observed by Mr. Hobhouse, had a reference to what had been asserted by Mr. Pitt, who had spoken a second time in explanation, on the present subject. Mr. Pitt said, that, before the order to Lord Keith went out, there was no supposition that Sir Sidney Smith was then in Egypt, nor that he would be a party to the treaty between the Ottoman Porte and the French general. When he did take a part in that transaction, it was not a direct part. He did not exercise any direct power: if he had done so, he would have done it without authority. He had no such power from his situation: for he was not commander-in-chief. Large powers, for obvious reasons, must be given to the commander-in-chief, subject to the discretion of the person with whom they were intrusted. But that neither was nor ought to be the case with every officer of inferior station. Such person, however great his talents, should not go beyond a specified point; for otherwise he might treat for whole provinces, and counteract his superior in command. Mr. Hobhouse observed, that if even a subordinate officer, intrusted with the direction of a particular enterprise, entered, as Sir Sidney Smith had done, into a convention, which, strictly speaking, he had no powers to conclude, many examples could be found, of cases in which the commander-in-chief thought himself bound to ratify what the subordinate officer had done, and in which government had ratified the consent of the commanding officer. Was not this the case at Cape Nicola Mole, when General Whitelock, though a subordinate officer, without any specific powers, and without the consent of the commander-in-chief, agreed to a convention which General Williamson, the commander-in-chief, afterwards thought himself bound to ratify, and which was afterwards ratified by government? An objection had been made to the form in which the motion was worded. This, indeed, Mr. Hobhouse did not think quite so accurate, and recommended it to his honourable friend to make some alteration in it.

Mr. Yorke, after observing that the motion was not of a parliamentary form, because Parliament could have no power over a letter which must be in the possession of General Kleber, expressed his astonishment that any one could have the confidence to say, in that house, that the British fleet was in the least degree injured by that which took place, on our behalf, in Egypt; and that the more especially, after we had been in possession of the intercepted French correspondence on that subject.

Mr. Percival said, that the English, after the orders from government had been communicated to them by Lord Keith, had done nothing to break the treaty. The English committed no act of hostility. But the French, on receiving the communication from Lord Keith, had chosen to break it themselves. If there was any breach of faith, it was on the side of the French. When government heard that the French had trusted and acted on the belief that this country would consent to the convention, it sent out orders not to ratify, but to respect it. With regard to the motion before the House, he could not recollect that he had ever heard one supported by less argument. He readily allowed that the publication of a letter was not a sufficient means of information for the purpose of founding on it any specific motion. But, if this was the intention, the supporters of the motion ought to have argued 'from the contents of the letter, that it would afford ground on which to rest a motion.

Mr. Jones, as a proof that this country was a party in the convention of El-Arisch, stated, that it was an article in this, that passports should be given to the French by the Porte, and by its allies, Russia and England.

"As to the form of the motion," said Mr. Jones, "I am prepared. On such occasions as these I generally go doubly armed, and now move, That an humble address be presented to his Majesty, that he will be graciously pleased to give directions that copies of all letters from the commander-in-chief of the fleet in the Mediterranean to General Kleber be laid on the table of this house." This motion was rejected by eighty noes against twelve ayes.

Lord Holland also failed in the Upper House to bring this matter in full light, his motion being negatived by twelve votes to two.

Mr. Pitt, in his speech, distinctly avers that Sir Sidney Smith had no authority to sign the treaty—a sentence that must convey a severe condemnation upon the conduct of that officer. The question then is, what authority had he? Did he possess the usual powers of a plenipotentiary—or were those powers so circumscribed, that for every delicate conjunction of circumstances—when slaughter that ought to have been stopped was going forward—when the miseries of a whole friendly nation, that ought immediately to have been alleviated, were increasing—was he, thus situated, to wait for months for instructions? Common sense decides in the negative. Even the ordinary powers of a commanding officer on the spot were, in our opinion a sufficient justification for the course that he adopted.

Well, we will grant, that neither as a plenipotentiary fully accredited, nor as a commander-in-chief fully endowed with the usual discretionary powers, had he authority to sign the convention. But was he, was Great Britain, the only parties to it? Who were the most concerned? Against whom did the sharp edge of war come in actual contact? Whose provinces were occupied? whose subjects plundered and slain? The Sultan's an independent sovereign of himself, perfectly competent and free, by his proper ministers, without the sanction of the British government, to make what treaty or convention he pleased, that was not, according to the terms of his alliance with England, an actual peace with the enemy. Such a justifiable convention he made to rid his provinces of a consuming host, and his diadem of a galling insult; and Sir Sidney Smith did no more than agree to the act on the part of his own government. What a mockery to say that he had not full powers to do so small a thing!

But we now come to the second category; and in that Sir Sidney stands in a still more triumphant light. What he did was eminently well done, and the undoing of it very nearly proved the undoing of England's pre-eminence on the southern shores of the Mediterranean; for, after the loss of some of our best generals, and many of our best officers, together with a dreadful slaughter of some of our bravest troops, our authorities at home were obliged to do tardily, and not very gloriously, that which Sir Sidney Smith had before done, with honour to himself and with glory to the English name, without, in the slightest manner, committing an outrage upon humanity.

It was this transaction that called forth, some time after, the honourable testimony to the great merits of Sir Sidney Smith, from one from whom eulogium must at all times have been most gratifying and distinguishing: we mean the good, the philanthropic, and the pious Mr. Wilberforce. After mentioning our gallant officer's exploit at Acre, in which he observes, "that if he, Sir Sidney, had had with him regular officers of engineers, he must have reported the place untenable and abandoned it," he goes on to state, that "the extraordinary achievements of that gallant officer had been but ill requited," with many observations to the same effect.

Mr. Wilberforce spoke truly. Sir Sidney Smith was not adequately rewarded. The peerage was, at that time, plentifully lavished upon individuals who required that distinction to make them stand apart from their fellow men Sir Sidney Smith did not.

As we have been just reverting to parliamentary proceedings, it may not be misplaced to mention that our late sovereign, William IV., when Duke of Clarence, thus spoke of Sir Sidney in the House of Peers: "The first important check which the formidable army of French invaders met, was from a handful of British troops, under Sir Sidney Smith, long before the landing of the army which became, in their turn, the conquerors of Egypt."

CHAPTER XVIII

BEFORE we proceed further in these Memoirs, we shall briefly state the appearance of their subject at this juncture. It is a very natural curiosity, that of being anxious to be acquainted with the looks and bearing of those who have been able, by their merits, to stand separate from their fellow men. But alas, man is still more variable in his physical than in his mental identity. The portrait of the youth of fourteen presents but little similitude to the man at the mature age of thirty, and the virility of thirty would look with disgust upon the lineaments of the same individual when he had numbered the average years allotted to humanity, three score and ten.

We have described Sir Sidney Smith's appearance as the fresh, amiable, and rosy-cheeked boy. We now, upon the testimony of one who was in daily communication with him, portray him in the vigour of his manhood, shortly after he had effected the expulsion of the French from Acre. Then, though small in stature, he had all the appearances that indicate a brave and generous hearted man, with a fine dark countenance, and eyes that sparkled with intelligence. His very appearance showed that he possessed an ardent imagination, which naturally prompted him to form and execute bold and important enterprises: he seemed, as it were, to be born to deserve glory and to acquire it.

This testimony to the dignity of his presence is from a Frenchman, and, so far as his public character was concerned, an enemy; and as the narrator was allowed, on all hands, to be a person of probity and honour, we must place implicit belief that he has put upon record the actual impression that Sir Sidney Smith made upon him.

But let us have recourse to other and less refined evidence. It is that of a worthy old Greenwich pensioner, who held an office about our officer's person, and who had the fullest opportunities of seeing him in all situations and in all moods, in full dress, in undress, and in no dress at all, and such is nearly the words of the veteran.

"Why, sir, after we skivered the mounseers away from Acre, Sir Sidney was looking as taut set up as the mainstay by a new first lieutenant; but, for all that, Sir Sidney was a weaselly man—no hull, sir—none; but all head, like a tadpole. But such a head! It put you in mind of a flash of lightning rolled up into a ball; and then his black curly nob—when he shook it, it made every man shake in his shoes."

"Was he then handsome?"

"Blest if I can tell! You know, sir, as how we don't say of an eighteen-pounder, when it strikes the mark at a couple of miles or so, that's handsome, but we sings out 'beautiful;' though, arter all, it's nothing but a lump of black iron. You're laughing, sir. And so you thinks I'm transmogrifying Sir Sidney's head into a round lump of iron shot! Well, I'm off like one. All I can say is, that he was most handsome when there was the most to do."

This worthy old sailor's notions of the line of beauty being rather tortuous, we have only to endeavour to reconcile the two accounts, which may be done by the single word "soul." It predominated in the expression of his features, and that, we conceive, is the noblest kind of beauty.

At the time of which we write, the use of the eat-o'-nine-tails was general throughout the navy, and as lavish as it was general. It therefore highly redounds to the humanity as well as to the good sense of Sir Sidney, that he was very sparing of the revolting infliction, but rarely having recourse to this brutal *ultima ratio* of naval commanders; and, when compelled to it by absolute necessity, never inflicting more than twenty-four lashes at one punishment. He had gained the entire confidence, and, though the word looks a little effeminate, we must add, the affection of all those who were so happy as to serve under him. Sir Sidney appears to have been distasteful only to those superior officers placed in command immediately over him.

Having thus been a little diffuse upon that which is merely personal to our celebrated commander, we must now proceed to trace the splendid course of his services, which in order the more fully to appreciate, we must turn our attention to the state of Egypt after the flight of Bonaparte, and the atrocious assassination of General Kleber. At this time, the fair average of the French troops occupying Egypt was twenty-six thousand men, with something more than eleven hundred Greek and Copt auxiliaries. In this average must be included sailors acting with the forces, commissioned and non-commissioned officers, the sick, the artillery, the commissariat, and every description of persons attached to the army.

This force was at once both dispirited and exasperated; for, pining for their homes, and being deprived of the stimulus of spirituous liquors, they could hardly be prevailed upon to work on the fortifications, or even to throw up the necessary entrenchments for the safety of the posts of the army, yet, remembering the supposed injuries that they had received at the hands of the English, they were prepared to and actually did fight, when the occasion offered itself, like so many furies.

We know it to be admitted on all hands that General Menou had not the force of character or the martial intelligence of his predecessors in command. The dispositions for the defence of Egypt have been severely animadverted upon, and very generally condemned. He should have, before he thus dared the enmity of the English, either have possessed more military strength, or have been conscious of more military talent, before he attempted to wield it.

Whatever was the cause of all the misunderstandings with respect to the treaty of El-Arisch, or to whomever censure ought to have been justly charged for thus prolonging a needless and a bloody strife, our government was not wanting in promptitude in taking steps to remedy these mistakes, and to clear Egypt from the presence of the French. The Turks were stimulated to fresh exertions, and several of their corps put in motion in various points, whilst Sir Ralph Abercromby was appointed to the command of an efficient body of English troops, destined to act, in conjunction with Sir Sidney Smith and our Turkish allies, against Menou, now in the chief command of the republican forces.

After receiving some reinforcements in the Mediterranean, and collecting a very respectable train of artillery at Gibraltar, the British army proceeded to its destination, but certainly not with that celerity which was expected from it, or which the urgency of the occasion seemed to demand. After various harassing and unexpected delays, the armament, in conjunction with Lord Keith, at length proceeded to the coast of Egypt, and arrived off Alexandria on the 1st of March, 1801, and the next day sailed for Aboukir Bay.

Alexandria being then in possession of the French, and there being but two or three spots on the coast accessible to invasion, Aboukir Bay was necessarily chosen for the disembarkment of the British troops, and at a most favourable period, for, at this time, the force of the Mamelukes in the French pay seems almost to have been subdued, and the Arabs, after the manner of their tribe, trafficked equally with both parties, and waited for the termination of the contest, to side with the victorious party. The French, as we have before stated, dispirited by the flight of Bonaparte and the assassination of General Kleber, had fallen under the command of Menou, a man confessedly inferior to his predecessors in all great and wise qualities, and of so little moral influence with those whom he commanded, that he had not the power to overawe into obedience the various parties into which his army had split themselves.

By a singular oversight, Menou, instead of concentrating all his strength to prevent the landing of the English at Aboukir, divided his forces and sent bodies of them to oppose the Turks, and retained a large corps in garrison at Alexandria. This want of policy was the more absurd, as the Turks did not arrive on the confines of Egypt until the 27th of April, fifty days after the landing of the British.

However, when the English fleet had arrived at Aboukir Bay, they found so high a sea running, and so violent a surf breaking upon the beach, that it was the 8th before any disembarkation could be attempted. On this occasion the incapacity of Menou was strikingly exemplified. He employed these six days of the inactivity forced upon the English, neither by sufficiently fortifying the coast, nor by moving up fresh bodies of men, so that the sixteen thousand troops of the British found only four thousand men opposed to them. However, the French were most advantageously posted, and made a most creditable resistance to the disembarkation. The difficulties with which the English had to contend were neither few nor insignificant. They had to be conveyed, directly under the fire of the enemy's artillery, for a long space in open boats, and, when they neared the beach, to receive the incessant volleys of musketry that played upon them, whilst they were obliged to remain seated in a state of inactivity. The landing, under the superintendence of the Honourable Captain Cochrane, was brilliantly effected, and with a loss much less than was calculated upon, and immediately after, the enemy were driven from their posts, and their defeat made the more humiliating and disastrous by the loss of several pieces of artillery.

Sir Ralph Abercromby was struck with admiration at the admirable coolness and tact evinced by the naval officers and men on this all-important service. He bestowed upon them the highest praises, and openly declared that, without their eminent services, he never could have brought his brave troops into action.

It certainly was a most desperate service, and it is the opinion of the highest military authorities, that the event of this invasion would have been extremely doubtful if the whole French army, with their great superiority in cavalry, had been brought down to the coast, before their opponents were clear of the sea, and, even had they effected a landing, before they could have gained time to organise and arrange their order of battle.

The personal services that Sir Sidney Smith performed were, among others, the taking charge of the launches which contained the field artillery. After the debarkation and consequent victory of our troops, Sir Sidney Smith, who had landed and reconnoitred this ground the year before, proposed that the battery at the entrance of Lake Maadie should be maintained when carried, or its assault, at all events, combined with the operations of the landing. Sir Robert Wilson confesses that this would have been a masterly movement, yet it was not adopted.

After the action of the landing, the army employed itself in finding water, as Sir Sidney assured the troops that wherever date trees grew water must be near. This assertion proved true, and thus Sir Ralph Abercromby found himself relieved from an anxiety which might have determined him to relinquish the expedition. On the 20th of March an Arab chief sent in a letter to Sir Sidney Smith, acquainting him with the arrival of General Menou with a large army, and that it was his intention to surprise and attack the British camp the next morning; but much confidence was not placed in this communication at head-quarters, although Sir Sidney was, in his own mind, convinced of the honesty and truth of the information, and assured his friends that the event would take place.

This little trait shows of what vast importance was the presence of our hero with the army, and how useful were his counsels, for the next day the memorable battle of Alexandria took place. We shall not describe the technical movements of the respective armies, but confine ourselves to the stating of the manner in which the commander-in-chief met with the wound that was fatal to him. On the first alarm of the surprise which Sir Sidney foretold, and who was not believed, Sir Ralph, finding that the right was seriously engaged, proceeded thither. When he came near some ruins near which it was stationed, he despatched his aide-de-camp with some orders to the different brigades, and, whilst thus left alone, some French dragoons penetrated to the spot, and he was unhorsed: one of them was supposed to be an officer, from the tassel attached to his sword; but just as the edge of the weapon was descending, his natural heroism and the emergency of the moment so much invigorated him, that he seized the sword, and wrested it from the hand of his adversary, who, at the very moment, was bayoneted by a soldier of the 42nd.

Sir Ralph did not perceive that he was wounded when he received the musket-ball in his thigh, but complained greatly of a contusion on his breast, supposed to have been received from the hilt of the sword in the scuffle. Sir Sidney Smith was the first officer who came to Sir Ralph, and who, by an accident, had broken his own sword, which Sir Ralph observing, he instantly presented him with the one which he had so gloriously acquired from the French dragoon. This sword Sir Sidney intends to place upon his monument.

A singular circumstance happened almost immediately afterwards. Major Hall, aide-de-camp to General Cradock, whilst going with orders, had his horse killed. Seeing Sir Sidney he begged of him permission to remount himself upon the horse of his orderly-man. As Sir Sidney was turning round to the man, he was saved the trouble of giving directions, by a cannon-ball sweeping off the dragoon's head.

"This," exclaimed Sir Sidney, "is destiny! Major Hall, the horse is yours."

Very shortly after, Sir Sidney Smith himself received a violent contusion from a musket-ball, which glanced on his right shoulder.

But to return to the wounded commander-in-chief. As the French cavalry was by this time repulsed, Sir Ralph walked to the redoubt on the right of the Guards, from which he could command a view of the whole field.

At ten o'clock in the morning the action ceased by an orderly and unmolested retreat of the French to the position from which they had emerged, and it was not until their defeat was thus absolutely assured, that Sir Ralph Abercromby, who had remained on the battery, where several times he had been nearly killed by cannon shot, could be prevailed upon to quit the field.

He had continued walking about, paying no attention to his wound, only occasionally complaining of a pain in his breast from the contusion. Officers who went to him in the course of the action returned, without knowing, from his manner or his appearance, that he was wounded, and many ascertained it only by seeing the blood trickling down his clothes. At last, his spirit, when no longer stimulated by exertion, yielded to exhausted nature; he became faint, was placed in a hammock, and borne to the depot, cheered by the feeling expressions and the blessings of the soldiers as he passed. He was then put into a boat, accompanied by his aide-de-camp and esteemed friend, Sir Thomas Dyer, and conveyed to Lord Keith's ship.

On the evening of the 23rd, Sir Sidney Smith went with a flag of truce to the outposts, and demanded to be permitted to communicate with the commandant of Alexandria. An answer having been returned that no person could be permitted to pass the outposts, Sir Sidney sent in his letter, as from Sir Ralph Abercromby and Lord Keith, proposing an evacuation of Egypt by the French, by which they might return to France without being considered as prisoners of war; but that their shipping, artillery, and material must be placed in the hands of the allies. This was angrily refused.

On the 29th, Sir Sidney Smith again went with a flag of truce to the outposts, as on the part of the Capitan Pasha, Sir Ralph Abercromby, and Lord Keith. Admittance into the town was refused, and no answer was returned to the despatch.

It was on the morning of this day that the death of Sir Ralph Abercromby was known. He had borne painful operations with great firmness, but the ball could not be extracted. At length, mortification ensued, and he died on the evening of the 28th, having always expressed his solicitude for the army, and irritating his body, through his mind, from the first moment of his accident, with a desire to resume his command. He died as should a brave officer—at a good old age, loved and honoured. His fate was a happy one.

On the 31st of this memorable March, eleven Arab chiefs came to Sir Sidney Smith. They were all very intelligent men, with uncommonly fine countenances, and they were well clothed. It was impossible to regard these chiefs without thinking of the wise men of the land, and to see the simplicity of their manners without remembering the patriarchs.

On the 13th of April, we find Sir Sidney, with a party of dragoons, reconnoitring a position, and shortly after proceeding up the Nile with an armed flotilla, so far as El-Arisch. This ubiquity seems astonishing. On the 18th, we next meet with him cannonading Rosetta from four dgerms that he had equipped with wonderful despatch.

We now come to the termination of his invaluable services on shore in Egypt. Sir Robert Wilson thus pays an honest tribute to his merits:

"Sir Sidney was endeared to officers and men by his conduct, courage, and affability. With pride they beheld the hero of Acre; with admiration they reflected on the convention of El-Arisch; they had witnessed his exertions, and calculated on his enterprise. The Arabs regarded him as a superior being. To be the friend of Smith was the highest honour they courted, and his word the only pledge they required. No trouble, no exertions, no expense, had been spared by him to obtain their friendship, and to elevate, in their opinions, the national character. But the order was given, and remonstrance would have been unworthy; it is true, as a seaman he could not complain of being ordered to reassume the command of his ship; but the high power he had been invested with, the ability he had displayed as a soldier and a statesman, entitled him to a superior situation in this expedition, and the interest of the service seemed to require that the connexion he had formed with the Mamelukes should, through him, be maintained. The army, therefore, saw Sir Sidney leave them with regret, but he carried with him their best wishes and gratitude."

It is thus that General Hutchinson mentions Sir Sidney in his despatch:

"Sir Sidney Smith had originally the command of the seamen who landed from the fleet; he continued on shore till after the capture of Rosetta, and returned on board the Tigre a short time before the appearance of Admiral Gantheaume's squadron on the coast. He was present at the three actions of the 8th, 13th, and 21st of March, when he displayed that ardour of mind for the service of his country, and that noble intrepidity, for which he has ever been so conspicuous."

CHAPTER XIX

CURSORY SKETCH OF THE TERMINATION OF THE EGYPTIAN CAMPAIGN
• SIR SIDNEY FETED BY THE CAPITAN PASHA • ANECDOTE OF ANOTHER
SIMILAR HONOUR • BONAPARTE'S IMPIETY • SIR SIDNEY RETURNS TO
ENGLAND WITH DESPATCHES • CIVIC HONOURS.

AS we have thus far glanced at the military operations of the combined forces in Egypt, it will not be thought superfluous to give a rapid sketch of the proceedings of the allied army, up to the treaty for the evacuation of Egypt.

These proceedings were marked by most singular delays and procrastinations. After the battle of the 21st of March, which was fought about four miles distant from Alexandria, we waited until the 14th of April before we presented ourselves at the gates of Rosetta, which were flung open at our approach. We remained content with this advantage until the 5th of May, when we again commenced military operations by investing the Fort of St. Julien, garrisoned by only two hundred and sixty men, which we reduced in two days.

On the 5th of May, we commenced our march for Cairo from El Hamed, which was distant only one hundred and twenty miles, yet it occupied us forty-two days in the march. The only opposition that we experienced was at Rhamameth, where we lost twenty men, the French suffering a defeat. This took place on the 9th of May. From this place the French retired from before General Hutchiuson, and reached Cairo in three days. However, we moved more deliberately, occupying thirty-eight days to overcome the same distance, without seeing an enemy or firing a shot the whole of the way.

Cairo capitulated on the 20th of June. We then proceeded against Alexandria, at which place Menou had stationed himself with the main body of the French army, and fifty days after the fall of Cairo, during which time not an hostile shot was fired, we opened the siege, and re-duced the place in fifteen days.

After this success, so long protracted, Menou consented to the evacuation of Egypt, upon precisely the same terms as those which formed the original evacuation of El-Arisch, and the republican army, with its baggage, was conveyed in ships of the allied powers to the near-est French ports.

As we have before stated, it was only at the commencement of this campaign that Sir Sidney Smith served with the allied army. Is it hazard-ing too much to say, that if he had continued with it, he would have in-fused into its commanders some of the same spirit of enterprise that made the defeat of Acre so successful? There is no doubt but that the conquest of Egypt was glorious to our arms, but still we think that we did not reap the full measure of honour in the field that lay before us.

Be this as it may, when the allied army advanced towards Cairo, by a very unworthy compliance with the antipathies of the Capitan Pacha, Sir Sidney was sent on board his ship. The following, reason is assigned by Sir Robert Wilson for the aversion of the Capitan towards Sir Sidney.

"Sir Sidney, on receiving Lord Keith's refusal to the convention of El Arisen, instantly sent off an express with it to Cairo, as he knew that General Kleber was immediately to evacuate that city on the faith of the treaty; thus preferring the maintenance of his own and his country's honour to a temporary advantage. The messenger arrived a few days be-fore the evacuation was to have been completed, and the consequences are well known. But certainly, the Turks had so fully depended on its exe-cution, that they had advanced without artillery and ammunition."

We can well conceive this to have been a mortal offence to the Capi-tan, as he could have but a slight conception of the chivalrous character of Sir Sidney; but, great as was the umbrage taken by the Turks, we should not have suffered the ignominy of permitting our barbarous allies to dictate to us what officers we should or should not employ. Of this we are well assured, that the presence of Sir Sidney Smith with the army was of more importance to its success than that of the Capitan Pacha and all his forces.

Whatever might have been the pique on the one hand by the Turkish commander, and the resentment on the other, we find, shortly after the evacuation of the French, the naval Capitan Pacha giving a grand enter-tainment on board the Sultan Selim, to Sir William Sidney Smith, to whom, with strong expressions of admiration and attachment, he pre-sented a valuable scimitar, and, what was considered as the greatest compliment that he could confer on him, one of his own silk flags, a badge of distinction which claims from all Turkish admirals, and other commanders, an equal respect to that which they owe to his highness the Pacha; such as the obligation of personally waiting on him previously to their departure from, and on their rejunction with, the fleet.

Honours of this sort seem to have been lavished on our officer with a prodigality that merit only such as his could have justified. Having, in 1799, rendered himself of much importance to the Grand Seignior, he received the Ottoman order of the Crescent from Constantinople, accompanied with a firman and seal from the Sultan, delegating to him unlimited authority over his subjects in the sea of the Archipelago, and of his Asiatic provinces—a power which Sir Sidney can exercise at any time by virtue of the seal and document above mentioned. The seal, the turban, and the aigrette, are the same with the Sultan's, with the exception of the inscription which surrounds it, a text from the Koran in Arabic, of which the following is a translation.

Speaking of the Christians, the Koran says, "They are a people which exist. They read of the wonders of God during whole nights, and they adore Him with bended knees. They believe in God and in the last day. They order the doing of good deeds, they forbid evil ones, and they are eager in works of charity; therefore are they (the Christians) good."

The Pacha, who was, on this occasion, the envoy of the Sultan to Sir Sidney Smith, having formerly incurred Sir Sidney's displeasure, was extremely troubled in his mind with apprehension and fear all the time that he was investing him with the order, and performing the other requisite commands; and, when finally he buckled on the rich sword, he fully expected to see the glittering blade flash in the light, and that, in the next twinkling of his eye, his head would fly off from his shoulders. Had this been the case, it would not have excited the smallest surprise in the bystanders; for it is quite customary in Turkey, and among the Mahometans generally, in sending an embassy to a powerful prince or a pasha, to replace another, or, as in this instance, on a mission of importance, bearing honours and presents from the Sultan, to select an individual who has offended the person whom the Sultan thus deigns to notice with favourable marks of confidence; and immediately after the unfortunate ambassador makes his salaam, he "is either relieved of his head by the ready Damascus blade, or, with equal promptitude and facility, strangled by the mutes with the bowstring.

No such fate, however, awaited the pasha sent by the Sultan to Sir Sidney. The commodore certainly enjoyed his embarrassment, and was highly amused at the trepidation and alarm which the old Turk displayed, and which he, in turn, endeavoured to conceal by an appearance of cheerfulness, a vivacity so awkwardly assumed, that even his own followers were quite surprised at his strange gestures and grimaces. The obstinate resistance that the muscles of his face made to represent anything like a genuine smile, and his fruitless attempts to force them to relax, were perfectly frightful, and provoked the laughter of the whole assembly. This mirth was the means of reassuring him a little, for he took it for granted that such a man as Sir Sidney Smith could not look upon the depriving of a poor Turk like himself of his head, to be the most fitting subject in the world for merriment, and, on daring to look up into his face, he was convinced that he had conjectured rightly. Upon a more earnest survey, his astonishment equalled his joy when he found not the slightest indication of resentment, or even of displeasure, in the admiral's countenance, as he turned his eyes upon him with an expression that he well understood, and began greeting him with words of peace and goodwill, thus entirely removing from him any doubts or fears with which he might still be harassed concerning his personal safety. As a still further assurance of Sir Sidney's kindly intention, and because he knew that there were valuable qualities in the man, he made him, a few days afterwards, the governor of Cyprus.

To return to our narrative. After the surrender of the French army, Sir Sidney Smith seized the opportunity of visiting the holy city of Jerusalem, where the following anecdote of Bonaparte was related to him by the superior of a convent. People may place what reliance they choose upon its authenticity, and either conceive it to be of no more value than is generally affixed to a monkish tale, or give it full credence, on the score that, at that time, so strong was the current of infidelity among the French people, that Bonaparte, who wished to float to power on its stream, might well have been guilty of the ascribed impiety.

When his general, Damas, had advanced with a detachment of the army, within a few leagues of Jerusalem, he (Damas) sent to his commander-in-chief for permission to make an attack upon the place. Bonaparte replied, that "when he had taken Acre, he would come in person, and plant the tree of liberty on the very spot where Christ suffered; and that the first French soldier who fell in the attack should be buried in the holy sepulchre."

At this period, when men's minds are less excited, such fanaticism of infidelity as is here displayed seems altogether incredible. However, whether this anecdote be true or not, as it was uttered to suit the temper of those times, it is a curious record of the exasperation that was entertained, either by the one party or the other. That much of this kind of senseless bravado on the score of religion was promulgated by Bonaparte in his Egyptian career is but too certain, yet this man died a certified good Catholic, and in a faith the most credulous that ever existed.

Sir Sidney Smith was the first Christian who was ever permitted to enter Jerusalem armed, or even in the customary dress of a Frank. By his means, his followers also, and all who visited it through his influence, were allowed the same privilege.

On the 5th of September of the current year, the transactions of which we have been narrating, Sir Sidney Smith and Colonel Abercromby embarked at Alexandria on board the Carmen frigate, with the despatches relative to the late campaign. Every one will concede that this honourable mission was justly devolved upon the naval commander; and not the less so was 'it shared by Colonel Abercromby, whose meritorious services had been of the most valuable description, to say nothing of the selection of the herald of the intelligence that was to complete his father's fame being gracefully and properly assigned to a son that was assiduously following in his parent's steps. These two accomplished officers arrived in London on the 10th of November following.

We must presume that Sir Sidney Smith's diplomatic character had now altogether ceased on his accepting this mission with the despatches, even if they had not been supposed to have terminated at the disavowal, on the part of our government, through Lord Keith, of the convention of El-Arisch, which we maintain that he so wisely signed. However, we have it upon good authority, that, up to the present time, he was never pecuniarily remunerated for his ambassadorial functions.

Sir Sidney, some very considerable time after, finding himself at Vienna, when the late Marquis of Londonderry, then Lord Castlereagh, was settling the affairs of the European world, stated to his lordship the disagreeable position in which lie found himself, and dwelt forcibly upon the injustice of letting claims for services so valuable as those which he had performed in Egypt remain so long unsettled. Lord Castlereagh immediately assented to the hardship of the case, and proceeded directly to make use of the best remedy, by amply satisfying the demand. "But,"as Sir Sidney expressed it himself, "as he thought proper to terminate his existence shortly afterwards, and neglected to leave an official memorandum of the transaction, I was obliged to refund the money, and up to the present moment, although I have been perpetually promised by the different ministers that I should be indemninified and settled with, I have never received one farthing."

Upon Sir Sidney Smith's return to England, one of the first honours with which he was greeted, and at which we have before hinted, was displayed in the following manner.

The Corporation of London, anxious to exhibit a proof of their admiration of the gallant achievements of Sir Sidney Smith at the siege of Acre, resolved to bestow upon him the freedom of their ancient city, and to accompany it with the present of a valuable sword; on the 7th instant, the naval hero attended at Guildhall, in order to be invested with the civic privileges of which he had been deemed worthy, and to receive the symbol of valour he had so justly merited.

The Lord Mayor, the Chamberlain, and several of the Aldermen were ready to receive him. He made his appearance between one and two, and was ushered into the Chamberlain's office. The Lord Mayor received him with the utmost courtesy, and introduced him to Mr. James Dixon, the gentleman who had done himself the honour of voting the thanks of the court of common council in his favour. The Chamberlain then addressed the distinguished officer in the following terms:

"Sir Sidney Smith—I give you joy, in the name of the Lord Mayor, Aldermen, and Commons of the City of London, in common council assembled, and present you the thanks of the Court for your gallant and successful defence of St. Jean d'Acre against the desperate attack of the French army under the command of General Bonaparte. And, as a further testimony of the sense the Court entertains of your great display of

valour on that occasion, I have the honour to present you with the freedom of the city and this sword. [Sir Sidney received the sword, and
pressed it with fervour to his lips.] I will not, sir, attempt a panegyric
upon an action to which the first oratorical powers in the most eloquent
assemblies have been confessed unequal; but I cannot help exulting on
this happy occasion at the vast acquisition of national reputation acquired by your conduct at the head of a handful of Britons, in repulsing
him who has been justly styled the Alexander of the day, surrounded by a
host of conquerors till then deemed invincible. By this splendid achievement you frustrated the designs of the foe on our East Indian territories,
prevented the overthrow of the Ottoman power in Asia, the downfall of
its throne in Europe, and prepared the way for that treaty of peace, which
it is devoutly to be wished may long preserve the tranquillity of the universe, and promote friendship and goodwill among all nations. It must be
highly gratifying to every lover of his country that this event should happen on the very spot where a gallant English monarch formerly displayed
such prodigies of valour—that a celebrated historian, recording his actions, struck with the stupendous instances of prowess displayed by that
heroic prince, suddenly exclaimed, 'Am I writing history or romance?'
Had, sir, that historian survived to have witnessed what has recently
happened at St. Jean d'Acre, he would have exultingly resigned his
doubts, and generously have confessed that actions, no less extraordinary
than those performed by the gallant Coeur de Lion, have been achieved
by Sir Sidney Smith." This speech was followed by universal acclamations.

Sir Sidney Smith thus replied:

"Sir—Unconscious that I should have been thought worthy of being
addressed by you on the part of the city of London in terms of such high
and unqualified approbation, I am but ill prepared for replying in a manner adequately to express the sentiments with which I am impressed. My
confidence would be lessened, did I not feel that I was surrounded by
friends who are dear to me, and whose approbation I am proud to have
received. It shall be the object of my future life to merit the panegyric you
have been pleased to pronounce in my favour. For the freedom of your
city, with which you have honoured me, I return you my sincere thanks,
and shall implicitly conform to all the obligations annexed to it. Above
all, I accept this sword as the most honourable reward which could have
been conferred on me. In peace it will be my proudest ornament, and in
war I trust I shall be ever ready to draw it in defence of my country, and
for the protection of the city of London." [Loud applause.]

Sir Sidney Smith then took the usual civic oaths; and having made a
liberal donation to the poor's box, departed amidst the acclamations of
the populace.

CHAPTER XX

THE grateful countrymen of Sir Sidney Smith, eager to testify their feelings for his almost universal talents, showed him, on every occasion, the most marked respect. Civic honours followed those of the battle, the ocean, and the court. At the general election of representatives for the second parliament of the United Kingdom, the citizens of Rochester evinced their good taste by choosing our officer, in conjunction with Mr. James Hulkes, to watch their own interests and those of the empire in the House of Commons. Sir Sidney accordingly took his seat for that ancient city on the opening of the session, on the 16th of November, 1802.

At this period, the country was in a state of fitful repose, during a short and hollow peace; a peace that seemed to be more like a mutual cessation of hostilities, only obtained in order to afford all parties a little respite to enable them to recommence war with increased bitterness, fury, and devastation.

In his Majesty's address to his parliament, whilst he assured both Houses that he was, with a paternal anxiety, most solicitous to maintain peace, he spoke as apprehensive of approaching war, and breathed forth the accents of defiance and preparation. In the Upper House, Lord Nelson, fresh in the glories of the victory of the Nile, seconded the address to the throne. This was commendable to all parties, and honourable to the ministry.

At this distance of time it is impossible accurately to know, or if known, fully to appreciate, the various actuating motives of those who then ruled the destinies of England. But, looking to the services of Sir Sidney, and weighing how greatly his talents and activity had been the cause of gaining for England the peace, such as it was, we presume to think that he should have done that in the House of Commons, which Lord Nelson so gracefully performed in the House of Lords.

For the short time that he was enabled to attend to his parliamentary duties, the commodore was, though by no means obtrusive, diligent and attentive. At that period Pitt, Fox, and Sheridan, with other men who have identified themselves with the history of the country, were in the zenith of their glory. In the fields of oratory, competition with declaimers like these would have been vain. Besides, at that time, Sir Sidney conscientiously supported the party that was opposed to the latitudinarian principles of government, religion, and morals, that was then so lamentably gaining ground. The posts that a man of virtuous ambition would have been anxious to fill, were all occupied. Nothing was left for Sir Sidney, but to follow those who were so well able to lead; and to support by his vote, and strengthen by his countenance, those principles for which he had so gloriously fought, bled, and conquered.

Yet, though by no means a clamorous or even a garrulous member, when the opportunity occurred, by which the House might benefit by his nautical or military experience, he knew well how to impart that experience in a manner both dignified and impressive. On the debate on the navy estimates, when Mr. Alexander moved for a grant of fifty thousand seamen for the service of the ensuing year, Sir Sidney Smith expressed considerable regret at the great reductions which were so suddenly made, not only in the king's dockyards, but also throughout the naval service. He remarked, feelingly, that by this proceeding a prodigious number of men had thus been reduced to the utmost poverty and distress; and thus, being goaded by a sudden and undeserved misery, they would be compelled to seek for employment in foreign states, and the very sinews of our strength and safety be wasted. He knew that, however distasteful foreign service might be to the English sailor, dire necessity would oblige him to enter into it. Though he supported the vote, yet, on the grounds that he had stated, he earnestly wished that the number of seamen to be employed were considerably greater than it actually was; for he knew, from his own experience, that what was called an ordinary seaman could hardly find employment, at present, either in his Majesty's or the merchant service. He then proceeded to inform the House that he himself had been present at some of the changes which had lately taken place in France, and that they resembled more the changes of scenery at a theatre than anything else. In that versatile country everything was done for stage effect; and, whether it were the death of Caesar, the fall of Byzantium, or the march of Alexander, it seemed, to a Frenchman, almost indifferent. He looked only to the blaze of the moment, and the magic of effect. Knowing this trait in the Gallic character, he felt assured, that if the invasion of Britain were to be produced for the amusement and excitement of that nation, it would have the stage effect sufficient to draw four hundred thousand volunteers to join in the procession. Under these circumstances, he wished that this country should always be in a situation to call together speedily a strong naval force—a force equal to frustrate any attempts on the part of the enemy.

The salutary nature of this advice events were not slow in making apparent, for, in a few weeks subsequent to the delivery of this concise and sensible speech, our subject was in the command of a portion of the naval armament, the increase of which he had so wisely and powerfully advocated.

In all those acts that had philanthropy for their end, or which could tend to ameliorate human suffering, Sir Sidney Smith was always found in the foremost ranks of the beneficent. On the 2d of June in the year 1802, the anniversary of the Naval Institution was held at the London Tavern. On this occasion Lord Belgrave was the chairman, occupying that distinguished post in the room of Earl St. Vincent, who was compelled to be absent on account of ill health. There were present some of the most distinguished heroes of the country, hardly one of whom now lives, saving in the memories of their grateful countrymen, with the exception of Sir Sidney Smith. Sir Hyde Parker, Lord Nelson, Sir William Hamilton, with very many others, to whom the nation then looked up with confidence, graced this benevolent meeting. We have no space, nor is it our province to record, any of those proceedings, excepting those personally connected with our officer.

Upon the health of Sir Sidney Smith being drunk with the warmest and most enthusiastic applause, he thus addressed the meeting:

"He need not assure the company of his warm feelings towards them for that Asylum they had provided for the orphans of those brave men who had fallen in the late contest. Unfortunately for him, too many were in the list of his dearest friends." [Here Sir Sidney's feelings were too great for utterance his head sank the big tear rolled down the hero's cheek.*] A solemn silence prevailed for several minutes, and soft sympathy filled many a manly bosom, until Sir Sidney was roused by the thunder of applause which followed. He again addressed the company, stated that it was his intention to hand the governors a list of those sufferers; among them was his intimate friend Captain Miller, of the Theseus; they had served together as midshipmen under Lord Rodney. Captain Miller lost his life off Acre, and had left two children. The next was Major Oldfield, of the marines. He would tell the company where the dead body of this brave man was contended for, and they would judge where and how he died. It was in the sortie of the garrison of St. Jean d'Acre, when attacked by General Bonaparte, that Major Oldfield, who commanded the sortie, was missing. On our troops advancing, his body was found at the mouth of one of the enemy's mines, and at the foot of their works. Our brave men hooked him by the neckcloth, as he lay dead, to draw him off; the enemy at the same time pierced him in the side with a halberd, and each party struggled for the body; the neckcloth gave way, and the enemy

---

* This is an extract from the Naval Chronicle.

succeeded in dragging to their works this brave man; and here he must do them that justice which such gallant enemies are fully entitled to; they next day buried Major Oldfield with all the honours of war. This brave man has left children. In the list also is Captain Canes, late first lieutenant of the Tigre. He lost not his life in any of the numerous actions in which he was engaged, but in carrying despatches to the Mediterranean of the preliminaries of peace. He perished at sea with his ship and crew. This brave officer has left young orphans who want support." Sir Sidney concluded a most affecting address thus: "That their orphans, and the offspring of the many others who have so nobly fought and died in their king and country's service, may meet support equal to their claim, is the warmest wish of my heart."

On the 7th of January 1803, Sir Sidney obtained from his sovereign permission to bear the following honourable augmentations to the armorial ensigns borne by his family, viz. on the cheveron a wreath of laurel, accompanied by two crosses Calvary; and, on the chief augmentation, the interior of an ancient fortification in perspective; in the angle a breach, and on the sides of the said breach the standard of the Ottoman Empire and the union flag of Great Britain. For crest, the imperial Ottoman chelengk, or plume of triumph, upon a turban, in allusion to the honourable and distinguished decoration transmitted by the Turkish Emperor to Sir William Sidney Smith, in testimony of his esteem, and in acknowledgment of his meritorious exertions in defence of Acre; and the family crest, viz. a leopard's head, collared and lined, issuing out of an oriental crown, the same arms and crest to be borne by Sir William Sidney Smith and his issue, together with the motto "COEUR DE LION." And although the privilege of bearing supporters be limited to peers of the realm, the knights of the different orders, and the proxies of princes of the blood-royal at installations, except in such cases wherein, under particular circumstances, the king shall be pleased to grant his especial license for the use thereof; his Majesty, in order to give a further testimony of his particular approbation of Sir Sidney Smith's services, was also graciously pleased to allow him to bear, for supporters to his arms, a tiger gardant navally crowned, in the mouth a palm branch, being the symbol of victory supporting the union flag of Great Britain, with the inscription "JERU-SALEM, 1799,"upon the cross of St. George, and a lamb murally crowned, being the symbol of peace, supporting the banner of Jerusalem.

Honoured thus by his king, and thus prized by his country, shortly after his Majesty's declaration against France, dated at Westminster, May the 18th, Sir Sidney hoisted his broad pennant as commodore on board of the Antelope, of fifty guns, with the command of a squadron to be employed on the French coast. His appointment to this ship bears the date of the 12th of March, 1803.

Of the fatigue, the irksomeness, and the danger of this service, a landsman can form no adequate opinion. The very seas in which the vessel is forced to remain, sailing hither and thither, within a very circumscribed compass, are replete with dangers. The pilot and the master have no longer to contend with the open sea, of which the dangers are, comparatively speaking, frank though great. But in the waters that wash the French, Flemish, and English shores, the soundings are variable, the sandbanks multitudinous, and continually shifting their positions. When we add to all these the impetuosity of the tides as they rush through the narrow races, and whirl round the low headlands, it will be most apparent that the shot and shell of the enemy are to be reckoned among the least of the dangers to which a ship is exposed in the service on which the Antelope was employed when under the command of Sir Sidney Smith.

The vessel was always either lying off the Texel, Ostend, or the coast of France opposite to England, sometimes at sea, sometimes at single anchor, excepting on those occasions when she was obliged to repair to Yarmouth Roads for the necessary refits.

When on the enemy's coasts, scarcely a day passed but some skirmish ensued, now with the ship, then with the boats. The prizes made were numerous, but singly of too little importance to call for observation. Sometimes these harassing services were performed by the crew of the Antelope alone, sometimes assisted by other vessels.

Very much of this fatiguing service consisted of taking soundings in the mouths of the harbours, and under the guns of the batteries. The danger and the damage encountered in these useful but little valued services, so far as either emolument or fame is concerned, are of an extent as little understood as it is appreciated. Arms and legs may be shredded off, and yet no room afforded even for five lines of glory to the sufferers in a despatch published in the Gazette. We acknowledge that the pension will be paid, but the man may be disabled for life, and all his hopes of future advancement in his profession destroyed. We have been induced to make these remarks, in order to impress upon the general reader that naval officers may have deserved well of the country, though they could never boast of having contributed to the success of a general action, or to the glory of some well-contested single encounter.

Our officer soon made his presence felt by the enemy, for by his vigilance he kept them in a state of continual alarm. At this time, the French were employing all their skill and activity in preparing, in the various seaports contiguous to Great Britain, a vast armament for the invasion of those shores that have never seen a successful enemy upon them since the Norman conquest. Nothing now was spoken of on one side of the Channel but praams, flat-bottomed boats, and flotillas; and, on the other, sea fencibles, corps of loyal volunteers, and catamarans.

The service on which our commodore was now employed gave but little scope to his ambition, and he performed nothing brilliant, solely because the enemy would give him no opportunity. But his untiring watchfulness, though it brought him no increase of glory, insured the safety of his country, and security to the commerce of England in the Channel.

But he was not wholly confined to the duties of vigilance, for on the 17th of May, 1804, he made an attack on a French flotilla lying at anchor off Ostend. This was a bold, well planned, but unsuccessful attempt to prevent the junction of the enemy's flotilla at Flushing with that of Ostend. The failure principally arose from the want of a sufficient number of gunboats, which, from the shallowness of water in which these vessels move, could alone act against the enemy with effect. Fifty-nine sail of the Flushing division reached Ostend in safety; and the English force, on the falling of the tide, were compelled to haul off into deep water, after being nearly the whole day engaged, and with considerable loss.

We shall give the narrative of this little affair in his own words, in a despatch addressed to Lord Keith.

"MY LORD, Information from all quarters, and the evident state of readiness in which the enemy's armaments were in Helvoet, Flushing, and Ostend, indicating the probability of a general movement from those ports, I reinforced Captain Manby, off Helvoet, with one ship, and directed Captain Hancock, of the Cruiser, stationed in-shore, to combine his operations and the Rattler's with the squadron of gunboats stationed off Ostend. The Antelope, Penelope, and Amiable, occupied a central position in sight both of Flushing and Ostend, in anxious expectation of the enemy's appearance. Yesterday, at half-past five A.M., I received information from Captain Hancock, then off Ostend, that the enemy's flotilla was hauling out of that pier, and had already twenty-one one-masted vessels, arid one schooner outside in the roads; and at half past seven the same morning I had the satisfaction to see the Flushing flotilla, of fifty-nine sail, viz. two ship-rigged praams, nineteen schooners, and thirty-eight schuyts, steering along-shore from that port towards Ostend, under circumstances which allowed me to hope I should be able to bring them to action. The signal was made in the Cruiser and Rattler for an enemy in the E.S.E. to call their attention from Ostend; the squadron weighed the moment the flood made, and allowed of the heavier ships following them over the banks; the signals to chase and engage were obeyed with alacrity, spirit, and judgment by the active and experienced officers your lordship has done me the honour to place under my orders. Captains Hancock and Mason attacked this formidable line with the greatest gallantry and address, attaching themselves particularly to the two praams, both of them of greater force than themselves, independent of the cross fire from the schooners and schuyts. I sent the Amiable by signal to support them. The Penelope (having an able pilot, Mr. Thornton) on signal being made to engage, Captain Broughton worked up to the centre of the enemy's line, as near as the shoal water would allow, while the Antelope went round the Stroom Sand, to cut the van off from Ostend. Unfortunately our gunboats were not in sight, having, as I understood since, devoted their attention to preventing the Ostend division from moving westward. The enemy attempted to get back to Flushing; but being harassed by the Cruiser and the Rattler, and the wind coming more easterly against them, they were obliged to run the gauntlet to the westward, keeping close to the beach under the protection of the batteries. Having found a passage for the Antelope within the Stroom Sand, she was enabled to bring her broadside to bear on the headmost schooners before they got the length of Ostend. The leader struck immediately, and the crew deserted her: she was, however, recovered by the followers. The artillery from the town and camp, and the rowing gunboats from the pier, kept up a constant and well directed fire for their support; our shot, however, which went over the schooners, going ashore among the horse artillery, interrupted it in a degree; still, however, it was from the shore we received the greatest annoyance; for the schooners and schuyts crowding along could not bring their prow guns to bear without altering their course towards us, which they could not venture; and their side guns, though numerous and well served, were very light. In this manner the Penelope and Antelope engaged every part of their long line, from four to eight, while the Amiable, Cruiser, and Rattler continued to press their rear. Since two o'clock the sternmost praam struck her colours and ran on shore; but the artillery-men from the army got on board, and she renewed her fire on the Amiable with the precision of a land battery, from which that ship suffered much. Captain Bolton speaks much in praise of Lieutenant Mather, who is wounded. Several of the schooners and schuyts immediately under the fire of the ships were driven on shore in the like manner, and recovered by the army. At eight, the tide falling and leaving us in little more water than we could draw, we were reluctantly obliged to haul off into deeper water to keep afloat, and the enemy's vessels that were not on shore, or too much shattered, were thus able to reach Ostend—these and the Ostend division having hauled into the basin. I have anchored in such a position as to keep an eye on them; and I shall endeavour to close with them again, if they move into deeper water. I have to regret that, from the depth of water in which these vessels move, gunboats only can act against them with effect: four have joined me, and I have sent them in to see what they can do with the praam that is on shore. I have great satisfaction in bearing testimony to your lordship, of the gallant and steady conduct of the captains, commanders, officers, seamen, and marines under my orders. Captains Hancock and Mason bore the brunt of the attack, and continued it for six hours against a great superiority of fire, particularly from the army on shore, the howitzer shells annoying them much. These officers deserve the highest praise I can give them. They speak of the conduct of their lieutenants, officers, and crews, in terms of warm panegyric. Messrs. Budd and Dalyell, from the Antelope, acted in the absence of two lieutenants of those ships. Lieutenants Garrety and Patful, commanding the Favourite and Stag cutters, did their best with their small guns against greater numbers of greater calibre. Lieutenant Hillier, of the Antelope, gave me all the assistance and support on her quarter-deck his ill state of health would permit. Lieutenant Stokes and Mr. Slesser, acting lieutenants, directed the fire on the lower and main decks with coolness and precision. It would be the highest injustice if I omitted to mention the intrepid conduct of Mr. Lewis, the master, Mr. Nunn and Mr. Webb, pilots, to whose steadiness, skill, and attention, particularly the former, I shall ever feel myself indebted for having brought the Antelope into action within the sands, where certainly the enemy could riot expect to be met by a ship of her size; and for having allowed her to continue engaged with Commodore Verheuil, to the last minute it was possible to remain in such shoal water, with a falling tide. It is but justice to say, the enemy's commodore pursued a steady course, notwithstanding our fire, and returned it with spirit to the last. I could not detach open boats in the enemy's line, to pick up those vessels which had struck and were deserted, mixed as they were with those still firing. Captain Hancock sent me one schuyt that had hauled out of the line and surrendered. She had a lieutenant and twenty-three soldiers of the forty-eighth regiment, with five Dutch seamen, on board. She is so useful here, I cannot part with her yet. Enclosed is a list of our loss, which, though great, is less than might have been expected, owing to the enemy's directing their fire at our masts. The Rattler and Cruiser have, of course, suffered most in the latter respect, but are nearly ready for service again. The smoke would not allow us to see the effect of our shot on the enemy; but their loss, considering the number of them under our guns for so long, must be great in proportion. We see the mastheads above water of three of the schooners and one of the schuyts which were sunk.

W. SIDNEY SMITH

Lord Keith, K. B. &c. &c. &c

In this little skirmish, Sir Sidney's squadron sustained a loss of two petty officers, ten seamen, and one boy killed; and two officers, four petty officers, twenty-five seamen, and one marine wounded.

This despatch will give the reader a tolerably accurate idea of the nature of the warfare that we were then compelled to carry on. It was of a most harassing nature, attended with great privation and suffering, and involving a loss of limb and life, that seems no way commensurate to the combatants, either in fame or in advantage, even when the operations were the most successful.

CHAPTER XXI

AT this momentous period, war was raging in almost every quarter of the civilised world; and after Sir Sidney's term of command in the Antelope had expired, his services were of a nature far too valuable to permit them to remain, longer than the rules of the navy permitted, uncalled for. But his past conduct merited much more distinction, and far greater rewards, than it had yet received, though, about the beginning of the year 1804, he was promoted to the highly honourable and somewhat lucrative appointment of a Colonel of Royal Marines, and, on the 9th of November 1805, was advanced to the rank of Rear-Admiral of the Blue.

During this interval, as he was not employed afloat, we do not find his name mentioned in the public records. He was assiduously and successfully cultivating the arts of peace, and laying the foundation for that scientific proficiency, for which he afterwards became, in many branches of useful knowledge, so conspicuous.

The progress of Bonaparte towards universal European dominion had now become most alarming. He had nearly overrun the continent, and had really hardly anything to do but to look around him for fresh pretences for aggression, and such a pretence the imprudence of the Neapolitan government readily afforded him.

By a treaty ratified by the King of Naples on the 8th of October of the year 1805, the French troops agreed to withdraw from the occupation of the Neapolitan territory; and the king engaged, in return, to remain neutral in the war between France and the allies, and to repel by force every encroachment on his neutrality. He more particularly became bound not to permit the troops of any other great power to enter his territories, or to confide the command of his armies or strong places to any Russian or Austrian officers, or to any French emigrant, and not to permit any belligerent squadron to enter into his ports.

Hardly had six weeks elapsed when every one of the stipulations of the treaty had been violated. On the 20th of November, an English and Russian fleet appeared in the Bay of Naples, and landed a body forces in that city and the vicinity. The French ambassador immediately took down the arms of France from over the gate of his hotel, and demanded his passport.

The Russians, who were in number about fourteen thousand men, under General Lacey, landed at Naples, and the English, amounting to about ten thousand, under Sir James Craig and Sir John Stuart, landed at Castell-a-Mare. The Neapolitans now openly abetted these operations.

But it was not long before the Court of Naples was made sensible of the full extent of its imprudence. On the morning after the signature of the peace of Presburg, Bonaparte issued a proclamation from his headquarters at Vienna, declaring that "the Neapolitan dynasty had ceased to reign,"and denouncing vengeance against the family, in terms that left no hope for accommodation or pardon.

From reasons only to be discovered in the arcana of those who conducted the political operations of England, immediately after this denunciation of vengeance, the principal cause of it, the Russian and English troops, withdrew from Naples, and left the King and his advisers in dismay, to repent of their folly as they best could. The immediate consequence of all this was, that the King of Naples, with his court, was forced to fly a second time to Palermo, whilst Joseph Bonaparte was crowned, in his stead, at Naples, and all the constituted authorities took the oath of fidelity to him. No sovereign was, perhaps, more easily manoeuvred out of his kingdom than was this unfortunate King of Naples.

The assumption of the royal dignity in Naples by Joseph Bonaparte, and the defection of so many persons of distinction, excited the liveliest indignation at the court of Palermo. Though driven from Naples by their inability to resist the French arms, they were eager to attempt the recovery of that kingdom, and thus they continued to excite the Neapolitans to rebellion against their *de facto* sovereign.

These attempts only produced defeat and slaughter; and though Abruzzo and Calabria were delivered, for a short time, from the French yoke, the French prevailed in the end; and after a fruitless waste of blood, and the perpetration of atrocities by both parties, disgraceful to humanity, those provinces were again compelled to acknowledge Joseph Bonaparte as their sovereign.

Notwithstanding these disasters, a fresh insurrection was decided upon; but so great was the universal dread of the French arms, that the court would not have attained its ends, had not an English army landed on the coast of Calabria, and begun its military operations by a most splendid and glorious victory.

It was to forward these operations on an extensive scale that induced our government to select some enterprising officer. The choice naturally fell upon Sir Sidney Smith. About the middle of April he had arrived at Palermo in the Pompée of eighty-four guns, and had taken the command of the English squadron destined, among other things, for the defence of Sicily, consisting of five ships of the line, besides frigates, transports, and gunboats.

With this force at his disposal, the gallant rear-admiral proceeded to the coast of Italy, and began his operations by introducing into Gaeta supplies of stores and ammunition, for the want of which its garrison had been greatly straitened. This operation produced the very best effects, as, through it, the enemy, though the besiegers, were immediately compelled to act on the defensive.

Having performed this important service, and left at Gaeta a flotilla of gunboats, under the protection of a frigate to assist at the defence of the place, he proceeded to the Bay of Naples, spreading consternation and alarm all along the coast, and so much intimidated the French, that they, in much haste, conveyed the greater part of their battering train from Gaeta to Naples, in order to protect the capital from insult, and secure it, if possible, from attack.

By these operations, the rear-admiral thus virtually raised the siege of Gaeta, as all the battering trains were removed from the trenches, and the attack was totally suspended.

It happened that, at the very moment when he approached Naples, the city was splendidly illuminated, on account of Joseph Bonaparte being proclaimed King of the Two Sicilies. Indeed, with a fickleness that is much the character of the unthinking multitude, there was every demonstration of joy evinced on the part of the populace, in which the nobility and gentry seemed to do more than share. The nobles were most eager to show their attachment to their new king, by soliciting from him all manner of offices and distinctions, at the same time most zealously proffering their services.

It was completely in the power of the English admiral to have disturbed these demonstrations of festivity, and to turn the place of rejoicing into a scene of mourning and desolation; but, as the sufferers from his hostilities must have been the inhabitants of Naples, and not the French troops or the new king, he wisely and humanely forbore to pour upon the city the devastations of war. He considered that the unfortunate inhabitants had evil enough already upon them, and that the restoration of his capital to the lawful sovereign and its fugitive denizens, would be but of little gratification, if it should be found a heap of ruins; and, lastly, that as he had no force to land and preserve order, in the event of the French retiring to the fortresses, he should leave an opulent city a prey to the licentious part of the community, who would not fail to profit by the confusion that the flames might occasion.

From the Bay of Naples, the rear-admiral proceeded with all despatch to the Island of Capri, determined to wrest that place from the enemy, which, by its position so effectually preserving their southern communications, were of a paramount object to the French to possess.

The commandant was accordingly summoned to surrender, and on his refusal, an attack commenced, in which he was slain. The army then beat a parley, a capitulation was subsequently signed, and the garrison marched out with all the honours of war.

The following is Sir Sidney Smith's despatch.

Letter from Sir Sidney Smith, dated Pompée, at anchor off Scalia, May 24, containing an Account of Proceedings in Calabria.

MY LORD, I arrived at Palermo in the Pompée on the 21st of last month, and took on me the command of the squadron your lordship has done me the honour to place under my orders. I found things in the state that may be well imagined, on the government being displaced from its capital, with the loss of one of the two kingdoms, and the dispersion of the army assembled in Calabria. The judicious arrangement made by Captain Sotheron, of the ships under his orders, and the position of the British army under Sir J. Stuart at Messina, had, however, prevented farther mischief. I had the satisfaction of learning that Gaeta still held out, although, as yet, without succour, from a mistaken idea, much too prevalent, that the progress of the French armies is irresistible. It was my first care to see that the necessary supplies should be safely conveyed to the governor. I had the inexpressible satisfaction of conveying the most essential articles to Gaeta, and of communicating to his Serene highness the governor (on the breach-battery, which he never quits) the assurance of farther support to any extent within my power, for the maintenance of that important fortress, hitherto so long preserved by his intrepidity and example. Things wore a new aspect on the arrival of the ammunition: the redoubted fire of the enemy, with red-hot shot into the Mole, (being answered with redoubled vigour,) did not prevent the landing of everything we had brought, together with four of the Excellent' s lower-deck guns, to answer this galling fire, which bore directly on the landing-place. A second convoy, with the Intrepid, placed the garrison beyond the immediate want of anything essential; and the enemy, from advancing his nearest approaches within two hundred and fifty yards, was reduced to the defensive, in a degree dreading one of those sorties which the Prince of Hesse had already shown him his garrison was equal to, and which was become a much safer operation, now that the flanking fire of eight Neapolitan gunboats I had brought with me, in addition to four his highness had already used successfully, would cover it, even to the rear of the enemy's trenches. Arrangements were put in a train for this purpose; and, according to a wise suggestion of his Serene highness, measures were taken for the embarkation of a small party from the garrison to land in the rear of the enemy's batteries to the northward. I confided the execution of the naval part of this arrangement to Captain Richardson, of H. M. S. Juno, putting the Neapolitan frigate and gunboats under his orders. His Serene Highness, possessing the experience of European warfare, and a most firm mind, having no occasion for farther aid on the spot, I felt I could quit the garrison without apprehension for its safety in such hands, with the present means of defence, and that I could best co-operate with him by drawing some of the attacking force off for the defence of Naples. I accordingly proceeded thither with the line-of-battle ships named in the margin.* The enemy's apprehension of attack occasioned them to convey some of the battering train from the trenches before Gaeta to Naples, The city was illuminated on account of Joseph Bonaparte proclaiming himself King of the Two Sicilies! The junction of the Eagle made us five sail of the line, and it would have been easy for their fire to have interrupted this ceremony and show of festivity: but I considered that the unfortunate inhabitants had evil enough on them; that the restoration of the capital to its lawful sovereign and fugitive inhabitants would be no gratification, if it should be found a heap of ruins, ashes, and bones; and that as I had no force to land and keep order, in case of the French army retiring to the fortresses, I should leave an opulent city a prey to the licentious part of the community, who would not fail to profit by the confusion the flames would occasion: not a gun was fired.

But no such consideration operated on my mind to prevent me dislodging the French garrison from the Island of Capri, which, from its situation, protecting the coasting communication southward, was a great object for the enemy to keep, and by so much, one for me to wrest from him. I accordingly summoned the French commandant to surrender: on his non-acquiescence, I directed Captain Rowley, in H. M. S. Eagle, to cover the landing of marines and boats' crews, and caused an attack to be made under his orders. That brave officer placed his ship judiciously; nor did he open his fire till she was secured, and his distance marked by the effect of musketry on his quarter-deck, where the first lieutenant, J. Crawley, fell wounded, and a seaman was killed. Although Captain Rowley regretted much the services of that meritorious officer in such a critical moment, he has since recovered. An hour's fire from both decks of the Eagle, (between nine and ten o'clock,) with that of two Neapolitan mortar-boats under an active officer, Lieutenant Rivers, drove the enemy from

* Pompée, Excellent, Athenienne, Intrepid

the vineyards within their walls; the marines were landed, and gallantly led by Captain Bunce; the seamen in like manner, under Lieutenant Morrell of the Eagle, and Lieutenant Redding of the Pompée, mounted the steps: for such was their road, headed by the officers, nearest to the narrow pass by which alone they could ascend. Lieutenant Carrol had thus an opportunity of particularly distinguishing himself. Captain Stannus, commanding the Athenienne's marines, gallantly pressing forward, gained the heights, and the French commandant fell by his hand. This event being known, the enemy beat a parley, a letter from the second in command claimed the terms offered, but being dated on the 12th, after midnight, some difficulty occurred, my limitation as to time being precise; but on the assurance that the drum beat before twelve, the capitulation annexed was signed, and the garrison allowed to march out and pass over to Naples with every honour of war, after the interment of their former brave commander with due respect. We thus became masters of this important post. The enemy not having been allowed time to bring two pieces of heavy cannon, with their ammunition, to Capri, the boat containing them, together with a boat loaded with timber for the construction of gunboats at Castilamare, took refuge at Massa, on the main land, opposite to the island, where the guard had hauled the whole upon the beach. I detached the two mortar-boats and a Gaeta privateer, under the orders of Lieutenants Faliverne and Rivera, to bring them off, sending only Mr. Williams, midshipman of the Pompée, from the squadron, on purpose to let the Neapolitans have the credit of the action which they fairly obtained; for, after dislodging the enemy from a strong tower, they not only brought off the boats and two thirty-five pounders, but the powder also (twenty barrels) from the magazine of the tower, before the enemy assembled in force. The projected sorties took place on the 13th and 15th in the. morning, in a manner to reflect the highest credit on the part of the garrison and naval force employed. The covering fire from the fleet was judiciously directed by Captains Richardson and Vicuna, whose conduct on this whole service merits my warmest approbation. I enclose Captain Richardson's two letters, as best detailing these affairs, and a list of the killed and wounded on the 12th.

On the 19th ult., the boats of the Pompée, under Lieutenant Beaucroft, brought out a merchant vessel from Scalvitra, near Salerno, although protected by a heavy fire of musketry. That officer and Mr. Sterling distinguished themselves much. The enemy are endeavouring to establish a land-carriage there to Naples. On the 23rd, obtaining intelligence that the enemy had two thirty-six pounders in a small vessel on the beach at Sealia, I sent the Pompée's boats in for them; but the French troops were too well posted in the houses of the town for them to succeed without the cover of the ship. I accordingly stood in with the

Pompée; sent a messenger to the inhabitants to withdraw; which being done, a few of the Pompée's lower-deck guns cleared the town and neighbouring hills, while the launch, commanded by Lieutenant Mouraylian, and Lieutenant Gates of the marines, and Mr. Williams, drove the French, with their armed adherents, from the guns, and took possession of the castle, and of them. Finding, on my landing, that the town was tenable against any force the enemy could bring against me from the nearest garrison in a given time, I took post with the marines; and, under cover of their position, by the extreme exertions of Lieutenant Carrol, Mr. Ives, master, and the petty officers and boats' crew, the guns were conveyed to the Pompée, with twenty-two barrels of powder.

W. SIDNEY SMITH

After placing an English garrison in Capri, Sir Sidney proceeded southward along the coast, giving the greatest annoyance everywhere to the enemy, obstructing by land, and intercepting by sea entirely, their communications along the shore, so as to retard their operations against Gaeta, which was the chief purpose of undertaking the expedition.

Encouraged by this success of our arms, several sorties took place from out of Gaeta, which we have stated Sir Sidney had so opportunely relieved.

All this had, however, but little effect upon the fate of the place, as it was enabled to hold out only until the 13th of July, and was then compelled to surrender to the French.

CHAPTER XXII

FURTHER OPERATIONS FOR THE RECOVERY OF NAPLES • THEIR INU-
TILITY • SIR SIDNEY SMITH RECEIVES THE ACKNOWLEDGMENTS OF
THEIR SICILIAN MAJESTIES • REMARKS ON NAVAL APPOINTMENTS.

ON the return of Sir Sidney Smith to Palermo, after the conclusion of this service, and a most harassing cruise to the enemy, the active turn and the sanguine temper of his mind induced him not only to enter into, but also to originate, projects that were, from time to time, suggested to the court, to second the King of the Sicilies' attempts for the recovery of Calabria from the invaders. Had all others, whose duty it was to carry these projects into execution, been actuated by half the zeal of Sir Sidney, and had they been possessed of enough humility and good sense to have followed in matters in which they were not qualified to lead, the re-conquest of Calabria would not have been long delayed.

The eager yet incompetent advisers of the King, finding the admiral thus favourably inclined towards the furtherance of their schemes, and the latter being most anxious to distinguish himself by some great exploit, their Sicilian Majesties invested him with the most ample authority to be exercised in Calabria, and they even went to the extent of constituting the British admiral their viceroy in that province.

But there were obstacles that even the energy of Sir Sidney Smith could not surmount. Though active and indefatigable in the duties of his new dignity, and successful in distributing arms and ammunition among the Calabrians, and a great deal of money among their leaders and influential men, he soon discovered, that unless an English army made its appearance in the country, there was not the remotest chance of producing an insurrection against the French.

It became, therefore, necessary for the court of Palermo either to abandon the fruit of all its intrigues and machinations, or to prevail on the commander of the English forces in Sicily to invade Calabria with the greatest part of his army. In this latter attempt the court succeeded.

The operations, after this, being strictly and almost exclusively military, they do not fall within our province to record. Of course, the admiral had to attend to the safe and convenient conveyance of the troops to their destination—to provide for their comfort on board, and their safe debarkation on shore. All this was duly effected, and Sir John Stuart, with an army of four thousand five hundred effective men, shortly after gained that victory, than which one more honourable to the combatants, or more glorious to the arms of any nation, was never recorded—the victory of Maida.

Major-general Sir John Stuart, in his despatch, dated, "Camp on the plain of Maida, July 6, 1806,"published in the London Gazette Extraordinary of September 5, of the same year, states as follows:

"The scene of action was too far from the sea to enable us to derive any direct co-operation from the navy: but Admiral Sir Sidney Smith, who had arrived in the bay the evening before the action, had directed such a disposition of ships and gun-boats as would have greatly favoured us, had events obliged us to retire. The solicitude, however, of every part of the navy to be of use to us, the promptitude with which the seamen hastened on shore with our supplies, their anxiety to assist our wounded, and the tenderness with which they treated them, would have been an affecting circumstance to observers, even the most indifferent: to me it was particularly so."

This victory led to the desired insurrection, but it proved transient and unsuccessful. So sensible was Sir John Stuart of his inability to maintain the ground he had won in Calabria, that very shortly afterwards he withdrew all his forces from that country, with the exception of a garrison left at Scylla, and a detachment of the seventy-eighth regiment, under Colonel M'Leod, which had been sent in the Amphion frigate to the coast near Catangaro, in order to countenance and assist the insurgents in that quarter.

General Acland was also despatched to the Bay of Naples; and though he was not absolutely prohibited from landing his troops, yet was he directed not to expose them to that danger, unless he had the prospect of effecting some object of real and permanent utility.

During all these operations, Sir Sidney Smith was most actively, if not judiciously, employed along the coast, assisting the insurgents with arms and ammunition, supplying them with provisions, and conveying them from one place to another, in the vessels under his command. Though we doubt that all this was a judicious acting, yet the manner in which the rear-admiral performed it was most judicious and effective.

He had nothing to do with the policy of this conduct he had only to see that it was well done—and well done indeed it was. His name became a very terror to the French.

By these unremitting exertions he contributed materially to extend the insurrection along the coast, and to expel the enemy from the watchtowers and the castles which they occupied upon the shore.

These spirited operations were, in some instances, of use, by securing a safer and better anchorage for his ships; but in others, we are bound to say, and it is with grief we say it, that the blood and treasure which they cost far exceeded the value of those temporary acquisitions.

In one of these adventures—for many of these exploits were more like the adventurous outbreaks of knight-errantry than the well-considered enterprises of modern warfare—he had in his own ship, the Pompée, a lieutenant and eight men killed, and thirty-four wounded, in an attack upon an insignificant fort on Point Licosa, which he destroyed when it fell into his hands.

It would, of itself, form a volume to detail all the services that he performed in this desultory warfare—services that really tended to no other result than to teach the seamen the art of gunnery, and to inure the ships' crews to the excitement of constant action. Gaeta was lost, the country became one scene of social disorganisation, and rapine and bloodshed prevailed wherever the human species congregated. The land was ruined and depopulated, whilst every place and post worth retaining still remained in the hands of the French. While things were in this state, Sir Sidney was called away to other duties.

The poor and despised court of Sicily was as grateful to Sir Sidney Smith as the bestowal of mere honours could prove them. The ex-viceroy of Calabria received the orders of the Grand Cross of St. Ferdinand and of Merit, accompanied by a letter from the then reigning Queen, expressive of the regret felt by the royal family at his departure, and the utmost gratitude for his exertions in their cause.

The subjoined is a translation of the letter (from the French) from the Queen of the two Sicilies to Rear-Admiral Sir Sidney Smith, dated Palermo, January 25th, 1837, and enclosed in a packet that conveyed the order.

My very worthy and dear Admiral,

I cannot find sufficient expressions to convey the painful feeling which your departure (so very unforeseen) has caused, both to me and among my whole family. I can only tell you that you are accompanied by our most sincere good wishes, and, more particularly on my part, by gratitude that will only cease with my life, for all that you have done for us; and for what you would still have done for us, if everything had not thwarted you, and cramped your zeal and enterprise.

May you be as happy as my heart prays for you! And may you continue, by fresh laurels, to augment your own glory and the number of the envious. I still cherish the hope of seeing you again in better times, and of giving you proof of those sentiments which, at the present moment, I cannot express; but you will find, in all times and places, (whatever may be the fate reserved for us,) our hearts gratefully attached to you, even unto the grave.

Pray make my sincere compliments to the Captain (Dacre) and to all the officers of Le Pompée, as well as my good wishes for their happiness. Assure them of the pain with which I witness their departure.

I am, most truly, for life,

Your very sincere and devoted friend,

CHARLOTTE

We are now going to inflict a digression upon the reader, but one intimately connected with the subject-matter of these volumes, and bearing individually upon the usefulness and the great talent of Sir Sidney Smith. It consists in a consideration as to the best method of giving merit, and merit only, that due preponderance in the naval service, so that, when the greatest object is to be effected, the very best man should be appointed to effect it.

We need not to be informed that a military autocracy, vested in one sole person—an autocracy of a character so absolute that no one of its acts could ever be called in question, would be the best principle for making either an army or a navy perfect: we mean such a power as Bonaparte so advantageously and universally exercised over the troops that he commanded. But this power can never be used in a free country, and may we never see an approximation to it; therefore, in a mixed government like that of the British Empire it is a most difficult question to solve, that of discovering the most efficacious method of rendering all public services the most available for the good of those for whom they should be instituted—the public. It is but seldom that one isolated mistake of a civil servant can produce disastrous, perhaps fatal consequences: he has only to swim forward, borne quietly down on the stream of office, with etiquette for his compass, custom for his helm, and precedent for his chart. So be it, for it is well that it is so.

But in the military, and still more stringently in the naval service, one act of incapacity, one moment's vacillation, and a ship is lost, a fleet destroyed, or the very salvation of a nation endangered. And how are these men appointed, on whom contingencies so awful depend? Like Cromwell's gallant Admiral, we meddle not with politics—we know it to be our primal duty, a duty sacred to good order and dear to humanity, to obey the powers that are legally constituted, however much we may condemn the policy of those who wield it, or despise their persons. We shall, therefore, without reference to this or that administration, fearlessly though briefly discuss a point so important in itself, and not irrelevant to our subject.

We freely confess that our hero, Sir Sidney Smith, sprang up to his glorious maturity from the very hotbed of corruption: but he was of a noble stock, and would have flourished in any soil. But this hotbed nourishes not only sluggish but poisonous weeds, and, for the sake of one Sir Sidney Smith, we are not willing to risk the honour and safety of the country to troops of such commanders-in-chief, naval or military, that one's heart burns to expose.

That promotion should take place in the navy solely by seniority is ridiculous. The sensible man and the fool, the gallant and cool sailor and the driveller and dastard, would have then equal chances of command, and the country be completely at the mercy of accident. Besides, to promote by seniority must necessarily throw the chief command into the hands of superannuated dotards, or, if these were to be provided for until the list showed an active man, the nation would be soon burthened with useless pensions, and the service made ridiculous by the then almost interminable multiplying of officers of rank. Seniority should have its weight in, but should not be the rule of, promotion. Yet as high commands are now gained by interests decidedly not naval, by courtly influences, by weight in parliament, by a bias most unjust, because carried to the extreme, in favour of the aristocracy, or to serve a party purpose, this system is still worse than the advancements of mere seniority. We have too often seen men in command of squadrons and of fleets, to whom we would not have entrusted the conduct of a flock of geese, even had they served seven years of apprenticeship to the humble but honest employment.

Well, then, it will be said, let merit determine the question. Alas, who shall decide what merit is? It is never the most distinguished officer that is the most meritorious, *"Palmam ferat qui meruit,"* [Ed. Let whoever earns the palm wear it] was a proud, a noble motto, and true also, and therefore the more noble. But it would be a libel, a gross calumny upon the British seamen of Nelson's glorious day, to say, though the hero bore the palm, that he the *most* deserved it—if mere merit had been the awarder.

A truly great man, as a naval commander, was the justly immortal Nelson. But we say it boldly, and we say it proudly, that in the fleet there were hundreds of men in every sense immeasurably better seamen, more skilful, and quite as brave as he the hero—whose memory no one can more deeply venerate than ourselves.

But who were they? It is a vain and an unfair question. The individuals cannot be pointed out, but they existed notwithstanding. They were hedged round by the rank weeds of favouritism—they were crushed down by the weight of authority—they lacked friends on shore and opportunities afloat accident, that was the midwife to others, was, to them, the cause of abortions. It is ten millions of chances to one, that the single grain of gold in the vessel filled with sand shall be the uppermost.

It would then seem that the officers should be elected and promoted by the votes of those who best understand, and are most immediately interested in their merit. That each ship should be, in itself, a floating, independent democracy, for certainly the crew of one vessel could not possibly be cognisant of the quantity or the quality of the talent in another. Already does the proposition begin to appear absurd, even before it is fully stated. The free discussion, the soliciting, the canvassing, the caballing—who would obey an irksome order, that knew he must be cajoled for his vote by the orderer? The notion would be preposterous; and yet the crews are the only witnesses, the only true appreciators of nautical merit. As a mass, the seamen of the royal navy have ever been, and still are, a rightly-minded and shrewd body—they best know when their ship is well worked, well disciplined, well navigated, and well fought.

Another great and insurmountable objection exists to the principle of the power of self-election to commands being vested in the navy. Valuable, nay, beyond all value as is the service, still, it must be a service—a subordinate body to defend, and neither to intimidate nor control the nation for whose good it was created. Directly that they were made an independent body, relying upon themselves for promotion, and all the good things the service has to bestow, they would soon cease to be a service, for they would no longer be subservient. It may be said, that there is always a check upon this fear of a naval usurpation, because the body of the people would cease to pay or to victual them, and thus, in a very short time, they must necessarily be subjugated.

But this reasoning would not hold good. Every one must perceive that, if the navy were to become a body distinct from and independent of the community, the army must become so too. The army, if the paramount power—as a military despotism—can always pay and victual itself from the resources of a prostrate country, and, in order to secure its power, it would immediately extend the privilege to the brother service, the navy.

Self-election must be vested in the members of neither the army nor the navy, if the liberties and the well-being of the community are to be preserved*

It then appears that those appointed by the forms of the country must still wield its naval and military powers—keep them under control—command them despotically—and distribute among their members all the prizes worth contending for. But, as yet, they have ever done, and must still do this, in comparative darkness and ignorance—a darkness and an ignorance that afford them the apology for the disgusting exercise of a patronage, that we boldly affirm is fast undermining the best interests of the navy. The high officials at home cannot tell who really the most deserve promotion, and thus, that promotion is bestowed, but too, too often on those who do not deserve it at all.

Now, these men in high places should no longer be permitted to shelter their gross and nefarious partialities under the plea of ignorance. The light should be brought to their very faces in spite of themselves, and then, if they wilfully and wickedly close their eyes against it, the country at large would know how properly to appreciate them.

To effect this, every ship's company, officers included, at stated intervals, should be called upon, as a duty, to recommend the most deserving among them as fit objects for promotion; at the same time it should be fully understood, that it was not to be looked upon as a rule that actual promotion should follow such nomination: the names of those persons thus virtuously distinguished should be published duly in the Gazette. This alone would be a great check upon unfair private patronage.

We well know that a system of secretly reporting to the Admiralty, by the captain of each vessel, has long existed; we also know,, that such reports are but seldom acted upon excepting the reporter have other influence, not connected with his official station. We are glad of this; for what is this reporting but nursing in the mind of the captain all bad tendencies, pandering to his spirit of favouritism, of pique, of revenge: he becomes, in reality, nothing better than a dignified spy—we will allow that the majority exercise this function with discrimination and impartiality—we sincerely believe that they do; but the mischief that the few evil-disposed among them may cause, by far outbalances the very uncertain good.

That accident, that seniority, and that blind patronage, have promoted admirals to important and extensive commands, is but too disgracefully true in the annals of our naval history. We have ourselves served under men at once tyrannical, brutal, and fatuous—animals of such limited intelligence, that we would not have entrusted to them the most insignificant command. We have seen such men manoeuvring fleets, with the safety and welfare of thousands at their disposal; and, still more revolting, with the power of life and death in their hands. We will mention no names, but only refer to those commanders-in-chief, who once were a byword and a mockery in the navy, of whom the most ridiculous stories were continually told, and who were really so stolid, that no story, however ridiculous, was too absurd to admit them as its heroes.

We deny not that even victories have been gained under the names of these men, and well written despatches have given a false impression to their countrymen of their worth and of their services. But if so much have been achieved under such imbecility, how much more would have been performed under men of activity and talent, and who had been recommended by those who knew them, to their respective commands, before they had been promoted to them.

We do not mean that this power of recommendation should be anything but a limited one. The navy must be under the control of the high civil authorities; it should be taught obedience to the constituted powers, and patriotism and loyalty impressed upon it to the utmost. We know all this, so much to be desired, might be fully attained, although the navy should be permitted at intervals, but not frequently, to name those of its own body who deserve well of their country, and upon whom promotion, if bestowed, would be bestowed worthily.

In resuming the course of our narrative, we think that it will be acknowledged, that, notwithstanding the great merit, and the enlightened bravery of the commander-in-chief, to whom the expedition against Constantinople was entrusted, had the conduct of it fallen to the lot of Sir Sidney, or the wish of the fleet been consulted, other and more brilliant results would have attended the British arms. We say this hesitatingly, for who can safely speculate upon mere probabilities? But we speak more decidedly when we say, that had it been demanded who, of all naval officers then fit for service, was the very best to have had the sole direction of this nice experiment upon the Turks, common sense would have replied "our officer," and the applause of the navy would have been the echo to the sentence. That we are not singular in our opinion, we quote the following extract from a publication cotemporary with the proceedings.

"As impartial observers, it seems to us that there were several circumstances which ought to have pointed out Sir Sidney Smith as the most proper officer that could be selected for the conduct of an expedition against Constantinople. His local knowledge of the country, it is thought, might have been an object of some consideration: he spoke the language; he had proved himself the saviour of the Ottoman empire, at St. John of Acre; and he had been accredited as a joint minister plenipotentiary to the then reigning sultan, Selim III. Yet, palpably absurd as it must appear, he was taken from the active station of Sicily, where he commanded, and placed, not *first*, nor SECOND, but THIRD in command of an expedition, of which he alone was competent to be the commander-in-chief! And, as an aggravation of this absurdity, when on the spot, he was not employed in the only diplomatic part of the proceedings which Sir John Duckworth entrusted out of his own hands! At the very time that the commander-in-chief was complimenting Sir Sidney Smith, Sir Thomas Louis was officiating as his deputed diplomatic agent!"

Let us again repeat, that we mean nothing invidious against Sir John Duckworth; his name stands deservedly high in the naval records of his country; more than one splendid victory have been gained under his flag, and the navy are indebted to him for many very facetious stories. Having thus done him all the justice that his warmest admirers can demand, we may be permitted to say, that he was not the best commander who could have been selected cunningly to display a force that he was not to employ, but under extremities, against a power in possession of much greater force, and possessing infinitely more cunning than himself.

On this delicate and very important subject we have been favoured with the enlightened and highly honourable opinion of Captain Montagu Montagu, who served under Sir John, as flag lieutenant, in the memorable expedition which we are about to relate. We had candidly submitted our idea to the Captain, that Sir Sidney Smith would have been, for that particular service, a more efficient commander. Captain Montagu's reply was as follows:

History is stern—she deals alone in facts, and makes no compromise with actions, as her business is—above all—truth. But, at the same time, she also estimates motives, as far as they can fairly be traced, and—still more—circumstances, which are, in fact, the deponing witnesses of that to which general reasoning is but the presumptive evidence. A Chief, and he alone, has upon him the responsibility of command, and which is not of a simple—but very compound nature—in the discriminating obedience he owes to his orders, the reference to public opinion—not that of the vulgar, and lastly—regard to his own conscience, which, to one of a mind suitable to his station, is most serious—an immense charge; considering that, in naval warfare, besides the ships' companies—numerous invaluable lives, the supremacy as well as the honour of his country's flag, are all confided to his care.

No one who has not been invested with command can sufficiently estimate its weight; and I will say more, that none can judge of the just line of conduct to be pursued in any specific case but he who has to decide upon it. Others, feeling their own powers, might perhaps fancy they would have done more than those who may be thought to have done too little, who, if in their place, would have found that more was not to be done. And, as for those who know not the seriousness of that responsibility—and—still less—juniors and subordinates, who have to fear neither condemnation—censure—nor self-reproach, with whom, naturally, every advance is a triumph and miscarriage is only ' the fortune of war,'—little store will be set on their opinions by those who have passed the age of first hope, who have added reflection to experience, and—above all—who are not interested in the decision.

That Sir Sidney would have 'dared all that may become a man' nobody will for a moment doubt. That he may have imagined that he might have accomplished more, is also possible; but even he cannot say he would have done so. It is not unlikely, that, certainly better acquainted as he was with the character of the Turks than Sir John Duckworth, and both more sanguine and more adventurous, he would, in negotiating with them, have used more of both cajolery and menace: he would have glittered brightlier, and have frowned more darkly: but it may be altogether doubted, whether this would have been one whit more successful than the dignified severity of his older chief; for it would not have been backed by one gun more, nor would all his skill, suavity, and determination have drawn one breath more wind to bring the British broadsides to bear on the Seven Towers.

So long as circumstances prevented the Squadron from acting, and every hour made that acting less to be feared—from the preparations making to resist it, the Turks were not to be hectored into submission; and Izaac Bey (whom I well remember) with all his long beard and his Mussulman impassibility, was, at short-handed diplomacy, a match for the most wily European.

This was the second time that Sir John Duckworth had been placed in these most trying and cruel circumstances; the first, two years before, in the presence of a French squadron; of appearing to decline an encounter with the enemy. But, in both, I am persuaded that Time, the great truth-teller and retributor—though often a sadly slow one, has done him ample justice; and re-echoed the voice of his own conscience, the noblest approver of a good man, as he was, who submitted to obloquy for doing what he felt to be right, where less scrupulous or reflecting men would have hazarded all for the gratification of their own personal vanity—for an applause that is seldom refused to an Englishman who fights, though with an utter disregard to the real interests of his Country.

From what I have said, then, you may infer my opinion on the subject; though, even if it were different, and I could incline to your view, you could not expect me to alter it, attached as I was to the good and brave man, whose conduct on this important occasion it goes to call in question. My conscientious persuasion—my conviction—is altogether in his favour and against your conclusion; as, I firmly believe, was that of all the senior officers of the squadron.

I must, then, leave you altogether to yourself in this matter; merely suggesting the danger, in all cases of this sort, of an over—though natural, as scarcely avoidable—partiality for one's hero.

As minutes of evidence are always of use, though those of a log-book or a ship's journal, from their cut and dry record of facts, are not very amusing, I send you a copy of the flagship's log for the time actually engaged, that is—from our appearing before to after repassing the Dardanelles," &c. &c.

The gallant officer thus concludes:

I will only add, that, with the exception of the greatly calamitous Walcheren expedition, this to Constantinople was the most crudely planned—rash—and insufficient, that—to use the term—ever left the British shores; and that, as it was, its escape from destruction was next to miraculous."

We are now about to narrate the expedition, and, if we still feel induced to suppose that it would better have prospered under the control of Sir Sidney Smith, we think so, solely because he had more accidental advantages for its happy accomplishment than Sir John Thomas Duckworth.

But before we proceed to it, we must devote one chapter to some very important affairs that were transacting in England at the time, and which materially affected the character of our officer.

CHAPTER XXIII

WHILE Sir Sidney Smith was thus actively and usefully employed in the service of his country abroad, men's minds were put almost into an universal agitation by a most delicate investigation at home, an investigation that deeply implicated the honour of the future Queen of England, together with that of many persons of high character, some of whom had made the nation their debtors by the value of their official exertions, and, among these, we are sorry to say, that our hero stood prominently forward.

It was the natural consequences of Sir Sidney's brilliant achievements, and his position in society, to be much sought for, and greatly admired.

To these advantages he added a graceful vivacity of manner, tinctured, at times, with an eccentricity as engaging as it was original. These physical advantages, and the fluency of his conversation, replete with anecdote, made him a dangerous man in female society, to which, we are bound to state, he was always most chivalrously partial.

His high connexions, and his deserved reputation, at length brought him within the circle over which Caroline Princess of Wales presided with so much imprudence and good-heartedness. His conduct, at that period, will ever be involved in an impenetrable darkness—a darkness made the more deep and inscrutable by the solemn and yet ridiculous attempts of commissioners and privy counsellors to dispel it. We have carefully perused and reperused all the depositions sworn to as affecting the continence of that unfortunate Princess, during her residence on Blackheath, and the only safe conclusion at which we can arrive is, that the laxity of morals, and the licentiousness of the manners of almost all concerned in that investigation, make us feel shame for the conduct, with but a few exceptions, for all the parties concerned.

Whether the attractions of Sir Sidney Smith, were only incitements to, or actually the cause of criminality with the Princess, he now only knows. That he was much in her society, that his conversation amused and his attentions pleased this unfortunate woman, cannot be doubted. It is also no less certain that he was discovered in her company at times, and in situations, that neither befitted her rank, nor his position as a future subject to the heir apparent.

This intercourse, of whatever nature it might have been, continued with unabated strictness for several months. To render it the more uninterrupted, Sir Sidney went and partly resided with his old companion in arms, Sir John Douglas, the husband of that Lady Douglas who, throughout these transactions, procured for herself an unenviable notoriety.

Having thus made himself conveniently proximate to the Princess, he was seen for weeks daily in her society; and being thus unguarded in his conduct, he gave too much scope for the voice of scandal to breathe guilt upon the fame of a person, already too much open to suspicion, and, as moralists, we are bound to say, to leave a stain of no very light dye upon his own.

We wish to tread lightly upon the ashes of the dead, who, when living, we think was hardly dealt with. We shall, therefore, not go into details of the evidence which imputed criminality to our officer, but merely state that, first, a coldness, and then a quarrel, having occurred between him and the object of his attentions, he shortly after forsook her society altogether, and was soon after found most actively employed in that scene so natural to his genius, and so conducive to his own fame and his country's glory.

The following is a description of Sir Sidney's appearance at the time of his acquaintance with the princess, to whom the world so generally gave him as a favoured lover. He had an air of general smartness, and was extremely gentlemanly in his deportment. He had a good-humoured, agreeable manner with him, with a certain dash and turn of chivalry that was very taking with the ladies. We are not using our own words, but the very expressive ones of a good judge upon these matters.

He used then to wear mustachios; they were not then vulgarised, as now; which fashion he had adopted when so much associated with the Turks. He was about the middle height, rather under than over, and of slender construction, which much helped his activity. He was generally very showily dressed, perhaps with some singularity; but there was not a particle of coxcombry about him. In features, he something resembled Bernadotte, though with not so prominent a facial angle. The countenance of Southey the poet still more closely resembled that of Sir Sidney Smith, when both were in their younger days.

The following is the best means in our possession of vindicating Sir Sidney Smith's character, being an extract from the letter dated 2d of October, 1806, that the Princess of Wales sent to his Majesty George the Third.

And I will begin with those which respect Sir Sidney Smith, as he is the person first mentioned in the deposition of W. Cole,

W. Cole says, "that Sir Sidney Smith first visited at Montague-house in 1802; that he observed that the princess was too familiar with Sir Sidney Smith. One day, he thinks in February, he (Cole) carried into the blue room to the princess some sandwiches which she had ordered, and was surprised to see that Sir Sidney was there. He must have come in from the park. If he had been let in from Blackheath he must have passed through the room in which he (Cole) was waiting. When he had left the sandwiches, he returned, after some time, into the room, and Sir Sidney Smith was sitting very close to the princess on the sofa: he (Cole) looked at her Royal Highness; she caught his eye, and saw that he noticed the manner in which they were sitting together; they appeared both a little confused."

R. Bidgood says also, in his deposition on the 6th of June, (for he was examined twice,) "that it was early in 1802 that he first observed Sir Sidney Smith come to Montague-house. He used to stay very late at night; he had seen him early in the morning there; about ten or eleven o'clock. He was at Sir John Douglas's, and was in the habit, as well as Sir John and Lady Douglas, of dining, or having luncheon, or supping there every day. He saw Sir Sidney Smith one day in 1802 in the blue room, about eleven o'clock in the morning, which was full two hours before they expected ever to see company. He asked the servants why they did not let him know Sir Sidney Smith was there; the footmen told him that they had let no person in. There was a private door to the park, by which he might have come in if he had a key to it, and have got into the blue room without any of the servants perceiving him. And in his second deposition, taken on the 3d of July, he says he lived at Montague-house when Sir Sidney came. Her (the princess) manner with him appeared very familiar; she appeared very attentive to him, but he did not suspect anything further. Mrs. Lisle says, that the princess at one time appeared to like Sir John and Lady Douglas. ' I have seen Sir Sidney Smith there very late in the evening, but not alone with the princess. I have no reason to suspect he had a key of the park-gate; I never heard of anybody being found wandering about at Blackheath.'

Fanny Lloyd does not mention Sir Sidney Smith in her deposition.

Upon the whole of this evidence then, which is the whole that respects Sir Sidney Smith, in any of these depositions, (except some particular passages in Cole's evidence, which are so important as to require very particular and distinct statement,) I would request your Majesty to understand, that, with respect to the fact of Sir Sidney Smith's visiting frequently at Montague-house, both with Sir John and Lady Douglas, and without them; with respect to his being frequently there at luncheon, dinner, and supper, and staying with the rest of the company till twelve, one o'clock, or even sometimes later, if these are some of the facts e which must give occasion to unfavourable interpretations, and must be credited till they are contradicted,' they are facts which I never can contradict, for they are perfectly true. And I trust it will imply the confession of no guilt, to admit that Sir Sidney Smith's conversation, his account of the various and extraordinary events, and heroic achievements in which he had been concerned, amused and interested me; and the circumstance of his living so much with his friends, Sir John and Lady Douglas, in my neighbourhood on Blackheath, gave the opportunity of his increasing his acquaintance with me.

It happened also that about this time I fitted up, as your Majesty may have observed, one of the rooms in my house after the fashion of a Turkish tent. Sir Sidney furnished me with a pattern for it, in a drawing of the tent of Murat Bey, which he had brought over with him from Egypt. And he taught him how to draw Egyptian arabesques, which were necessary for the ornaments of the ceiling: this may have occasioned, while that room was fitting up, several visits, and possibly some, though I do not recollect them, as early in the morning as Mr. Bidgood mentions. I believe also, that it has happened more than once, that walking with my ladies in the park, we have met Sir Sidney Smith, and that he has come in with us through the gate from the park. My ladies may have gone up to take off their cloaks, or to dress, and have left me alone with him: and, at some one of these times, it may very possibly have happened that Mr. Cole and Mr. Bidgood may have seen him, when he has not come through the waiting-room, nor been let in by any of the footmen. But I solemnly declare to your Majesty, that I have not the least idea or belief that he ever had a key of the gate into the park, or that he ever entered in or passed out at that gate, except in company with myself and my ladies. As for the circumstance of my permitting him to be in the room alone with me; if suffering a man to be so alone is evidence of guilt from whence the commissioners can draw any unfavourable inference, I must leave them to draw it, for I cannot deny that it has happened, and happened frequently; not only with Sir Sidney Smith, but with many, many others; gentlemen who have visited me; tradesmen who have come to receive my orders; masters whom I have had to instruct me in painting, in music, in English, &c., that I have received them without any one being by. In short, I trust I am not confessing a crime, for unquestionably it is a truth, that I never had an idea that there was anything wrong or objectionable in thus seeing men in the morning, and I confidently believe your Majesty will see nothing in it from which any guilt can be inferred. I feel certain that there is nothing immoral in the thing itself; and I have always understood that it was perfectly customary and usual for ladies of the first rank and the first character in the country, to receive the visits of gentlemen in a morning, though they might be themselves alone at the time. But if, in the opinions and fashions of this country, there should be more impropriety ascribed to it than what it ever entered into my mind to conceive, I hope your Majesty, and every candid mind, will make allowance for the different notions which my foreign education and foreign habits may have given me.

But whatever character may belong to this practice, it is not a practice which commenced after my leaving Carlton-house. While there, and from my first arrival in this country, I was accustomed, with the knowledge of his Royal Highness the Prince of Wales, and without his ever having hinted to me the slightest disapprobation, to receive lessons from various masters, for my amusement and improvement; I was attended by them frequently from twelve o'clock till five in the afternoon; Mr. Atwood for music, Mr. Geffadiere for English, Mr. Tourfronelli for painting, Mr. Tutoye for imitating marble, Mr. Elwes for the harp. I saw them all alone; and, indeed, if I were to see them at all, I could do no otherwise than see them alone. Miss Garth, who was then sub-governess to my daughter, lived certainly under the same roof with me, but she could not be spared from her duty and attendance on my daughter. I desired her sometimes to come down stairs, and read to me, during the time when I drew or painted, but my Lord Cholmondeley informed me this could not be. I then requested that I might have one of my bed-chamber women to live constantly at Carlton-house, that I might have her at call whenever I wanted her; but I was answered that it was not customary that the attendants of the royal family should live with them in town; so that request could not be complied with. But, independent of this, I never conceived that it was offensive to the fashions and manners of the country to receive gentlemen who might call upon me in a morning, whether I had or had not any one with me; and it never occurred to me to think that there was either impropriety or indecorum in it, at that time, nor in continuing the practice at Montague-house. But this has been confined to morning visits, in no private apartments in my house, but in my drawing-room, where my ladies have at all times free access, and as they usually take their luncheon with me, except when they are engaged with visitors or pursuits of their own, it could but rarely occur that I could be left with any gentleman alone for any length of time, unless there were something, in the known and avowed business, which might occasion his waiting upon me, that would fully account for the circumstance.

I trust your Majesty will excuse the length at which I have dwelt upon this topic. I perceived, from the examinations, that it had been much inquired after, and I felt it necessary to represent it in its true light. And the candour of your Majesty's mind will, I am confident, suggest that those who are the least conscious of intending guilt are the least suspicious of having it imputed to them: and therefore that they do not think it necessary to guard themselves at every turn, with witnesses to prove their innocence, fancying their character to be safe as long as their conduct is innocent, and that guilt will not be imputed to them from actions quite different.

The deposition, however, of Mr. Cole, is not confined to my being alone with Sir Sidney Smith. The circumstance in which he observed us together he particularises, and states his opinion. He introduces, indeed, the whole of the evidence by saying, that I was too familiar with Sir Sidney Smith; but as I trust I am not yet so far degraded as to have my character decided by the opinion of Mr. Cole, I shall not comment upon that observation. He then proceeds to describe the scene which he observed on the day when he brought in the sandwiches, which I trust your Majesty did not fail to notice, *I had myself ordered to be brought in.* For there is an obvious insinuation that Sir Sidney must have come in through the park, and that there was great impropriety in his being alone with me. And at least the witness's own story proves, whatever impropriety there might be in this circumstance, that I was not conscious of it, nor meant to take advantage of his clandestine entry from the park, to conceal the fact from my servant's observation. For if I had had such consciousness, or such meaning, I never could have ordered sandwiches to have been brought in, or any other act to have been done which must have brought myself under the notice of my servants, while I continued in a situation which I thought improper and wished to conceal. Any of the circumstances of this visit, to which this part of the deposition refers, my memory does not enable me in the least degree to particularise and recall. Mr. Cole may have seen me sitting on the same sofa with Sir Sidney Smith. Nay, I have no doubt he must have seen me over and over again, not only with Sir Sidney Smith, but with other gentlemen, sitting upon the same sofa; and I trust your Majesty will feel it the hardest thing imaginable, that I should be called upon to account what corner of a sofa I sat upon four years ago, and how close Sir Sidney Smith was sitting to me. I can only solemnly aver to your Majesty, that my conscience supplies me with the fullest means of confidently assuring you, that I never permitted Sir Sidney Smith to sit on any sofa with me in any manner, which in my own judgment was in the slightest degree offensive to the strictest propriety and decorum. In the judgment of many persons, perhaps, a Princess of Wales should at no time forget the elevation of her rank, or descend in any degree to the familiarities and intimacies of private life. Under any circumstances, this would be a hard condition to be annexed to her situation. Under the circumstances, in which it has been my misfortune to have lost the necessary support to the dignity and station of a Princess of Wales, to have assumed and maintained an unbending dignity would have been impossible, and, if possible, could hardly have been expected from me.

After these observations, sire, I must now request your Majesty's attention to those written declarations which are mentioned in the report, and which I shall never be able sufficiently to thank your Majesty for having condescended, in compliance with my earnest request, to order to be transmitted to me. From observations upon these declarations themselves, as well as upon comparing them with the depositions made before the commissioners, your Majesty will see the strongest reason for discrediting the testimony of W. Cole, as well as others of these witnesses, whose credit stands, in the opinion of the commissioners, so unimpeachable. They supply important observations, even with respect to that part of Mr. Cole's evidence which I am now considering, though in no degree equal in importance to those which I shall afterwards have occasion to notice.

Your Majesty will please to observe, that there are no less than four different examinations or declarations of Mr. Cole. They are dated on the 11th, 14th, and 30th of January, and on 23rd of February. In these four different declarations he twice mentions the circumstances of finding Sir Sidney Smith and myself on the sofa, and he mentions it not only in a different manner, at each of these times, but at both of them in a manner which materially differs from his deposition before the commissioners. In his declaration on the 11th of January, he says, that he found us in so *familiar* a posture, as to *alarm* him very much, which he expressed by a *start back* and a look at the gentleman.

In that dated on 23rd of February, however, (being asked, I suppose as to that which he had dared to assert, of the familiar posture which had alarmed him so much,) he says, 'there was *nothing particular* in our dress, *position* of legs or arms, that was extraordinary; he thought it improper that a single gentleman should be sitting quite close to a married lady on the sofa, and from that situation, and *former observations*, he thought the thing improper. In the second account, therefore, your Majesty perceives he was obliged to bring in his former observation to help out the statement, in order to account for his having been so shocked with what he saw, as to express his alarm by 'starting back.' But unfortunately he accounts for it, as it seems to me at least, by the very circumstance which would have induced him to have been less surprised, and consequently less startled by what he saw; for had his former observations been such as he insinuates, he would have been prepared the more to expect, and the less to be surprised at, what he pretends to have seen.

But your Majesty will observe, that in his deposition before the commissioners, (recollecting, perhaps, how awkwardly he had accounted for his starting in his former declaration,) he drops his starting altogether. Instead of looking at the gentleman only, he looked at us both; that I caught his eye, and saw that he noticed the manner in which we were sitting, and instead of his own starting, or any description of the manner in which he exhibited his own feelings, we are represented as both appearing a *little confused.* Our *confusion* is a circumstance, which, during his four declarations, which he made before the appointment of the commissioners, it never once occurred to him to recollect. And now he does recollect it, we appeared, he says, 'a little confused.' A little confused! The Princess of Wales detected in a situation such as to shock and alarm her servant, and so detected as to be sensible of her detection, and so conscious of the impropriety of the situation as to exhibit symptoms of confusion; would not her confusion have been extreme? would it have been so little as to have slipped the memory of the witness who observed it, during his first four declarations, and at last to be recalled to his recollection in such a manner as to be represented in the faint and feeble way in which he here describes it.

What weight your Majesty will ascribe to these differences in the accounts given by this witness, I cannot pretend to say. But I am ready to confess that, probably, if there was nothing stronger of the same kind to be observed in other parts of his testimony, the inference which would be drawn from them would depend very much upon the opinion previously entertained of the witness. To me, who know many parts of his testimony to be absolutely false, and all the colouring given to it to be wholly from his own wicked and malicious invention, it appears plain, that these differences in his representations are the unsteady, awkward shuffles and prevarications of falsehood. To those, if there are any such, who from preconceived prejudices in his favour, or from any other circumstances, think that his veracity is free from all suspicion, satisfactory means of reconciling them may possibly occur. But before I have left Mr. Cole's examinations, your Majesty will find that they will have much more to account for, and much more to reconcile.

"Mr. Cole's examination before the commissioners goes on thus: 'A short time before this, one night about twelve o'clock, I saw a man go into the house from the park, wrapt up in a greatcoat. I did not give any alarm, for the impression on my mind was, that it was not a thief.' When I read this passage, sire, I could hardly believe my eyes; when I found such a fact left in this dark state, without any farther explanation, or without a trace, in the examination, of any attempt to get it further explained. How he got this impression on his mind, that this was not a thief? Whom he believed it to be? What part of the house he saw him enter? If the drawing room, or any part which I usually occupy, who was there at the time? Whether I was there? Whether alone or with my ladies? Or with other company? Whether he told anybody of the circumstance at the time? Or how long after? Whom he told? Whether any inquiries were made in consequence? These, and a thousand other questions, with a view to have penetrated into the mystery of this strange story, and to have tried the credit of this witness, would, I should have thought, have occurred to any one; but certainly must have occurred to persons so experienced and so able in the examination of facts, and the trying of the credit of witnesses, as the two learned lords unquestionably are, whom your Majesty took care to have introduced into this commission. They never could have permitted these unexplained, and unsifted hints and insinuations to have had the weight and effect of proof. But, unfortunately for me, the duties, probably of their respective situations, prevented their attendance on the examination of this, and on the first examination of another most important witness, Mr. Robert Bidgood—and surely your Majesty will permit me here, without offence, to complain that it is not a little hard, that, when your Majesty had shown your anxiety to have legal accuracy, and legal experience assist on this examination, the two most important witnesses, in whose examinations there is more matter for unfavourable interpretation than in all the rest put together, should have been examined without the benefit of this accuracy, and this experience. And I am the better justified in making this observation, if what has been suggested to me is correct that if it shall not be allowed that the power of administering an oath under this warrant or commission is questionable, yet it can hardly be doubted that it is most questionable, whether, according to the terms or meaning of the warrant or commission, as it constitutes no *quorum*, Lord Spencer and Lord Glenville could administer an oath, or act in the absence of the other Lords; and if they could not, Mr. Cole's falsehood must be out of the reach of punishment.

Returning then from this digression, will your Majesty permit me to ask, whether I am to understand this fact, respecting the man in a great-coat, to be one of those which must necessarily give occasion to the most unfavourable interpretations; which must be credited till decidedly contradicted? And which, if true, deserve the most serious consideration? The unfavourable interpretations which this fact may occasion, doubtless are, that this man was either Sir Sidney Smith, or some other *paramour*, who was admitted by me into my house in disguise at midnight, for the accomplishment of my wicked and adulterous purposes. And is it possible that your Majesty—is it possible that any candid mind can believe this fact, with the unfavourable interpretations which it occasions, on the relation of a servant, who, for all that appears, mentions it for the first time four years after the event took place? And who gives, himself, this picture of his honesty and fidelity to a master whom he has served so long, that he, whose nerves are of so moral a frame that he starts at seeing a single man sitting at mid-day in an open drawing-room, on the same sofa with a married woman, permitted this disguised midnight adulterer to approach his master's bed without taking any notice, without making any alarm, without offering any interruption? And why? Because (as he expressly states) he did not believe him to be a thief: and because (as he plainly insinuates) he did believe him to be an adulterer.

But what makes the manner in which the commissioners suffered this fact to remain so unexplained, the more extraordinary, is this: Mr. Cole had, in his original declaration of the 11th of January, which was before the commissioners, stated, 'that one night, about twelve o'clock, he saw a person wrapped up in a great-coat, go across the park into the gate at the green-house, and he verily believes it was Sir Sidney Smith.' In his declaration then, (when he was not upon oath) he ventures to state, ' that he verily believes it was Sir Sidney Smith.' When he is upon his oath in his deposition before the commissioners, all that he ventures to swear is, "that he gave no alarm, because the impression upon his mind was, that it was not a thief!' And the difference is most important, ' The impression upon his mind was, that it was not a thief!' I believe him, and the impression upon my mind too is, that he *knew* it was not a thief—that he knew who it was and that he knew it was no other than *my watchman*. What incident it is that he alludes to, I cannot pretend to know. But this I know, that if it refers to any man with whose proceedings I have the least acquaintance or privity, it must have been my watchman, who, if he executes my orders, nightly, and often in the night goes his rounds, both inside and outside out of my house. And this circumstance, which I should think would rather afford, to most minds, an inference that I was not preparing the way of planning facilities for secret midnight assignations, has, in my conscience, I believe, (if there is one word of truth in any part of this story, and the whole of it is not pure invention,) afforded the handle, and suggested the idea, to this honest, trusty man, this witness, ' who cannot be suspected of any unfavourable bias' ' whose veracity in that respect the commissioners saw no ground to question' and 'who must be credited till he received decided contradiction'—suggested, I say, the idea of the dark and vile insinuation contained in this part of his testimony.

Whether I am right or wrong, however, in this conjecture, this appears to be evident, that his examination is so left, that supposing an indictment for perjury or false swearing would lie against any witness examined by the commissioners, and supposing this examination had been taken before the whole four. If Mr. Cole was indicted for perjury in respect to this part of his deposition, the proof that he did see the watchman would necessarily acquit him; would establish the truth of what he said, and rescue him from the punishment of perjury, though it would at the same time prove the falsehood and injustice of the inference, and the insinuation, for the establishment of which alone, the fact itself was sworn.

Mr. Cole chooses further to state, that he ascribes his removal from Montague-house to London to the discovery he had made, and the notice he had taken of the improper situation of Sir Sidney Smith with me upon the sofa. To this I can oppose little more than my own assertions, as my motives can only be known to myself. But Mr. Cole was a very disagreeable servant to me; he was a man who, as I always conceived, had been educated above his station. He talked French, and was a musician, playing well on the violin. By these qualifications he had got admitted, occasionally, into better company, and this probably led to that forward and obtrusive conduct which I thought extremely offensive and impertinent in a servant. I had long been extremely displeased with him; I had discovered, that when I went out he would come into my drawing-room, and play on my harpsichord, or sit there reading my books; and, in short, there was a forwardness which would have led to my absolutely discharging him a long time before, if I had not made a sort of rule to myself, to forbear, as long as possible, from removing any servant who had been placed about me by his Royal Highness. Before Mr. Cole lived with the prince, he had lived with the Duke of Devonshire, and I had reason to believe that he carried to Devonshire-house all the observations he could make at mine. For these various reasons, just before the Duke of Kent was about to go out of the kingdom, I requested his Royal Highness the Duke of Kent, who had been good enough to take the trouble of arranging many particulars in my establishment, to make the arrangements with respect to Mr. Cole; which was to leave him in town to wait upon me only when I went to Carlton-house, and not to come to Montague-house except when specially required. This arrangement, it seems, offended him. It certainly deprived him of some perquisites which he had when living at Blackheath; but, upon the whole, as it left him so much more of his time at his own disposal, I should not have thought it had been much to his prejudice. It seems, however, that he did not like it; and I must leave this part of the case with this one observation more—That your Majesty, I trust, will hardly believe, that if Mr. Cole had, by any accident, discovered any improper conduct of mine towards Sir Sidney Smith, or any one else, the way which I should have taken to suppress his information, to close his mouth, would not have been by immediately adopting an arrangement in my family, with regard to him, which was either prejudicial or disagreeable to him; or that the way to remove him from the opportunity and the temptation of betraying my secret, whether through levity or design, in the quarter where it would be most fatal to me that it should be known, was by making an arrangement which, while all his resentment and anger were fresh and warm about him, would place him frequently, nay, almost daily, at Carlton-house; would place him precisely at that place from whence, unquestionably, it must have been my interest to have kept him as far removed as possible.

There is little or nothing in the examinations of the other witnesses which is material for me to observe upon, as far as respects this part of the case. It appears from them, indeed, what I have had no difficulty in admitting, and have observed upon before, that Sir Sidney Smith was frequently at Montague-house—that they have known him to be alone with me in the morning, but that they never knew him to be alone with me in an evening, or staying later than my company or the ladies; for what Mr. Stikeman says, with respect to his being alone with me in an evening, can only mean, and is only reconcilable with all the rest of the evidence on this part of the case, by its being understood, to mean alone, in respect to other company, but not alone in the absence of my ladies. The deposition, indeed, of my servant, S. Roberts, is thus far material upon that point, that it exhibits Mr. Cole, not less than three years ago, endeavouring to collect evidence upon these points to my prejudice. For your Majesty will find that he says, 'I recollect Mr. Cole once asking me, I think three years ago, whether there were any favourites in the family. I remember saying that Captain Manby and Sir Sidney Smith were frequently at Blackheath, and dined there oftener than other persons.' He then proceeds: 'I never knew Sir Sidney Smith stay later than the ladies; I cannot exactly say at what time he went, but I never remember his staying alone with the Princess.'

As to what is contained in the written declarations of Mr. and Mrs. Lampert, the old servants of Sir John and Lady Douglas, (as from some circumstance or other respecting, I conceive, either their credit, or their supposed importance,) the commissioners have not thought proper to examine them upon their oaths, I do not imagine your Majesty would expect that I should take any notice of them. And as to what is deposed by my Lady Douglas, if your Majesty will observe the gross and horrid indecencies with which she ushers in and states my confessions to her, of my asserted criminal intercourse with Sir Sidney Smith, your Majesty,

I am confident, will not be surprised that I do not descend to any particular observations on her deposition. One, and only one, observation will I make, which, however, could not have escaped your Majesty, if I had omitted it. That your Majesty will have an excellent portraiture of the true female delicacy and purity of my Lady Douglas's mind and character, when you will observe that she seems wholly insensible to what a sink of infamy she degrades herself by her testimony against me. It is not only that it appears, from her statement, that she was contented to live in familiarity and apparent friendship with me, after the confession which I made of my adultery, (for by the indulgence and liberality, as it is called, of modern manners, the company of adulteresses has ceased to reflect that discredit upon the characters of other women who admit them to their society, which the best interests of female virtue may perhaps require;) but she was contented to live in familiarity with a woman, who, if Lady Douglas's evidence of me is true, was a most low, vulgar, and profligate disgrace to her sex; the grossness of whose ideas and conversation would add infamy to the lowest, most vulgar, and most infamous prostitute. It is not, however, upon this circumstance that I rest assured no reliance can be placed on Lady Douglas's testimony; but after what is proved, with regard to her evidence respecting my pregnancy and delivery in 1802, I am certain that any observations upon her testimony or her veracity must be flung away.

Your Majesty has, therefore, now before you the state of the charge against me, as far as it respects Sir Sidney Smith. And this is, as I understand the report, one of the charges *which, with its unfavourable interpretations, must, in the opinion of the commissioners, be credited till decidedly contradicted.*

As to the facts of frequent visiting on terms of great intimacy, as I have said before, they cannot be contradicted at all. How inferences and unfavourable interpretations are to be decidedly contradicted, I wish the commissioners had been so good as to explain. I know of no possible way but by the declarations of myself and Sir Sidney Smith. Yet we, being the supposed guilty parties, our denial, probably, will be thought of no great weight. As to my own, however, I tender it to your Majesty in the most solemn manner; and if I knew what fact it was that I ought to contradict, to clear my innocence, I would precisely address myself to that fact, as I am confident my conscience would enable me to do, to any, from which a criminal or an unbecoming inference could be drawn. I am sure, however, your Majesty will feel for the humiliated and degraded situation to which this report has reduced your daughter-in-law, the Princess of Wales; when you see her reduced to the necessity of either risking the danger that the most unfavourable interpretations should be credited; or else of stating, as I am now degraded to the necessity of stating, that not only no adulterous, or criminal, but no indecent or improper intercourse whatever, ever subsisted between Sir Sidney Smith and myself, or anything which I should have objected that all the world should have seen. I say degraded to the necessity of stating it; for your Majesty must feel that a woman's character is degraded when it is put upon her to make such statement, at the peril of the contrary being credited, unless she decidedly contradicts it. Sir Sidney Smith's absence from the country prevents me calling upon him to attest the same truth. But I trust, when your Majesty shall find, as you will find, that my declaration to a similar effect, with respect to the other gentleman referred to in this report, is confirmed by their denial, that your Majesty will think that in a case where nothing but my own word can be adduced, my own word alone may be opposed to whatever little remains of credit or weight may, after all the above observations, be supposed yet to belong to Mr. Cole, to his inferences, his insinuations, or his facts. Not, indeed, that I have yet finished my observations on Mr. Cole's credit; but I must reserve the remainder till I consider his evidence with respect to Mr. Lawrence; and till I have occasion to comment upon the testimony of Fanny Loyd. Then, indeed, I shall be under the necessity of exhibiting to your Majesty these witnesses, Fanny Loyd and Mr. Cole, (both of whom are represented as so unbiased, and so credible,) in flat, decisive, and irreconcilable contradiction to each other.

After all the deliberations and meetings of the commissioners, as far as regards Sir Sidney Smith, and other questions in connexion with the Princess, his Majesty says:

On the other matters produced in the course of the inquiry, the King is advised that none of the facts or allegations stated in the preliminary examinations, carried on in the absence of the parties interested, can be considered as legally or conclusively established. But in those examinations, and even in the answer drawn in the name of the Princess by her legal advisers, there have appeared circumstances of conduct on the part of the Princess, which his Majesty never could regard but with serious concern. The elevated rank which the Princess hold in this country, and the relation in which she stands to his Majesty and the royal family, must always deeply involve both the interests of the state and the personal feelings of his Majesty, in the propriety and correctness of her conduct. And his Majesty cannot, therefore, forbear to express, in the conclusion of the business, his desire and expectation, that such a conduct may in future be observed by the Princess, as may fully justify those marks of paternal regard and affection which the King always wishes to show to every part of his royal family.

His Majesty has directed that this message should be transmitted to the Princess of Wales, by his Lord Chancellor, and that copies of the proceedings which have taken place on the subject should also be communicated to his dearly beloved son, the Prince of Wales.

Therefore, from the charge of levity and imprudence, the Princess must still be deemed as not exonerated.

We should not have adverted, in the slightest degree, to the affair narrated in this chapter, had it not assumed, to all intents and purposes, the features of a public transaction. We have called these volumes by a name no more pretending than that of "Memoirs;" and having meant to do no more than the title warranted, we have only given so much of our hero's private adventures and family concerns as was needful to form something like continuity in the narrative. Indeed, we are well aware, so replete as Sir William Sidney Smith's life has been of "moving accident by flood and field,"—so rife has been his prolonged days with private enterprise and wonderful surprises—in a word, the feats he has performed and witnessed have been so numerous and so strange, and his memory is stuffed so full of anecdote, that none but himself could be his biographer: for no one can tell the tales of himself that he can; and if any one could, disappointment would still be the result, for to achieve his happy manner of telling them would be utterly impossible.

Many of these anecdotes have found their way into the public periodicals: generally speaking, they do not read well, because the hero did not himself write them. They are turgid and overstrained, being miserably bloated and swelled out with too much panegyric. We shall quote a few of them at the end of these volumes, and endeavour to divest them a little of their inflated laudation.

We may just now, moreover, observe, that to write a good life, in the extended sense of the word, of the gallant veteran, would be a matter of no small difficulty, were it rigidly a true one; and a biography, however amusing, if not true, could not be good. It is in this that the difficulty lies—the impossibility to find a person sufficiently impartial. Were Sir Sidney himself to attempt it, much of it would appear, from him, like gasconade, simply because his adventures have been so singular that it would be hazardous for a man to publish them of himself; and unfortunately, such are his qualities, that his friends are very friends indeed, and verge too much upon idolaters; and his enemies are contemning sceptics of anything good or great about him. Whilst the one party would extol him, as the *ne plus ultra* of heroism, the other would designate him merely as a successful charlatan—brave, but without conduct, cunning without being sensible—arrogant and supercilious in his youth, and, in his after life, immersed in the vapours of his intolerable vanity; that all that ever was sterling in the man is totally evaporated, and that nothing remains of him but a gaudy shell, tricked out with ribbons and stars, and all the blazonry of which beggarly monarchs are so lavish, and fools so greedy.

That Sir Sidney has nothing of the latter character about him, those who attentively read these memoirs must be convinced. They must also be convinced that he is, properly speaking, truly a great man, and had more favourable opportunities presented themselves, would have been a much greater, perhaps the very greatest man of his time or nothing. We have always thought, and always said, that he possessed wonderful but dangerous faculties; that he is a sort of warrior Lord Brougham, though a much pleasanter fellow. We do not mean to say that his lordship is not a very pleasant man; but still, after his public avowal of his inability to play the courtier, he will not consider us as libellous in saying, that it is possible there may be pleasanter men, and that our fine old admiral is one of them, though we fear he will not take the comparison altogether as a compliment.

We must resume our narrative in the next volume.

END OF VOLUME I

VOLUME TWO

CONTENTS OF
VOLUME TWO

CHAPTER I

SIR SIDNEY APPOINTED TO ACCOMPANY SIR JOHN DUCKWORTH • IN-
STRUCTIONS TO SIR JOHN • SIR SIDNEY SMITH'S LETTER TO THE SUB-
LIME PORTE.

WE must now convey the reader again to the Mediterranean, and view
Sir Sidney Smith as about to be transferred from his command in chief
on the Neapolitan coasts, to the third only in authority, in the expedition
against Constantinople.

We have, in a former part of this narrative, seen him the active and
energetic friend of the Mahometans, assisting them in building their
ships, teaching them navigation and maritime warfare, strengthening
them with his advice, and successfully fighting their battles; but now,
such is the instability of human policy, we are to contemplate his employing all his talents, and calling forth all his energies, to harass and destroy
his ancient friends—and to know that this duty devolved upon him, because the friendship of other days had afforded him the best opportunities to injure a people who had learned to esteem and honour him.

A revolution which was in accordance with the rule, and not the exception of the order of things in Turkey, deposed Sultan Selim, and
placed his nephew Mustapha at the head of the faithful. This catastrophe
was altogether unconnected with politics, and totally antichristian, both
in the religious and political sense. It, however, brought in its train very
serious political consequences. Both Russia and France solicited the
friendship and co-operation of the new Sublime Porte against their respective enemies, denouncing hostilities if this should be withheld.

The Russians said that they wished to save the Ottoman empire from
the grasp of the French; the French conjured the Ottomans to beware of
the treacherous friendship of the Russians. Both parties were in the right;
so the Porte sent troops into Moldavia and Wallachia to watch them. The
French envoy, Sebastiani, tried many fruitless efforts to make the Turks

break off all peaceable intercourse with Russia and her ally Great Britain. He then assumed a more lofty tone, and threatened hostilities. Mr, Arbuthnot, the English minister at the Porte, did not fail to make the English government acquainted with these proceedings.

Similar intelligence was communicated to the British government by the Russian ministry, accompanied with a recommendation to send a British fleet to Turkey, with a large military force, which might defeat the ascendency of the French counsels at the Porte, and cause a powerful diversion of the force of France in favour of Russia.

A negotiation for a state of stricter amity with the Porte was commenced by the Russian, in conjunction with the British, government. To give weight to this, a fleet, under the command of Sir John Duckworth, was sent to force the passage of the Dardanelles, and, if certain terms should not be acceded to by the Ottomans, to bombard Constantinople.

It appears by the secret instructions given to Sir John Duckworth, that he was directed to proceed, without loss of time, to the neighbourhood of Constantinople, and there to take such a position as would enable him to effect the object of the expedition. Immediately on his arrival, he was to communicate with the British ambassador, to send him certain despatches, and consult with him on the measures that might then be necessary to be taken.

Should he find that the subject of difference had been amicably settled between the Sublime Porte and the English legation, he was to preserve the relations of amity; if not, he was to commence offensive operations; having previously demanded, in the case of their detention, the ambassador and his suite, together with all the persons connected with the British factory; and, in the event of the demand not being complied with, he was to proceed to measures of hostility against the city.

Should the result of his communications with Mr. Arbuthnot be such as to render the commencement of hostilities necessary, he was to demand the surrender of the Turkish fleet, with a supply of stores sufficient for its equipment. This demand was to be accompanied with a menace of the immediate destruction of the city; and, should any negotiation be proposed by the Turks, as it would probably be only with a view of preparing means of resistance, and of securing their ships, this negotiation was not to be continued more than half an hour.

In the event of an absolute refusal on the part of the Turks, Sir John Duckworth was to cannonade the town, and to attack the fleet wherever it might be; holding it in his mind, that the getting the possession of, and next to that, the destruction of the ships, was the first object of consideration.

Such, and so delicate, was the import of the admiral's secret instructions; and the vastness of the objects that they embraced was to be equalled only by the delicacy necessary to effect them, so that some diplomatist not inferior to a Metternich was required for the one, and one of England's largest fleets, with a corresponding army, demanded for the other.

However, so differently thought the directors of England's resources, that the armament which they despatched to carry out so momentous an object, consisted only of seven ships of the line, besides a few frigates and bomb vessels, and the diplomatic proceedings were conferred upon its admiral, Sir John Duckworth, assisted by our ambassador, Mr. Arbuthnot. Means so feeble, both morally and physically, were scarcely ever employed to effect ends so great and so complicated. Consequently the expedition failed.

Even the arrangements that were made, which were as judicious as the force employed to make them effective was insignificant, were much disturbed by the fears and the precipitancy of the ambassador. At his request, a naval force had been previously despatched for his protection, and in aid of his negotiations; in conformity to which, Rear-Admiral Sir Thomas Louis had anchored with a small squadron between the outer and inner castles of the Dardanelles, and sent the Endymion frigate up to Constantinople.

She had not been long there, before the ambassador, under the impression of alarm for his personal safety, (produced by secret information, which was doubtlessly false, and thus treacherously furnished by the French party,) that the Turkish government meant to confine him to the castle of the Seven Towers, went on board, and prevailed upon the commander to send a sudden invitation to the whole of the British factory to meet Mr. Arbuthnot at dinner. They were no sooner arrived, than the Endymion's cable was cut, her anchor left behind, and the company carried off *en masse* to the Dardanelles: a conciliatory preliminary this, to negotiations for a renewed and stricter amity, and a high compliment to the civilisation and honour of the Sublime Porte.

After Mr. Arbuthnot had thus ostensibly abdicated his functions by deserting his post, he sent a letter to the Reis Effendi, committing the protection of the British property to the Turkish government. From the Endymion he removed to the Canopus, and from the Canopus into the Royal George, the flag-ship of Sir John Duckworth, where he remained during the whole of the progress of the negotiations.

Having received his final orders, the vice-admiral proceeded off Tenedos, where he found Sir Thomas Louis's division at anchor off the Hellespont.

That Sir Sidney Smith had the honour of his country and the success of this expedition at heart, will be readily perceived by the following remonstrance which he drew up a few days before the passage was attempted, and which he wished immediately to be forwarded to the Sultan.

On board of His Majesty's Ship Pompée, off the
Dardanelles, 12th February, 1807.

May it please your Imperial Majesty,

SIRE,

In approaching your imperial seat of government, I feel the same respect for your Imperial Majesty personally, the same desire to promote your happiness, and to preserve your tranquillity, that I did eight years ago, when I was sent to cement the ancient friendship which, I trust, still subsists between your Imperial Majesty and my august sovereign, George the Third, by signing a treaty of alliance, on which basis the combined forces afterwards acted against the common enemy, and secured the integrity of your imperial Majesty's dominions.

It was hoped that the peace of Paris, which was the result of these labours, would have been permanent for the advantage of all parties; but the immeasurable ambition of Bonaparte continued to oppress and absorb the surrounding states for his own and his family's aggrandisement; and by the mission of M. Sebastiani (as it is avowed in that embassy's report) he sought to effect in Syria and Egypt, by intrigue and influence, that which the French arms had failed to accomplish.

The British government, true to the principles on which the triple alliance was established, and trusting that, as the interests of the Sublime Porte were the same, its conduct would be so likewise, resisted these encroachments, and this fresh aggression, by all the means in its power; and although the principal ground of the war was that very proof of the continued intention of Bonaparte to pursue the original plan, subversive of the integrity of the Ottoman empire, Great Britain, feeling herself strong enough to resist France single-handed, purposely declined committing the neutrality of the Sublime Porte by an act which might justify a new French invasion, and deprive it of the tranquillity necessary for the restoration of its resources.

Little could it be thought that such delicate conduct would be repaid by allowing the French agent, who had failed in his attempt to regain a footing in distant provinces by intrigue, to acquire an ascendency in the councils of the government in the capital, equal to the direction of the whole empire, and the consequent annihilation of the power of the august sovereign whom I have now the honour of addressing. Surely his will never could have assented to such a degradation! Shall the magnificent Ottoman Sultan, who (from respect to his great ancestors and his own high situation) so long cautiously avoided the humiliation of corresponding with an Asiatic usurper, or an African rebel, allow himself to be dictated to on his throne, to his utter ruin, by a man he resisted successfully in the campaigns; who, whatever he may denominate himself, or be denominated by servile flatterers, is, in fact, no more than a successful rebel, who has usurped, by violence and bloodshed, the throne of his master, the ancient ally of the Sublime Porte, and the palace of his benefactors, whose bounty taught him the art of war, by which he in vain attempted to prevail against the Ottoman arms? Shall it be said that Bonaparte, who could not succeed by force in the provinces, has succeeded to obtain the dominion of the entire Ottoman territory by arts of another kind—by fallacious reasoning, and by bribing your imperial Majesty's servants to desert and betray their master as he did his? No! Let it rather be recorded, that Sultan Selim the Third proved himself worthy of his ancestors, his throne, and his people, by nobly stepping forward to assert, establish, and secure their honour, splendour, and prosperity; joining hands with those who have the power, as well as the will, to protect and to punish.

The door is still open for your imperial Majesty to pursue this dignified line of conduct, by causing the French ambassador to withdraw from your imperial residence, recalling those of the two sovereigns whose friendship you have found advantageous to your security, and employing the resources of your great empire to the preservation of its integrity and independence. The time is come for your imperial Majesty to decide, for the interval of negotiation will soon, very soon, be at an end; and if you decide that the resources shall be at the disposal, or within the reach of the French, our common enemy, your imperial Majesty cannot doubt but that we shall deprive that enemy of their all. Should I ever see that fleet which your Majesty was graciously pleased, at one time, to confide to my fostering care, destroyed by the unavoidable events of war, I shall feel the same pain a man must feel, who sees the house he built, and the trees his hands planted and watered, in ruins and in ashes; yet that pain he must submit to, rather than see them in the hands of his declared enemy; for he. must consider that as the least of the two evils, and bow to dire necessity.

Think, most gracious sovereign, whilst it is yet time, and place your fleet, your capital, your palace, and your person, out of the reach of such events as must follow the continuance of the line of conduct that your present counsellors are pursuing, by a prompt acquiescence to the reasonable propositions of his Britannic Majesty's ambassador, for your imperial Majesty's and the general good, and by placing your interests in the keeping, and your fleet under the protection, of an ally whom your imperial Majesty well knows to be just and merciful even to his enemies, and to be most faithfully attached to your imperial Majesty.

In these sentiments, I have the honour to subscribe myself, with the most profound respect,

Your imperial Majesty's most sincere friend,

&c. &c. &c.

WILLIAM SIDNEY SMITH

We think this document, though a little too oratorical and egotistical, well calculated to have made some favourable impression in the quarter to which it was directed. We think its efficacy should have been tried; yet, although it was sent to the commander-in-chief, and an Italian translation of it forwarded to the British ambassador, Mr. Arbuthnot, it never reached the Sultan. As it partook more of the nature of a private and friendly remonstrance than of an official despatch, it could have compromised no one, and the probabilities of benefit were all in its favour.

We cannot account for this omission, as Sir John Duckworth always expressed the highest opinion of Sir Sidney's talents in affairs of this nature, which will be at once evident by an extract of a letter sent to him, dated Royal George, off the Dardanelles, February 10th, 1807. It is to this effect:

> Should a gauntlet with the minister be necessary for me to run, I shall have two powerful motives to call for your assistance; first, as *I know no man more equal to the undertaking,* and, when there, *your knowledge of diplomacy must be highly beneficial.*

We will add another letter on the same subject after Sir Sidney's document had been received.

> In the name of Mr. Arbuthnot, who is just going into the boat, and myself, we thank you for the attention that you have shown in thus addressing the Sultan; and we shall judge from events, whether it will be right to put the Sultan in possession of it, which you will, in course, be acquainted with.

> I am, with esteem, &c.

> J. T. DUCKWORTH.

This fully proves that the commander-in-chief had the option of availing himself of this spur in the side of the insensible Sultan—insensible, at least, to all that the ambassador and Sir John could produce to move him into acquiescence.

CHAPTER II

The Dardanelles forced • A division of the Turkish fleet destroyed by Sir Sidney Smith • His despatch • Other official documents • His letter to Captain Dacre.

OUR fleet passed the Dardanelles on the 19th of February. It was now that Sir Sidney Smith's talents and enterprise were called into action. He was directed, in case of anticipated opposition and resistance on the part of the Ottomans, with the rear division to destroy a Turkish squadron off Point Nagara Burun (or Pesquies.) This was effected by Sir Sidney Smith with three ships of the line, which led the invading fleet.

At a quarter before nine o'clock, the whole of the fleet had passed the outer castles without having returned a shot to the Turkish fire, which did our ships but little injury. This forbearance was intended to express the pacific disposition and anxiety of our sovereign and government towards the Sublime Porte. But this mild and amicable demeanour the British force was not able long to maintain. In passing the narrow strait between Sestos and Abydos, our squadron sustained a very heavy fire from both castles. A tremendous cannonade was now opened by our ships of war in return, and with such an effect that the firing of the Turks was considerably slackened, and all our ships passed the fortifications without sustaining much injury.

It was at this crisis that the small Turkish squadron within the inner castles was attacked by Sir Sidney Smith, driven on shore, and burnt, and the guns of a formidable battery, to the number of more than thirty, on a point of land which our squadron had yet to pass, were spiked by a detachment of marines.

The following is a copy of the Rear-Admiral's report to Sir John T. Duckworth, concerning this brilliant affair.

Edward Howard

His Majesty's Ship Pompée, within the Dardanelles,
Feb. 20, 1807

Sir, In reporting to you the entire completion of the service you were pleased to order should be executed by the rear division under my immediate directions, I need not inform you that the ships were anchored in the thick of the Turkish squadron, and in close action with them, as you must have observed it; but as the intervention of the land, after you passed the point, prevented your seeing the subsequent operations, it is my duty to acquaint you therewith. The Turks fought desperately, like men determined to defend themselves and their ships as long as they could; but the superiority of our fire, within musket-shot, obliged them in half an hour to run on shore on Point Pesquies, or Nagara Burun. As the redoubt on the point continued to fire, also as the ships kept their colours up, and the part of their crews which had deserted them remained armed on the beach, while a considerable body of Asiatic troops, both horse and foot, appeared on the hills, it was necessary to make an arrangement for boarding them with some precaution; at the same time that it was of consequence to press them closely before they recovered from the impression and effect of our cannonade. A few shells from the Pompée dispersed the Asiatics, and convinced them that we commanded the ground within our reach, and that they could not protect the green standard they had hoisted, which I caused to be brought off by Lieutenant Oates, of the Pompée's marines, that they might not rally there again. The Standard's guns bearing best on the frigates on shore, I sent the Thunderer's boats to that ship, to be employed with her own under the direction of Captain Harvey, making the signal to him to destroy the enemy's ships in the N.E. The Active's having been previously made to follow and destroy a frigate which had cut her cable to get from under the Thunderer's and Pompée's fire, and run on shore on the European side, in the N.W.; at the same time, Lieutenant Beecroft, of the Pompée, was detached to take possession of the line-of-battle ship on which the Thunderer's and Pompée's guns could still bear, under the protection likewise of the Repulse, which you had ^considerately sent to my aid: that officer brought me the captain and second captain, the latter of whom was wounded; also the flag of the rear-admiral, who had escaped on shore, which I shall have the honour of presenting to you. The whole of the Turks were landed, in pursuance of your orders, including the wounded, with due attention to the sufferings of our misguided opponents, as I must call them; for the term enemy does not seem applicable, considering their evident good disposition towards us nationally. The ship was then set on fire by the Repulse's and Pompée's boats, and completely destroyed.

"Captain Harvey, in making his report to me of the conduct of the boats' crews, under the command of Lieutenants Carter, Waller, and Colby, of his Majesty's ship Thunderer, and of the marines employed with them, to board and burn the frigates and corvettes under the command of Captain Nicholls, speaks in strong terms of the gallantry and ability of them all. The latter, whom I have long known to be an intelligent and enterprising officer, after destroying the frigate bearing the flag of the Capitan Pasha, which is preserved to be presented to you, sir, landed; and, profiting by the consternation of the Turks from the explosions on all sides of them the effects of which occasioned no small risk to him, Lieutenants Fynmore, Boileau, and the party, he entered the redoubt, (the Turks retreating as he approached,) set fire to the gabions, and spiked the guns, thirty-one in number, eight of which are brass, carrying immensely large marble balls: as, however, the expected explosion of the line-of-battle ship made it impossible for the boats to stay long enough to destroy them effectually with their carriages, or to level the parapets, the wicker of the gabions being too green to burn, I have directed Lieutenants Carroll and Arabin of his Majesty's ship Pompée, and Lieutenant Lawrie of the marines, to continue on that service, with the Turkish corvette, and one gunboat, which, you will observe by the return, were not destroyed; and to act under the protection and direction of Captain Moubray, of his Majesty's ship Active, whose name I cannot mention without expressing how highly satisfied I am with the able and gallant manner in which he executed my orders to stick to the frigate with which he was more particularly engaged, and to destroy her. Captain Talbot placed his ship admirably well in support of the Pompée, thereby raking the line-of-battle ship and the frigate we were engaged with, when I made his signal to anchor, as the Pompée had previously done, under the directions I gave for that purpose to Captain Dacres, which were promptly and ably executed; Mr. Ives, the master, applying his local knowledge and experience, as I had a right to expect from his long tried abilities, while Lieutenant Smith made my signals to the squadron in rapid succession, and with precision. Captain Harvey merits my entire approbation for placing the Standard in the manner in which he did, and for completing the destruction of the others. Much as I must regret the loss of the Ajax, as a most efficient ship in my division, I have felt that loss to be, in a great degree, balanced by the presence of my gallant friend Captain Blackwood, and the surviving officers and men, whose zeal in their voluntary exertions on this occasion does them the highest credit: in short, all the captains, officers, and men concerned, merit that I should mention them in high terms to you, sir, as their leader, whose example we humbly endeavoured to follow.

The signal success that has attended the general exertion under your direction, speaks more forcibly than words.

I have the honour to be, &c. &c.

W. SIDNEY SMITH

Vice-Admiral
Sir John Thomas Duckworth, K.B.

The Turkish squadron consisted of a sixty-four gun ship, four frigates, mounting altogether one hundred and forty-four guns, five corvettes and brigs, mounting sixty-eight guns, and two gunboats. Of these, one corvette and one gunboat were taken, and all the rest destroyed, together with a redoubt. The number of guns in favour of the Turks was fifty-three.

The following are the orders which Sir Sidney Smith received, in reference to this very brilliant service:

Royal George, off the Dardanelles,
February, 1807

Sir, As it appears, from the best information, that a Turkish squadron, consisting of one ship of the line, some frigates, and corvettes, are at anchor off Pesquis, above the upper castles of the Dardanelles; it is my directions, in case the castles and forts should hostilely oppose our going up, and the ships and vessels of war should continue at their anchorage, that, with the Thunderer, the Standard, and the frigates, you bring to and destroy them; letting as many of their crews as their own boats can contain land, and receiving the remainder on board of his Majesty's ships, till an opportunity offers to put them on shore.

I have the honour to be, Sir,

Your most obedient

humble Servant,

J. T. DUCKWORTH.

To Rear-Admiral Sir W. Sidney Smith, &c.
Pompée

Some further particulars of this action may be gleaned from the following letters on service, from Captain Harvey to Sir Sidney Smith:

Standard, Sea of Marmora,
February 20, 1807

Sir, Agreeably to your directions yesterday for destroying the Turkish frigates and corvettes on shore, near the Standard, I beg leave to report the very able and gallant manner in which the officers employed on that service performed it.

Previous to the Thunderer's boats arriving, I had despatched Captain Nicholls, of the royal marines, who very handsomely volunteered his services on the occasion, with Lieutenant Fynmore, royal marines, and Lieutenant de Bouille, Dillon's regiment, in a boat, to set fire to the frigate bearing the flag of the Capitan Pasha; in performing which service, one man was dangerously wounded in the boat. I have given you Captain Nicholls's report of the proceedings.

The Thunderer's boats, under the direction of Lieutenants Carter, Waller, and Coleby, of that ship, I sent to destroy the other frigates and corvettes, which they very ably and gallantly performed; and I trust that the conduct of the officers employed in that service will meet your approbation.

I have the honour to remain

Sir, your most obedient

humble Servant,

THOMAS HARVEY

Sir Sidney Smith, Knt., &c

Captain Nicholls boarded the ship bearing the flag of the Othman admiral, under a fire of musketry from the shore. After striking the flag and setting fire to the ship, he proceeded to destroy the battery on the point, on which he found thirty-one guns, eight of which were of brass, carrying a ball weighing upwards of two hundred pounds. The rest were thirty-two and twenty-four pounders, all of which he spiked, and blew up the magazine. He gave the admiral's flag to Captain Blackmore to send to Sir John Duckworth, and his jack he sent to Captain Harvey; by whom, as it appears by the subjoined letter, it was forwarded to Sir Sidney Smith.

Standard, 21st Feb. 1807

Dear Sir, I send you the names of the officers of the Standard and Thunderer employed in destroying the frigate and corvettes under my own eye, and I assure you they merit your approbation; and, had not the Standard's two cutters been disabled by shot, and our yard tackles shot away, the officers of the Standard would have had a more active part.

I send you the Capitan Pasha's jack. The ensign was shot away. The flag at the masthead was unfortunately, through mistake, given to Captain Blackmore.

I shall do myself the honour of waiting on you at three, if we remain quiet, and will bring Captain Nicholls.

Believe me, dear Sir,

Your faithful humble Servant,

THOMAS HARVEY

To Sir Sidney Smith, Knt

The following official communication relates to the close of the service off Point Nagara.

> *Active, at anchor off Pesquies,*
> *21st February, 1807.*

Sir, The battery on Point Pesquies having been rendered unserviceable by the destruction of the gun-carriages, and spiking and filling the guns thereon, as were those in the wreck, I do myself the honour to communicate to you the completion of this service; and it is a very satisfactory part of my duty to bear testimony to the gallant and judicious conduct of Lieutenant Carroll of the Pom pee, who speaks in the highest terms of praise of the officers and men under his direction.

The Turks were in general kept in check by the fire of the Active and her launch; but they made one resolute push, whereby two men were wounded.

I enclose a list of the officers and petty officers employed under Lieutenant Carroll's orders on the occasion, and a list of the wounded.

> I have the honour to be, &c.
> R. M. MOUBRAY.

To Rear-Admiral
Sir W. Sidney Smith, Knt., &c.

In this action, so spirited, and so completely successful, Captain Richard Dacres was Sir Sidney Smith's flag captain, and consequently in command of the Pompée.

It is highly creditable to our officer's character, that his urbanity and exceedingly gentlemanly deportment so much attached his officers to him, that they had always towards him the affection of a personal friendship. In Sir Sidney Smith's early career he had served under Captain Dacres, and on his promotion to the command of the Diamond, he wrote to the then lieutenant the following letter, so full of excellent feeling:

> *Swallow-street, London, 3rd April, 1794*

My dear Sir—It has quite grieved me to see you hang so long on the lieutenants' list, and I have often wished that it were in my power to give you a lift towards that promotion that your character and services so justly entitle you to; and, though I have ever named you as you deserved, when I thought that I could do you service, I have not positive interest enough to get you made. The only thing immediately in my power has afforded me an opportunity of mentioning your name at the Admiralty; and I sincerely hope that it may be a stepping-stone to your promotion, in case we should be so fortunate as to make additional claims from the situation that it is in my power to offer you.

I am appointed to the Diamond, a fine eight-and-thirty, just launched in the river. Lord Chatham is so good as to allow me to name my officers, and I have, at a venture, named you FIRST; trusting that your confidence in my friendship will induce you to sacrifice all recollection of my being now placed as the commander of the man I was once happy to obey, and that you will accept the appointment.

I, for my own part, freely confess, I make a sacrifice in making you the offer, feeling, as I do, for the delicacy of our mutual situation. In this k respect, however, I know the goodness of your heart, temper, and good sense, and have no doubt but that we shall continue to add new links to that chain which first attached me to you,

As your sincere friend,

W. SIDNEY SMITH

Lieutenant Dacres did not, however, remain long with his friend, but they, on that account, lost not sight of each other, and we now find the former sharing in this expedition, in that part of it only which was glorious.

CHAPTER III

THE COMMENCEMENT OF THE NEGOTIATIONS WITH THE TURKS • SIR
SIDNEY'S ADVICE ASKED BY THE COMMANDER-IN-CHIEF • THE TURKS
PROCRASTINATE AND ARM • THE ENGLISH RESOLVE TO RETURN.

ON the 20th of February, in the evening, our squadron come to an anchor near Prince's Islands, about eight miles distant on the south-east from Constantinople. A novel, and almost a ridiculous process now began on the part of the English minister and the admiral; a kind of menacing courtship—a wooing by the mouths of heavy ordnance. The first step was taken by Mr. Arbuthnot sending a letter by a flag of truce to the seraglio, and to the Turkish government, recapitulating the efforts that had been made, by an amicable negotiation, to preserve the relations of peace and friendly intercourse which had unfortunately been interrupted by the intrigues of a party inimical to both Turkey and England.

Previously to Sir John Duckworth despatching this public letter, he desired to see Sir Sidney Smith, who accordingly waited on the vice-admiral. On hearing it read, Sir Sidney offered a remark on the unnecessary introduction of a lieutenant of the Repulse into the drama, which had been going on well, and would have gone on better without his interference, he having lately pretended to act under superior authority to that of the lieutenant of the flag-ship of the rear-admiral, who was furnished with proper instructions to prepare everything for the ignition of the Turkish sixty-four, to hoist a flag when ready, and to wait for the affirmative answer from the Pompée, on the signal to put the match to the preparations.

She was set fire to previously to the signal, which was suspended, to allow time for the battery on the point to be completely destroyed, under the cover of the prize's guns, for the Standard to withdraw from the sphere of her explosion, and for the Pompée and Thunderer to pass her before she should be in flames.

The precipitation of the lieutenant of the Repulse, in firing the vessel too soon, was attributed to eagerness for the destruction of the sixty-four, as the signal to that effect was made by the Royal George. This complaint Sir Sidney did not urge, nor would he accept of Sir John Duckworth's offer to investigate his conduct, as it was not attended by any bad consequences, further than some risk to the Standard, some delay in junction of the Pompée and Thunderer with the van, and the impossibility of our maintaining the battery on Pesquies Point long enough to level it, though the guns were spiked.

Indeed, this was not fitting time to agitate nice points of precedence in command. We think that the blame, if any, would have been traced to the Royal George, in making the signal prematurely, which we do not see how the lieutenant of the Repulse could have disobeyed.

After this incidental subject was disposed of, the letter was again taken into consideration, which, after dwelling much on the amicable sentiments of the English government, asserted that there could be no clearer or more satisfactory proofs of the pacific disposition of his Britannic Majesty, than that the admiral had not immediately proceeded to the execution of his orders, though the wind was fair for that purpose, but had consented to keep his fleet at a distance from the capital for so long a time as would be necessary to receive an answer to the letter. If that answer should be received to-morrow, (21st February,) before the setting of the sun, with satisfactory assurance that his Britannic Majesty's just demands were agreed to, then all demonstrations of hostility on the part of his Majesty should cease; but if not, the British admiral would act, in the event of war, according to the orders he had received from his government.

At the same time, a letter in a similar spirit was sent by Sir John Duckworth to the Reis Effendi—but a little more to the point, for he proposed to the Turkish government, as a condition of peace and amity, that the Sublime Porte should immediately deliver into his hands all his ships and vessels of war, with all necessary stores and provisions. The vice-admiral was graciously pleased to allow the space of half an hour after his note should be translated into the Turkish language, for the divan to deliberate and decide upon his proposition, protesting that, if he should be reduced to the hard necessity of seizing the ships, and all vessels of war, by force, and proceed to the destruction of Constantinople, for the accomplishment of which he possessed ample means, the blame would lie on the Sublime Porte, and and not on the King his master.

A vessel bearing these notes was despatched with a flag of truce, on the morning of the 21st; but the officer who had charge of them was not permitted to land. Mr. Arbuthnot then sent the flag of truce once more, with a short additional note, that, from an ardent desire for peace, he had thought it right to make another effort for the delivery of the propositions before sent, and expressing in a few words to the Reis Effendi the contents of the rejected notes, which were to give the Sublime Porte the option of declaring himself either on the side of the French or the English;

and that if he should prefer the former alternative, still the British admiral would spare the city, on condition of the whole of the Turkish fleet being surrendered to him, with a sufficiency of naval stores.

The diplomacy continued to be most signally one-sided. The Turks chose the wiser part; for whilst Mr. Arbuthnot was writing, they were arming—each to his occupation. Accordingly, in the middle of the night, between the 21st and 22d of February, our ambassador wrote another note to the Reis Effendi, stating that the English officers had discovered, by means of telescopes, how the time was employed that had been allowed to the Sublime Porte for coming to a decision on the subject of the former notes from himself and the British admiral. It stated that it had been observed that its subjects were busily engaged in withdrawing the ships of war from their usual stations to places more capable of defence, and in constructing batteries all along the coast. His highness the Sultan should give an assurance, in two words, that the good understanding should not be destroyed.

To these repeated notes, the Reis Effendi replied, that the proffered negotiation was considered merely as an artifice for gaining time. This was the retort courteous; the cunning Turk was doing exactly the thing of which he accused his opponents.

At this, which was probably intended, the old admiral's blood became of the fever heat, and he repelled with indignation the unfounded charge, observing, that they who could be guilty of such base suspicions, were themselves the very objects that merited to be suspected. He renewed the alternative that had already been repeatedly offered. He declared, upon his honour, though the English were prepared for war, they were desirous of peace, which, on the terms proposed, might be concluded in half an hour. He finished by stating, that if the Sublime Porte were really desirous to avert the calamities that were ready to be accumulated upon his capital, it would send a plenipotentiary on board of his ship early next morning for the purpose of concluding a peace. This took place on the 23rd.

It is evident that, in all this, the Turks were gaining the advantage. The ambassador and the naval commander did not amalgamate Avell. Sir John Duckworth was for as much fighting and as little protocolling as possible; Mr. Arbuthnot for as little fighting as need be, provided it could be warded off by protocolling. Without meaning anything disrespectful to either character, we think that Sir Sidney Smith most excellently and efficaciously united the functions of both in his own person; he would have fought as manfully as the vice-admiral, and diplomatised more successfully than the ambassador. He knew the Turks well, and they knew him. They had a friendship for, and a confidence in, him; if there was a man in existence who could have adjusted this nice point, that man was our officer. But the rules of the service to which he was an ornament, and the forms of official etiquette, which ought then to have been laid aside, were opposed to his taking the chief part in these operations, the termination of which produced so little of advantage or of honour to the British nation.

After the receipt of Sir John Duckworth's imperative and hostile demand for peace and amity, early on the morning of the 24th of February, a letter was forwarded to the English admiral from the Reis Effendi, signifying the wish of the Sublime Porte to enter immediately into a negotiation for a definite treaty of peace, and requested that a person invested with full powers on the part of the English might be sent to meet the Ottoman plenipotentiary.

A great source of contention now arose as to the precise spot where the conference should be held. The Turks wished for some place on shore under their control and command—the English either the Isle of Princes, or on board of their own flag-ship, or the Endymion frigate, lying at anchor before Constantinople, with a flag of truce. The most effectual negotiators, the line-of-battle ships and the bomb-vessels, were still windbound at the distance of eight miles from the city. Their presence would have had more weight than Mr. Arbuthnot and all his attaches.

It has been said that the admiral, when too late, saw his error, and moved his fleet four miles nearer the city. This is a mistake, as the wind did not permit him to move. Threats and cajoleries still continued to be inflicted upon the Turks, who, in the mean time, persevered most assiduously, night and day, in working at their fortifications, fully determined that the English should not depart from, so easily as they entered into, their narrow seas. Even acts of courtesy and generosity made no impression, but seem to have been received only to be resented; for, whilst the English sent back to the Seraglio some Turks who had been taken in actual hostilities against the English, the Turks kept close prisoners five English seamen that had fallen into their hands, having gone some distance from their ship (the Endymion) in the jolly boat..

Both the European and Asiatic shores, and the narrows of Constantinople, now bristled with the guns of batteries. The havoc made by Sir Sidney Smith on the 19th of February seemed to have exasperated rather than intimidated them. The ships were burned and the redoubt taken, and the guns spiked in vain. Even the Grand Seignior himself, conducted by the French ambassador, General Sebastiani, appeared at the places most proper for the construction of fortifications and batteries.

The whole male population began to work—even the clergy put their sacred hands to the spade and wheel-barrow. The members of the divan and other grandees were on the busy scene day and night; they took their necessary repose in tents. The Grand Seignior fared no better. At the end of four days, batteries, with excellent breastworks, mounted with five hundred pieces of cannon and one hundred mortars, were completed. The English had constructed a few more diplomatic notes.

Whilst the two lines of coast thus presented the spectacle of an almost continuous battery, completed in many parts, and in a state of great forwardness, in all, twelve Turkish line-of-battle ships, two of them three-deckers, and nine frigates, filled with troops, lay in the canal, with their sails bent, apparently ready for action. An immense army destined to march against the Russians was in the city and the suburbs, and very numerous gun-boats and troops were also prepared to act against the hostile negotiators.

The whole force of the British then consisted only of eight ships of the line, two frigates, and two brigs; an enormous disproportion, and tending more to provoke aggression than to inspire intimidation.

When it was wholly too late, that question so indicative of weakness of mind, and infirmity of purpose, was asked of Sir Sidney Smith, "What ought we to have done?" A string of questions was propounded to him from the vice-admiral, bearing date the 27th of February.

From the queries and answers alluded to, we find that Sir Sidney Smith did not conceive that it would have promoted his Majesty's service to cannonade the city of Constantinople, on the first arrival of the British squadron. "There being reason to hope that the object in question might be gained by negotiation, when an immediate hostility would have precluded intercourse, and all possibility of amicable discussion and arrangement."

From various causes, such as the circuitous eddies within the harbour, the prevalence of the northerly current of the Bosphorus, which, setting directly on the Seraglio Point, would prevent a disabled ship from extricating herself—the Turkish mode of warfare, every man using a rifle, &c.,—Sir Sidney Smith was also of opinion, that it would not have been advisable to have led the squadron to an attack on the arsenal.

Again, Sir John Duckworth asks:

"The negotiation with his Majesty's minister, Mr. Arbuthnot, having failed of success, do you consider the present squadron equal to forcing the Turkish government into terms, or to destroy their navy, and afterwards be in a state to pass the Dardanelles?"

To which the following answer was returned:

Being necessarily in a state of hostility, as well from the engagements existing with Russia, as from the distinct menaces which have been held out to the Turkish government, in case of its not yielding to amicable representations, it seems advisable to try the effect of bombardment without, in the first instance, committing the line-of-battle ships to the fire under the new batteries which have been raised under the directions of the French engineers. If this should provoke the Turks to risk their navy outside the harbour, we shall, therein, find our advantage. The effects of such bombardment, at the seat of government, may induce the divan to concede some points as the price of its cessation. It will divide the parties in the town more distinctly, and I think, isolate the war or French party from the other, to which it is presumed that the Sultan is most inclined; who will endeavour to re-open intercourse and negotiations with the ambassador, through which means our free intercourse with our resources on the other side of the Dardanelles may be conceded to us, as the price of our equivocal concession to the capital, for a limited time; for it is to be remembered, that this immense city is supplied from day to clay by water in small boats, chiefly from Asia, with all kinds of provisions, corn coming by way of the Dardanelles: consequently, the position of the squadron, immediately off the town, shortens the duration of time the government can possibly hold out.

Their magazines cannot have anything like four months' provisions, and the authority which sent this squadron hither, will, no doubt, take care that supplies are sent up, which can reach us in the same way we reached this spot; and this being a key port, I think it ought not to be relinquished without an order counter to that by which it was occupied.

The Turks, having their attention and resources directed to the defence of the capital, cannot execute the suggestions which, no doubt, the French engineers will make to them, of increasing their means of a cross fire in the Dardanelles. His Majesty's government is in possession of a plan of securing the European side of that entrance, in a manner to oppose the fire of those castles to the castle on the Asiatic side, by landing a body of troops behind the former, in the gulf of Saros; and having ordered this small squadron hither, must necessarily consider of and supply the means of supporting and extricating it.

So long as the capital is closely blockaded and menaced by the squadron in its immediate vicinity, its councils are paralysed, and its authority weakened with respect to all the distant parts of the empire. His Majesty's officers employed elsewhere, can act, in the name of, and for, the Sultan, by representing him, as he is, a prisoner to the French faction; and it may not be impossible to get him secretly to convey his consent to us, in order that he may, by our means, preserve the Asiatic and best part of his empire, when he sees the northern portion of it a prey to immediate invasion.

To preserve terms with him personally, and prevent a greater degree of distress bearing on the peaceful inhabitants than need be, a warning to his Majesty, personally, to quit the Seraglio with his family, and our indication of Gallipolis, Lemnos, or Tenedos, as neutral places of refuge, might be sent officially, previously to the bombardment, and publicly circulated in the town with good effect.

This counsel, judicious as it appears to be, must have been very barren of consolation to Sir John Duckworth, in the straits in which he found himself. His extrication depended, if this advice were followed, entirely upon the prudence and foresight of our government at home—and he showed his good sense in not relying upon it. However, as Sir

Sidney was more sanguine in this respect than his commander-in-chief, "his voice was still for war," for in a letter to him, dated on the first of March, he thus expresses himself:

> I should be wanting towards you, after the desire you have expressed to receive such suggestions as arise in my mind, if I omitted to submit to your consideration the utility of making a demonstration while the squadron is under way, on the west end of the city, between the Seven Towers and the Western mosque; the effect of remaining in which position might make the government more apprehensive, which is averse to receiving the effect of our fire, than it is, of the party whose presumption or policy tends to provoke it, and prevents the Sultan listening to the ambassador's propositions. At any rate, it would induce the government to re-open intercourse, and give an opportunity of claiming a free passage for the ambassador through the Dardanelles, as was allowed to M. Italinski. I dare say they would gladly compound for getting rid of the whole of us, and consequently, that no orders exist at the forts below for firing on ships bound down; a firman, however, would be the best security for masts and yards, which are not to be had at Malta, even for a frigate. If you should decide to anchor again, the north coast of Marmora has the best anchorage.

Sir Sidney himself subsequently wrote to the governor of the castle at the Dardanelles, to dissuade him, individually, from hostilities; but, as it soon will be seen, with no successful result. In the rest of his letter, after mentioning some subordinate points, such as the conveyance of letters, &c. he proceeds thus:

> I mention these things, in consequence of our conversation, merely as means of doing what you may project, without urging or proposing any new measure, as I am persuaded that the Sultan's disposition, and that of the persons in his council, who were originally the parties of the triple alliance, remain the same, but that they are under the coercion of the French faction, who have found means to excite a fanatic mob to insurrection, and consequently that the government rather look to us for protection, in aid of a counter insurrection of the Sultan's adherents.

> Being sincerely anxious for your credit, I will venture to mention, before you repass the Dardanelles, (as I presume to be your intention,) by your getting under way with a north-east wind, that it is possible the courts of Petersburgh and England may have combined a military operation for possession of this capital, by means of the two fleets, one to the northward and the other to the southward, and a Russian army; in that case, the order that will come up will be positive, grounded on your having passed the Dardanelles upwards, which will be taken for granted from your known intrepidity, and the talent you have often evinced, as well as on this occasion, of attaching your followers to

you, in emulation of your spirit of enterprise; in that event we shall have to pass them upwards again.

In a postscript to this letter, he remarks, "that the eddy runs from west to east, along the town wall; so that the fire-ships from the Bosphorus would not drift on us, as they would in our former berth in the stream, northerly."

But Sir John was not to be cajoled into remaining where he then was, either by the military display of an Anglo-Russian force, or by the well-turned compliments of the hero of Acre.

Sir Sidney's balked appetite for fighting was again excited, for spying the powder manufactory and magazine of the enemy, he pointed it out to Sir John, and thus endeavoured to inflame him to share in his longings.

"The ships," he observes, "can anchor at any distance from the shore the range of the mortars may require, or fire random shells under way with a chance of blowing the whole up, which will, of course, paralyze their fleet, as it is not allowed to have powder on board in the arsenals, nor do they venture to keep much at the depot at Tophanna."

Sir John Duckworth thus declines all these friendly and well-meant invitations for a little repast in this style, for he answers, "That no man could feel more sensible of these strong modes of friendship, which he Sir Sidney Smith had evinced towards him, by his various suggestions in his two letters; and most truly desirous was he to benefit by the aid of such talents, for he certainly knew that he had his all at stake; yet, with the decided manner in which the Porte had acted since their *projet*, it seemed impracticable to obtain any communication with it; and he really conceived, from delay, that great evil must arise, and his Majesty's service be considerably injured, without the most distant prospect of advantage; and to combat with an empire which appeared so positively hostile in a sea where the squadron was shut out from all possible resource, could not be attended with any advantage, but might eventually tend to the destruction of our squadron, which, in the present state of the Mediterranean, he felt could not be justified. As to the magazine, he certainly should be well disposed to destroy it, but from various information he had learned, that as fast as the powder was manufactured it was deposited in a place of safety; and it was not possible to suppose, when he had been off the town ten days, that the Turks, knowing that vulnerable part, would not have provided against our doing them so essential a mischief."

CHAPTER IV

SIR JOHN DUCKWORTH LEAVES THE DARDANELLES • HIS OFFICIAL
ACCOUNTS OF HIS PROCEEDINGS.

ON the 1st of March, Sir Thomas Duckworth weighed and made sail, in order to extricate himself from his perilous situation.

Although, up to the 27th of February, he had deluded himself with the vain hopes of peace, believing, notwithstanding the display of enthusiasm on the part of the populace, that the desire of the Sublime Porte to negotiate was sincere; yet whether this were the case or not, it seems that the heavens were as unpropitious to him as the obstinacy of the Turks, for, up to this day, such had been the adverse state of wind and weather, that he could not have left his dangerous situation, nor was it till the morning of the 1st of March that he could have occupied a station which would have enabled the squadron to have commenced offensive operations against Constantinople.

Even if this had not been the case, the English, after encountering a force which the resources of an empire had been employed for weeks in preparing, they would not have been able to maintain a successful conflict with the enemy, and then have repassed the Dardanelles. Indeed, had the delay been much longer protracted, the repassing of the Dardanelles would have been impossible. The fire from the two inner castles on our ships in the outward passage had been most severe; but, on their return, they found their defences to have become doubly formidable. Huge blocks of marble, of immense weight and size, were fired at our ships from stationary mortars. One of these, weighing eight hundred pounds, cut in two the mainmast of the Windsor Castle, and it was not without great exertions that the ship was saved. The course of these masses of stone being easily discovered, contact with them was avoided by the men slipping aside, and thus opening for them a clear passage.

-221-

The total loss sustained in this fruitless expedition was forty-two killed, two hundred and thirty-five wounded, and four missing; the Pompée's (Sir Sidney Smith's ship) share of which was only five seamen wounded.

We now proceed to give the vice-admiral's own version of the matter, in his three official letters to his commander-in-chief, Lord Collingwood.

Royal George, off Constantinople, Feb. 21

"My Lord, I had the honour of transmitting to your lordship, by the late first lieutenant of the Ajax, the various details relating to the transactions of the squadron till the 17th ult. Your lordship will, from thence, have been informed of my resolution of passing the Dardanelles the first fair wind. A fine wind from the southward permitted me to carry it into effect on the morning of the 19th. Information had been given me by his Majesty's minister, Mr. Arbuthnot, and Sir Thomas Louis, that the Turkish squadron, consisting of a sixty-four gun ship, four frigates, and several corvettes, had been, for some time, at anchor within the inner castle; and conceiving it possible they might have remained there, I had given orders to Rear-Admiral Sir Sidney Smith to bring up with the Thunderer, Standard, and Active, and destroy them, should our passage be opposed. At a quarter before nine o'clock, the whole of the squadron had passed the outer castles, without having returned a shot to their fire, (which occasioned but little injury.) This forbearance was produced by the desire of his Majesty's minister, expressed, to preserve every appearance of amity, that he might negotiate with the strongest proof of the pacific disposition of our sovereign towards the Porte; a second battery on the European side fired also with as little effect. At half-past nine o'clock, the Canopus, which, on account of Sir Thomas Louis's knowledge of the channel, joined to the steady gallantry which I had before experienced, had been appointed to lead, entered the narrow passage of Sestos and Abydos, and sustained a very heavy cannonade from both castles, within point-blank shot of each. They opened their fire on our ships as they continued to pass in succession, although I was happy in observing that the very spirited return it met with had so considerably diminished its force, that the effect on the sternmost ships could not have been so severe.

"Immediately to the north-east of the castles, and between them and Point Pesquies, on which a formidable battery had been newly erected, the small squadron which I have already alluded to, were at anchor. The van division of our squadron gave them their broadsides as they passed, and Sir Sidney Smith, with his division, closed into the midst; and the effect of the fire was such, that, in half an hour, the Turks had all cut their cables to run on shore. The object of the rear-admiral was then to destroy them, which was most rapidly effected; as in less than four hours the whole of them had exploded, except a small corvette, and a gun-boat, which it was thought proper to preserve. I enclose to your lordship a statement of their number; and when I add also an account of the loss his Majesty's ships have sustained, I cannot help expressing my satisfaction that we have suffered so slightly; as, had any of their stone shot, some of which exceeded eight hundred weight, made such a breach between wind and water, as they have done in our sides, the ship must have sunk; or had they struck a lower mast in the centre, it must evidently have been cut in two; in the rigging, too, no accident occurred that was not perfectly arranged in the course of next day. The sprit-sail yard of the Royal George, the gaff of the Canopus, and the maintopsail-yard of the Standard, are the only spars that were injured. It is with peculiar pleasure that I embrace the opportunity which has been at this time afforded, of bearing testimony to the zeal and distinguished ability of Sir Sidney Smith; the manner in which he executed the service entrusted to him was worthy of the reputation which he has long since so justly and generally established. The terms of approbation in which the rear-admiral relates the conduct of Captains Dacres, Talbot, Harvey, and Moubray, which, from my being under the necessity of passing the Point of Pesquies before the van could anchor, he had a greater opportunity of observing than I could, cannot but be highly flattering; but I was a more immediate witness to the able and officer-like conduct which Captain Moubray displayed in obedience to my signal, by destroying a frigate with which he had been more particularly engaged, having driven her on shore on the European side, after she had been forced to cut her cables, from under the fire of the Pompée and Thunderer. The sixty-four having run on shore on Pesquies Point, I ordered the Repulse to work up and destroy her, which Captain Legge, in conjunction with the boats of the Pompée, executed with great promptitude and judgment. The battery on the point, of more than thirty guns, which, had it been completely finished, was in a position to have annoyed the squadron most severely in passing, was taken possession of by the royal marines and boats' crews of the rear division, the Turks having retired at their approach, and the guns were immediately spiked. This service was performed under the direction of Captain Nicholls, of the Standard's marines, whose spirit and enterprise can never be doubted; but as circumstances rendered it impracticable to effect the entire destruction of the Redoubt, orders were given by Sir Sidney Smith to Captain Moubray, which I fully approved, to remain at anchor near the Pesquies, and to employ Lieutenants Carrol and Arabin, of the Pompée, and Lieutenant Lawrie, of the marines, to complete the demolition of the redoubt and guns, which when performed, the Active was to continue in the passage of the Dardanelles till further orders.

"At a quarter past five P.M. the squadron was enabled to make sail; and on the evening of the next day, the 20th, came to an anchor at ten o'clock, near the Prince's Islands, about eight miles from Constantinople, when I despatched Captain Capel, in the Endymion, to anchor near the town, if the wind, which was light, would permit the ship to stem the current, to convey the ambassador's despatches to the Sublime Porte, in the morning, by a flag of truce; but he found it impracticable to get within four miles, and consequently anchored at half-past eleven P.M. I have now the highest satisfaction to add, that the conduct of the officers and ships' companies of the squadron, under my command, has fully supported the character of the British navy, and is deserving of my warmest eulogium. Having endeavoured to pay just tribute to those whose duty necessarily called them into this service, I should feel myself very deficient if I omitted to mention that his Majesty's minister, Mr. Arbuthnot, and Lord Burghersh, (who had requested to take a cruise with me,) were amongst the most animated in the combat. To Captain Blackwood, who, after the unfortunate loss of the Ajax, volunteered to serve in the Royal George, great praise is due for his able assistance in regulating the fire of the middle and lower decks; and when the Royal George anchored, he most readily offered his services to convey a message to the Endymion, of great moment, her pilot having refused to take charge of the ship. From thence he gave his assistance to arrange the landing of the troops from the sixty-four, and setting her on fire: indeed, where active service was to be performed, there was his anxious desire to be placed. His officers, too, requested to serve in the squadron, and their services, in passing the Dardanelles, met with approbation.

I have the honour to be, &c.

J. T. DUCKWORTH

In another letter to Lord Collingwood, dated the 28th of February, Sir John mentions "an unfortunate attempt of the marines and boats' crews of the Canopus, Royal George, Windsor Castle, and Standard, who, under the command of Captain Kent, were sent to take a party of Turks who were erecting a battery on the island of Prota. Captain Kent had positive orders not to pursue the object, if he found it attended with any hazard; but it appeared that the information of a few Turks only having remained on the island was entirely false, as nearly a hundred of them had retired to an old convent, from loopholes in the walls of which they defended themselves with musketry. In this affair we had Lieutenant Belli, a young officer of the fairest promise, and four seamen, one officer, and one private marine, killed; two officers, three petty officers, and five seamen; one officer, two non-commissioned officers, and six private marines, wounded."

On the 6th of March the Vice-Admiral writes thus to his commander-in-chief:

Royal George, without the Dardanelles
March 6th.

My Lord Together with this letter, I transmit to your lordship
two letters of the 21st and 28th ult., the former of which will have
informed you of my arrival with the squadron near Constantinople, and the latter, of an unlucky attempt, in which the marines
and boats' crews of the Canopus, Royal George, Windsor Castle,
and Standard, had been engaged.

It is now my duty to acquaint your lordship with the result of
the resolution which, for the reasons I have already detailed, I
had adopted, of forcing the passage of the Dardanelles. My letter
of the 21st is dated at anchor eight miles from Constantinople,
the wind not admitting of a nearer approach; but the Endymion,
which had been sent a-head with a flag of truce, at the request of
the ambassador, was enabled to anchor within four miles. Had it
been then in our power, we should then have taken our station
off the town immediately; but as that could not be done from the
rapidity of the current, I was rather pleased than otherwise with
the position we had been forced to take; for, in the conferences
between Mr. Arbuthnot and the Capitan Pacha, of the particulars
of which your lordship is in possession, it was promised by Mr.
A. that even when the squadron had arrived before Constantinople, the door to pacification should remain open, and that he
would be willing to negociate on terms of equality and justice. In
consideration of this promise, and as it would convince the Porte
of his Majesty's earnest desire to preserve peace, as well as possess its ministers with a confidence in the sincerity of our professions, it was the opinion of Mr. A., in which I concurred, that it
was fortunate we had anchored at a little distance from the capital, as a nearer approach might have given cause for suspicion
and alarm, and have cut off the prospect of an amicable adjust-
ment of the differences which had arisen.

"At noon of the 21st, Ysak Bey, a minister of the Porte, came
off; from whose expressions Mr. Arbuthnot thought it impossible
not to believe, that in the head of the government (for in the present instance every circumstance proved that between him and
the armed populace a great distinction is to be made) there really
existed a sincere desire for peace; and the negotiation was carried on, as will appear by the documents transmitted to your
lordship, till the 27th; but from the moment of our anchorage till
we weighed, on the morning of the 1st of March, such was the
unfortunate state of the weather, that it was not at any time in
our power to have occupied a situation which would have enabled the squadron to commence offensive operations against
Constantinople. On Sunday the 22nd alone, for a few hours, the
breeze was sufficient to have stemmed the current where we
were placed; but such was its rapidity on the shore where the

Endymion was at anchor, that Captain Capel thought it very doubtful whether the squadron could have obtained an anchorage, though it had been held in preparative readiness, by signal, from daybreak; but the peculiarly unsettled state of the weather, and the minister's desire that I should give a few hours for an answer to his letter, through Ysak Bey, prevented me from trying. Before five o'clock P.M. it was nearly calm, and in the evening the wind was entirely from the eastward, and continued light airs or calm till the evening of the 28th, when it blew fresh from the N.E., and rendered it impossible to change our position.

Two days after our arrival near Constantinople, the ambassador found himself indisposed, and has been ever since confined with a fit of illness, so severe as to prevent him from attending to business. Under these circumstances, he had delivered in on the 22nd, to the Turkish minister, a projet, as the basis on which peace might be preserved; and, at his desire, the subsequent part of the negotiation was carried on in my name, with his advice and assistance; and while I lament most deeply that it has not ended in the re-establishment of peace, I derive consolation from the reflection, that no effort has been wanting on the part of Mr. Arbuthnot and myself to obtain such a result, which was soon seen, from the state of the preparations at Constantinople, could be effected by negotiation only, as the strength of the current from the Bosphorus, with the circuitous eddies of the port, rendered it impracticable to place ships for an attack without a commanding breeze, which, during the ten days I was off the town, it was not my good fortune to meet with.

I now come to the point of explaining to your lordship the motives which fixed me to decide on repassing the channel of the Dardanelles, and relinquishing every idea of attacking the capital; and I feel confident it will require no argument to convince your lordship of the utter impracticability of our force having made any impression, as, at this time, the whole line of the coast presented a chain of batteries; that twelve Turkish line-of-battle ships, two of them three-deckers, with nine frigates, were with their sails bent, and apparently in readiness, filled with troops; add to this, near two hundred thousand were said to be in Constantinople, to march against the Russians; besides, there were an innumerable quantity of small craft, with boats; and fire-vessels had been prepared to act against us. With the batteries alone we might have coped, or with the ships, could we have got them out of their stronghold; but your lordship will be aware, that after combating the opposition which the resources of an empire had been many weeks employed in preparing, we should have been in no state to have defended ourselves against them as described, and then repass the Dardanelles. I know it was my duty, in obedience to your lordship's orders, to attempt every thing (governed by the opinion of the ambassador) that appeared within the compass of possibility; but when the unavoidable sacrifice of the squadron committed to my charge, (which must have arisen, had I waited for a wind to have enabled me to cannonade the town, unattended by the remotest chance of obtaining any advantage for his Majesty's service,) must have been the consequence of pursuing that object, it at once became my positive duty, however wounded in pride and ambition, to relinquish it; and if I had not been already satisfied on the subject, the increased opposition in the Dardanelles would have convinced me I had done right, when I resolved on the measure as indispensably necessary. I therefore weighed with the squadron on the morning of the 1st; and as it had been reported that the Turkish fleet designed to make an effort against us, to give them an opportunity, if such was really their intention, I continued to stand on and off during the day, but they showed no disposition to move. I therefore, as every hour was of importance, bore up at dusk with the squadron: we arrived off Point Pesquies towards the evening of the 2nd instant; but the daylight would not admit of our attempting to pass the castles, and the squadron came to anchor for the night; we weighed in the morning, and, when I add that every ship was in safety outside of the passage about noon, it was not without the most lively sense of the good fortune that has attended us.

The Turks had been occupied unceasingly, in adding to the number of their forts; some had been already completed, and others were in a forward state. The fire of the two inner castles had, on our going up, been severe; but, I am sorry to say, the effects they have had on our ships returning, has proved them to be doubly formidable; in short, had they been allowed another week to complete their defences throughout the channel, it would have been a very doubtful point whether a return lay open to us at all. The manner in which they employed the interval of our absence has proved their assiduity. I transmit your lordship an account of the damages sustained by the respective ships; as also their loss in killed and wounded, which your lordship will perceive is far from trifling. The mainmast of the Windsor Castle being more than three-quarters cut through by a granite shot of eight hundred weight, we have found great difficulty in saving it.

I have the honour to be, &c.

J. T. DUCKWORTH.

P. S. I am sorry to observe, that, in the course of this letter to your lordship, I have omitted to mention, that having placed the honourable Captain Capel, in the Endymion, which had been advanced in the stream of the Bosphorus, for the purpose of ascertaining when the squadron could stem the current, and for a watchful observation of the movements of the Turks, as well as to facilitate communication with the Porte, I feel myself indebted to that officer for his zealous attention and assiduity during the time he was placed in that arduous situation.

J. T. D.

CHAPTER V

ACTING under the command of another, Sir Sidney Smith, whilst he escapes all the unpleasantness of the failure of this ill-advised expedition, may justly claim the full credit of the little part of it which proved successful.

On the 4th of March, Sir John Duckworth issued the following letter of thanks to the officers, &c., under his command:

> Although unforeseen and insurmountable obstacles prevented the squadron under my command from effecting, at Constantinople, the objects which it had in view, I cannot refrain from offering my most heartfelt acknowledgments to all who have so nobly contributed their exertions throughout the arduous service in which we have been engaged. To Rear-Admiral Sir Thomas Louis, who, with the gallantry and cool judgment which marked his character, led the squadron, and to Rear-Admiral Sir Sidney Smith, I beg to present my sincere thanks for their able assistance, as well as to the captains, officers, seamen, and royal marines, for the steady bravery which has been so eminently displayed in forcing and returning through a passage so strongly fortified by nature and by art, and which had, till now, been deemed impregnable."

The copy of this document, addressed to the subject of this memoir, was accompanied by the following lines:

> Feeling that the want of ultimate success should not restrain me from doing that justice I owe to those who have so handsomely supported the honour of their country, I enclose you a

copy of thanks I think it my duty to issue, as a tribute of my approbation and obligation to the squadron, and to none more than you, my dear Sir; for which I again offer you my thanks, as I am, with high esteem and regard, &c. &c.

J. T. DUCKWORTH.

Sir W. S. Smith

Before we take leave of this expedition, it is not out of place to remark, that Sir John Duckworth did all that ever was expected from him. The affair itself was so ill contrived, that its failure was all but a moral certainty. The whole transaction fully reminds one of the very sensible reply made by the Turkish envoy to Charles VII. of France, when asked his opinion of a grand tournament exhibited for his amusement. He remarked that, "if it was in good earnest, there was not enough of it done; but, if it was in jest, too much."

Indeed, this very defeat was an advantage to us; for had we succeeded in partially destroying Constantinople—to get possession of it was out of the question and have deprived the Turks of their fleet, we should only have drawn upon us fresh evils by the enduring exasperation and enmity of the Turks, at a period, too, when it was of the utmost consequence to secure their good will. The fleet might have been some little acquisition to our naval resources, but the partial destruction of the town, whilst it would have proved a stinging and unpardonable insult to the Turks, would have been laughed at as an injury, so simple and so slovenly is the construction of the generality of their houses.

The conflagration threatened by Sir John Duckworth only calls to our recollection an offer made by a former Dey of Algiers to a similar menace. "How much," said he, "will it cost to put it in practice? I will myself undertake to do it for half the price."

The squadron, after leaving the Dardanelles, proceeded to the coast of Egypt, where it arrived a few days after the surrender of Alexandria and its forts to the naval and military forces under the respective commands of Sir Benjamin Hallowell and Major-General Fraser. Thus, in the lapse of a very few years, we twice took this place from the French, formerly as the ally, and now as the enemy of the Turks. Such are the mutations of human policy!

As it is of great consequence to know what was the opinion of this expedition of a commander so renowned and so able as is Sir Sidney Smith, and of one, too, actually on the spot and actively serving in the affair, we may, with justice, still continue to dwell upon it, by giving our hero's impression of this unfortunate transaction.

This opinion should be studied with care, and indeed the whole course of the proceedings well weighed throughout. If the reader be professional, the advantage must be great to him; and even as regards the civilian, nothing will tend more to make officials zealous in their duties, and enlightened as to their manner of performing them, than a general, not a technical knowledge, of military and naval affairs, spread throughout the community at large. Incapacity ought never to be permitted to shelter itself under the screen of national ignorance.

This extract from a letter of Sir Sidney Smith well expresses what he thought upon the conduct of this unsuccessful business.

Pompée, off the Island of Tenedos
March 11, 1807

I have written at length to ——, to ——, and to ——, as I could seize moments in the midst of my occupations; amongst which throwing in hints my experience dictates, to prevent things going from bad to worse, has been an unceasing one, though, I fear, a thankless office.

However, a sense of duty makes me act conscientiously, and my motives are not doubted by those who do not follow the advice, or take the early warnings I have given. 'Tis poor consolation to me to see the result sometimes justify my predictions; 'tis painful to see so much within our reach, whilst our means of realising any object are inapplicable, notwithstanding their apparent magnitude, 'Tis painful to look back, and see our ascendency in these countries lost by the political experiment of sending new diplomatic men, who (whatever their talents) had to buy their local experience, and, during their noviciate, were totally in the hands of a deep man, who, if not in the French interest, was in that of the Turks, which becoming blended, latterly, by the march of the Russians into Moldavia and Wallachia, enabled Buonaparte to induce the Turks to see their safety in the success of the French arms, and not to listen to the counsels of the British ambassador, who could no longer speak as an ally after the expiration of our treaty, which was, as you know, signed by S— — and me on the 6th of January, 1799.

The Turks are wrong in their calculations after all, for they have more to fear from French pretended friendship, than from the passage of the Russian troops through two provinces that hardly belonged to them. I am quite sure that I could have made you see this, if I had been allowed to open a collateral intercourse with those who could have overruled the fanatic junta and mob by our aid. These latter will be the victims in the end. *Quem Deus vult perdere, prius dementat,* [Ed. Whom the gods would destroy, they first make insane] you will have said on the first knowledge you had of this rupture; the Sultan knows better, but the ecclesiastical and judicial bodies being in one, and having a vote in everything, he cannot act as sound policy dictates.

S— — can explain this to you, and will agree with me in the advice I sent the poor Sultan, by his confidential messenger Isack Bey, viz. to employ the three fleets combined to chastise the rebels, and guard his capital against the French. I am convinced he was personally sorry to see us go, &c.

In the postscript to this letter, he thus acknowledges the services of a meritorious young officer. "I ought not to omit to say, for your satisfaction, that your son T. proved himself to be of a good breed, by steady, clear-headed conduct, in the situation I entrusted to him, of signal lieutenant with me on the poop, where we could see round us, and know the worst."

In some of these remarks, we think that our officer was a little mistaken, for the enthusiasm against the English was almost general, and the Sultan must have been a most accomplished hypocrite, if he did not possess more than his share of it. That Sir Sidney Smith much disapproved of the whole of this expedition we have made tolerably evident; and it is probable, as we have before ventured to express, had the whole conduct of it have been left to him, its termination would have been very different—either eminently triumphant to the British arms, or but the probabilities did not lie this way—ruinously disastrous. He was not the man for temporising measures.

He was, however, more inclined to ascribe the original cause of its failure to the mismanagement of Mr. Arbuthnot, than to any error of the commander-in-chief. Indeed, from a private letter from Sir John Duckworth to Sir Sidney Smith, it appears that, even after their return to England, and at the very time of the height of the public outcry at the failure of the expedition, a perfect harmony and general good feeling continued to be preserved between the two flag-officers.

From the letter alluded to, it appears Sir John Duckworth was on the point of setting out for Bath, in the hope of obtaining relief from a rheumatic complaint, and he returned thanks to Sir Sidney for his kind attention in transmitting to him certain documents, on service, which related to events that had occurred since their separation; and he also expressed his happiness in having a man of his honour and character to bear him out in his representation of not having had the power to destroy the Turkish fleet, or to effect a political change in the government. Sir John much regretted the contention of parties, and the freedom of abuse which had been exercised; but he says, "Feeling confident that the good of our country governed all my actions, I must endeavour to bear it with patience, though it is cruel to be put to such a trial."

But we are not always to regard our hero, Sir Sidney Smith, as the hero with the sword in his hand, and the speaking-trumpet to his lips, not always as an aquatic Mars; but sometimes we must contemplate him as an Apollo, in a rear-admiral of the blues full-dress uniform, after having ordered the boatswain's mate to pipe to dinner, himself piping on the melodious reed: he conquers, and then commits the account of his deed, not to the flames, as he did the Turkish squadron, but to immortal verse.

We must premise, that many years ago, when the Turks would neither be beaten into peace nor compliancy, there was just enough of superstition in the navy to make omens half believed and half derided. Shortly after this splendid achievement of Sir Sidney's, many very brave and wise officers were commenting upon their favourite oracle, Francis Moore, physician, astrologer, and almanac-maker, and how very apposite were his mystic leaves to the passing events, for, for that very year he had prognosticated, "About this time the Turkish emperor dies, or, it may be, he hides liis head; his people are tumultuous; let him save his life if he can. I give him fair warning of it."

Kind and considerate Francis Moore! How much was the Sultan obliged to you, how much more we! For this accurate prophecy was the cause of the following effusion from the gallant hero of Acre.

> AJAX, [1] alas ! devouring flames destroy!
> His ashes left before the walls of Troy.
> CANOPUS [2] led the way 'twixt neighbouring strands,
> 'Tween Sestos and Abydos, throng 'd with Turkish bands.
> Dreading REPULSED [3] the Turks dar'd not assail;
> The British STANDARD [4] turn'd the Crescent pale;
> On Caesar's allies, Pompée [5] vengeance wreaks,
> And rushing in amidst, their line he breaks;
> Whilst showers of deadly bolts the THUNDERER [6] hurl'd;
> The anchor drops—again the sails are furl'd;
> Whilst ASIA [7] trembles with explosions dire,
> An ACTIVE [8] torch in Europe spreadeth fire:
> The Pasha's fleet in fragments on the coast,
> Propontis now doth bear the British host: [8]
> Its dread approach each Turkish heart appals,
> For WINDSOR CASTLE'S [9] at Byzantium's walls!
> Grim LUCIFER [10] his brimstone doth prepare,
> Whilst fiery METEOR [11] glows to darken'd air.
> Th' astonished Turks, who ne'er beheld the like,
> Fear ROYAL GEORGE'S [12] a final blow should strike.
> Mercy they beg. ENDYMION [13] stands between—
> The hand of power to mercy still doth lean.
> A truce [14] requested, and obtained, they break,
> Loud tumults Sultan Selim's throne do shake; [15]
> The fate of empires but a thread doth bear,—
> Suspended hangs the blow of death in air. [16]
> "Tis not yet time' (saith Moore,) 'the spell to break
> That shackles Greece—'tis not yet time to take
> Revenge on Europe's scourge—Mahomet's race,'
> A greater scourge for them his wand's lines trace.
> The curse of hell—the greatest man hath seen!
> 'Tis Buonaparte's friendship he doth mean.

With all deference to Sir Sidney Smith, Francis Moore did not say all that is imputed to him. He would have been a happy man if he could have said it. To understand the full beauty of this Homeric burst of poetry, the reader must observe that all the words printed in small capitals designate the ships employed in the action. We dare not longer dwell upon this fascinating subject; but, for the better understanding this effusion, we shall subjoin the following explanatory notes from an already-named officer, who shared in the conflict which the poem describes.

It is not necessary to point out the play on words that prevails throughout these lines, in reference to the ships' names; which, without the amphibology being in the least sought for by the writer, would naturally suggest itself where it was intended to say but little, and there was but little else essential to fill the space. With this admission, the piece is by no means deficient in either poetical conception or metrical beauty; and the close, however strongly worded, is an expression of genuine English—and one may say—philanthropic feeling that does the gallant poet real honour.

1. The Ajax was destroyed by fire accidentally.

2. The Canopus was the leading ship of the squadron. "Twixt neighbouring strands' perhaps also alludes to the Canopian branch of the Nile, whence she takes her name.

3. The Repulse was the next ship, the second in the line of sailing.

4. An officer from the Standard, with some other ships' boats, took the Capitan Pasha's flag.

5. The Pompée, with the Thunderer and the Standard, ran in and anchored in the midst of the Turkish squadron.

6. She also anchored.

7. The Active, in a manner worthy of her name, engaged, drove on shore, and burned a very large Turkish frigate. All the Turkish ships blew up, soon after being fired, with terrible explosions. A furnace for heating shot was also blown up.

8. The rest of the squadron, after passing the batteries, anchored below them whilst the above service was being performed.

9. She anchored, with the rest of the squadron, off Constantinople.

10. Their fears unfortunately proved vain—meaning the British squadron. The Royal George bore the admiral's flag, and had also the British ambassador on board.

11, 12. The Lucifer and Meteor were two bomb-ships. Orders had been given from the flag-ship to make every requisite preparation for bombarding and firing the town.

13. The Endymion was the medium of intercourse by flag of truce. She was anchored between the squadron and the city of Constantinople, just without gunshot of the Seven Towers.

14. Before any British act of hostility had been committed since forcing the passage of the Dardanelles, on the 26th of February, the Turks made prisoners a midshipman and four men, (the jolly-boat's crew of the Endymion,) who were purchasing stock on the Island of Prota. The melancholy consequences of our retaliation are known the loss of an officer—and several men killed, and many more wounded.

15. The day after our appearance off Constantinople, all the shops were shut up, and nobody thought of anything but arming against the common enemy. On the night of the 27th the malcontents burned down a large square of new buildings, intended to be occupied by the Janissaries; a token of disapprobation of the measures of government not uncommon, and very well understood.

16. The movements of the British squadron depended on the wind."

As we are now on classic ground, it is not foreign to our subject to state, that though geographers commonly assert the castles of the Dardanelles to be built on the ruins of the ancient Sestos and Abydos, yet they are evidently mistaken, for these towns are on the western entrance of that narrow strait where, on the Asiatic shore, there is a sort of rising ground, similar to a rampart, which has the appearance of the ruins of a castle. There is also a hillock on the European side; to the northward of which is a castle in ruins, called by the Turks "Allack," which is used as a habitation by a dervise, and may probably be a fragment of Sestos.

Following the coast for between three or four miles, there is a Cape, called by the Turks "Kepos Bornou," and by the Europeans, Cape Berbier, which is most likely the site of the ancient "Promontine Dardanium" of the ancients. There is there an artificial eminence, which is very likely to be the remains of the ancient little town of Dardanum; its name would now have been buried in oblivion, but for the peace which was there made between Mithridates and Sylla, generals of the Roman army.

To the northern side of Dardanum there is a valley which stretches itself towards the Levant, where probably was "Orphrynium," Hector's wood, which writers place near Dardanum, and the Lake Pteleus; for a sort of marsh is there observable.

Farther south are the high white mountains, which stretch in a northerly direction from the plains of Troy, and near the sea. It must have been on one of these hills that Rhaetium was situated, as it is said to have been built on a mountain.

For these remarks we are indebted to an intelligent traveller, Mr. M'Kenzie.

But to return to Sir Sidney Smith.

It would naturally be judged, that even in the command off the Sicilian coast, Sir Sidney Smith was not adequately placed by the Lords of the

Admiralty; indeed, Earl Grey acknowledges that the appointment was not given him as one commensurate with his professional skill and acknowledged general ability. In one of the Earl's letters it is stated that lie was nominated to that command "till a more active scene of exertion should present itself."

That Sir Sidney Smith had some great political or military views of his own, prior to his receiving the command in Sicily, is evident from the letter alluded to, in which Earl—then Mr. Grey—at that time the first lord of the Admiralty, observes, that he was "altogether ignorant of the nature of the service which Sir Sidney had stated had been agreed upon between him and Lord Nelson, there being no paper affording the least trace or explanation of it at the Admiralty. Upon the expediency of continuing this plan I cannot, at present, venture to express my opinion; in general, I must confess, that the ill success of the attempts that have already been made, has given me rather an unfavourable impression with respect to attacks of this nature, in which ships and men have always been exposed to great dangers, and sometimes lost to their country, without any advantage, hitherto, to compensate the sacrifice. A part of the service, too, is precluded by the unfortunate events of the war on the Continent, which have left no opportunity of acting, at present, against the French armies."

None but Sir Sidney Smith, and those whom he consulted, can now tell us the nature of the service contemplated; but, under the circumstances, Mr. Grey recommended Sir Sidney to submit his plans to Lord Collingwood, with whom would rest the decision as to the propriety of carrying them into effect. "I know all," said Mr. Grey, "that is expected from your general knowledge, activity, and resources; and I beg you to remain in the Mediterranean; and my wish will be to find you immediate employment in the Channel fleet: for that service we shall be greatly in want of officers of experience, and I am confident you will readily give your service where it is most desired. I have, therefore, written to Lord Collingwood, to tell him that you will be wanted for the Channel service, and have desired his lordship, accordingly, to send home the Pompée, conceiving that you will probably be desirous to retain the same ship in which your flag is at present hoisted. I have, consequently, to hope very soon to have the pleasure of seeing you here, upon your return to the Mediterranean, before you proceed to join the Channel fleet."

This letter was forwarded in one from Lord Collingwood, dated February 26th, in which his lordship says, "I have enclosed the orders for that purpose to Sir Thomas Louis, as I conclude Sir John Duckworth will have left you before this can arrive. I have, at present, great anxiety to know what part the Turks have taken. If hostilities had been necessary, your local knowledge would have been highly beneficial in the service to be performed."

This eagerness for giving our officer a more extended sphere of service, and to place him in that spot where most difficulties abounded, is highly flattering to his reputation. At the time these transactions with the Turks were taking place, it was not known at home that Sir Sidney Smith had been called upon to take any part in them, for the first Lord of the Admiralty who succeeded Mr. Grey, thus writes to the rear-admiral, in a letter dated 2nd February, 1807.

"When I had the honour of being first called to the naval department, I understood that it was probable that Lord Collingwood would either himself have taken the command at Sicily, or that he would have sent Vice-Admiral Duckworth thither. Very soon, however, it appeared to be desirable that Vice-Admiral Duckworth should proceed to Constantinople, and it had been my intention to have proposed to you to have you there with him. More recent events have since changed those destinations, and with the very large army which is now in Sicily, it hardly can be necessary to keep, for that island, a rear-admiral's flag and four sail of the line, besides frigates. In concert, therefore, with the king's servants, I have recommended to Lord Collingwood no longer to appropriate to Sicily so extensive a naval force as that which is now under your flag, but to divide his attention and means between the defence of Sicily and the blockading of Toulon."

Sir Sidney Smith did not of course receive the first lord of the Admiralty's letter till after his arrival at Alexandria, to which place he proceeded with the squadron, after the repassing of the Dardanelles.

In consequence of this recall, Sir Sidney Smith, with the Pompée, arrived in England in June, 1807.

When thus returned to his own country, instead of being permitted to retain the Pompée, and being employed in the Channel, he saw that fine ship transferred to Vice-Admiral Stanhope, in order that she might proceed to the expedition against Copenhagen. This was, undoubtedly, the result of some political manoeuvre; but it was a proceeding not very flattering to Sir Sidney Smith, or grateful to the feelings of the captain and officers of the ship he had so lately commanded. Thus was our hero precluded from sharing in the dangers and the glory of the very questionable attack upon the Danes. In the ignominy of the design, those who so brilliantly executed the latter cannot be made to share in the former.

CHAPTER VI

THE SITUATION OF PORTUGAL AS REGARDED ENGLAND AND FRANCE •
THE PORTUGUESE COURT THROW THEMSELVES UNDER THE PROTEC-
TION OF THE BRITISH FLEET • THE PORTUGUESE FLEET JOIN SIR SID-
NEY SMITH'S SQUADRON IN THE FIRST INSTANCE, AND FINALLY SAIL
FOR THE BRAZILS WITH THE PRINCE REGENT • THE OFFICIAL DES-
PATCHES.

REAR-ADMIRAL Sir William Sidney Smith, as we mentioned in the last chapter, returned to England, where he arrived in the month of June.

There was but a short respite for repose left to Sir Sidney before he was again employed in active service. During this period of inaction as a public character, how he was employed, as it was peculiarly of a private nature, we do not deem it necessary to record. It is only sufficient for us to state that his popularity went before him as a herald, ushering him with the greeting of welcome into all ranks of society, among which he soon became as much noticed for his amiable manners and great powers of conversation, as he was admired for the conspicuous and glorious part that he had played on the theatre of the world.

On the 27th of October, 1807, he was appointed commander-in-chief of a squadron destined for particular service, the nature of which was not long in transpiring. The coast of Portugal was his destination, and his squadron was soon after put into requisition, to expedite a very important, but, owing to the agitated state of the world, no longer an isolated act, among the rulers of the earth. We have lately lived in times, in which dynasties of the greatest antiquity have been overthrown, kingdoms and principalities made and unmade, with as little remorse as the enactment and the repeal of a turnpike-bill—indeed, the standing rule seems to have been that of eternal change. Whether the mutation shall be for the good or evil of mankind in the aggregate, posterity only will be able to tell. The advantage *may* be theirs—the certain misery is ours.

After the peace of Tilsit, Buonaparte, with ambitious insatiability, and an unrelenting animosity towards England, turned his eyes towards the small, but ancient and respectable, kingdom of Portugal, and commenced with the arbitrariness too often attendant upon intoxicating success, to demand, firstly, that the Prince Regent should shut up all the Portuguese ports against England; secondly, that he should detain all Englishmen as prisoners who were then residing in his dominions; and, lastly, that he should immediately confiscate all British property upon which he could lay his hand. The alternative of a concession to these arrogant and unjust proposals was an immediate war; and, to prove how serious he was in his determination to have all his demands complied with, Buonaparte commenced by giving orders that all Portuguese merchant vessels should be detained that were then in any port under the domination of France.

The Prince Regent, knowing his inability to contend with so powerful an opponent, or to resist an aggression so wanton and insulting, attempted to temporise, in hopes, ultimately, to escape the storm that was gathering for his destruction. He, therefore, acceded to shutting up his ports against England, but hesitated to comply with the two other requisitions, as being contrary to the principles of public law, and in direct violation of the treaties then subsisting between the two nations.

These measures, however, were too doubtful to place any reliance of safety upon them, and the Portuguese court began to make active preparations for the evacuation of their European dominions, and to secure to itself a last and a safe retreat to its South American possessions.

In furtherance of these views, the Prince Regent ordered all vessels of war that were in order sufficiently good to keep the sea, immediately to be fitted out, at the same time warning all the English in Portugal to make as quick a sale of their property as circumstances would admit of, and then immediately to quit his dominions, in order, should the worst ensue, to save them from the miseries of a long captivity, or, very probably, from a great effusion of blood.

Whilst he was thus providing for the safety and welfare of allies that he dared not own, yet wished to cherish, he resolved, if possible, to conciliate the Emperor of the French, and to obey his mandate, deeming it riot to be impossible to soften him down so that he might a little moderate his pretensions. But all these attempts proved fruitless, for Buonaparte peremptorily insisted not only on the shutting up of the ports, but also on the imprisonment of British subjects wherever they could be found, the total confiscation of their property, and an immediate abandonment of the project of the royal family to remove themselves to America.

Seeing himself thus at the mercy of one who knew not how to be merciful to any who thwarted his vast projects, and firmly believing that all the English had not only sold their property, but removed the proceeds of it, and themselves from the kingdom, the Prince Regent at last determined to comply unlimitedly with the demands of France, at the same time making a solemn declaration that the moment the French troops should enter the confines of Portugal, that moment he would remove the seat of government to Brazil, which he considered to be beyond the reach of the grasping ambition of his oppressor.

But the harassed Prince Regent was soon made to feel that there were other parties who were to be conciliated besides the French, and that the toleration of the English court had its bounds. It had been frequently urged on the cabinet of Lisbon, by the English minister, Lord Strangford, that the King of Great Britain, in agreeing not to resent the exclusion of 'British commerce from the ports of Portugal, had gone to the utmost extent of political forbearance, that, in making this concession to the peculiar circumstances of the Prince Regent's situation, his Majesty had done all that friendship could justly require; and that a single step beyond this modified hostility on the part of the Prince, must necessarily lead, on the part of the King, to the extremity of actual war. Notwithstanding this English declaration, the Regent, in the fond hope of conciliating France, on the 8th of November signed an order for detaining the few British subjects, and the very inconsiderable portion of British property, that then remained in Lisbon.

On the promulgating of this order, Lord Strangford immediately removed the arms of England from the gates of his residence, sent in a final remonstrance, demanded his passports, and then proceeded, on the 17th of November, on board the British squadron commanded by our hero, who, at his lordship's suggestion, established a most rigorous blockade at the mouth of the Tagus.

In this predicament, the Prince Regent now found himself placed between two enemies—he had to make his choice on which to throw himself for protection; he, therefore, very wisely renewed his intercourse with Lord Strangford, who, on the 27th, after receiving assurances of protection and security, again proceeded to Lisbon. It is a point of dispute, which perhaps will never be satisfactorily settled, whether our minister did or did not recommend the next step that the Prince Regent was induced to take.

The English government, of that time, was most willing to have all the credit of suggesting the measure, though to that credit they never openly made claim. Be this as it may, the Prince Regent had to decide immediately between the tender mercies of a French army, and the protection and liberality of the English squadron commanded by Sir Sidney Smith. No time was to be lost, for already had the Emperor's troops entered Portugal.

His decision in favour of the English was strengthened by Buonaparte having published, in his official journals, that "the house of Braganza had ceased to reign." He was the more confirmed in this, as Lord Strangford promised his royal highness, on the faith of his sovereign, that the British squadron before the Tagus, or a sufficiently strong portion of it, commanded by Sir Sidney Smith, should be employed to protect his retreat from Lisbon, and insure the safety of his voyage to the Brazils. Reassured by this, on the 28th of November he published a decree, by which he announced his intention of retiring to the city of Rio de Janiero until the conclusion of a general peace, and of appointing a regency for the administration of the government at Lisbon during his absence from Europe.

On the morning of the 29th, the Portuguese fleet sailed from the Tagus, with the Prince of Brazil and the royal family of Braganza on board, accompanied by many of his faithful councillors and adherents, as well as by other persons attached to his present fortunes. This fleet consisted of eight sail of the line, four large frigates, several corvettes, brigs, and ships of war, besides twenty-five sail of merchantmen, forming in all a fleet of thirty-six sail. Whilst they passed through the British squadron, our ships fired each a salute of twenty-one guns, which was returned by an equal number.

The following is a description of the scene by a spectator.

"At seven, on this remarkable day, it was a beautiful morning: a fine breeze blew from the eastward, which wafted the Portuguese ships directly out of the Tagus. Signal was made for two sail, which shortly afterwards was repeated for three ships of the line, and we saw Portuguese colours. At nine, the signal was repeated for six sail, at ten for nine; arid a telegraph from the Confiance announced, that the royal standard was flying on board one of the ships. Signals were repeated for several ships of a smaller class, which were composed of brigs, schooners, and merchant ships, together with the Lisbon packet.

"We had now the heartfelt satisfaction to see that our hopes and expectations were realised to the fullest extent; the whole Portuguese fleet arranged itself under the protection of that of his Majesty, whilst firing a reciprocal salute of twenty-one guns, which announced the friendly meeting of those powers, who were but one day before on terms of hostility.

"To any heart but a Buonapartist's, the scene was sublimely beautiful; impressing every beholder, except the French army on the hills, with the most lively emotions of gratitude to Providence, that there yet existed a power in the world capable, as well as willing, to protect the oppressed. A more interesting spectacle than that afforded by the junction of the two fleets, has been rarely beheld.

"Lord Strangford, who had hitherto accompanied the Prince, now repaired to the Admiral on board the Hibernia, but returned immediately, accompanied by him, whom he presented to the Prince, and was received with the most marked and gracious condescension. His royal highness expressed every sentiment, that the most cordial feelings of gratitude to, and confidence in, his Majesty and the British nation, could be supposed to dictate. He informed the Admiral, that himself, his family, and fleet, came out to place themselves under the protection of his Britannic Majesty's ships, and that his intention was to proceed to Rio de Janeiro; trusting that part of the squadron would be allowed to convey him to the place of his destination.

"Sir Sidney answered his royal highness in the name of his king, that every assistance should be given; that the British nation were his *real friends*, and that the whole kingdom would have been distressed, had the French seized on his royal highness's person.

"The Portuguese men of war presented a wretched appearance, as they had only three days to prepare for their escape; scaffolds were still hanging by their sides, and in short, they rather resembled wrecks than vessels of war. Signal was now made from the commander-in-chief's ship, for the marines of the London to repair on board his Majesty's frigate Solebay."

The junction of the two so lately hostile fleets, under the peculiar circumstances, was imposing, and calculated to call up deep reflections, and some very painful as well as some gratulatory feelings. To those who contemplated the act only, this self-expatriation had all the appearance of a sublime sacrifice at the altar of patriotism. Of the motives we much doubt. We will not examine too closely into the matter in this place. England did her duty, and we shall not here argue whether the royal house of Braganza did theirs to a nation that had so long respected and cherished it.

The British admiral ordered four English ships of the line to form an escort for this royal cortege, with orders to the commanding officer to see them in safety to Brazil. We are inclined to think this precaution needless, for we very much doubt whether a superior French force would have meddled with them at all.

Lord Strangford accompanied the Portuguese royal family a part of the way to their new destination, as appears by the following letters, sent by the secretary of state and first lord of the admiralty to the lord mayor.

Foreign Office, half-past two P.M.
Dec. 19, 1807

My Lord, I have the honour to acquaint your lordship that Lord Strangford, his Majesty's minister plenipotentiary to the court of Lisbon, has just arrived, having left the Portuguese fleet on the 5th instant, between Madeira and the Western Islands, under convoy of a British squadron, steering for the Brazils.

I have the honour to be, &c.

GEORGE CANNING.

The other letter, from the Admiralty, is of the same date.

My Lord, I have great satisfaction in acquainting your lordship that Captain Yeo, of his Majesty's sloop Confiance, arrived this afternoon at this office, with despatches from Rear-Admiral Sir Sidney Smith, dated December 6th, stating that the Prince Regent, with the whole of the royal family, consisting of fifteen persons, had embarked for the Brazils on the 24th ult., with seven sail of the line, four frigates, three armed brigs, and upwards of thirty Brazilian merchant vessels.

The Portuguese fleet is attended by his Majesty's ships Marlborough, London, Monarch, and Bedford, under the command of Captain Moore.

Only one serviceable line-of-battle ship and three hulks remained in the Tagus. Eight Russian line-of-battle ships remained in the Tagus, only three of which were in condition for sea.

Rear-Admiral Sir Sidney Smith has resumed the blockade of the port of Lisbon with five sail of the line, and will probably, by this time, have been joined by an additional line-of-battle ship.

I have the honour to be, &c.

MULGRAVE.

J. Ansley, Mayor

The following are the official despatches concerning these transactions:

A Despatch this day received from Lord Viscount Sir Stangford, his Majesty Minister Plenipotentiary at the Court of Lisbon, by the Right Honourable George Canning, his Majesty's Principal Secretary of State for Foreign Affairs.

His Majesty's Ship Hibernia, off the Tagus
November 29, 1807

Sir, I have the honour of announcing to you, that the Prince Regent of Portugal has effected the wise and magnanimous purpose of retiring from a kingdom which he could no longer retain, except as the vassal of France; and that his royal highness and family, accompanied by most of his ships of war, and by a multitude of his faithful subjects and adherents, have this day departed from Lisbon, and are now on their way to the Brazils, under the escort of a British fleet.

This grand and memorable event is not to be attributed only to the sudden alarm excited by the appearance of a French army within the frontiers of Portugal: it has been the genuine result of the system of persevering confidence and moderation adopted by his Majesty towards that country; for the ultimate success of which I had, in a manner, rendered myself responsible; and which, in obedience to your instructions, I had uniformly continued to support, even under appearances of the most discouraging nature.

I had frequently and distinctly stated to the cabinet of Lisbon, that in agreeing not to resent the exclusion of British commerce from the ports of Portugal, his Majesty had exhausted the means of forbearance; that in making that concession to the peculiar circumstances of the Prince Regent's situation, his Majesty had done all that friendship and the remembrance of ancient alliance could justly require; but that a single step beyond the line of modified hostility, thus most reluctantly consented to, must necessarily lead to the extremity of actual war.

The Prince Regent, however, suffered himself for a moment to forget that, in the present state of Europe, no country could be permitted to be an enemy to England with impunity, arid that however much his Majesty might be disposed to make allowance for the deficiency of the means possessed by Portugal of resistance to the power of France, neither his own dignity, nor the interests of his people, would permit his Majesty to accept that excuse for a compliance with the full extent of her unprincipled demands. On the 8th instant, his royal highness was induced to sign an order for the detention of the few British subjects, and of the inconsiderable portion of British property, which yet remained at Lisbon. On the publication of this order, I caused the arms of England to be removed from the gates of my residence, demanded my passports, presented a final remonstrance against the recent conduct of the court of Lisbon, and proceeded to the squadron commanded by Sir Sidney Smith, which arrived off the coast of Portugal some days after I had received my passports; and which I joined on the 17th instant.

I immediately suggested to Sir Sidney Smith the expediency of establishing the most rigorous blockade at the mouth of the Tagus; and I had the high satisfaction of afterwards finding, that I had thus anticipated the intentions of his Majesty; your despatches (which I received by the messenger Sylvester on the 23rd) directing me to authorise that measure, in case the Portuguese government should pass the bounds which his Majesty had thought fit to set to his forbearance, and attempt to take any farther step injurious to the honour or interests of Great Britain.

Those despatches were drawn up under the idea that I was still resident at Lisbon; and though I did not receive them until I had actually taken my departure from that court, still, upon a careful consideration of the tenor of your instructions, I 'thought that it would be right to act as if that case had not occurred. I resolved, therefore, to proceed forthwith to ascertain the effect produced by the blockade of Lisbon, and to propose to the Portuguese government, as the only condition upon which that blockade could cease, the alternative (stated by you) either of surrendering the fleet to his Majesty, or of immediately employing it to remove the Prince Regent arid his family to the Brazils. I took upon myself this responsibility in renewing negotiations after my public functions had actually ceased; convinced that although it was the fixed determination of his Majesty not to suffer the fleet of Portugal to fall into the possession of his enemies, still his Majesty's first object continued to be the application of that fleet to the original purpose of saving the royal family of Braganza from the tyranny of France.

I accordingly requested an audience of the Prince Regent, together with due assurances of protection and security; and upon receiving his royal highness's answer, I proceeded to Lisbon, on the 27th, in his Majesty's ship Confiance, bearing a flag of truce. I had immediately most interesting communications with the court of Lisbon, the particulars of which shall be more fully detailed in a future despatch. It suffices to mention in this place, that the Prince Regent wisely directed all his apprehensions to a French army, and all his hopes to an English fleet; that he received the most explicit assurances from me that his Majesty would generously overlook those acts of unwilling and momentary hostility to which his royal highness's consent had been extorted; and that I promised to his royal highness, on the faith of my sovereign, that the British squadron before the Tagus should be employed to protect his retreat from Lisbon, and his voyage to the Brazils.

A decree was published yesterday, in which the Prince Regent announced his intention of retiring to the city of Rio Janeiro until the conclusion of a general peace, and of appointing a regency to transact the administration of government at Lisbon, during his royal highness's absence from Europe.

This morning the Portuguese fleet left the Tagus. I had the honour to accompany the Prince in his passage over the Bar. The fleet consisted of eight sail of the line, four large frigates, several armed brigs, sloops, and corvettes, and a number of Brazil ships, amounting, I believe, to about thirty-six sail in all. They passed through the British squadron, and his Majesty's ships fired a salute of twenty-one guns, which was returned with an equal number. A more interesting spectacle than that afforded by the junction of the two fleets has been rarely beheld.

On quitting the Prince Regent's ship, I repaired on board the Hibernia, but returned immediately, accompanied by Sir Sidney Smith, whom I presented to the Prince, and who was received by his royal highness with the most marked attention.

I have the honour to enclose lists of the ships of war which were known to have left Lisbon this morning, and which were in sight a few hours ago. There remain at Lisbon four ships of the line, and the same number of frigates, but only one of each sort is serviceable.

I have thought it expedient to lose no time in communicating to his Majesty's government the important intelligence contained in this despatch. I have therefore to apologise for the hasty and imperfect manner in which it is written.

I have the honour to be, &c.
STRANGFORD

Despatches, of which the following are Extracts and Copies,
were received at the Admiralty Office, on Saturday, Dec. 21,
by Captain Yeo of his Majesty's sloop the Confiance, from
Rear-Admiral Sir William Sidney Smith, addressed to the
Hon William Wellesley Pole.

His Majesty's Ship Hibernia, 22 leagues
west of the Tagus, Dec. 1, 1807

Sir, In a former despatch, dated the 22nd November, with a postscript of the 26th, I conveyed to you, for the information of my lords commissioners of the Admiralty, the proofs contained in various documents of the Portuguese government being so much influenced by terror of the French arms, as to have acquiesced to certain demands of France operating against Great Britain. The distribution of the Portuguese force was made wholly on the coast, while the land-side was left totally unguarded. British subjects of all descriptions were detained; and it therefore became necessary to inform the Portuguese government, that the case had arisen which required, in obedience to my instructions, that I should declare the Tagus in a state of blockade; and Lord Strangford agreeing with me that hostility should be met by hostility, the blockade was instituted, and the instructions we had received were acted upon to their full extent. Still, however, bearing in recollection the first object adopted by his Majesty's government, of opening a refuge for the head of the Portuguese government, menaced as it was by the powerful arms and baneful influence of the enemy, I thought it my duty to adopt the means open to us, of endeavouring to induce the Prince Regent of Portugal to re-consider his decision 'to unite himself with the continent of Europe' and to recollect that he had possessions on that of America, affording an ample balance for any sacrifice he might make here, and from which he would be cut off by the nature of the maritime warfare, the termination of which could not be dictated by the combination of the continental powers of Europe.

In this view Lord Strangford having received an acquiescence to the proposition which had been made by us, for his lordship to land and confer with the Prince Regent under the guarantee of the flag of truce, I furnished his lordship with that conveyance and security, in order that he might give to the Prince that confidence which his word of honour as the King's minister plenipotentiary, united with that of a British admiral, could not fail to inspire towards inducing his royal highness to throw himself and his fleet into the arms of Great Britain, in perfect reliance on the King's overlooking a forced act of apparent hostility against his flag and subjects, and establishing his royal highness's government in his ultra-marine possessions, as originally promised. I have now the heartfelt satisfaction of announcing to you, that our hopes and expectations have been realised to the utmost extent. On the morning of the 29th, the Portuguese fleet (as per list annexed) came out of the Tagus with his royal highness the Prince of Brazil and the whole of the royal family of Braganza on board, together with many of his faithful counsellors and adherents, as well as other persons attached to his present fortunes.

This fleet of eight sail of the line, four frigates, two brigs, and one schooner, with a crowd of large armed merchant-ships, arranged itself under the protection of that of his Majesty, while the firing of a reciprocal salute of twenty-one guns announced the friendly meeting of those who but the day before were on terms of hostility; the scene impressing every beholder (except the French army on the hills) with the most lively emotions of gratitude to Providence, that there yet existed a power in the world able, as well as willing, to protect the oppressed.

I have the honour to be, &c.
W. S. SMITH

Eight ships of the line, four frigates, three brigs, and one armed schooner, came out of the Tagus with the royal family.

His Majesty's ship Hibernia, twenty-two leagues
west of the Tagus, Dec. 1, 1807.

Sir, In another despatch of this day's date, I have transmitted a list of the Portuguese fleet that came out of the Tagus on the 29th ultimo, which I received that day from the admiral commanding it, when I went on board the Principe Reale to pay my visit of respect and congratulation to his royal highness the Prince of Brazil, who was embarked in that ship. I here enclose the list of those left behind. The absence of but one of the four ships is regretted by the Portuguese, (the Vasco de Gama,) she being under repair; her guns having been employed to arm the Freitas, sixty-four, a new ship, and one of those which came out with the Prince. The other three were mere hulks; and there is also one ship on the stocks, the Principe Regent, but she is only in frame.

The Prince said everything that the most cordial feelings of gratitude towards, and confidence in, his Majesty and the British nation, might be supposed to dictate.

I have by signal (for we have no other mode of communicating in this weather) directed Captain Moore in the Marlborough, with the London, Monarch, and Bedford, to stay by the body of the Portuguese fleet, and render it every assistance.

I keep in the Hibernia close to the Prince's ship. I cannot as yet send the Foudroyant, Plantagenet, and Conqueror on to Admiral Purvis, according to their lordships' order of the 14th, which, I trust, will be the less felt as an inconvenience off Cadiz, as they appear to have been ordered thither with reference to the Russians being within the Straits, before it was known they were on my station.

I have the honour to be, &c.
W. SIDNEY SMITH

There remained at Lisbon four sail of the line and five frigates, all out of repair, and some of them quite past service.

Hibernia, at sea, lat. 37. 47. ; long. 14. 17.
Dec. 6, 1807.

Sir, I have the satisfaction to acquaint you, for the information of my lords commissioners of the Admiralty, that I succeeded in collecting the whole of the Portuguese fleet, except a brig, after the gale, and that the weather was such as to allow the necessary repairs, and such distribution of supernumeraries and resources to be made, as to enable Vice-Admiral Don Manuel d'Acunha, sotto-mayor, to report to me yesterday all the ships capable of performing the voyage to Rio Janeiro, except one line-of-battle ship, which he requested might be conducted to an English port. I meant to escort her part of the way, but she did not quit the fleet with me last night as settled. I hope, however, she may arrive safe, as she is not in a bad state, being substituted for the Martino de Freitas, which was at first destined to go to England, in consequence of a fresh arrangement made yesterday, on the latter being found in the best state for the voyage of the two. I have detached Captain Moore in the Marlborough, with the London, Monarch, and Bedford, to attend the Portuguese fleet to the Brazils. I have thought it my duty, in addition to the usual order to take the above ships under his orders, to give Captain Moore one to hoist a broad pendant after passing Madeira, in order to give him greater weight and consequence in the performance of the important and unusually delicate duties I have confided to him. I feel the most perfect reliance in that officer's judgment, ability, and zeal.

The Portuguese ships did not, after their reparation, want more provisions or slops from us than the list enclosed, which I supplied from this ship and the Conqueror.

This despatch will be delivered by Captain Yeo of his Majesty's sloop Confiance, who has shown great address and zeal in opening the communications by flag of truce, which it was the interest of those in power; who were against the measure of emigration, to obstruct. Lord Strangford speaks of his conduct in terms of warm approbation; on this ground I beg leave to recommend him to their lordships, to whom his general merits as an officer are already well known. Having been in Lisbon without restraint during the intercourse, he is qualified to answer any questions their lordships may wish to put to him.

I have the honour to be, &c.
W. SIDNEY SMITH

We must remark, in this place, that glorious to our arms and gainful to our interests as this step of the Portuguese court seemed to be, it was precisely the very step that Buonaparte wished us to take. Nothing could have more completely forwarded his interests, or been more inimical to our own.

Much, very much, of turgid eloquence has been displayed, and many the attempts made upon our feelings to excite sentiments of admiration in our bosoms at the sublime and solemn spectacle of the Prince and most of the magnates of the land nobly expatriating themselves, rather than see the land of their fathers overrun by the invader and the oppressor. If the land had been so dear to them, the fugitives should have staid and consecrated their attachment to it by the enriching the soil with their blood. As they did not act heroically, they had no right to claim the reputation of heroes. They thought only of themselves, and sought only their personal safety in flight.

Had they staid and borne the brunt of Buonaparte's hostility, the event would have been doubtful, but their own honour secure. By flying, Portugal, for a time, became a province of France, and the South American colonies did *not* fall into the possession of England. That they would do so, was Bonaparte's greatest fear. The Portuguese dynasty was preserved, and England lost a most favourable opportunity of turning the channels of South American commerce towards our own shores exclusively. They must have fallen under our protection, had not the Portuguese family gone to them and encumbered them with an European court, and disgusted them by European prejudices.

That our minister acted most skilfully, no one who has marked the course of these events can, for a moment, doubt. The ends that a minister must seek in a foreign court to obtain are definite; he has but to work them out, whilst the initiative of all such important movements must proceed from those who direct the foreign policy at home.

We think that the family of Braganza should have staid in their capital until the very last moment, and then have retreated no farther than the friendly fleet that lay off it. The Peninsular war, so skilfully conducted, and so gloriously concluded, by the Duke of Wellington, might then have begun most auspiciously, and what was afterwards effected by sacrifices so great of blood and treasure, have been purchased with infinitely less loss, and the honour, the heroism, and the patriotism of the Regent of Portugal remained untarnished.

Had he staid by his subjects, who afterwards proved how capable they were of staying, to the death, by their country, how many factions would have never seen the light, how much French interest would have been prevented from distracting and dividing the people; and with what energy would all the nation, in its integrity tinder their legitimate prince, have acted with their too generous allies, the English!

The retreat of the Braganza family did not prevent their country from being made the battlefield of nations, nor avert from it all the attendant miseries of foreign armies struggling upon the soil, and making waste the face of the country; but their remaining would, in all human probability, have made the war of much less duration, and the struggle less fatal to that unhappy and demoralized kingdom.

From the expelled, let us return to the authors of the expulsion. The Portuguese fleet had not fairly left the Tagus, when the French, with their Spanish auxiliaries, appeared on the hills above Lisbon, under the command of General Junot. Though the Portuguese had long been under the apprehension of a visit, they were surprised by their sudden arrival. The entrance of the French troops into Portugal was not known in Lisbon till their advanced guard had reached Abrantes. The greatest professions of friendship were made on the part of the French army for the people of Portugal. In defiance of all this, their country was treated as a conquered one; severe laws and heavy contributions were imposed upon high and low, and the French system as to subdued countries put inexorably into force.

It was on the occasion of this invasion that the Marquis of Alorna returned the following laconic answer to the invading enemy, the commander of which asked for safe passage and supplies, wishing at the same time to know if he and his troops would be received as friends or enemies. "We are unable to entertain you as friends, or to resist you as enemies."

Sir Sidney Smith continued to blockade the coast, and, as usual with his enterprising mind, to cause great annoyance and vexation to the enemy, until the 15th of January, 1808, on which day he was superseded in his command of the squadron by Sir Charles Cotton.

While off Lisbon, Sir Sidney Smith was appointed, by the following document, to the chief command on the South American station.

To Sir William Sidney Smith, Knight, Rear-Admiral of the Blue, hereby appointed Commander-in-Chief of a squadron of his Majesty's ships and vessels, to be employed on a particular service.

Whereas we have thought fit to appoint you commander in-chief of a squadron of his Majesty's ships and vessels to be employed on a particular service; these are to will and enjoin you forthwith to take upon you the charge and command of the said ships and vessels as Commander-in-chief; accordingly, hereby charging all captains, commanding officers, and companies, belonging to his Majesty's said ships and vessels, to be obedient to you, their commander-in-chief; arid you, likewise, to follow such orders and directions as you shall, from time to time, receive from us, or from any other your superior officer, for his Majesty's service. For which this shall be your warrant. Given under our hands, and the seal of the office of Admiralty, 27th October, 1807, in the forty-eighth year of his Majesty's reign.

MULGRAVE.
R. BICKERTON.
WM. JOHNSTONE HOPE.
By command of their lordships,
W. W. POLE

On the 24th of the same month, Sir Sidney had the satisfaction of receiving despatches from the Admiralty, conveying their lordships' high approbation of his whole conduct in the management of the important and delicate service committed to his charge, and on the punctual and successful execution of the various orders which he had received from time to time.

The light in which Sir Sidney Smith's services was viewed at home, in this momentous affair, is sufficiently evident from the subjoined copy of a letter from Mr. Secretary Pole.

Admiralty Office, Dec. 28, 1807

Sir, I lost no time in laying your despatches, brought by Captain Yeo, of H.M.S. Confiance, and by the Trafalgar letter of marque, before my lords commissioners of the Admiralty; and I am commanded by their lordships to express their high approbation of your judicious and able conduct in the management of the service entrusted to your charge, and in the execution of the various orders you have received from time to time.

Their lordships are strongly impressed with the propriety of the whole of your conduct towards the royal family of Portugal; the respectful attention which you appear to have shown to the illustrious house of Braganza has been in strict conformity to their lordships' wishes, and they have desired me to express their complete satisfaction at the manner in which you have, in this as well as in every other respect, obeyed their instructions.

My lords are pleased to approve of your having supplied the necessary succours to the Portuguese fleet from his Majesty's ships; and I am commanded to acquaint you, that, under the peculiar circumstances of the case, their lordships are satisfied of the necessity of your resuming, in person, the strict blockade of the Tagus, and they approve of your having detached from your squadron four sail of the line, under the command of Captain Moore, to escort the royal family of Portugal to Rio Janeiro.

My lords concur in the propriety of your directing the officer in command of the squadron destined for this important service, to hoist a broad pendant after he had passed Madeira, and they approve of the instructions to Captain Moore, and of the selection you have made of that distinguished and judicious officer.

I have the honour to be, &c.

W. W. POLE

Rear-Admiral Sir Sidney Smith

CHAPTER VII

SIR CHARLES COTTON arrived off Lisbon on the 15th of January, and superseding Sir Sidney Smith in his command, hoisted his flag in the Hibernia. Sir Sidney was thus obliged to shift his flag, and as Sir Charles Cotton vacated the Minotaur, Sir Sidney chose that ship in preference to turning the captain out of any other; not then knowing what kind of vessel the Minotaur was. However, he was not long in the dark as to her qualities, for two days after he had joined her, a gale of wind coming on, in the early part of the night, she lost her maintopmast, and great confusion prevailed on board. The gale lasted two days, the ship making a great deal of water, and on the third day, the fleet being all separated, the Minotaur fell in with the Foudroyant, on board of which ship Sir Sidney Smith thought proper to shift his flag; in which change Sir Charles Cotton afterwards acquiesced, the Minotaur really not being fit for service.

When in this ship, the officers were a long while in expectation of being ordered somewhere, but whither was a matter of the wildest conjecture, the various reports being so contradictory. At length, orders arrived from England for Sir Sidney Smith to proceed to the Brazils, with liberty for him to choose any ship for his flag excepting the Foudroyant. Sir Charles Cotton recommended to him the Hercule, an old French prize, fitted out merely for the Copenhagen expedition, and the want of a poop rendered her particularly inconvenient for an admiral.

This ship our hero accepted, but requested that she might previously be surveyed before she proceeded to her destination across the Atlantic. This was done, and she was reported absolutely unfit for sea, and in proof of which a fragment of her timbers was exhibited, almost in a state as pulverised as snuff. This arrangement was thus, of course, broken off. It was then attempted to place Sir Sidney in the Agamemnon, an old sixty-four; and as there was no other ship in the squadron fit for a flag, except the Conqueror, he applied for her, but as she was a very desirable ship, and commanded by the captain of the fleet's brother-in-law, every persuasion was used to make him take another. Added to this, she was then away for water, and it was studiously asserted that she would not be back for three months; but, on the very day that Sir Sidney had come to the resolution to go in any ship rather than lose time to the detriment of the service, the Conqueror joined company.

Private interest was then called into operation, and, rather than displace the then captain of the Conqueror, it was determined upon to infringe the Admiralty orders. The result of this was, that Sir Sidney Smith, in the Foudroyant, accompanied by the Agamemnon, arrived at Gibraltar on the 20th of February, and there refitted for his American voyage, having taken in a new foremast, and caulked the ship throughout. Sir Sidney sailed from Gibraltar on the 13th of March.

The truth of all this vacillation will be borne out by the following official documents. The first is from Sir Sidney Smith to Sir Charles Cotton, and runs thus:

Minotaur, at Sea, Jan. 24, 1808

Sir, Having fallen in with the Confiance this morning, and finding Captain Yeo charged with a letter on his Majesty's service, addressed to you or to me, and learning from its contents that the Rochefort squadron is at sea, I lose no time in forwarding it to you, together with another from Sir John Duckworth, addressed to Vice-Admiral Lord Collingwood, which, being put into my hands by Captain Yeo, at the same time, I merely opened, under the idea that it was similarly addressed. I send it you in its present state, in order that you may inform yourself of its contents, if you think proper; but I have not presumed to proceed farther, considering your vicinity.

The Minotaur having suffered in the gale, and being by no means an efficient ship in any respect, I meant, at any rate, to have requested your permission to shift my flag on board the Foudroyant; but, under the circumstances of the enemy being at sea, and the Russian fleet being supposed to be in readiness, and with the intention to come out, I think the honour of the flag requires that I should immediately do so, in order that I may be able to give you that support on this service, which it is as much my wish as it is my duty to do. Under the hope that you will please to approve of this step, it is my request, further, that you will please to consider this as a permanent arrangement, as, under the present circumstances, as, indeed, under any, until the Minotaur has been put into repair, and in an efficient state, she is the last ship in the squadron on board which I should choose to have my flag.

I have the honour to be, Sir,

Your most obedient, "humble Servant,
W. SIDNEY SMITH.
To Vice-Admiral Sir Charles Cotton, Bart.

To which Sir Sidney received the following answer:

Hibernia, off the Tagus, 15th Feb. 1808

Sir, I am to acquaint you that the lords commissioners of the Admiralty have, by Mr. Secretary Pole's letter of 25th ult., directed me to put any two line-of-battle ships under my orders, with the exception of the Foudroyant and the Confiance, under your command, in order to augment the squadron of his Majesty's ships which have been detached to accompany the Prince Regent, and of which you are to take upon yourself the chief command; and, in consequence thereof, I propose, as soon as the Elizabeth, Plantagenet, and Conqueror, join the squadron, to recommend your hoisting your flag on board her Majesty's ship Hercule, then with the Agamemnon and Confiance, to proceed to Brazil in execution of the service for which I presume you have received your orders.

"I further intend, from the very low state of the water in the squadron, to take as much from the Hercule as can possibly be spared, aware that you must touch at some place to complete, in your passage to Brazil.

I have the honour to be, &c.

CHARLES COTTON

Sir Sidney, on the same day, stating his objections to the above arrangement, forwarded to Sir Charles the following letter.

(Secret.)

H.M.S. Fondroyant, 15th Feb. 1808

Sir, In obedience to orders from my lords commissioners of the Admiralty, dated 25th ult., of which I enclose a copy for your information, I am to proceed to Rio Janeiro as commander-in-chief of the squadron stationed on the coast of Brazil, under the authority of their lordships' commission, bearing date the 27th of October last, in my possession, taking with me two ships of the line, which, I am informed by their lordships, you have been directed to place under my orders, to the end that the squadron, of which I was, and am again, appointed commander-in-chief, may amount to the number of six sail of the line stated by Mr. Canning, as originally assembled and placed under my command.

I have, therefore, to request you will be pleased to enable me to proceed, and signify when I may part company with you.

I beg leave to state to you, as I shall to the lords commissioners of the Admiralty, that I consider the honour of the British flag to require that it should be enabled to meet that of a French flag-officer in a ship of equal force; and, under the circumstances of a French squadron having passed these latitudes to the southward, which may possibly be bound to Brazil, the commanding officer of which was in a three-decker, I trust I may not be deemed unreasonable in expressing my earnest desire that I may be enabled, sooner or later, to meet him on equal terms; meanwhile, as long as I may be in a two-decked ship, I am quite satisfied with the rate and qualities of the Foudroyant, and feel confident, from what I have observed of the abilities and conduct of the officers arid men, that I shall be able to do my duty in her to the extent of her powers, as a good eighty gun ship.

I have to request you will bear in recollection, in making the arrangement which depends on you for the completion of the squadron under my orders, that Commodore Moore may possibly have withdrawn from the Brazil in the Marlborough, or have sent home some other ship, in pursuance to the authorisation to that effect contained in my order to him of the 5th of December; also, that the Solebay, at best a very inefficient ship, with a sprung foremast, and many men sent to England in prizes, will be soon on her way home; so that, of the three frigates destined, in my original order, to be under my command, with three smaller vessels, I shall not have one to cope with the frigates of the enemy, or to keep a proper look-out to cover a coast of thirty-three degrees of latitude, from the river Amazon to the southern limit, in the neutral ground between Brazil and the Spanish settlements; and farther, to keep a look-out on any armaments that may be equipped in the latter for the annoyance of our infant trade; for which purpose it will not be advisable to detach the line-of-battle ships, lest an enemy's force from Europe should suddenly make its appearance in those seas, which is to be expected, if it is not already therein.

I am satisfied with the Confiance as one of the smaller ships, and under her present commander she will, no doubt, act against a frigate to the utmost of her powers, but not to advantage. The Viper and Pitt will, I trust, now follow their destination.

W. S. S., &c.

The same day Sir Charles Cotton sent Sir Sidney the following answer:

Sir, I have the honour to acknowledge the receipt of your letter of this day's date, enclosing a copy of your order to proceed to Rio Janeiro, which, the moment the ships join that were mentioned to you in my letter of this morning, I shall feel as happy in enabling you to put in execution, as I shall to meet your wishes in any way the arrangement left in my power enables me to do; but the directions respecting the Foudroyant are positive and pointed, as you may observe by the two letters herewith transmitted for your perusal.

The Elizabeth and Conqueror, commanded by the two senior captains in the squadron, whom I cannot think of dispossessing of their commands, are absolutely essential, and but sufficient, to enable me to cope with the enemy, which you, as well as myself, know to be in the Tagus, and who, there is good reason to suppose, may shortly be on the move from thence. The Ruby's crew, being unfortunately affected by the smallpox, leaves only the Agamemnon to be spared, while the Hercule, (recently fitted foreign,) being next in point of quality to the two senior captains' ships, will, I trust, appear effective to convey your flag to Brazil, and where, I hope, agreeably to your desire, a three-decked ship may speedily follow for its reception.

With respect to the smaller vessels, you will observe, by the enclosure, the great want of such craft for this station. The Viper I always intended for you, if detached; and although no orders to that effect have been received by me, she shall accompany you.

The Pitt is most likely at Gibraltar, but about such vessel I have received no particular directions, nor was she under my orders, otherwise than as a transport of the convoy. You will therefore, in the event of proceeding to Gibraltar, and falling in with her, use your own discretion.

I have the honour to be, Sir

&c. &c.

The reader may gain some insight, by this correspondence, into the eagerness with which commanding officers are prone to keep all the force they can to themselves, and the heedlessness with which the authorities at home sometimes dispose of ships that are not disposable. Sir Sidney Smith tells Sir Charles Cotton that he fears to be met, in his transit across the Atlantic, by a superior force, and well beaten; and produces his orders to be supplied with a competent force to maintain the dignity of the flag; and, in reply, Sir Charles offers him the worst ships of his fleet, telling him, when he gets to Brazil, he trusts a competent force will be sent after him, (when the danger is over,) and he produces his orders also for the justification of his conduct.

On the 20th of February, Sir Sidney received the following letter from Sir Charles:

Sir, The Conqueror having yesterday, as you may perceive, lost an anchor and two cables, and being now far to leeward, the time she may again join the squadron quite uncertain, I cannot think (after the several urgent representations you have made to me, stating the great importance your speedy appearance in Brazil may be of to his Majesty's service and government) of longer detaining you; and as no other ship in this squadron appears so well, or indeed at all, calculated for a foreign voyage as the Foudroyant, you have my permission to part company in such ship, taking with you the Agamemnon, whose captain is ordered to put himself under your command, and proceed, agreeably to the orders you have received from the lords commissioners of the Admiralty.

> I have the honour to be, &c.
> CHARLES COTTON

Thus Sir Sidney gained one portion of the object for which he contended; but this success was saddled with the Agamemnon, a very incompetent sixty-four, and, from her force, hardly admissible into the line-of-battle. Sir Sidney thus speaks on the subject:

> *H.M.S. Foudroyant, off the Tagus,*
> *20th February, 1808*

"Sir, I have been much gratified by your decision, communicated to me by your letter of this day's date, giving me leave to part company in a ship so well calculated for foreign service as the Foudroyant, which I am persuaded will be more advantageous to the King's service than my going in a ship of less force at a later period, considering the new circumstances known to us here, and the necessity of my speedy arrival, after the delay that has taken place since the signification of the first arrangement.

> I have the honour to be, &c,
> W. SIDNEY SMITH

How very much Sir Sidney's wishes were disregarded at home, and how much he was bandied about, may be inferred from another private letter from Sir Charles Cotton, in which he tells Sir Sidney that he does not wonder at his preferring the Foudroyant to the Minotaur, as the latter ship "had certainly some good qualities, but she was hurried out of dock at Chatham without having justice done to her." Yet he hoped Sir Sidney would still take her, in the belief that it would have excited some zeal in the officers and crew to show themselves worthy of such a distinction. A pleasant reason, truly, which, if acted upon, should have induced Sir Sidney to embark himself in the most inferior and badly officered and manned ship in the navy.

Yet, with these gentle recommendations, he adds, in order the more pointedly to contrast the reality with the just expectation, that in his last conversation with Lord Gambier, his lordship had positively said, that "the Victory was Sir Sidney Smith's, and was to come out to him, with his own officers and men, from the Pompée."

We have seen how our hero was served with respect to his favourite ship and cherished crew.

It is most certain that Sir Charles Cotton was anxious to meet Sir Sidney's wishes, for in another private letter he tells him, "As to the Foudroyant, I wish it was in my power to indulge you, for which I have every disposition that friendship and the high estimation in which I hold you can dictate. If left to the original order I had respecting your flag-ship, there could not be a doubt; but the repetition of their lordships' order is too strong a push to parry."

We see, however, that the push was parried, and in the Foudroyant Sir Sidney went to the Brazils, "good-humouredly thanking his stars for a double escape from drowning in the rickety Minotaur, or the rotten Hercule."

CHAPTER VIII

SIR SIDNEY SMITH ARRIVES AT RIO JANEIRO • GIVES A GRAND ENTERTAINMENT TO THE ROYAL FAMILY OF PORTUGAL • THE SPEECHES AND PROCLAMATION.

ON the 13th of March, as before stated, Sir Sidney Smith, with his rear-admiral's flag flying on board of the Foudroyant of eighty guns, he proceeded to South America, on which station he assumed the chief command.

On May 17th, Admiral Sir Sidney Smith, in his flag-ship, accompanied by the Agamemnon, Captain Jonas Rose, arrived at Rio Janeiro. The admiral was received by all the officers with the greatest joy; his royal highness the Prince Regent particularly expressed the satisfaction he felt on the admiral's joining him.

On May 24th, orders came on board the London from the commander-in-chief, to employ every artificer in the fleet to prepare that ship for the reception of the royal family, who had been invited by him to dine on board, on the 4th of June, in commemoration of his Britannic Majesty's birthday; and which invitation they had condescendingly accepted. Accordingly, all the guns from the middle deck and upper cabin, as also from the quarter-deck, were removed. The cabins were decorated with the English, Portuguese, and Spanish colours, and with a picture containing the likenesses of all our naval heroes; and, in honour of the royal visitors, the deck was covered with French flags.

The royal table was placed in front of the upper cabin, and tables for the reception of the nobles attending the royal family were set the full length of each side the quarter-deck. A platform was raised from the main to the foremast, the railing of which was ornamented with English, Portuguese, and Spanish colours. In the centre, a table was placed with one hundred and sixty covers; the awnings, the full length of the ship, were lined with English and Portuguese ensigns united, the borders of which were festooned with different coloured signal flags; the sides of the ship on the quarter-deck were covered with the royal standards of England, in the front of which were his Britannic Majesty's arms over the royal table. On the poop was raised a marquee, for the reception of the attendants of the illustrious visitors; and no pains were spared to render the appearance of the ship most nautically magnificent.

On the 4th of June, the standard of England, in conjunction with that of Spain, was hoisted. At two o'clock, the Regent and his family embarked, under a royal salute from the ships and batteries; and upon his highness's arrival on board, the standard of Portugal was hoisted at the fore, when they were received with sincere demonstrations of heartfelt respect. His highness remarked, that the decks were covered with the colours of the French nation. The admiral answered in the affirmative, and the Prince replied, that he was indebted to his faithful ally and his brave subjects, who enabled him to trample them under his feet; a reply which feelingly evinced his grateful sentiments for British friendship.

At four o'clock the royal family placed themselves at table, the admiral superintending, until commanded by his highness to sit at the table, which was placed at his right hand, with Mr. Hill, the British *charge d'affaires*, the nobility taking their places according to their rank; and the royal family were attended by British naval officers.

In front of the table was placed the memorable standard which the Prince had flying on board the Principe Real, when he was compelled to quit his native country; the arms of Portugal and Spain were suspended over the royal guests, and when the English and Portuguese officers were seated, nothing could exceed the happiness his highness and family manifested, and the whole of their misfortunes seemed to have been forgotten.

On this festive occasion, various appropriate toasts were given, which the reader may, perhaps, not be displeased to peruse, as they serve to convey, more accurately than description could effect, the grateful sentiments of the royal visitors. His highness the Prince Regent, the Princess of Brazil, and the Princesses, severally gave:

"The King of Great Britain, and may he live till time shall be no more!"

The Infante of Spain gave "Prosperity to the British, who are fighting for my family's cause."

The Infanta gave: "May our father and his family ever retain the esteem of all his British Majesty's officers."

These were returned with royal salutes. At sunset, his royal highness requested that the royal standard, which had been flying on board the London, might be brought before him. This request being complied with, his highness commanded that the standard should be laid on the deck, and then addressed the admiral in the following impressive manner:

"Admiral, the honour that you and the British officers have this day conferred on me and my family is more than we ever expected, when so short a period has elapsed, and I had the gloomy prospect before me of being surrounded by my enemies; to prevent which, and procure my neutrality, I was constrained to shut my ports against the British nation, with a hope that it would satisfy the exorbitant demands of the French Emperor; yet my compliance did not secure my country from being invaded.

"Such extremity was, to my mind, a source of the most poignant sorrow—that I should be forced to break off an alliance which had so long subsisted between my mother's court and that of his Britannic Majesty; but the snares of Buonaparte compelled me, as his perfidious conduct gave me reason to suppose, in the event of my refusal, he would invade my mother's kingdom. On the part of Great Britain I had not anything to fear, the honour of that nation being unquestionable.

"Admiral, your advices, which I received by despatch, gave me information that Portugal had, in part, been taken possession of by the French. Such intelligence convinced me I was betrayed.

"But to you, admiral, I and my family owe our liberty, and my mother her crown and dignity. We are this day come on board the London to celebrate his British Majesty's birthday; and on this joyful occasion my royal standard has had the honour to fly in conjunction with that of England. It now lies on the deck; and permit me to return you and the officers thanks for all the services you and they have conferred on me, my family, and my faithful subjects.

"As a mark of my respect, accept this standard from me; and from henceforth, quarter the arms of my house with those of your own: it will remain as a memorial for your posterity, that your exertions preserved us from falling into the snare which Buonaparte had laid for our destruction."

This address was honoured with a salute from all his Majesty's ships. It was most truly affecting to see the princesses, the princes, and the

Infante of Spain, while his royal highness was addressing the admiral; and, although the entertainment was the most magnificent that was ever given on board any of his Majesty's ships, yet when a sovereign addressed the British admiral in such terms of respect, it was sufficient to cause a retrospective sigh to be heaved at the calamities his highness and his family had been compelled to undergo, and the loss of their ancient hereditary dominions. But the admiral revived their cheerfulness, by recommending the British officers to drink "Prosperity to his royal highness and his dominions;" which was most graciously received by the royal visitors.

At eight in the evening, these illustrious personages left the ship, and invited the admiral, captains, and officers, to attend them to the opera; which had been previously commanded on the occasion, in honour of the day, boxes having been provided for their reception.

An address, by way of prelude to the opera, was delivered on the occasion; of which the following translation will, it is hoped, be found to exhibit a tolerably accurate idea.

"This day has been a joyful one: our sovereign has cordially united in celebrating the birthday of George the Third, the sovereign of. the British Isles the father of his people, and the protector of the house of Braganza! May his flag always continue triumphantly to sway over the heads of his enemies! The laws of Britain are just, their sovereign governs with justice and humanity. All ranks of oppressed men address him, whose views are just, and are sure to obtain relief; and those whose designs are base and dishonourable, his arms can scourge, and cause them to dread the name of a Briton. Don John, Prince Regent, enjoys his liberty, which he owes to the arms of England. May it never be disturbed by any power of the universe May the two sovereigns and their posterity live in peace and friendship, until time shall be no more! And may the ill-acquired power of the usurper meet a rapid fall, and the united powers avenge their countries' wrongs.

"Unhappy Spain! Thou hast been deceived. Thy country has been robbed of its sovereign, and that sovereign and his family have been dragged from their faithful subjects, and doomed to ignominious imprisonment; for what end the Omnipotent can only decide.

"Don Carlos, Prince of Spain, should ever Providence restore you to your country, and place you on the throne of your ancestors, remember the protection of Britain: her amicable connexions will ensure your country's happiness; your commerce will flourish, your arms by land and sea will regain their original power, and the brave Spaniards will then remember their ancient dignity.

"Illustrious princess,‡ descended from a long line of Spanish sovereigns, and you the descendants of the royal house of Braganza, may your offspring ever learn to venerate the royal house of Brunswick!

"And now, on the evening of the 4th of June, a day of joy, a day of grateful respect, as our royal master and family have honoured us with their illustrious presence, may our performances afford to their august audience equal pleasure, and be crowned with success, like the British flag, which has hitherto protected and preserved our royal master!"

It might very reasonably be supposed that Sir Sidney Smith would have been most acceptable to the court of Brazils, in the elevated office which he went to fill, not only for the protection of British interests, but for the safety and even for the existence of the transplanted Portuguese dynasty. When, afterwards, Lord Strangford arrived, who had co-operated with Sir Sidney Smith in rescuing the Braganza family from the thraldom of France, it soon became evident that, with the Brazilians, British interests would now be sedulously studied, and British influence become paramount.

---

‡ The consort of the Prince Regent.

In the first instance, owing to the well directed exertions of Lord Strangford, regulations very favourable to British interests were adopted in our commercial relations with the Brazilians. Indeed, these were looked upon as giving so much advantage to England and the commercial and shipping interests of the United Kingdom, that the committee of merchants trading to the Brazils forwarded, officially, to Sir Sidney Smith their most grateful thanks, for so well carrying out, by the assistance of the naval force under his command, those beneficial arrangements with Brazil that his lordship had completed, in the "Treaty of Commerce and Navigation" which he negotiated and signed.

After a long-protracted silence, the court of Portugal put forth its justificatory manifesto, on its passing over to the Brazils. This delay is not to be imputed as matter of blame to the Prince Regent, since the manifesto could not be promulgated without the previous concurrence of his ally, the King of Great Britain. It begins by stating abhorrence of the French revolution, and reprobates the domineering deportment adopted by France towards states less powerful than itself. It then cites many grievances—the confiscation of Portuguese shipping in 1801, with many other unjust measures.

Afterwards, it proceeds to animadvert on the conduct of Buonaparte at the breaking out of the war between England and France, when Portugal thought itself fortunate by purchasing, with great sacrifices of money, the treaty of 1804, wherein France promised by the sixth article a neutrality thus: "The first consul of the French republic consents to recognise the neutrality of Portugal during the present war, and he promises not to oppose any of the measures which may be adopted with regard to any of the belligerent nations, not at variance with the principles or general laws of neutrality." Notwithstanding this, France made Portugal declare war against England, without the Portuguese having the least complaint to make against the latter power. The protest enumerates the alternations of aggressions and humiliations that it received, until the royal family were compelled to sail for the Brazils; and concludes thus "His royal highness breaks off all communication with France, recalls his mission collectively and individually, and authorises his subjects to make war by land and by sea upon those of the Emperor of the French. "His royal highness declares all the treaties that the French emperor has forced him to conclude, and especially those of Badajoz and Madrid, in 1801, and of neutrality, in 1804, which the said emperor has infringed and never respected, to be null and void.

"His royal highness will never lay down his arms, but in conjunction with his ancient and faithful ally, his Britannic Majesty; and, in any case, will not consent to the cession of Portugal, which forms the ancient part of the heritage and rights of his august royal family.

"When the Emperor of the French shall have satisfied the just claims of his royal highness the Prince Regent of Portugal on all these points, shall have abandoned the absolute and imperious tone with which he rules oppressed Europe, and shall have restored to the crown of Portugal all he has despoiled her of by an unprovoked invasion in the midst of peace, his royal highness will be ready to renew the ties that have always subsisted between the two countries, when not divided by principles of unlimited ambition, which the experience of ages has but too clearly shown to be alike contrary to the welfare and the tranquillity of those by whom such principles are adopted."

We have thus much insisted upon Brazilian affairs, because it has been generally supposed that Sir Sidney Smith, in conjunction with Lord Strangford, had great influence in determining the conduct of the expatriated court. If this be the case, the above document, though vilely drawn up, and in despicable taste, betrayed something like a proper spirit under the wrongs and insults that were heaped upon those from whom it emanated.

This manifesto was followed up by a demonstration of actual hostilities against the allies of Napoleon. An expedition against Cayenne was proposed to the Brazilian court by Sir Sidney Smith, and consisted of about seven thousand Portuguese, supported by a detachment from the British fleet under the command of Sir James Yeo, and proved completely successful. At the time of the Vienna negotiations, in 1814, this conquest turned out to be a very important acquisition. As commander-in-chief of the British forces employed at Cayenne, Sir Sidney Smith subsequently advanced his just claims upon the restored Bourbons, especially for having rescued from Buonaparte the celebrated plantation called "La Gabrielle,"which was the private property of the French royal family. These claims are, we believe, to this very day, still unsettled.

It has been also published, that, notwithstanding the active and judicious exertions of Lord Strangford, British interests seemed gradually to decline at the court of the Brazils; and that though the Prince Regent continued to express himself as happy and grateful in the protection of England, his conduct towards her was both petulant and unthankful; that even the just weight that ought to have been attached to the personal and public character of Sir Sidney Smith seemed to have been disregarded, and insult and annoyance to have superseded respect and accommodation in the conduct of the Brazilian authorities towards him. We give this a most strenuous denial; for, so far from this being the case, there was not a single case of just complaint, which, on application through Lord Strangford or the rear-admiral, was not promptly and amply redressed, nor a single just demand which was not successfully maintained. There certainly were sundry absurd and unreasonable pretensions (not on the part of British merchants alone) which our minister could not, with any degree of propriety, sanction or sustain; and hence, perhaps, arose the unfounded impression to which we have alluded.

Much stress has been laid upon the following symptom of jealousy manifested by the Brazilian court. His Majesty's ship London, in going out on a cruise, owing to a sudden flaw of wind, was obliged instantly to drop her anchor under one of the forts. In this predicament, her boats were observed to be taking soundings, as it is customary, and was then absolutely necessary.

This act was made the subject of a formal complaint to Sir Sidney Smith, and represented, with much bitterness, to be a breach of hospitality, and a violation of the respect due to the house of Braganza. To this representation the rear-admiral coolly answered, that the duty of the ships under his command must be carried on according to the rules of the service in all parts of the world; and as to the asserted impropriety of surveying the coast, (supposing such survey actually to have taken place,) as he was charged with the responsibility of defending it, it was only just and reasonable that he and his officers should take every opportunity of becoming intimately acquainted with it. This is the answer heroical, and one which must be pleasing to naval vanity; but let us look to both sides of the question.

We have given the English version of this transaction, but it should be remembered, that this sounding was not an isolated case, for the boats of the squadron had made themselves acquainted with every depth of water of every part of the harbour, and about the fortifications. It could hardly be expected that any government, claiming to be independent, could submit to such an infraction of its territorial rights by any foreigners. Were a French or Russian squadron enjoying our hospitality at Plymouth or Portsmouth, we should be somewhat astonished should they commence taking soundings, without even the previous civility of asking our permission.

CHAPTER IX

NAPOLEON having placed his brother upon the throne of Spain, and thus made one more step towards planting his own dynasty as the sole sovereigns of Europe, this proceeding very naturally aroused the members of the old legitimate royal families into active but fruitless exertion. Spanish and Portuguese princes had nothing but manifestoes and declarations to oppose to Gallic victories, and at the instigation and by the advice of Sir Sidney Smith, to these they had recourse.

But still, the British admiral, commanding in the southern seas of America, thought he had an imperative duty to perform in endeavouring to preserve the allegiance of the Spanish colonies to the expelled family of Spain; and, with that view, he was extremely successful in distributing the declarations and manifestoes to which we have just adverted. Whether, in so doing, he was performing a work of supererogation, it is not easy to decide. That he had been over zealous was more than rumoured—it was publicly affirmed. The apparent course of duty is not always the one that the secret councils of the cabinet will approve of. Whether Sir Sidney Smith's zeal was judiciously manifested we know not—we know it was, to some parties, most vexatiously.

Intimately connected as was our officer with all the political movements in the quarter of the world in which he exercised his command, it becomes our province to state that the Princess of Brazil, and her cousin, the Spanish Infante, who followed the court of Portugal, published joint and separate protests against the usurpation of Napoleon's family, which usurpation was in prejudice of their rights as possible heirs to the crown of Spain. Even supposing that the Buonaparte dynasty should prove stable, they deemed this step advisable to secure to themselves the succession of those parts of the Spanish monarchy which were beyond the reach of the French imperial power. This document is headed by the words "Just claim," and is addressed by "The representatives of the royal house of Spain, Donna Carlotta Juaquina de Bourbon, Princess of Portugal and Brazil, and by Don Pedro Carlos de Bourbon y Braganza, Infante of Spain, to the Prince Regent of Portugal, to the end that his royal highness may vouchsafe to take into consideration to protect and preserve the sacred rights of their august house to the throne of Spain and the Indies, which throne the emperor of the French has obtained by means of an abdication and renunciation, extorted by the most atrocious and detestable violence, from the hands of the King Don Carlos IV., and their royal highnesses the Prince of Asturias and the Infantes Don Carlos and Don Antonio."

The memorial then gives a brief history of how Buonaparte contrived to get possession of the meek King of Spain, characterising the *coup de politique* with every epithet that tends to give it the colour of treachery and perfidiousness. It then "implores the aid of the Prince Regent of the Brazils as their guardian and natural protector, supplicating his succour against the propagating of this usurping system that absorbs the states of Europe one after the other, beseeching his royal highness to employ his power and influence in favour of their house, so that they may be thereby enabled (as the nearest relations of the king) to preserve his rights, and with them, to secure their own; combining the Portuguese, Spanish, and English forces, to hinder the French from practising, with their armies, the same violence and subversion that they have committed almost over the whole extent of Europe.

It then tells his royal highness, that "in consideration of the state and situation in which their father and uncle, together with the rest of the family of the august house of Spain, are placed, his royal highness cannot but approve of this their present proceeding, founded on the principles and the fundamental laws of the Spanish monarchy, from which they will never separate themselves; a proceeding authorised by the irresistible principles of divine and natural justice, and which, as such, we hope will merit the approbation of their beloved uncle, the King of the Two Sicilies, that of his royal family, and of all personages interested. They consider the step that they are taking as expected of them by the members of their unfortunate family who are in a state of restraint, oppressed by force, and that they surely feel most painfully the separation from the bosoms of their much loved vassals, the faithful, the constant, and the generous Spaniards."

The memorial then adverts to the words employed by the ex-king of Spain when he abdicated, and thus comments upon them: "This mode of expression appears to us to offer evident proofs, first, of the compulsion that has been exercised to make those princes write, without allowing them to write their own sentiments; secondly, that, in case Spain was not placed in such circumstances as are therein described, they would not deem useless an effort of the inhabitants to recover their rights; and thirdly, that, when this should follow with respect to the colonies, they would be lost to the mother country. In these words we perceive a tacit though very clear insinuation, addressed to ourselves, and to such of our most faithful countrymen as are still at liberty, that we should, by unanimous consent, endeavour to defend and preserve our rights."

The memorialists then appeal to the King of Sicily, and to the sovereign pontiff, intimating that their cause is that of the church and of religion.

It then proceeds, "As for us, we deem ourselves happy in being on this side of the Atlantic, neither in a state of subjection, nor liable to it; if, laying aside all party spirit, we cultivate that perfect union and alliance whereby community of sentiment will consolidate those resources that are capable of forming a respectable force sufficient in itself to resist whatsoever invasion, and to secure our interests, our liberties, and our lives against French ambition.

"We cannot, for a single instant, doubt of the loyalty and love that the inhabitants of the Americas have at all times shown towards our august house, and more particularly to our much honoured father; for whom, *in recent times, they have sacrificed their lives* and their fortunes, and given the greatest proofs of fidelity. With this knowledge, and certain that the misfortunes of our family will have saddened the minds of those who have always interested themselves for the conservation of our rights, we hope that, by the means of the interference and help of your royal highness, it may be practicable to realise a perfect alliance with the King of Spain's subjects in America; and, by that just and salutary measure, frustrate the enemy with ease, as well as avoid those rival dissensions which continue too frequently to be excited between the subjects of the two kingdoms, of which the consequences are always more or less fatal.

"In order to realise these our just and sound intentions, we are desirous of a secure opportunity for communicating them to the respective tribunals, and other legitimate depositaries of the authority of our Lord the King, which we would in no wise alter or diminish, and which can be preserved and defended only by freeing it from the power of France. To which end, we hope that your royal highness will interest yourself with the admiral of our strong and powerful ally, the King of Great Britain, that he may so order and dispose of the forces under his command, as, without weakening the defence of your royal highness, and of the Brazilian coasts, to contribute to that of the shores of the river Plata, and the other dominions of Spanish America; without in any way prejudicing the navigation and commerce between the inhabitants of those parts and this and other parts of this principality, the protection for which trade, we doubt not, will be immediately confirmed by the generosity of the King of Great Britain's noble character, and that of his powerful nation.

"Lastly, we request of your royal highness to place at our disposal all the means that may be necessary for us to communicate our intentions to the chiefs, tribunals, and civil as well as ecclesiastical authorities, in which dwells the authority of our Lord the King, and to whose loyalty we commend the rights of our royal house, which we desire to support inviolate during the continuance of those misfortunes with which French ambition has afflicted the royal family of Spain.

"Written in the Palace of Rio de Janeiro, 1st August, 1808."

(Signed) &c.

He must be grave indeed, who, casting the eye of deliberate reasoning upon this document, forbears to smile—and yet, the next sentiment must be of a much sadder cast. This crying out of the frogs to king Log for protection against king Stork is ludicrous, but the invitation to civil war throughout the Spanish colonies is a miserable instance of arrogant and selfish ambition. The young colonists were, however, all this time taking counsel among themselves, and the spirit of Freedom presided at their deliberations.

These princes' reliance on the "love and loyalty "of a people who were on the eve of casting off the supremacy of the mother country for ever, betrays a weakness, excessive even in those advantaged by the "divine right" doctrine. They appear not to have been able to discern anything beyond the precincts of their own little court, or if they ventured a glance a little more extended, it was only with the eye of the most inveterate prejudice. Their appeal to the Americans was wholly too late, for their coveted subjects were thinking of federal, while the princes were thinking of feudal, system.

However, the Regent of Portugal gave the memorialists a very favourable answer; for, among other gracious things, he acquaints them and the world, that he judged, like them, that the time was come for union against the common enemy. He says, "I hope that, in concert with my allies, (amongst whom ought to be comprised Sicily, and so consider itself,) we shall be able to oppose a barrier to the extension of those conquests France may undertake against us. At least, I will do all that shall depend upon me to effectuate this salutary combination and alliance which your royal highnesses have proposed to me. And I wish the American Spaniards, knowing that we are of one accord on the great necessity of protecting them, to unite their resources with our forces, in order to give full and entire effect to my intentions for procuring them that peace and prosperity of which their position renders them capable and susceptible of the fullest enjoyment."

It took eighteen days to concoct this magnanimous answer, virtually transferring the allegiance of all Spaniards, and American Spaniards more particularly, from the *de facto* King of Spain, to Joaquina, Infanta of Spain and Portugal.

Now, it is fully understood, that the appeal made in the first document to Sir Sidney Smith, for the co-operation of the naval force under his command, entirely met the gallant commander's views, for the best of all reasons, that they originated with himself. In the aspect of affairs at that period, these movements, though they now seem feeble and puerile enough, were thought of great moment, though they were certainly not in accordance with British policy at the time. Indeed, nothing could have been more fatal to the relations of England as regarded Spain, where, by this time it had been discovered that the battle was to be fought, and has been decided. It was then our interest to cultivate the confidence of the Spanish provisional government, acting in the name of Ferdinand VII. These proceedings in South America, authorised, as they were erroneously supposed to be, by the British government, excited suspicion and alarm; and, for a long time, it was difficult to persuade the Spanish authorities at Cadiz that we were not acting a double part, and that, while we affected to support the rights of Ferdinand VII. in Europe, we were not secretly intriguing to transfer their colonies in America to their old natural enemies, the Portuguese. But Sir Sidney Smith had neither the authority nor sufficient force to attempt anything of consequence in their favour, in the quarter of the globe in which he found himself.

Indeed, from the different views in politics entertained by Sir Sidney Smith and the ministry at home, his command was about to be abruptly terminated, but not before he had done his country essential service, and, though no important military exploit distinguished his presence in the Brazils, in many instances, himself great honour.

Not only had he made the commerce of his country a paramount object, but his advice and assistance were found most beneficial in the employment of British capital, in developing the resources of the rich country confided to his protection. But as the subject is foreign to our purpose, we can only just allude to it.

That, during his stay in this country, Sir Sidney Smith was personally very acceptable to the Prince Regent, is evidenced by that august personage presenting him with a very pleasant villa on the banks of the river, with a good deal of land attached to it. To this residence Sir Sidney gave the name of Chacara de Braganza.

CHAPTER X

ALMOST from the very beginning of Sir Sidney Smith's command, the court of the Brazils had split into two distinct parties—that of the Prince, and that of the Princess. Sir Sidney was considered to be the leader of the latter, the chief political object of which was to place the Princess at the head of an independent government, (under the name and representing the authority of her brother, Ferdinand VII) to be established in the provinces of La Plata.

This project was discountenanced by the British government, and was also very distasteful to the Prince of Brazil, and, consequently, Sir Sidney's position at the court ceased to be so agreeable to him as might have been expected from all that previously occurred before our hero became mixed up with politics.

Previously to that time, the sovereign bestowed every public mark of honour and approbation upon our officer that was possible in their relative situations. The project of reviving the ancient order of the Tower and the Sword had been sometime suggested to the Prince by Don Rodrigo de Souza, his minister for foreign affairs. This order was originally instituted by Alphonso V., surnamed the African, in 1459.

This revival was not carried finally into execution until the 17th of December, 1808, the anniversary of the Queen of Portugal's birthday, on which occasion a great number of British naval officers had the order conferred upon them, whilst the admiral himself was made a Knight Grand Cross.

In unison with the promise made to Sir Sidney by the Prince Regent, on board the London, on the 4th of June, 1808, he solicited permission to quarter the arms of Portugal with his own, and the prince graciously met his views by ordering his minister to forward the following document to England.

Palace of Rio Janeiro, 6 Aug. 1808

His royal highness the Prince Regent, our sovereign lord, very desirous to show the estimation in which he holds the merit, abilities, and valour of Sir Sidney Smith, rear-admiral and commander-in-chief of his Britannic Majesty's naval forces in the southern seas; his royal highness has been pleased to grant him the honour of enabling him to bear the arms of Portugal quartered with his own, and to bear them, as the French express it, on *shield and banner*;* that he and his descendants may use them, and in default of issue, his representatives in both the male and female lines; but as the said Sir Sidney Smith cannot do this without his Britannic Majesty's license, his royal highness orders that your Excellency will request this faculty through Mr. Canning, his minister of state for foreign affairs, signifying the great pleasure and satisfaction his royal highness will receive by his Britannic Majesty's being pleased to accede to this his particular desire. Your Excellency will make known this minister's answer as soon as possible. His royal highness flatters himself that this just request will not meet any difficulty.

God preserve your Excellency.

D. RODRIGO DE SOUZA COUTINHO

To Don Domingos Antonio de Souza Coutinho,
London

These honours fully evince how high had been the esteem of the Regent for Sir Sidney's great worth as a commander, and that he could not afterwards have borne him a great degree of pique as an adverse partisan. The political dissensions of the time have long since been forgotten, obliterated as they are by the events of a nature so surprising that followed. The honour bestowed on Sir Sidney remains.

Whilst at Rio de Janeiro, Sir Sidney could boast, with a few exceptions from political motives, of the friendship of every man who had the slightest pretensions to come within his extensive circle of acquaintance, for from the high station which he held, his boundless hospitality, as well as from his courtesy, kindness, and agreeable manners, he had, to use a very common yet expressive term, "won all hearts."

Though generally at anchor in his flag-ship at Rio, the naval commander-in-chief sometimes proceeded in the Foudroyant to the different places within the limits of his jurisdiction, which partook greatly the character of naval pageants; for, as he could find no enemies to overcome, he had nothing to do but to create new friends, to conciliate the

---

* En ecusson et banniere

inhabitants, and to implant the feelings of love and respect for the country that he so honourably and so profitably served.

Every one, excepting those in the political secret, was surprised at the recall of our hero from these seas; but it cannot be expected that any ministry would, or ought to, keep an officer in a *high* command, when he has publicly testified that he has essentially different political views from those of his government.

We wish this remark to be understood generally; but in Sir Sidney's case the application of the ministerial rule had other accessory circumstances to help it out, and in some manner to justify it. It is most true, that in all Sir Sidney's actions nothing ever appeared but magnanimity, probity, and the most chivalrous courage. He served his country at the Brazils with advantage, and was, on his return to his native shores, as we shall hereafter show, received with accumulated honours.

But still Sir Sidney Smith was removed from his command before the usual period; and such removal alone, until fully arid satisfactorily explained, will always carry with it something like a slur upon the character of the displaced officer We believe the step was never explained, and we can only offer a conjecture upon the subject, and which we should hesitate to offer at all, did we not think that the probabilities are very strongly in its favour.

It is well understood that Sir .Sidney Smith was as conscious of his diplomatic astuteness as of his high naval and military talents, and we must not be surprised if he felt a little disinclination to allow them to remain unexercised in a field so wide and so tempting as was then afforded him by the Brazilian court, which contained, at the same time, so many members of the expatriated families of Spain and Portugal.

On the subject of these families, and especially the claims of the Spanish portion of it, as we have before mentioned, Sir Sidney took his own peculiar views; and would also, if he had been permitted, have taken measures which would very much have embarrassed the cabinet at home. In these he was opposed by the British minister, Lord Strangford, at Rio de Janeiro, who was content to act solely upon the instructions that he had received from Mr. Canning, the secretary of state at the time.

This opposition of his lordship was solely on public grounds, for, privately and personally, no two persons could have been in a more friendly position; each respected the talents and the character of the other; and had their political views been in unison, they could not, as individuals, have been upon better terms.

Of this we may be assured, that Mr. Canning was not the person to permit any one to retain a command, who might feel inclined to thwart his policy, or even to disapprove of it. Sir Sidney believed that his course of acting was best suited to the interests of his country, whilst some of those in power at home deemed that out of his own peculiar province he should not act at all; and, to prevent him from so doing, he was superseded in his command. We mention this with a great deal of diffidence, for acts which partake so much of the nature of opinions assume different names according to the views taken of them by different parties. However, Sir Sidney Smith's proceedings became, towards the end of 1808, the subject of a confidential letter to George III from the Prince Regent, which letter, most probably, led to the recall of Sir Sidney Smith, and to the appointment of another officer to succeed him.

In all this, we see nothing in the least discreditable to our hero, as a zealous officer and a gallant man. His political views might have been the correct ones; he was too manly to disguise them; and he thus placed himself voluntarily in a position, in which it was impossible for him to retain his command.

On the 7th of August, 1809, Sir William Sidney Smith, having left the Brazils in the Diana frigate on the 21st of June, once more arrived on his native shores, and shortly after struck his flag. Whatever might have been the opinion of the ministers as to the value and extent of our officer's exertions to promote the honour and the interests of his country, the merchants of great Britain more immediately concerned with our South American commerce, on the arrival of Sir Sidney Smith, were eager to testify their respect to him personally, and the high sense that they entertained of his activity and intelligence officially. They presented him with the following address—a spontaneous tribute highly honourable to all parties.

"The committee of merchants of London trading to, and who have establishments at Brazil, beg leave to congratulate Sir William Sidney Smith on his safe arrival in England from his command on the coast of that country.

"Impressed with a lively sense of the essential services rendered by him to the commercial and shipping interests of the United Kingdom in general, and more particularly to those immediately concerned in the Brazil trade, of the protection that he has always so eminently and uniformly afforded them, and of the judgment with which his conduct has always been regulated, upon all occasions in which the interests of his correspondents and connexions have required his interference; the committee consider it to be their duty to return Sir Sidney their most grateful thanks, which they request him to accept, accompanied by their warmest wishes for his health and prosperity."

This spontaneous tribute of respect to our officer produced from him the following very appropriate reply:

Royal Hotel, Pall Mall,
Sept. 4, 1809

Sir, Mr. Buckle, secretary to the committee of British merchants trading to the Brazils, having this day put into my hands your letter, containing an extract of the proceedings of that respectable body, of the 17th ult., together with the very flattering proof of my earnest endeavours to promote the commercial interests of our country having been favourably considered by them, I lose no time in requesting you to convey to them my best thanks for this distinguished mark of their approbation.

I assure you and them, that nothing could be more gratifying to me than the unanimous address from so respectable a body of my countrymen, to whose service, in general, my whole attention and care have ever been, and ever will be, devoted.

A sense of duty induced me to labour for the extension and security of the commerce of my country. All other modes of securing it being denied me by the circumstances of my situation, my first care was to cement the friendship of our allies, the Portuguese; my next, to extinguish the enmity of our opponents in the Spanish part of that vast continent, and to show the latter, that the enlightened views of the British government and nations in Europe, with regard to Spain, entitle us to the confidence of her colonies, with which I succeeded in opening, and have since maintained, a degree of amicable intercourse that cannot fail to cement the bonds of friendship, and augment the resources of both states towards enabling them to bear the expenses of the war, on the success of which depends their safety, and even their existence.

If, in pursuing these great objects, I have collaterally been enabled to further the interests of the British trade in general, I am sincerely rejoiced; and the proof that you have kindly given me of my endeavours having been crowned with success, is (next to the approbation of those to whom I am responsible, and which, I am happy to find, is not to be denied me,) the most gratifying circumstance that could occur, and amply balances the painful struggles I have sometimes had against prejudice and egotism.

I beg leave, sir, to thank you for the very obliging manner in which you have conveyed this most flattering and unexpected address. I cannot, however, in accepting it, omit to acknowledge the labours and merits of his Majesty's consul-general, Sir James Gambier, with whom I acted most cordially in all things, when the interests of the merchants trading to the Brazils were concerned.

I have the honour to be, &c.

Your most obedient,

humble servant

W. SIDNEY SMITH

To J. Princep, Esq., Chairman
of the Society of British Merchants trading
to the Brazils

But he was not, during this cessation of naval service, idle; for, on the 11th of October of the same year in which he arrived in England from his

Brazilian command, he married the widow of Sir George Berriman Rumboldt, Bart., formerly British consul at Hamburgh. This Sir George Rumboldt had drawn the public attention very much towards him, on account of a most unjustifiable persecution that he endured from the arbitrary proceedings of the satellites of the French emperor. Indeed, at one time, his life was in imminent danger. He left a family with his widow, who have found in Sir Sidney Smith all the affection and care of a father.

Though, at this time, our fleets were actively employed in keeping the enemy blockaded in their various harbours, from private political motives Sir Sidney Smith was not again employed until the summer of 1812.

On the 31st of July, 1810, Sir Sidney Smith was promoted to the rank of Vice-Admiral.

Among other honours, which seemed to have no end in their multiplying, Sir Sidney Smith had, about this time, the distinction conferred upon him, at Oxford, of Doctor of Civil Law. He was not alone in this honour, for he shared it with Isaac George Manly, Esq., rear-admiral of the Blue, and Captain Thomas Fremantle, of the royal navy. These academic honours were bestowed upon these celebrated officers at the Oxonian Encaenia, and the applause at the ceremony was universal and enthusiastic, particularly so with respect to our hero.

The *grace* for Sir Sidney Smith's degree passed the senate of the university in the year 1805, during the vice-chancellorship of the Reverend Doctor Whittington London, provost of Worcester College, as a tribute of respect to the "Christian Knight," whose merit had already served for a theme to a bard of whom Oxford is justly proud.

The degree that was thus proposed for the admiral during his absence, only awaited his return from foreign service to receive the *placets* of the convocation. This honorary distinction is really *honourable*, and, from Sir Sidney Smith's high cultivation of mind., not at all misplaced; for, although he gained his qualification in sterner fields than any of those that are proximate to the groves of Oxford, they are not the less sterling and exalted, and the degree is every way appropriate to the character which bears it.

On this occasion, a very valuable contemporary periodical is facetious, though not very original, in the following remark: "Now that Sir Sidney Smith is made a doctor of civil law, we hope that he will not abandon the practice of the cannon law, in which he has hitherto been so eminent."

CHAPTER XI

IN every place of any populousness, in which Sir Sidney Smith showed himself, he was always received with enthusiasm. We make the following extract from the "Pilot," respecting his reception at Liverpool.

"This town is at present (September 12th, 1810) favoured with the company of Admiral Sir Sidney Smith. This distinguished officer, whose exploits have procured him the admiration and attachment of the whole nation, passed through Manchester on Saturday. He was there waited upon by a deputation of gentlemen, and invited to a public dinner at the Exchange, on which occasion the principal inhabitants of that town were present. When he arrived at Warrington, the horses were taken from his carriage, and he was drawn through the streets amidst the congratulations of a vast concourse of people. Sir Sidney arrived at Liverpool on Monday evening, and yesterday morning waited upon the mayor and stewards, and afterwards, accompanied by several gentlemen, inspected the Town Hall, the Athenaeum, the Lyceum, the Rotundo, and the Union Rooms. After this, he returned to the Exchange, where he was met by the body of merchants there assembled, and hailed by repeated cheers.

"Upon entering the Exchange room, he was again most heartily saluted by incessant cheers, and he received the same compliment at the underwriters' room. On the following Saturday he dined in public with the mayor in the Town Hall. With these tokens of respect every heart beats in unison. They call forth our warmest congratulations."

After which, the gifted editor proceeds to perpetrate some fine writing on the subject, to the effect that "the laurel which decks the brow of the patriotic warrior is ever green; it is not blasted by envy, nor corroded by time; but it becomes a more pleasing decoration when joined with the festive wreath entwined by the hands of a grateful country. It was the, lot of many ancient heroes that their merits were left only for posterity to appreciate; but it may be the boast of the heroes of England, that, whilst they erect a name and an example for future years, yet living they are honoured with the honest applause and the warm feelings of their fellow citizens."

This would have been most pleasant to our hero, and all others of our nation, if true; but another contemporary writer thinks very differently as to the laurel and the ever-green wreaths, with other more substantial advantages, that ought to have been bestowed upon the defender of Acre. In a letter to Sir Sidney Smith, on his installation as a doctor of civil laws at Oxford, this writer tells him: "So great, indeed, so characteristically great have been your achievements, that we must, in charity, suppose our different administrations, under which they have been performed, despairing adequately to estimate them, have withheld the rewards which lesser merits might be understood to claim;" and have received, he might have very truthfully added. The writer, warming with his subject, thus proceeds:

"Your country, sir, has long beheld with mingled emotions of shame, anger, and indignation, the affronting neglect with which the brilliant character of Sir Sidney Smith has been insulted; but the same country has, at length, in a plenitude of opportunity, bestowed upon you the proudest reward which any age or any nation could by popularity have bestowed. History, indeed, quietly at her post, was collecting for her brightest pages the materials for your fame; but it was in the theatre of Oxford, sir, that the splendid arid living attestation of your merit burst upon us."

That is to say, that his country, "in a plenitude of opportunity," withheld from him a peerage or a baronetcy, and gave him the proudest reward that any nation could possibly bestow, by making him, "a man-of-war's man, a doctor of civil law."

After this, the writer makes Caesar, Rome, and the dagger of Brutus, dance in mazy confusion around the couch of Socrates, and finishes with the sententious Franklin sighing with sensibility, as, at his bidding, the electric spark descends from the atmosphere to show that none of these were equal in celebrity to the act of making Sir Sidney a doctor.

The writer, then, very naturally diverges to commendations of the university and all there, unto belonging, and tells Sir Sidney, that before her venerable chiefs he was crowned with "immortal honours."

"Yes," he continues, "at that hour, your numerous escapes and hardships; your daring snatches at fame, amid the waves of the Baltic; your eruption from the prisons of France; your resourceful defence of Acre; your genius as a statesman in your projected recovery of Egypt by treaty; your assistance along its streams, and upon the plains of the Delta, in its actual recovery; your protecting of the house of Braganza in its escape from perpetual enthralment; all these bright deeds, and all these severe exertions, were at once *compensated* and rewarded by this deputation from our empire, *not more mighty in force than in intellect."*

But awful as was this display on the part of the university, it would have wanted its climax, had it not been for the death of Mr. Windham. His eulogy follows, and Horace and Sir William Draper are enlisted among those forming the funeral pageant. Indeed, so taken up is the author with his *peroration*, that Sir Sidney has only the distinction to be lugged into it in the very last words, styling him the defender of Ptolemais, where he is ranked with Nelson, Montrose, Wellesley, Coeur de Lion, and Wallace.

We have only noticed this effusion as an instance of the very general spirit of admiration which the character of Sir Sidney Smith at this time excited. We have but to remark, that he fully deserved all that is sensible in these eulogiums, and much better eulogists.

In the month of August, the Lord Provost and magistrates of the city of Edinburgh unanimously voted the freedom of the city of Edinburgh to our officer; and on the 22nd he dined with them, the council, and clergy, and a number of gentlemen, in the new rooms, Royal Exchange. On the following day, he and other strangers, accompanied by several gentlemen belonging to the city, visited Heriot's Hospital.

The grandeur of the building, the excellent management of the institution, exemplified by the clean and healthy appearance of the boys, attracted, in a particular manner, the attention of the admiral, as well as of the other visitants, After witnessing the embarkation of the forty-second regiment at Leith, Sir Sidney returned to Edinburgh, and in the afternoon dined with the Lord Provost, at his seat, View Forth, in company with a select party.

In this year more honours were showered upon Sir Sidney Smith, and the knight of Palestine was received with acclamations worthy of his glory among the learned fraternity of Cambridge.

In addition to the academical distinction conferred upon him at Oxford, he was now vested with the degree of Master of Arts, the highest that the statutes of Cambridge university admit of, *honoris causâ*, amidst universal acclamation. In his Latin harangue on the occasion, the public orator introduced, most happily, the name of the conqueror of the conqueror of Europe. The admiral's appearance in the senate-house, on the recent installation of the Duke of Gloucester as chancellor, was the signal for a general salute. The whole ceremony was as gratifying to him who was its object, as it was honourable to those with whom it originated.

At this time his popularity seemed, if possible, on the increase, for it enabled the very indifferent poem of Mrs. Cowley, called "The Siege of Acre," to appear in a new and greatly amplified edition. This poem, its editor tells us, "was written after Buonaparte had abandoned his army and returned to France, but before the English army had beaten it in Egypt; at a time, therefore, when the military event of the expedition of the highest import was, "The Defence and Siege of Acre." The author's object was, whilst the threats of invasion were revived, to assist in teaching Britons—before the proofs which they have given under Sir John Stuart at Maida, and repeatedly under Lord Wellington in Portugal and Spain—had dissipated the "dastard doubt," which had existed in the minds of a few, whether Englishmen, on shore, could keep their accustomed lead of the enemy, that they could, notwithstanding his improved state, conquer those whom others cannot resist.

We may take this opportunity of our officer's cessation from naval employment to introduce to our readers

SIR SIDNEY SMITH'S INVENTION

It has generally been remarked, that, in men of extraordinary genius, the inventive faculties have always been well developed. The mind that conceived, and the patience that executed, "Paradise Lost," had it turned its energies to mechanism, would, perhaps, have anticipated the use of steam, or made progress towards the discovery of the longitude by the means of improved chronometers. Indeed, invention may be characterised as a ready appliance by the mind of the resources within its reach, and the power of doing that circuitously that cannot be directly done. In the defence of Acre, Sir Sidney evinced a great degree of this tact, so distinguishing to the possessor, and so valuable to mankind. Need we then be surprised that, at the time when the nation, or a great part of it, trembled under the threat of an invasion, the preparations of which were so gigantic that fear was not reprehensible in the calmest temperaments, Sir Sidney Smith turned his attention to the means of conveying aid rapidly from one destination to another. To effect this, much to the amusement of the suburban and waterside residents of the metropolis, he treated them with the following nautical exhibition.

It was a construction adapted to convey large bodies of troops, in shallow water, without noise or confusion, under the enemy's batteries.

The model of this vessel was very completely put together, and the first experiment made with it was on the 23rd of August, 1805. About ten o'clock, ante meridian, for we must now speak nautically, Sir Sidney Smith, a naval lieutenant, and six men, independently of four others who were stationed at the oars, got on board the vessel, proceeded up to Chelsea, and from thence sailed down to Greenwich.

The form of this raft resembled two wherries placed alongside each other, but separated by means of a platform twenty-four feet wide and twenty-four feet long, to which the wherries were attached. Eight spritsails were used to impel the construction through the water. These sails were so cut as to be capable of forming a complete tent, under which the regulating officer and men were to be stationed.

Everybody must be aware that this contrivance is very ingenious, and would tell admirably, as to effect, upon a smooth river. We think that, in some few cases of rare occurrence at sea, it might be rendered serviceable, but it certainly would not live through a surf—would be snapped asunder in a short sea, and be rolled under water, tents and stationed men and officer, in a long one.

But this essay must only be looked upon as a rudiment of something more complete, and which, we doubt not, would have been effected, had not Sir Sidney's attentions been called to loftier and more weighty matters. Most heartily do we wish that some of our rear-admirals and post-captains would, in these piping times of peace, thus usefully employ their time—for in one thing they would be certain of success—the amusement of the citizens of London.

And, shortly after, his teeming mind did produce something much more effective, and calculated for a wider sphere of operations. It was in the construction of vessels to form a flotilla, and the practicability of his invention was first essayed on the 2nd of September, 1805.

It was altogether a sort of military triumph. He arrived at Dovor from Ramsgate in the Diligence revenue cutter, under a salute of six guns. He landed in a pilot wherry, and was received on shore by a discharge of three more guns. Accompanied by several naval officers, he retired for the night to the York Hotel.

The next day, at a very early hour, the two gunboats, newly constructed under his directions, were brought from their moorings to the mouth of the harbour for his inspection, and for the purpose of making some further improvements in them.

They were much on the same plan as the united wherries we have just described that were tried on the river, but differing in a few particulars, and on a scale much more extensive. One of the boats was called the Cancer, the other the Gemini. The Cancer was formed of a galley, forty-eight feet in length, cut exactly in two, from stem to stern. Those two parts were joined to the ends of four pieces of timber, which crossed them, and were made secure by braces of iron. Upon these four beams a platform was raised, in the centre of which was placed a three-pounder, ready mounted, with ammunition boxes, and all the necessary apparatus for the gun's service. The wheels of the light piece of ordnance stood in a groove, upon a sort of framework, which ran out some feet beyond the bows, so that, the moment the vessel was run ashore, the cannon could be landed and be instantly put in use.

In the centre of each of the two extreme beams which joined the two half galleys, masts were stepped, each of which carried a large square sail with proper rigging, and a foresail also projected from the beam which was fixed to the frame. There were four rudders, one to each extremity of the half galleys, two only of which to be worked at a time, by a cord connected with a larger one in the centre, and managed by a person on the platform. These four rudders could be shipped and unshipped in a moment, and the half galleys being equally sharp at both ends, the construction could progress, with the same facility, either backwards or forwards.

The half galleys were decked, with eight holes cut along each, large enough to admit a man's body. To the mouth of each hole was fixed a canvass bag, so as to prevent the water penetrating, and with a running string at the top. In these bags the sixteen men who pulled at the oars seated themselves, and tied them on tightly above their hips, which sufficiently lashed them to the body, and also prevented them from being washed overboard.

Besides these sixteen persons at the oars, and the other sailors who managed the sails, this vessel was capable of holding fifty soldiers; her sides were entirely lined with cork, so that it was impossible to upset her, and the heavy seas passed over her, doing no other injury than wetting that part of the men which was not encased in the painted canvass bags.

The other boat, the Gemini, was of a nearly similar construction, but much larger, and with this difference: she was formed of two entire galleys, fastened together, as was the Cancer, with sixteen holes in each galley, for the rowers were inside in the other; the sixteen outside men pulled with oars, whilst those in the middle were furnished with a sort of spade, in the shape of the paddle of an Indian canoe, the blade of which was made of iron, a place being left between the platform and the galleys to work these paddles. The paddles might also be used in clearing away the sand, mud, or gravel, and thus facilitate the landing of the cannon.

The Gemini carried a six-pounder, and a proportionate number of men more than the Cancer. Those vessels, when laden at the heaviest, drew only eighteen inches of water, so that they could be made most useful in running into shallow places, and landing guns with expedition.

At one o'clock, Sir Sidney Smith, accompanied by Major Chubley, of the East York militia, and some naval and military officers, went on board the Cancer, whilst the rest of his party embarked in the Gemini; and it being then flood-tide, and the wind at north-north-east, they proceeded out of the harbour, steering a south-west course.

Both the piers were crowded with company to witness this interesting spectacle. In short, all the fashionables of the town, as well as most of the population, had assembled to behold our hero; whilst the oldest of the inhabitants, who prided themselves in fancying Dover to be his native place, hailed him as the ornament and honour of their town. Many of these remembered him as a little boy; and he recognised his old friends, as he passed among them, with that kindness and affection that proved he deserved their love and approbation.

These vessels were attended by a ten-oared galley and the Diligence cutter. Having stood for some miles out to sea, they tacked and went before the wind. Here one of the greatest perfections of these boats was displayed. They ran before the wind with the greatest rapidity, outstripping even the cutter and galley, which were the swiftest sailing vessels then belonging to the harbour.

Whilst Sir Sidney was directing these movements, the Utilité frigate, of thirty-eight guns, belonging to the Boulogne squadron, passed under full sail from the Downs for that station, and when she came abreast of the harbour, fired a gun for her pilot. Soon after, the Desperate gunbrig hove in sight, from the Downs. This vessel was ordered to attend upon Sir Sidney, having on board twenty privates of the royal artillery, sent from Ramsgate to work the guns on board the newly-invented boats.

All this, with the addition of a most beautiful day, and a distinct view of the French coast, made the *coup d'oeil* [ED. glance] enchanting. After trying these boats in every way in which they could possibly be managed, through the whole of which they appeared to work with great ease and convenience, the artillery from the Desperate was put on board them, and several shots were fired in different directions, without having any visible effect upon the vessels. They were then brought into the roads, and ran on shore on that part of the strand where the brigade usually parade, near to the cottage then occupied by Sir Sidney Smith's aunt.

The cannon were landed in a moment, with the greatest ease, and several shots being fired by way of experiment, they were again, in the shortest space of time, shipped with the greatest facility; and whilst Sir Sidney and his party retired to regale themselves on shore, the boats were brought again out of the harbour to their original moorings.

It was rumoured that Admiral Lord Keith was to have been of this experimentalizing party, but, for some reasons that have never transpired, he did not attend.

We think that the same objections apply to this larger, as we thought were applicable to the smaller experiments. It answered beautifully in fine weather, and on smooth water.

The invention was a combination of the double Indian canoe of the southern seas, the Laplander's small seal-skin constructed coracle, and the modern lifeboat, with the addition of the negro's paddle. It was a most clever contrivance, but much too elaborate ever to have come into general use.

CHAPTER XII

AS we have before stated, Sir Sidney Smith was promoted to the rank of vice-admiral on the 31st of July, 1810, but he did not hoist his flag at the fore until the summer of 1812, when he was appointed the second in command in the Mediterranean, under Sir Edward Pellew, afterwards Lord Exmouth. He proceeded to his station in the Tremendous seventy-four, and, on arriving off Toulon, he shifted his flag to the Hibernia, a first-rate, where it remained until the close of the war. This service had but little in it that was captivating to so ardent and zealous an officer as Sir Sidney. The blockading of the French fleet in Toulon in the fine months of the year, and lying in the excellent harbour of Port Mahon in the tempestuous ones, were the usual alternations of employment, now and then varied by a skirmish with the blockaded force, and a storm of more or less fury.

Sir Sidney Smith, with his flag flying on board the Hibernia, led the lee-line, and for wearying months together nothing further took place than stretching off the port and harbour of Toulon at the approach of night, in order to stretch in next morning.

Sometimes, when the coast became a lee-shore to the British fleet, Sir Edward Pellew was obliged to haul off, and then the French fleet would seize the opportunity of stealing out of their harbour, in order to train the seamen to the different nautical evolutions—a discipline of which they stood much in need. Having their port, with its formidable batteries, directly under the lee to run into, they used, on these occasions, to play very ostentatious pranks; clapping on all sail as if in pursuit of their enemies, making signals with a rapidity quite imposing, and from time to time firing innocuous broadsides over the seas that they claimed as their own, but on which they dared not remain, though always in greater force than the enemy of whom they stood so much in awe. This was all very well and very pleasant, so long as the wind remained dead on the Toulon shore, but sometimes it would suddenly change, and then the eagerness with which they made for their port was perfectly amusing.

But the English had always an in-shore squadron, that, hugging the western shore, were sometimes enabled to intercept them in their retreat, or at least, by firing upon them, throw them into confusion, and thus retard their recovery of their port.

In the midst of this, up would come, heavily plunging through the water, every stitch of canvass crowded upon them, first one and then another, and then two or three together of the largest and finest three-deckers from the English fleet, in the world. They would arrive in the fray without order, or any losing of time in forming the line. But, unfortunately, when they could get within range, they were generally in the very centre of the outer harbour, and all but surrounded with batteries; and in this situation, fighting, almost literally, under a canopy of shell and shot, they would pour in their farewell broadsides upon the retreating Frenchmen, who, when huddled up in the inner harbour, would immediately set about writing self-satisfactory despatches—procure *Te Deums* to be sung for their signal success—whilst the shops of the town would teem with caricatures of the English, in which their own navy was held up for admiration and the public gratitude for having baffled the enemy, by safely getting away from an inferior force.

There is no exaggeration in all this. We ourselves have read the French despatches, and seen the French caricatures concerning these futile skirmishes that were so provoking to the British tars, because their foes would not permit them to be anything else.

It would be ridiculous to enter more into detail on these trifling encounters, in which Sir Sidney's high talents and great professional skill could not, by any possibility, be brought into action.

When lying in the harbour of Mahon, during the severe gales of the winter months, the Hibernia was the focus of all that was hospitable and social. The mania of the day consisted in theatrical exhibitions, and we believe we are strictly in truth when we say that they were patronised, and, as far as liberality of purse was concerned, mainly assisted by Sir Sidney.

These performances took place in a dismantled church at Mahon, and what was formerly the altar now became the stage and proscenium of the theatre. The wings of the church, that had once been appropriated as chapels to the saints, were metamorphosed into saloons, where very excellent segars and very bad grog were sold by ladies who were more liberal in their moral notions than in their mercantile dealings. The Spaniards of the Balearic Islands are very good and orthodox Catholics; yet they never objected to all this, but generally made the greater part of the audience.

Acts of parliament not being in force in Mahon, money was openly taken at the doors for admission to this theatre, and the proceeds applied to the purchase of luxuries and indulgences for the sick of the fleet, and to the assistance of the poor of the town. The characters were filled, of course, by the junior officers of the navy; if they performed them well, it was well—if ill, still better, for the amusement, because the more exhilarating.

On board of the Hibernia, also, we have witnessed histrionic performances, which, though they were not so effective as those exhibited in the deserted church in the town, might well compete in excellence with the efforts of any company of strolling players that were ever great in a barn.

But Sir Sidney took means less questionable for the amusement and improvement of the future captains and admirals of the British fleet. In order to encourage habits of study, he promulgated the following document:

"Sir Sidney Smith allows the officers of his ship, gentlemen, his or their guests, passengers, gentlemen petty officers, and young gentlemen volunteers, free access to his books, maps, and charts, in the portion of the fore-cabin that will be generally opened as a reading-room, between the hours of ten A.M. and one hour before the dinner hours at sea and at harbour, as it may be; which will be notified by these rules being hung up in a conspicuous place therein, and the shutters of the fore-bulkhead being opened; access being then to be had by the starboard-door, the larboard one being reserved for communication with the admiral on service, or otherwise.

The following regulations are to be observed for general convenience.

1st. The most absolute SILENCE is to be maintained; salutations are mutually dispensed with; messages and answers are not to be conveyed within the reading-room.

2nd. Any gentleman selecting a book, with the intention of reading it through, will mark his place with a ticket inscribed with his name, and the date of his having so selected it; and although another may take it up for perusal in his absence, and also mark his place therein in like manner, the first ticket is not to be removed, and the occupant is to make over the book to the person whose marking ticket is of prior date, on his appearance in the reading-room, without his claiming or requesting it.

N.B. The Encyclopaedia, Hutton's Mathematical and Philosophical Dictionary, and all other dictionaries; the Naval Chronicle, Panorama, and other periodical publications, are excepted from this rule, and to be generally accessible when out of hand.

3rd. No books or newspapers to be taken out of the reading-room.

4th. All books are to be replaced on the shelves, or in the chest from which they were taken; and generally, on the removal of these rules from their place at the hour appointed, observing that they are arranged on the shelves according to their comparative sizes, in gradual succession, without reference to their contents, and in their boxes according to their classification, with reference to the subject or characteristic marked thereon.

5th. Should any gentleman wish to call the attention of any other to any particular rule, the mode of so doing, without a breach of the first rule, is, by exhibiting to him the card containing the rule in question.

6th. Any gentleman inclined to leave a book of his own for general perusal, will please to put his name on the title-page, and insert its title and his name in the book appropriated for that purpose.

"Printed on board the Hibernia, January, 1813.

We may, in this place, inform the reader that both the flag-ships, the Caledonia, bearing the flag of the commander-in-chief, and Sir Sidney's ship, had on board of them very complete printing presses, with all the necessary types and furniture.

There is now in the Bodleian library at Oxford a book which was printed on board the Hibernia, which was presented to it by our officer.

CHAPTER XIII

WHILST Sir Sidney was assisting at this wearisome blockade, Buonaparte was precipitating his vast and gallant army upon the snows of Russia, and soon found in its annihilation that adverse turn of fate from
which he never recovered, though he rallied manfully against his destiny.

In this state of doubt as to the security of his power, anarchy made its
appearance in the south of France, many portions of which, long before
the lion was caught and chained, showed a disposition to hoist the white
over the tricolour flag. This was a juncture of circumstances peculiarly
fitted for the exercise of the various talents of Sir Sidney Smith.

Unfortunately, if there be any reliance on rumour, our officer was not
on the most cordial terms with Sir Edward Pellew. Sir Sidney was so well
fitted to be a commander-in-chief, that the consciousness of it made him
less suited to act a secondary part. *Aut Cesar aut nihil*, [Ed. Either Caesar
or nothing] if not his motto, the sentiment it expressed seemed, at least,
to be paramount with him. Just before the re-establishment of the Bourbons in their ancient power, Sir Sidney separated from the fleet with the
Hibernia, and repaired to Cagliari, no doubt for the purpose of forwarding the legitimate movement that was then beginning so generally to display itself On this occasion, the King of Sardinia and suite dined on board
his flag-ship. At this *fete*, not only were the usual captains and commanders invited to meet royalty, but the vice admiral bid, as his guests,
with his accustomed liberality, all the senior lieutenants and midshipmen
of his squadron. From this munificent act, the last named class of officers
augured very wisely, that a general peace was most certainly on the eve of
being proclaimed.

Shortly after this, Sir Sidney returned to England, and struck his flag. This was the last time in which he was employed afloat in the service of his country. Soon after his arrival in England, the mayor and commonalty of the borough of Plymouth voted him the freedom of their corporation, which was presented to him in a silver box. This took place on the 7th of July, 1814, as indicated by the following document:

At the common hall of the mayor and commonalty of the borough of Plymouth, held at the Guildhall of and within the said borough, on Thursday, the 7th day of July instant, in pursuance of a regular notice of three clear days from Henry Woolcombe, Esq., mayor, for the purpose hereinafter mentioned.

The mayor and the commonalty, in common hall assembled, being desirous of recording their sense of high desert, and their gratitude for the eminent services to their country, more especially on that branch of his Majesty's service with which, from local circumstances, they are more immediately connected, have taken in their consideration the meritorious actions of Vice-admiral Sir William Sidney Smith, now arrived at this port, from his command on the Mediterranean station, at the conclusion of a war of unexampled importance, through the long course of which this gallant officer has been actively and eminently engaged.

In this eventful war, in which the naval and military renown of Britain has been extended to a pitch, not only exceeding the recorded glory of former ages, but even the most ardent expectations of the present times; a war, not more distinguished by the stupendous victories of fleets and armies, than by the most brilliant instances of individual prowess. No exploit has surpassed the astonishing defence of Acre.

To Sir Sidney Smith it was given, by fortitude, perseverance, conduct, and valour, to revive and augment the glories of England in Palestine, and, on the plains of Nazareth, to defeat the gigantic ambition of France, meditating the destruction of British power in India.

Nor were the ability and valour of the chieftain more distinguished on this memorable occasion than his humanity; that humanity which, in the moment of victory, has ever adorned the brightest examples of British heroism, and which, in this instance, admitted of no check from the recollection of unmerited sufferings and indignities in a captivity unauthorised by the usages of war, and inflicted in revenge for the exercise of that zeal, intrepidity, and spirit of enterprise, which should have commanded the admiration rather than the detestation of his foes. We have, therefore, unanimously resolved to confer the freedom of the said borough on the said Sir William Sidney Smith, Knt. Grand Cross of the military order of the Sword in Sweden, &c., and Vice-admiral of the red squadron of his Majesty's fleet, in testimony of his high, distinguished, and meritorious services; and it is ordered that the same be presented to him in a silver box by a committee of the commonalty.

Resolved, that the following gentlemen, viz; Sir William Elford, Bart., recorder, John Arthur, Esq., justice, Richard Pridhomme, Esq., Robert Butler Bennet, M.D., and George Bellamy, M.D., be a committee for the above purpose, and that any three of them be competent to act.

Resolved, that the mayor be requested to communicate the above resolutions to Sir William Sidney Smith, and to acquaint him that the deputation will wait on him with the freedom when he shall next come within the borough.

JOSEPH WHITEFORD
Town Clerk

Peace was not permitted to check our hero's activity in doing good. He now took up the cause of philanthropy in its noblest sense, by endeavouring to put an end to the white slavery that had been so successfully carried on, for generations, by the piratical states of the northern shores of Africa. He immediately set about establishing a society, in which he sought to enrol the names and to secure the protection and assistance of all the European potentates. To effect this, being still in England, he published the following document, which, at the time, excited a very great sensation. This is the first of the papers relative to the reports of the President of the re-union of all knights of all the European orders, which took place at Vienna on the 29th of December, 1814.

Memorial upon the necessity and the means
to exterminate the pirates of the barbarian nations

London, August 31, 1814

Whilst the means of abolishing the slave-trade of the negro on the western coast of Africa are discussed, and whilst civilised Europe is endeavouring to extend the benefits of commerce, and of the security of person and property into the interior of this vast continent, peopled with a race of men naturally mild and industrious, and capable of enjoying the highest degree of civilisation, it is astonishing that no attention has been turned to the southern coast of this same country, which is inhabited by Turkish pirates, who not only oppress the natives in their neighbourhood, but carry them off, and purchase them as slaves, in order to employ them in armed vessels, to tear away from their firesides the honest cultivators of the soil, and the peaceable inhabitants of the shores of Europe. This shameful piracy is not only revolting to humanity, but it fetters commerce in the most disastrous manner, since, at present, mariners can neither navigate the Mediterranean nor the Atlantic in a merchant-vessel, without the fear of being carried off by pirates, and led away into slavery in Africa. The Algerine government is composed of an orta, or a regiment of Janissaries, revolted soldiers, assuming not to recognise, even in appearance, the authority of the Ottoman Porte, who, however, does not acknowledge their independence. The Dey is always that individual of the orta who has the most distinguished himself by his cruelty. He is now at the head of the regency or divan, enriching his confederates, that is to say, permitting them to practise all manner of violence in Africa, and piracies at sea, against the weaker European nations, or those whose immediate vengeance it does not fear.

Even the Ottoman flag itself is no protection for its Greek subjects, in sheltering them from the Algerine corsairs. Lately, the Dey, either through the caprice of cruelty, or by a barbarous policy, the end of which is to destroy the rival commerce of Tunis and Tripoli, has hung the crews of some ships that have fallen into his power, from the Archipelago and Egypt, and which were laden with corn.

The Pacha of Egypt, in his just anger, has caused all Algerines found in his territories to be imprisoned, and demands in vain the restitution of the cargoes so unjustly seized by the Dey of Algiers.

The Sublime Porte sees with indignation, and even with umbrage, that a revolted vassal dares to perform the most outrageous and the most atrocious acts against his peaceful subjects, and that it cripples a commerce, of which he was never more in need, in order to be enabled to pay the troops of the pachas employed upon the eastern frontier of the Ottoman empire, in order to oppose the Wachabites, and the other numerous Arabian tribes, which, under sectarian influence, cease not, by their invasions, to threaten the existence of his tottering government.

On the other side, Europe is interested in the support of the Ottoman government, as an acknowledged authority, and as a power which is able to restrain the pachas and the revolted beys, and preventing them from following the example of Algiers, in becoming sea-robbers. This interests Europe the more particularly, in the need that is often experienced for the import of corn from the Black Sea and from the Nile, countries where there is always a superabundance; whilst, in the Ottoman empire, the bad season of the north is always counterbalanced by the good season of the south in the same year, and *vice versâ*.

Thus, if a barbarian, calling himself an independent sovereign, though not acknowledged as such by the Turkish sultan, his rightful sovereign, may, as he thinks fit, threaten, coerce, and hang the Greeks, imprison the mariners of the small European states, who alone carry on a trade that the ships of the greater powers do not find sufficiently advantageous to follow, because they cannot navigate at so small an outlay; if this bold chief of pirates may, at his own good pleasure, intercept cargoes of corn destined for Europe, civilised nations are, in this respect, dependent upon a chief of robbers, who can, unknown to them, increase their distress, and even famish them in times of scarcity.

This barbarian has also another formidable method of extorting money from Christian princes; he threatens them, as he has just served Sicily, to put to death all their subjects that may fall into his power; his well-known cruelty rendering these threats the more formidable, because to him the means of making use of the money of one Christian prince to carry on the war that he has declared against another; he can thus place all Europe under contribution, and force, in a manner, nations, each in its turn, to pay tribute to his ferocity, in purchasing from him the lives of the unfortunate slaves, and peace.

It is useless to demonstrate that such a state of things is not only monstrous but absurd, and that it no less outrages religion than humanity and honour. The progress of knowledge and civilisation ought, necessarily, to dispel it.

It is evident that the military capabilities employed by Christian princes, up to this moment, to keep in check these barbarous states, have been, not only insufficient, but more often have been operative to consolidate still more this barbarian power. Europe has, for a long period, appeared to rely on the efforts of the Knights of St. John of Jerusalem, and not sufficiently to have understood that this order of chivalry had not, latterly, the power, and perhaps not the energy ^ sufficient to counterbalance and repel the continually recurring aggressions of these numerous pirates. Besides, through the nature of its institution, the order of Malta, forbidden to have any intercourse with infidels, cannot turn to advantage all political resources, in making treaties of alliance with those among them who are rather the victims of this piratical system than pirates themselves; as, for example, Tunis and Morocco, both of them governed by princes born in these states, and who have, for a long time, shown themselves well disposed, and are quite capable of maintaining with European powers social and commercial relations.

Thus, the revival of this order, after the political suicide that it has committed, would not be sufficient to accomplish the object proposed. This object is to secure Europe for ever from the assaults of the African corsairs, and to cause these states, essentially piratical, because barbarous, to establish governments useful to commerce, and in harmony with civilised nations.

Now, what are the means to be employed? The undersigned wishes to make Europe share in his conviction, the result of thirty years of study and of profound examination. He never ceased, during his mission to the Ottoman court, and in his command in the Levant, to occupy himself with the subject on which he is now speaking. It was ever present to him, both in the fields and on the waves of this same power, and during the whole course of those relations, that are publicly enough known, which he had with the nations and the territories of Asia and Africa.

This internal conviction of the possibility of promptly putting an end to this system of brigandage of those barbarian states, cannot better be proved than by the offer that he makes to take upon himself the direction of the enterprise, provided that the necessary means be placed at his disposal.

Animated by the remembrance of his oaths as a knight, and desiring to excite the same ardour in other Christian knights, he proposes to the nations the most interested in the success of this noble enterprise, to engage themselves, by treaty, to furnish each their contingent of a maritime, or, more properly speaking, amphibious force, which, without compromising any flag, and without depending on the wars or the political events of the nations, should constantly guard the shores of the Mediterranean, and take upon itself the important office of watching, pursuing, and capturing all pirates by land and by sea. This power, owned and protected by all Europe, would not only give perfect security to commerce, but would finish by civilising the African coasts, by preventing their inhabitants from continuing their piracy, to the prejudice of productive industry and legitimate commerce.

This protective and imposing force would commence its operations by the vigorous blockade of the barbarian naval forces, wherever they might be found; at the same time that ambassadors from all the sovereigns and states of Christianity ought mutually to support each other, in representing to the Sublime Porte, that she cannot be otherwise than herself responsible for the hostile acts of her subjects, if she continues to permit the African garrisons to recruit in her territories, which are of no utility to her, whilst these forces would be better employed against her enemies than against European and armed powers; and in requiring from her a formal disavowal, and even an authentic interdiction against the wars that these rebel chiefs declare against Europe.

The Ottoman Porte might be induced to grant promotion and rewards to those of the Janissaries, captains of frigates, and others, Algerine mariners, who should obey the Sultan's command, and, by these means, the Dey would soon find himself abandoned, and without adequate means of defence.

The other details will be easily developed when the sovereigns shall have adopted the principle, and when they shall have deigned to grant to the undersigned the confidence and the authority necessary to the success of the enterprise.

Received, considered, and adopted at Paris, September, 1814; at Turin, October 14th, 1814; and at Vienna, during the meeting of the Congress of the allied sovereigns.

WM. SIDNEY SMITH

At this time it was understood that the allied sovereigns on the continent were already subscribers to a charitable fund towards the abolition of the white slave trade in North Africa, as well as of the black slave trade in West Africa, and that all bankers received subscriptions for the *caisse* in the hands of Messieurs Gaulifreres at Genoa, on whom the consuls in Africa were authorised to draw.

Sir Sidney Smith, accompanied by his family, at the restoration of Louis XVIII., repaired to Paris, and there took up his residence, at which place, with the exception of occasional tours, he has, up to the present time, remained.

CHAPTER XIV

PARTICULARS CONCERNING CAPTAIN WRIGHT • THAT OFFICER TAKEN
BY GUNBOATS • IS WELL TREATED IN THE FIRST INSTANCE • THE SUB-
SEQUENT PERSECUTIONS TO WHICH HE WAS SUBJECTED.

WE have, in the course of this memoir, stated, and that without meaning
the least disrespect to Captain Wright's memory, that he was generally
employed by Sir Sidney Smith to collect for him information, to arrange
the minor details of treaties and compacts, to aid him in diplomacy; in
fact, to be his coadjutor in all manner of head-work, and that, the more
effectually to perform this, he was often habited in other dresses than the
uniform prescribed by the Admiralty. These services, and the singular
positions in which Sir Sidney Smith found himself when he called for
their employment, as we have before mentioned, made the lower grades
of the navy, who are apt to give the shortest, though perhaps not the most
just appellation to the person so occupied, designate Captain Wright as a
spy. This is a harsh term, but its signification must altogether change
with the parties who use it.

If Captain Wright volunteer on a dangerous service—a service that
involves, if unsuccessful, not only certain death, but great obloquy, his
country, for whom this risk is run, applauds the self-sacrifice, and honours the private and clandestine seeker for information, as a patriot and a
hero, whilst the hostile party covers him with opprobrium, and hangs
him up with as little ceremony, and with much less compunction, than
they would a mangy dog. To the English, therefore, Captain Wright is a
bold, an intelligent, and self-devoted patriot; and one who was selected
for this kind of delicate and adventurous service, because he possessed
more judgment, and as much courage as his brother officers. That he was
a most estimable man, one upon the knowledge of whom love and respect were bound to attend, all who have read his memoirs, or whoever
met him in private life, must eagerly testify. Sir Sidney esteemed him to a
degree that might have been termed romantic, had he been a less deserv-

ing object; and as soon as he found himself on the scene of their mutual sufferings, he commenced an inquiry into the details of his friend's mysterious death with all the ardour and the intelligence of his character.

We have before stated it as our opinion that this meritorious officer was not sacrificed to the vengeance of Buonaparte, or perished the victim of a miserable and detestable state policy. He fell either by his own act, or by the operations of private malice. We will, notwithstanding, implore the reader to judge for himself; and in order that he may do so the more effectually, we submit to him the following documents, interesting in themselves, and throwing all the light that has yet been obtained upon this dark and terrible transaction.

These documents are abridged from the "Naval Chronicle;" and we again take the opportunity of acknowledging how much we are indebted to that valuable work for many of the materials of these memoirs. In order to preserve the continuity of the narrative, we shall throw into one form the whole of Sir Sidney's researches into this affair, and, disregarding dates, go through with it at once.

As it is not our intention to give an abstract of the life of this very meritorious and unfortunate officer, we shall merely take up the narrative at the time of his second capture, which led to his imprisonment and death; and then proceed with the inquiry instituted by his friend Sir Sidney Smith, in order to arrive at the truth of the circumstances that led to his mysterious end.

On the 7th of May, 1804, toward the evening, Captain Wright, accompanied by the surgeon, Mr. Lawmont, went on shore on the Isle of Houat. The night was dark and hazy, and it blew a gale. On returning, he nearly missed the brig, but at last got on board, and ordered her to be steered in the direction of Porto Navallo. Towards morning the wind had died away, and at daylight there was a dead calm. Seventeen gun-vessels, perceiving his situation, took advantage of it, and rowed out in pursuit of the Vincejo, then completely becalmed near the mouth of the harbour.

Every exertion was made by the officers and crew to sweep or tow her off, but the flotilla rapidly gained on her—opened their fire, and when she arrived near the Teigneuse rock, the flood-tide met her, and she was drifted back into the bay. The action now began, and was continued nearly two hours, under every advantage on the part of the enemy, when, after a heavy loss of men, Captain Wright was obliged to surrender; and thus, under circumstances similar to those which consigned him to his former captivity, was he again placed in the hands of the enemy.

Captain Wright had a strong presentiment of the fate that awaited him, and, without recurring to supernatural influence, his former experience of the enmity of those who were now to dispose of him, would be sufficient to account for it. He was entreated by his officers to escape on board the Fox cutter, which was then sweeping out of the bay, at no great distance; but he firmly opposed their importunities, and insisted on sharing the fate of his officers and gallant ship's company. Had there been no reason to apprehend worse than the ordinary treatment of a captured commander, the persuasions of his officers would have borne the character of insult; but their fear was too well founded, that his fate would be *particular*!

The French carried their hard-earned prize into Porto Navallo, a small harbour in the mouth of the river Vilaine, and treated the officers with polite attention. In the evening, the whole of the prisoners were conveyed in boats to Auray, where also they were kindly treated, the officers being lodged in private houses; the men were sent to a prison. The wounded were conveyed to the hospital, and, on their passing through the streets, the inhabitants were seen flocking round them from the houses, and offering them wine.

After remaining here several days, orders arrived for their being conducted into the interior of France; and some of the principal inhabitants evinced their respect to Captain Wright, by accompanying him a considerable way from the town. He proceeded, with the surgeon, to Vannes, in a small cart, and the whole were guarded by a few gendarmes, and some of the national guard, under the command of a Swiss officer.

Soon after reaching Vannes, he went, accompanied by Lieutenant Wallis, and his nephew, Mr Wright, to pay a visit to General Julien, then prefect of the department of the Morbihan. This officer had been wounded and made prisoner in Egypt, and was treated with a brotherly kindness by Captain Wright, who resigned to him his cabin on board the Tigre, off St. Jean d'Acre, where he remained on board several months, and parted with him under protestations of eternal friendship. To the disgrace of General Julien we record it, he returned all this kindness with ingratitude: he ordered Captain Wright to be arrested at the inn, where he had stopped, and sent him to Paris in charge of a gendarme, treacherously pretending that he adopted this mode of proceeding from a regard to his comfort. To add to the atrocity of this act, he, at the same time, addressed a letter to Fouché, the minister of police. He began his letter by saying, that having heard the crew of an English corvette, which had been captured a few days before by a division of the national flotilla, was passing through Vannes, he had repaired to the spot to examine if there were among them any traitors like those who had lately been vomited on the coasts; but what was his surprise, when in the commander he recognised the celebrated Captain Wright, who had landed Pichegru, &c., and whom he had formerly known in Egypt; and as he thought he might make some useful revelations, he had sent him forward by the gendarmerie, with a very young nephew, and his servant. He next represented Captain Wright as a most artful and dangerous adventurer, who thought himself destined to act some high part that he affected to set all interrogatories at defiance, as he acted under the orders of his government, and was accountable only to it—but, added the General, if he is *properly* questioned, he will make revelations of much importance to the Republic.

The crew of the Vincejo were drawn up without the gates of Vannes. Captain Wright there took an affectionate leave of them, many of whom shed tears. He said, as he passed before them, that in whatever situation he might be placed, he should never forget that he was a British officer.

On his arrival at Paris, he was subjected to many interrogatories, to all which he firmly answered, that he had no account to render to the French government, and that he would answer none of the questions put to him. He was then conveyed to the Tower of the Temple, and confined in a very small room in one of the upper turrets of that state prison, two soldiers being placed with him in the cell.

Thus lodged and guarded, he remained until he was brought forward at the public trial of Georges Cadoudal, the Marquis de Riviére, Moreau, and others, termed conspirators by Buonaparte, and with them he was confronted. Georges, De Riviére, and some others, denied positively any knowledge of him, and Captain Wright, though suffering extremely from a wound in the thigh, nobly persisted, in answer to all the insidious questions of the grand judge and others, that he was accountable to none but his own government for his public conduct, would answer no questions, and insisted on the treatment due to a prisoner of war of his rank.

In spite of the awful police of this tribunal, a thunder of applause burst from the crowd of spectators in the galleries, and being faint with his exertions, and the pain of his wound, he was allowed to withdraw, which he did, bowing to the spectators, who again applauded him. His nephew, then not fourteen years of age, was also questioned, and answered with a coolness and firmness that again excited the applause of the spectators, whom the all-powerful police could not awe into silence.

The firmness of Captain Wright seems to have procured him better treatment from his enemies, or the semblance of it, preparatory to their final purpose: he was now allowed a room to himself in the Temple, with the company of his nephew, and the system of rigour was to be next adopted against the officers of the Vincejo, for the like purpose of extorting the important *revelations* which the honourable General Julien had represented as attainable, if *properly* questioned.

These gentlemen were all conveyed to Paris, and subjected to various interrogatories; first in the prison of the Abbaye, and afterwards in the Tower of the Temple, where they were confined in separate cells, without any communication with each other, or with any of the other prisoners of the Temple, This solitary imprisonment was continued twenty-six days, with bread and water for their sole nourishment, and without being allowed to quit their cell an instant. During this period, they were repeatedly interrogated in the night-time by agents of police, accompanied by gendarmes, relative to the supposed mission of Captain Wright. At length they were permitted to lodge together in one large room, and they had now, by stealth, some intercourse with their captain; but the interest he took in contemplating and advising the future conduct of the young gentlemen of his ship, whom he called his *admirals in embryo*, seemed to render him totally unmindful of his own critical situation.

About the middle of July, all his officers were ordered from the Temple. By connivance of the keeper, they had an interview with the captain, who seemed cheerful, though evidently impressed with a strong presentiment of the melancholy fate that awaited him. On taking leave of the surgeon, Mr. Laumont, he said impressively, "I hope we may meet again under more favourable circumstances; but, at all events, whatever may happen to me in my present position, I will behave, believe me, whatever reports may be sent abroad, like a Christian and a British officer." The following letter from him soon after reached the first lieutenant at Verdun, and is strongly characteristic of his excellent and affectionate heart:

Dear Wallis, In order to intrude but little on the translator in office, and to favour an early delivery of my letter, I send you this time merely a short one, in acknowledgment of your kind perseverance, which procured me the pleasure of receiving yours of the 29th, a few days ago.

Accept my thanks for your congratulation on my promotion, which is, however, become indifferent to me, farther than to demonstrate the liberality and justice of government, of which I never entertained a doubt. I beg you to bear in mind, that I have every proper feeling on the occasion, and the handsome manner in which it has been conferred has not escaped my observation, or failed to have due weight; although it has been in my contemplation to resign my commission, through an official channel here, in order to relieve government from the embarrassment my extraordinary situation must have placed it under, and to prevent a practice which I forbear to characterise, bearing upon other victims on either side; but I felt, on further reflection, that although I was willing to forego its protection, yet no act of mine, thus situated, could absolve my government from the performance of its duty to a British subject.

I rejoice to hear that you are within the immediate jurisdiction of a liberal-minded man; for I was under some anxiety as to the *regimé* you might be subject to. I think I had already prepared you to expect benevolence from individuals, when they might be at liberty to exercise that benign principle: give it the fullest credit, make much of it, as one fair means of giving it farther extension, and make use of the custom under your eye to obliterate from the young mind of my poor boys unfavourable impressions, to which they may already have yielded.

I rejoice also to hear at length that you are near those dear boys, in whose progress my whole solicitude at present centres: give them my best wishes, and recall to their memory what has been so often pressed on them; I must have no idleness, no indecorous boyish tricks, no habits of riot or inebriety, no deviation from truth, no adoption of prejudice, no tendency to exaggeration, no indiscriminate censure or proscription *en masse*; but a liberal, gentlemanly conduct, and a steady persevering assiduity, which will alone surmount the difficulties that are before them. Remind them often of their destination; of the precious leisure they have but momentarily on their hands: let the mainspring of all their outward actions be the character of our dear country, and repeat how much I expect from them. If Mr. Trewin's son be amongst them, let him partake of all the advantages I purpose securing to my own three boys, but with such delicacy as will neither hurt his own nor his parent's feelings; in the mean time, apply to my authority when the pecuniary means are attainable, which in the course of our correspondence, should it continue, I shall specially appropriate.

I am not unaware, my dear Wallis, that I am thus imposing a difficult task, and laying a heavy burthen on you; but I am sure you undertake the one cheerfully, and will bear the other with patience. Give my best wishes to all my officers individually, and tell the doctor I take it for granted he makes good use of his time. I recommend him to walk the public hospitals, if there are any in the neighbourhood, and to follow up his chemistry with ardour. I shall be glad to hear from any of my officers, when they are in a scribbling mood. If it be possible, let my servant Henry attend on the boys, and tell him I have begged you to take care of him. Is poor Mr. Brown recovered? The last time I heard of him was before your departure, and that was unfavourable. Pray give me an account nominally of all my people; poor old Sampson, you know, is no more. Is that poor creature, whose wishes death seemed unwilling to accomplish, still living?

I have a little amiable cat, that has just taken the caprice of laying her whole length on my paper, and purs to me as nearly as I can guess, ' mercy on the translator;' so all that I can say is, that I have taken the liberty to make you a sort of foster-father to my little admirals in embryo; you must assume a gravity suitable to the weighty occasion: you perceive that I am not without amiable society; and I must tell you, for the comfort of my other little amiable creatures, who may weep for my misfortunes, that I can bear them, however great or multiplied; but that I am less ill off than people at a distance, whose apprehensions magnify evil, are aware of; for I have within a few months had the faculty of procuring books, and subscribing to the ' Moniteur,' whose foibles and prejudices, I assure you, I am in no danger of adopting. Now, fare you well, and believe me, most faithfully and unfeignedly, your friend,

J. W. WRIGHT.

P. S. Tell me particularly all the boys have done; tell them I continually think of their progress; let no partiality, except that inspired by excellence or superior merit, be shown to one above another; for a favourite has no friend.'

It seems strange that our government had hitherto made no attempt to save our much lamented countryman, by threatening retaliation on the prisoners of rank in their power. At last, however, the British ministers, through the medium of the Spanish ambassador, remonstrated against the severity of Captain Wright's treatment, as authorised by the French government, and was answered by the French minister, Talleyrand, with promises, couched in the most insulting terms, no doubt dictated by Buonaparte himself, styling Captain Wright a person of the most frightful character, (*un homme affreux,*) whom they could not deign to treat as a prisoner of war, being sure that no French officer would consent to be exchanged against him, and proposing to send him to some neutral port, there to be placed at the disposal of the British government. But there is reason to believe, that at the time these fallacious promises and propositions were made, Captain Wright had ceased to exist. A paragraph shortly after appeared in a minor paper, the ' Gazette de France,' stating, "Captain Wright, of the English navy, a prisoner in the Temple, who had debarked on the French coast Georges and his accomplices, has put an end to his existence in his prison, after having read in the 'Moniteur' an account of the destruction of the Austrian army."

The absurdity of this statement was alone sufficient to divest it of all credit. There existed strong ground to presume that he was put to death by the orders of Buonaparte; that he was brought to a mock trial, and condemned to be shot; and that this sentence was executed in private. An officer of the imperial guard asserted, in the hearing of Mr. Laumont, that he was present at this odious transaction. Before this information, it was believed that he was, like Pichegru, strangled in his cell. One thing certain is, that in the Temple he was attended by the man who was universally believed by the other prisoners of the Temple to have been the assassin of Pichegru. This has been repeatedly stated by some who had been confined there at the time this unfortunate general was also said to have committed suicide.

The following account was the almost universal impression in England of this gentleman's fate. We shall now proceed to show what means were taken by Sir William Sidney Smith to unravel this mystery.

"The catastrophe of our former narrative," says our authority, "was sufficiently final, but not equally demonstrative. It is owing to the recent exertions of Sir Sidney Smith, that additional evidence has been procured, which, although it does not yet leave the fact of his murder positively incontrovertible by those whom nothing but direct evidence, or the personal confession of the assassins, can satisfy, it does not leave a doubt on our minds. The evidence is in some particulars contradictory, but the contradiction is on one side so evidently absurd, that in our opinion it rather tends to confirm than to confute the opposing testimony.

"The active benevolence and humanity of Sir Sidney Smith, (principles essential to the perfection of true heroism, and which have completed that gallant knight's title to chivalric distinction,) while engaged in projecting the suppression of barbaric tyranny, and the final redemption of Christian captives from slavery and torture, prompted the equally honourable, though less conspicuous, design of ascertaining, by a diligent inquisition, the circumstances relative to the death of his late pupil, fellow-prisoner, and friend. Accordingly, previous to his leaving London for Vienna in 1814, he wrote to Madame B— —, the widow of the gaoler, (Concierge,) who was keeper of the Tower when he and Captain Wright escaped in 1798, requesting of her such information as she could give or procure of his unfortunate friend's fate.

"When Sir Sidney entered Paris with the Allies last July, Madame B— — came to him, and told him, that she had written an answer, in consequence of his request: it had, however, never been received by Sir Sidney, arid she recapitulated her information in a letter, which letter will form one portion of the recently collected evidence.

"In the prosecution of this very laudable design, Sir Sidney has been sedulously employed at Paris. The French government have likewise, at his request, very honourably afforded him every becoming facility. The offices and officers of the police have been rendered immediately accessible to his search and inquiry, which, judiciously directed, has produced the recovery of all the captain's papers, and such evidence of his assassination as seems to have left no doubt on the mind of Sir Sidney—(we repeat it)—no doubt on ours; and we presume it must carry equal conviction to every mind not impenetrably callous to circumstantial evidence, which in most cases of murder is all that can possibly be obtained, but by the voluntary confession of the parties concerned.

"The regal government of France, as we have already observed, has aided Sir Sidney in his inquiry, and has given up, on the claim of that officer, everything connected with the name of his late friend; viz. 1st. Copies and translations taken by the police of all his correspondence, as it passed through the hands of office. 2ndly. Documents and other papers taken violently from his person and room, at a domiciliary visit in the prison. 3rdly. Every scrap of paper found in the apartment after his death, so very minute and miscellaneous, as to justify the integrality of this collection, all regularly numbered by the proper officer, and stitched together at the corner, affording a curious specimen of the accuracy of French administration, compared with the careless, slovenly way in which such matters are, or would probably be, transacted here. 'They manage these things better in France,' as Sterne says. These papers are in two sets: viz.

Marked G, and numbered 1 to . . .	208
Under one numerical entry, 8866 . .	15
Total pieces . .	223

of every size, from a folio sheet to fragments two inches long by half-inch broad; a reading mark, a servant's account, or even the title of a book.

"The greater part of the mass of papers above numerically stated, appears in its contents to have been the mere ways and means of speeding the lingering hours of captivity; but it also contains a proof, that however indifferent to the menaces of death with which that captivity was embittered by his enemies, he was sensibly alive to the preservation of his honour in the eyes of his countrymen, and assiduously desirous of leaving a fair fame behind him; a desire so natural to true magnanimity, that inferring the principle from the existence of its concomitant, we are warranted in construing his conduct by correspondent motives, and in allowing the claims he was so anxious to justify. We here allude to a written justification of his conduct in the Vincejo, previous to her capture, as connected with a narrative of his subsequent treatment by the government of France; from which it may be inferred that he had been accused of pusillanimity!—an accusation which would imply that the same man could exhibit the character of a coward possessed of power, and a hero, destitute, and in the power of a rancorous enemy a manifest contradiction to all ordinary experience of human conduct; for be it observed, that the firm behaviour of Captain Wright was not the momentary daring of final desperation, but a consistent display of fortitude under various instances of trial. In fact, it was all but the last resort of a mean, inglorious tyranny it was to blast the hard-earned reputation of an unfortunate captive, previous to his sacrifice as the victim of malice, that the "Moniteur" threw out its unjust and inconsistent aspersions; and it was to obviate its possible effects, that Captain Wright drew up the justificatory narrative or memorial which we shall now lay before our readers; it is valuable, as being a copy of the original relation in the captain's own handwriting, and apparently his farewell to the world.

CHAPTER XV

A Narrative by the late Captain Wright; containing a Justification of his Conduct in the Vincejo against certain Calumnies in the "Moniteur," &c., and an Account of his Treatment by the French Government, subsequent to his capture,
found among his papers, in his own handwriting, recently
claimed by Sir Sidney Smith, and given up by the present Government of France.

"HAD it ever occurred to me that blame could in any manner attach to
my conduct, under the closest scrutiny of a court composed of my
brother officers, famed for the severity of their criticism on all that concerns the honour of the country and the reputation of the navy, and who
are at least as good judges as the enemy, of the risks that a. brave and
enterprising officer ought reasonably to run in performing the king's
service; I confess that I should more readily have anticipated a charge of
temerity, than a censure of pusillanimity. If with, I may fairly assert, as
ill-manned a ship as ever sailed from England, a station was maintained
singly, with very little interval, for three months, without a pilot, within
the enemy's islands, in the mouths of their rivers, in the presence of an
extremely superior force, continually in motion; if his convoys, attended
by this force, were as often chased, forced out of their course, and obliged
to take shelter in ports they were not destined for; if that very weak and
inefficient ship's company was in that time, by unremitting attention and
exertion, brought to such a state of discipline as gave me sufficient confidence to wait for, and chase into her own port, an enemy's ship, in all
respects greatly superior to the brig I commanded; if lying-to a whole day
in the enemy's road at the mouth of a river, bidding defiance to two brigs,
each of nearly equal force with the Vincejo, a schooner, and fifty sail of
armed gunboats, brigs, and luggers, all under weigh, and occasionally
laying their heads off the land, but keeping close to their batteries; if after
having got ashore in the mouth of a river, within grape-range of the batteries, I had, I may well be permitted to say, the audacity to unrig the
Vincejo, get her guns out, and haul her high and dry into an enemy's port
in a small island, between Belle-Isle and the main, within four miles of

the continent, to examine her keel and repair her damage, making preparations in the mean time to fight a land battle, in case of a very probable attack, protected only by the presence of a frigate for a day or two; if taking and running on shore several of the enemy's vessels under the batteries, in sight of the above force; if unreeving and reeving double all my running rigging that was susceptible of it, and almost entirely rigging my ship anew, as much to increase my mechanical purchases, to supply the deficiency of hands in working her, as promptly to make sailors of my landsmen and boys, with whatever circumstances may be added to this catalogue, from my public account of the action, and the testimony of my immediate captors, be proofs of want of energy, bravery, intelligence, and seamanship, it must be acknowledged that I ought to take my place among arrant cowards and incorrigible lubbers.

"It is rather essential to observe, that the first account published of the capture was written by the general commanding at L'Orient. From his letter the value set upon this capture may be collected, and which manifestly arose from the enterprise and activity of the Vincejo, as he speaks in terms of gratulation of the consequent arrival of a convoy at L'Orient from the Morbihan, which had been blockaded by this single brig; the convoy amounted to one hundred sail, with provisions, &c. for the fleet, chiefly that of Brest: this letter describes the action as being very warm for two hours. It is not less worthy of remark, that the 'Moniteur,' a few days after, described the action as desperate, and stated my loss at upwards of thirty men, chiefly of the flower of my ship's company; and it was not until many months after, that the government, disappointed that their base treatment produced no other sentiment in me than contempt, that the favourable impression my conduct had made on the public mind, and this improper treatment, began to be spoken of in appropriate terms both in France and in England, where it excited the attention of parliament, had recourse to the infamous expedient of calumniating my public and private character, to stop the clamour in England, and allay the apprehension here of retaliation.

"The aspersion of pusillanimity must appear so absurd to any one acquainted with my standing and services in the navy, that, quite superior as I am to anybody's opinion, in a case where I am conscious of the strictest rectitude, I should be inclined not to notice it at all, or at most to treat it as one would any vulgar prejudice that occurs in one's intercourse with the world, and which must be borne, because it would be more ridiculous to controvert, than to appear tacitly to let it pass; but that the charge so obviously arises out of the enemy's systematic attack upon our national character, and the general reputation of the navy and army of England, and ceases therefore to be an object of mere individual concern.

"I might here dismiss this charge, trusting that my known character, my official letter, and other details, the testimony of those I fought, that of my own officers and ship's company, the 'Moniteur's' first remarks, which of course bore the impression received from the coast, of the obstinacy of the conflict, contrasted with its subsequent remarks, imagined

in Paris some months after to serve political purposes, and my deportment in the difficult and delicate scenes that have occurred since my confinement, would more than answer the aspersion to any impartial mind.

"The next in order are the numerous calumnies contained in the Prefect Julien's letter to the grand judge, which is a tissue of falsehood from
the beginning to the end; but as it carries contradiction with itself, all I
desire is that it may be read, and contrasted with the description I shall
give of my interview with him, and the manner in which I claimed his
acquaintance. To his assertion, that I am a fanatical enemy to Frenchmen, I have to observe, that, admitting for the moment the fact to be correct, there is nothing either criminal, or illegitimate, or unnatural, in an
Englishman being at enmity with the enemies of his country, during a
war; but I have had too wide an intercourse with the world to be subject
to fanaticism of any kind; and my habits of social intimacy with Frenchmen, added to the lenient manner in which it is proved I have treated
those enemies, by willingly wresting them from captivity, disease, and
despair, in the vile prisons of Constantinople and of Rhodes; saving them
from the rage of the Turks in Syria, and affording them prompt succour
when languishing upon the field of battle in Egypt, as well as my humane
conduct to them this war, must sufficiently invalidate that calumny as far
as it was meant to attach.

"As to the artifice he imputes to me, it cannot fail to appear to have
arisen from my good sense enabling me to see through his treachery, for
his conduct deserves no fairer epithet, and which he has clumsily discovered throughout his letter: and my demeanour in the critical circumstances I have since passed through, will perhaps have characterised a
manly and energetic character, not very commonly allied to such a disposition.

"The very first practical lesson of humanity I recollect to have received was when, yet a very young boy, serving as midshipman, and in
the character of a little aide-de-camp, to the now Admiral Sir Roger Cur-
tis, at the defeat of the floating batteries, commonly called junk-ships,
during the memorable siege of Gibraltar, the war before last. Under this
humane and good man, the urbanity of whose manners is very well
known, I, in a manner, received my early education, and probably the
first stamp of my more mature character. Having, on the occasion above
alluded to, boarded one of the enemy's ships, where there had been
dreadful slaughter, and which was then on fire in several places, he ordered me to occupy our sailors solely in saving the wounded, and being
near him, some time after, I saw him cut one of his own boats' crew,
found plundering, severely in the arm, several times with his sword, for
not giving immediate succour to the distressed enemy; and he ended this
example, in midst of the fire, by a most impressive lecture to all his people, in favour of the humane duties of a brave man. This very early impression fixed itself upon my young mind, and the principles then incul-
cated have since regulated my conduct: they have been strengthened and
extended in a later school of the navy, under a commander of most en-

lightened humanity, whose generous disposition and amiable manners are not less conspicuous than his heroic gallantry. But it is not necessary to serve in any particular school in the British navy, to imbibe principles of generosity and humanity towards a vanquished enemy, for they are uniformly practised, and are even positively prescribed by the naval articles of war, which annexes degradation and very severe punishment to the breach of them. All I have thus said may, I trust, counterbalance the vague, though official, charge of my being an atrocious man, impudently published in the 'Moniteur.'

"I am not without hope of having succeeded in proving:

"First, that I defended his Majesty's ship in a manner creditable to the British character, and the reputation of the navy, and honourable to my own fame; prolonging the fight until there was no hope of succour, no chance of escape, and no possibility of victory by further resistance, yielding only when the ship was disabled in a perfect calm, the flower of my men killed or wounded, and an enemy, ten times as numerous as the little remnant of my people, advancing to board. I surrendered with the concurrence of my officers, after destroying all my signals, and every public and even private paper.

"Secondly; That Mr. Prefect Julien's charges are basely false and malicious.

"Thirdly; That the 'Moniteur's' abuse is as absurd as it is unfounded, and was malignantly intended to serve a political end: and lastly; that I shall prove, that through the whole of this melancholy scene I have performed my duty to my king and country, and to individuals, in the widest latitude of the term, and, to the very utmost of my power, supporting the character of my country with the energy becoming a British officer, disdaining every personal and private consideration that could have presented itself.

"I must remark, that if my ship's company had been the best that could be supposed to exist in a brig of the Vincejo's class, all that could have been hoped for, under the peculiar circumstances she was unfortunately engaged in, would be to protract the moment of surrender for a very short time, and to do the enemy some little further damage. Their damage was comparatively less than the Vincejo's; they do not acknowledge to have had any men killed or wounded, although there is a strong presumption of their having, in this case, as is their uniform practice, concealed their loss; for several of my people, who were dispersed through the flotilla, reported to me that they had seen Frenchmen with their heads bound up, and their faces smeared with blood; and it appears to me next to impossible that all their men could have escaped unhurt, considering the direction some of my shot had taken fore and aft their crowded vessels, and the volleys of round and grape that had passed through their sails and rigging, leaving undeniable tokens of their passage. You very likely know that an English officer has it not in his option to conceal his loss; that he is forced, by the articles of war, to give true returns of it, which are published through the ' London Gazette;' and any one acquainted with the principles of our constitution, will readily see the reason of such instructions: so that the official account of our loss in battle, by sea and land, may always be considered as perfectly true, barring the trifling inaccuracies that are sometimes incidental to hurry, and the dispersion of corps, and ships in service, before the returns can be carefully revised, but which argue nothing against their general correctness.

"Two of my men took a boat from Houat, and deserted to the coast of France; another was shot by accident by the armourer's mate, in cleaning the arms, and a few useless men, under a master's mate, had been sent to England in a prize. No person on board, I will affirm, had an idea that we should be able to fight and work the ship at the same time with so weak a ship's company; for that circumstance had more than once been a subject of conversation and regret between me and my officers; but, by unremitting attention, they were brought to handle her on one occasion, in presence of an enemy I had chased under Belle Isle, in such a manner as to inspire more confidence, and give me hopes of being able, in time, to become even actively enterprising with them.

"It was a great misfortune that the first action I had in her happened to be very severe, and in a calm, against rowing gunboats. My public and private letters, written previous to my departure from England, will, I doubt not, have been read again since my capture; and they will be found but too prophetic. had not myself been blind to the danger, nor had dissembled it to those with whom it lay to parry it: the energy of my representations had even excited a menace from Lord Keith; so that I was placed in the dilemma of either resigning my command, at a moment when a zealous officer could least reconcile it to himself, or of proceeding upon a service of uncommon danger and difficulty, with means quite inadequate to the object. I was under the necessity of sending back a lugger, because she sailed extremely ill, and could not be risked alone to run so great a distance along shore, when the enemy's flotilla were everywhere in motion.

"The Lively Custom-house cutter I sent a very short chase, almost in sight of a point of rendezvous; so that I remained with the Vincejo, and only one small and almost defenceless cutter, having only one gun and small arms, in the presence of an enemy daily increasing his force, whom I was to prevent from suspecting my weakness, which, however, he learned, at length, from the two deserters.

"It remains to be explained, to me at least, why the Lively failed me at the appointed rendezvous; but as it is far from my intention to criminate, or attempt to establish my own justification upon the delinquency of others, I am willing to believe that Lieutenant Rowe, an officer to whose zeal and attention upon former services with me I am ready to bear handsome testimony, had good reasons for the conduct which prevented him from being present to support me with so efficient a vessel on the day of battle.

"I am not unaware that the master of the Lively, Mr. Smith, may be disposed to plead a scarcity of provisions, as a reason for not being able to remain at so great a distance from his own port; and to lay stress upon the uneasiness of his people, diverted from the service of the Custom-house, which they were alone engaged for, to be taken in the face of an enemy, in whose presence it would have required the rigour of the martial law, which he had not the power of exercising, to command them. But the Vincejo had already supplied him with provisions, and would have continued to afford all necessary supplies, as long as her provisions lasted, or the service might require him to keep that station. If the people had shown any disposition to be refractory, speedy measures could have been easily adopted, while the Lively had remained in company, to bring them to a proper sense of their duty. Had she been in company, it is more than probable that the flotilla would not have attempted to act offensively; or, in so doing, would have been repulsed: for her presence must have made a difference of nearly half the number that was opposed to the Vincejo; beside the advantage of dividing attention, and the powerful effect of a flanking fire.

"It is not my wish to glance blame at the officers who superintended the manning of the Vincejo: that part of her equipment was performed, during my absence on the public service, by draughts from different ships at the Nore, and no one can be ignorant of the nature of sudden draughts from ships in a course of equipment, whose officers take such opportunities of getting rid of useless hands, and reluctantly part with any good man. Some persons will possibly cavil at these observations, and oppose to them numerous regulations instituted for the prevention of such abuses: but I speak of the service, not as it stands upon paper, but as it is executed in reality; and dare appeal to any liberal-minded officer, who has followed up the details of equipment, for a confirmation of what has been advanced. The bare inspection of the list of my ship's company, and the comparison of it with even her reduced establishment, cannot fail to flash conviction on the mind, that, although destined immediately to be employed on very particular and eminently hazardous service, she was not manned in a manner adequate to the exigencies of even ordinary service. But, had her crew been the very best that could be imagined in a brig of her class, I will not be bold enough to affirm that, in the circumstances she fought under, I could have hoped to do more than protract the moment of surrender; and I am persuaded I shall hazard very little in asserting, that with four of such very manageable gun-vessels as were opposed to me, I would, under similar circumstances, attack a line-of-battle ship with well-grounded hope of completely disabling, if not finally subduing her. Some of my friends and my brother officers will, no doubt, recollect my having, previous to my departure, expressed such an opinion, and which my late experience has fully confirmed.

"Many attempts have been made to bribe and seduce my people from their allegiance to enter into the enemy's service. Mr. Keame, my gunner, a most valuable man, whose herculean form and intrepid countenance made the enemy covet his services, was repeatedly tampered with, and had large pecuniary offers made to him as a reward for becoming a traitor to his country; his conduct under this insult has been represented to me as highly loyal, manly, and energetic; and I am not aware that one of my ship's company swerved from his duty.

"It may perhaps be thought superfluous to have added anything to the details contained in my official letter, to prove that the Vincejo was defended to the last extremity, under eminently unfortunate circumstances, against a very superior force. But the impression which our obstinate resistance made upon the minds of our immediate antagonists, will possibly afford the very best testimony that could be desired, and the account written by me will derive a character of truth and impartiality from the corroborating speech addressed to me publicly and spontaneously by Monsieur le Tourneur, the enemy's commanding officer, upon my presenting my sword to him on board his ship. This speech was too remarkable at the time, and has since become too valuable a document, for me to feel unsolicitous for its preservation; some of my own officers were present, to whom I immediately repeated it in English, for their satisfaction. It follows nearly verbatim—'*Monsieur, vous avez noblement défendu l'honneur de votre nation, et la reputation de votre marine; nous aimons et estimons les braves, et l'on vous traitera, vous et votre equipage, avec tous les égards possibles.*' [ED. Sir, you have defended the honor of your nation nobly, and the reputation of your navy as well; we love and respect the brave, and we will treat you, you and your crew, with all the consideration possible.] The sincerity of the sentiments here expressed was manifest in all this officer's conduct: after treating me with great respect and attention, he sent me, with my officers, to Auray, accompanied by a single soldier, '*purement pour la forme,*' [ED. purely for form] as he declared upon taking leave of me in a very friendly manner. So little was I guarded, or under restraint, on my arrival at that place, that I spontaneously waited upon Monsieur Le Grand, commissaire de marine, unattended except by a woman as a guide to his house. This gentleman received me with great civility, and mistaking me for the commander of the French flotilla, complimented me upon the capture, conversing with me some moments under this illusion, until I undeceived him, which did not abate his attentions. I mention this circumstance, merely to characterise the honourable treatment I at first received. Of the favourable impression received of me at Auray, and the consequent attentions of the inhabitants, the mayor's letter to me offers the best evidence. I must, however, notice a circumstance that happened at this place, as the energetic conduct I was forced to adopt to save an innocent man's life may, in some measure, have been the cause of the prefect of Vannes' ill humour, and have given rise to the falsehood and impertinence contained in his letter to the grand judge concerning me. A paragraph will be noticed in my official letter, respecting a pilot, inserted there merely to serve as evidence in the poor man's favour, in case the letter should fall into the enemy's hands. The circumstance is perfectly true as it is related. This man, being found on board my brig after the action, was put in irons by the French officers, and intended to be tried for his life; but, upon my proving his perfect innocence, to the satisfaction of M. Le Tourneur, through the testimony of the lieutenant, whom I had ordered to bring him by force on board, he was set at liberty: at Auray, however, I was informed by an officer, that the pilot was then under trial before a military commission, and would be immediately shot. There had been a flippancy in this man's conversation, that I had previously found it necessary to check, as he repeatedly declared he was acquainted with me, had seen me on board some vessel where I had never been, and almost insisted that I was a Swiss: but, upon this occasion, I felt it my duty to proclaim the pilot's innocence, and seriously and formally to place it upon this officer's responsibility to prevent the execution, as he was acquainted with the fact; and finding that he discovered no disposition to interfere, to state the truth to the commission, I declaimed against the injustice of the proceeding, and threatened to pursue, as long as I lived, the authors of so atrocious a crime, and publish their names throughout Europe, coupled with all the circumstances of their infamy. I have reason to believe that my conduct alone saved the man's life, although it is probably the cause of some part of the persecution I have suffered, and which, on that account, I do not in the least regret.

"Hearing the name of Julien mentioned soon after my arrival at Auray, and, upon inquiry, that he had been in Egypt, I was naturally induced to express to the mayor and others my desire to see a person I was acquainted with. On the road to Vannes he became the subject of conversation between me and the officer commanding the escort, to whom I repeated my wish to see the prefect, and I was actually presented to him at my own request. He received me politely as an old acquaintance, invited me to pass the evening with him, as he expected company; and he even carried his pretended civility so far as to express his wish that I should dine with him the next day, provided I did not proceed upon my journey at an early hour. The fatigue of the journey, increased by the inflammation of my wound, alone prevented my being of his evening party. On my return to my inn, I found myself closely guarded by a perpetual sentinel in my room, and one at the door of the house; and observed, with regret, that the honourable treatment due to a prisoner of war was suddenly changed for that of a detestable inquisition. I was sent for the next morning by Mr. Julien, who, in the presence of the general commanding the department, had the effrontery to tell me, that for my better accommodation, on account of my wound, he had determined to send me to Paris by the diligence: but upon my declaring that it would be painful to me to quit my brave officers and seamen, with whom I preferred bearing the fatigue of the journey, in such a manner as to show that I was not the dupe of his artifice, he no longer dissembled his sinister motives, but told me that it was his intention to afford his government an opportunity to obtain information from me respecting conspirators and assassins which he said I had landed upon the French coast, and concluded by saying, those persons would probably wish to claim my acquaintance. I replied, that as I owed no account of my services to any authority but my own government, I would not answer any questions touching them, or give the least information to my enemy; that the adoption of any measures of rigour towards me would not, in the least, forward the end he professed to have in view; and I warned him not to depart from the customs of civilised nations, in their treatment of prisoners of war. Far from mingling with the crowd, or shrinking from public notice, to pass unobserved, as he falsely and basely insinuates, I was known to several naval officers at Port Navalo, the place we were first conducted to after capture, and I was everywhere in evidence at the head of my officers and ship's company, to support, encourage, and comfort them in misfortune, as it is the duty and practice of British officers.

"As the prefect Julien's letter before alluded to has been made an official document, given to the world as a sort of *pièce d'accusation,* to shed a colour of justice over the barbarous treatment I have received, I shall give it at length, from which, contrasted with the above description of my interview with him, and of the circumstances which led to it, it will plainly appear that he was insensibly drawing his own portrait, while he pretended to delineate mine; and that he scrupled not, even at the sacrifice of truth and honour, to flatter a known and puerile foible of his master, in attributing to the tutelary deity or fortune of Buonaparte my capture and rencontre with him, which is readily accounted for by natural causes, without the necessity of recurring to the aid of occult influence, or supernatural agency. The prefect, no doubt, imagined that the tide of his affairs was at the flood, and, seizing the golden moment, he'd swim gaily on to fortune, and no more remain in shallows and in penury."

Le Général de Brigade Julien, Préfect de
Vannes, au Grand Judge, Monsieur Regnier,
24 Floréal, 14 May, 1804.

Ayant appris que les officiers et l'equipage d'une corvette Anglaise prise, il y a peu de jours, par nos chaloupes canonnieres, passoient à Vannes pour se rendre à Epinal, je fis demander le capitaine dans l'intention d'obtenir adroitement de lui quelques aveux ou quelques renseignemens sur les traitres qui pouvoient le servir sur la côte, ou sur les complices de-la conspiration qui auroient pu se sauver à son bord et de-la passer en Angleterre. Je m'attendois peu à trouver dans le capitaine un personage assez important: c'est Mr. Wright, qui a jété Georges, Pichegru, et complices sur la côte de Dieppe; je l'ai beaucoup connu en Egypt, où il etoit Lieutenant de Sidney Smith, et chargé par le commodore de toutes ses negociations avec l'armée Française. J'ai pensé que ce Mr. Wright pourroit faire des révélations utiles, ou au moins déclarer, pour mettre sa responsabilité à l'abri, que c'est par ordre de son gouvernement qu'il a vomi sur nos côtes cette bande d'assassins, et fournir ainsi une nouvelle preuve authentique de la participation du cabinet Britannique à cette atrocité. J'ai donc cru devoir vous l'envoyer de suite par la diligence, et sous l'escorte de la gendarmerie, en recommandant toutefois d'avoir pour lui les égards dus à un prisonnier de guerre.

Mr. Wright est le même qui échappa du Temple, il y a quelques années, avec Sidney Smith; il est très fin et rusé, ennémi fanatique des Français, assez vain pour se croire destiné à jouer un rôle, insolent tant qu'il croira que la position le met à l'abri de tout danger, mais qui pourrait foiblier si on le plaçoit dans l'alternative de mettre authentiquement sa mission sur le compte de son gouvernement, ou de passer pour un conspirateur non avoué, et dès-lors justiciable. J'ai cru devoir vous soumettre ma manière de voir a cet égard. Il partira ce soir par la diligence de Rennes, et arrivera à Paris presque aussitôt que ma lettre; il est accompagné d'un très jeune neveu et de son domestique, que je n'ai pas cru devoir séparer de lui. Quoique j'ai voulu lui cacher le motif de la mesure extraordinaire que je prenois à son égard, il n'en, a pas été la dupe, et j'ai lieu de croire d'après la conversation que j'ai eu avec lui, qu'il a d'avance étudie son rôle, et qu'il est décidé à garder le silence, s'appuyant sur le principe qu'il ne doit compte de ses operations militaires qu'à son gouvernement. Au reste, de quelque utilité qu'il puisse vous être, ou quelles que soient les mesures que vous prendriez à son égard, j'ai pensé qu'à tout événement il seroit intéressant de vous envoyer un homme qui a joué un rôle dans l'affreuse conspiration qui vient d'alarmer toute la France, et que la Providence, toujours propice, afin de donner à Buonaparte un nouveau témoignage de sa surveillance, semble avoir jetté sur la côte du Morbihan, où son batiment bien armé a été pris par de simples batteaux, et lui-même reconnu dans la foule des prisonniers, parmi lesquels il auroit resté confondu dans tout autre endroit que celui-ci.

J'ose esperer, Citoyen Ministre, que vous approuverez la mesure qui j'ai prise.

J'ai l'honneur de vous saluer.

Julien

[Editor's Translation]

Brigadier General Julien, Prefect of
Vannes, to the High Judge, Mr. Reynier,
24 Floréal, 14 May, 1804

Having learned that the officers and crew of an English corvette taken a few days earlier by our gunboats, passed by Vannes on the way to Epinal, I sent a question to the captain, intending to obtain cleverly from him some admission or information about the traitors who could serve him on the coast or about the conspirators who could save themselves aboard his ship and from there reach England. I was hardly expecting to find the captain an important person: it is Mr. Wright, who landed Georges, Pichegru and the accomplices on the coast at Dieppe. I knew him well in Egypt, where he was Sidney Smith's lieutenant and charged by the commodore with all the negotiations with the French army. I thought that this Mr. Wright could reveal some useful information, or at least declare, to protect his own responsibility, that he disgorged this band of assassins on our shores by the order of his government, thus to furnish new, authentic proof of the participation of the British Cabinet in this atrocity. I therefore thought I should send him to you immediately by stagecoach under the escort of the gendarmerie, requesting, however, that you show him the consideration due to a prisoner of war.

This is the same Mr. Wright who escaped from the Temple a few years ago, together with Sidney Smith; he is very clever and tricky, a fanatical enemy of the French, vain enough to believe that he is destined to play a role, insolent in believing that position shelters him from all danger, but who might weaken if placed in the position of either ascribing his mission to his own government or being considered an unavowed conspirator and thus liable to the law. I thought I should tell you of my opinion in this matter. He will leave this evening on the stagecoach for Rennes and will arrive in Paris almost as soon as my letter. He is accompanied by a very young nephew and by his servant, whom I did not feel I should separate from him. Although I wanted to hide from him the reason for the extraordinary measure I am taking with regard to him, he was not deceived and, from the conversation I had with him, I believe that he studied his role in advance and that he decided to keep silent, on the grounds that he owes an accounting of his military operations only to his government. As for the rest, no matter how useful he might be to you and no matter what measures you take with regard to him, I thought that in any case it would be interesting to send you a man who played a part in the terrible conspiracy that has just alarmed all of France and whom Providence, always gracious, giving Napoleon yet another sign that it is watching over him, seems to have thrown onto the coast of the Morbihan, where his well-armed vessel was taken by simple ships, and he himself was recognised in the crowd of prisoners, among whom he would have remained unknown anywhere but here.

I permit myself to hope, Citizen Minister, that you will approve the measure I have taken.

I have the honor of saluting you.

JULIEN

Captain Wright thus describes the treatment that he experienced at Paris:

"Conducted by two soldiers, one by my side in the carriage, and the other upon the coach-box, I arrived in Paris after ten days' painful journey, accompanied by my little nephew and my servant, whom Julien had permitted to go with me. The agitation of the journey had extended the inflammation of my wound to the bladder, and produced an excruciating strangury that had nearly forced me to remain at Haudan, near Paris. In this situation, on the morning after my arrival, I was transferred from Real's police office to the Temple, and suddenly conducted, under a guard, before Judge Thuriot, presiding at a court of inquisition, attended by numerous secretaries, and surrounded by a military guard.

"This man's countenance and brutal demeanour brought to the memory the savages, who, issuing from the hotbed of the violent passions, the South of France, at a too memorable epoch of the late disgraceful revolution, rushed upon Paris to massacre thousands of innocent victims confined in its corroding prisons, without trial or even examination. He appeared, like another Jefferies, panting for blood, and cumulating insult, artifice, falsehood, and menace, to disconcert, betray, and intimidate the weak or unwary.

"To his first questions, 'my name, profession,' &c, I answered, that being taken in arms, I had perfectly satisfied the military men to whom I surrendered, upon all these points; that as this novel mode of proceeding was in direct hostility to received principles, and the practice of civilised nations towards their prisoners of war, I was determined not to give it the least sanction by my acquiescence, and should therefore decline answering any questions.

"A pretty animated conversation ensued, upon general principles, the law of nations, and customs of war, in which he very indecently loaded my government and country with the most unjust and gross abuse, and concluded by declaring, that the laws and customs of France alone should be applied to me. Waiving what immediately concerned my government, whose defence I observed it was unnecessary for me to undertake, as it was fully competent to justify its own measures, and would, no doubt, prove to Europe the falsehood of these aspersions, I pointed out to him the injustice of applying to me the laws of France, which I was totally unacquainted with, to which I owed no obedience, and would yield no submission; and confining myself within the sacred character of a prisoner of war, claiming personal inviolability in virtue of the law of nations, I denied the competency of any authority in France to interrogate me, and again declined answering any questions. This disappointment of his hopes increasing his brutality, and his rage getting the better of all judicial decorum, he had the insolence to couple me with persons he called conspirators and assassins, employed by the British government; and declared he would force me to answer, or send me before a military commission, to be instantly shot as a spy, if I persisted in my refusal. To this I answered, with a mixture of indignation and contempt, that I had never been afraid of my enemy's shot, that my person was in his hands, and he might do with it as he thought proper; but no power on earth should force me to betray my king and country, or dishonour myself. Finding at length that he was prepared for every violation, and, lest my total silence should, in case of my becoming a probable sacrifice to my principles, favour an induction of criminality, which this government would not fail to propagate for its own justification, I determined to leave behind me, consigned to the records of this country, such a statement of the battle in which I was overpowered, as would establish my claim, and that of my officers and ship's company, to the honourable treatment due to prisoners of war. With this view, I particularly described the action; and entirely confining my replies to what related to it, whenever he interposed, as he often did, any subject foreign to this, I referred him to my former answers, declaring my resolution not to reply to any questions of such a nature, either negatively or affirmatively. He strongly urged me to acknowledge having debarked conspirators and assassins in France; to recognise thirty or forty persons, who were confronted with me, and of whom he as falsely as impudently asserted, previous to their appearance, that they had all acknowledged having been landed by me, under orders from the British cabinet, for the purpose of murdering the first consul, overthrowing the government, and creating a civil war in France. I replied, that I would not recognise any person whatsoever that might be confronted with me; and should the whole emigration of France be brought before me, I would not acknowledge ever to have seen one, though I might have known many of them; that, ignorant as I was of the precise object of this extraordinary and obviously sinister proceeding, which I demanded to know, but was refused to be told, I would make no answer that could have even the remotest tendency to commit any unfortunate men; and he need not, under such circumstances, expect anything from my mouth that might, under his interpretation, attach delinquency to myself. I rejected, with indignation, those horrid imputations, and felt it necessary to exhibit the mayor of Auray's letter, in proof of the humane principles which governed my actions. With respect to my orders, I declared that I had been wherever they had led, but I would render no particular account of them to the enemies of my country. I was quite indifferent, I told him, as to what others might be described to have said of themselves or of me, and my conduct should be regulated alone by my own ideas of honour and rectitude; being in the presence of my enemies, I had reason to suspect the purity of their intentions, and should of course be upon my guard against their treachery.

"Of the persons confronted with me, three only said they knew me to be the captain who had landed them in France: two of these were suborned witnesses, who had been threatened with death if they did not affirm they knew me, and were screened from the effect of prosecution for having, under this menace, consented to give the evidence required: the third, in a letter to Real, afterwards explained away the whole force of what had been stated as his deposition, by asserting, that, far from declaring I was the captain of the ship in which he came from England, he meant to say, merely, he had been acquainted with me in London. This examination lasted almost five hours, until I was nearly exhausted by the fatigue of six days' journey, an increasing inflammation, the great heat of a close and crowded room, and the ebbs and flows of contempt and indignation excited by a succession of insult and provocation.

"It is necessary to remark, that Thuriot directed the secretary to commit to writing such parts only of this examination as suited his particular purpose, entirely omitting his menace to send me before a military commission, or my answers, which, on the one hand, would expose his departure from principle and decorum, or, on the other, might leave some favourable impression of my character and conduct. But, incorrect and mutilated as the written examination was, I thought proper to subscribe my name, as it really contained a narrative of the battle, and demonstrated the claims of myself and my people.

"General Savary, whom I had spoken of to the gendarmes during my journey, and expressed a desire to see, came to me soon after I was dismissed by Thuriot. After a vain attempt to draw from me some avowal injurious to the unfortunate men before mentioned, he endeavoured to irritate my feelings, to throw me off my guard, by an unjust and ungrateful attack on my friend Sir Sidney Smith, to whom thousands of his countrymen are under lasting obligations; but he managed this so clumsily, that in condemning my friend's politics as detestable, his heat betrayed him into an unwilling eulogium on Sir Sidney's private character. Finding me very unyielding, and quite prepared to support the public and private character of my friend, he shifted his ground, and pointed his attack at Mr. I. Spencer Smith, to whom he seemed resolved to give no quarter. He brought to my mind the fable of the wolf and the lamb, who, having proved his own innocence to the savage beast, was still doomed to expiate the faults of some remote part of the family. He vainly boasted of having formed his judgment of Sir Sidney Smith in two days; and I must confess it bore the stamp of a very hasty judgment. After menacing me, and threatening Sir Sidney, as well as other British officers who should be found equally devoted to the service of their sovereign and their country, he had the folly and atrocity to declare, *"Nous ne ferons plus la guerre aux Anglais honorablement et loyalement, mais nous sommes déterminés à leur faire tout le mal possible, par tous les moyens imaginables."* To this I replied, *"Dès que vous me faites cet aveu, il faut prendre son parti:"* he quitted me, saying, *"Vous pouvez m'ecrire."* [ED. "We will no longer make war on the English honourably and faithfully, but we are determined to do them all the harm possible, by all means imaginable." To this I replied, "As you make this admission to me, I will have to adapt myself to it." He quitted me, saying, "You can write to me."] but as his conduct had left an impression upon my mind extremely unfavourable to a military man, I entertained not the least idea of having any further communication with him.

"I was immediately locked up in an upper tower, guarded for about a week by a sentinel in my room, who was relieved every six hours: my nephew and servant were separated from me.

"Two days after the first examination, I was again conducted before Thuriot, who recurred to the same artifices, falsehood, and insult, through the course of an equally tedious and tiresome '*interrogatoire*,' under which I several times dozed in my chair; but changing the terms of his menace, he declared that I should be considered as a member of the conspiracy, and be tried for my life; coupled, he said, with conspirators and assassins, whom I had voluntarily landed in France, unauthorised by my government, who would disavow me, and to whose protection I could have no claim. I told him it was not difficult to answer him victoriously; repeating, that in the whole course of my services as a captain of the British navy, I had acted under orders which were ever eminently humane; but not being responsible to my enemy, I should decline entering any further into particulars: satisfied that I had honourably performed my duty, I was ready to meet the very worst consequences of it, and felt no apprehension of being disavowed by my government. I was again confronted with many persons whom I refused to recognise, and declined to answer any questions concerning them. As a last experiment, Thuriot affected to suspend over my head, *in terrorem*, a criminal prosecution, for having formerly escaped from the Temple, by means of a suppositions order for transferment. But I suffered nothing to warp me in the least from the line of conduct I had early prescribed to myself, and which is as follows: Deprived, as I was, of counsel, or communications of any kind; secretly immured, without access to any information of what had already taken place, or was even intended, with regard to the unfortunate but respectable men I was coupled with; equally ignorant whether I was to be shot as a spy, arraigned as a criminal, or exhibited as a witness, and brought from my cell, occasionally, as part of the mechanism of the political tragedy then getting up for representation, I determined generally to withhold all information which the enemy should appear solicitous to obtain; to recognise no person whatsoever that should be presented to me for that purpose; to decline making any declaration that could, even remotely, implicate others; and finally, to refuse to answer any question not immediately connected with the description of the battle in which I was taken. Thuriot, having completely failed in all his efforts, wound up his labours by saying, '*Il est donc inutile de vous interroger;*' to which I readily replied, '*Parfaitement;*' [ED. "So, it is useless to question you," to which I readily replied, "That's exactly right."] and was recommitted to secret confinement. My nephew and my servant were also interrogated by Thuriot, touching my services for some years back, my family and connexions, my nephew's family, &c., with an indelicacy that, I believe, has no parallel; and, I have reason to believe, with a view of serving the purposes of the police, through the medium of spies which this government entertains in England, hanging upon the skirts of society, to pick up and report private conversations. A few days after, my nephew was permitted to be with me.

"Considering it beneath the dignity, and inconsistent with the manly character of a British officer, to cover his personal responsibility by fable or artifice, I imagined no tale of deception, I disdained using the least prevarication, and stood alone upon the ground of the incompetency of the power that wished to subdue me to its authority; refusing to declare, either negatively or affirmatively, whether I had formerly been confined in the Temple, as had been proved before me by the evidence of many; and having reason to apprehend that my recognition of the persons who gave the evidence might become ground of prosecution, or persecution, against them, I equally declined saying whether I knew them or not. After some time the perpetual sentinel was withdrawn.

"In the course of the week, General Savary, accompanied by two superior officers, repeated his visit. He seemed disappointed that I had not written to him: he gave me to understand that my case was very critical, and insinuated a menace. I told him, with marked contempt, that it was impossible, in justice, to refuse my claims as a prisoner of war; but if the enemy must have a British victim to grace a triumph, I was ready to shed my blood for my sovereign and my country, but never would betray them, or sully my honour. He then changed his ground, saying, '*Je sais que vous ne craignez pas la mort, mais vous étes déshonnoré dans toute l'Europe; l'on vous regarde comme complice d'assassins, votre réputation est flétriée.*' [ED. He then changed his ground, saying, "I know that you do not fear death, but you are dishonoured in all Europe. You are considered the accomplice of assassins, your reputation has dwindled."] I replied indignantly, that my reputation was not in the power of my enemy; it was in the keeping of my country, and of my friends, who, being well acquainted with my character, would defend it; many of his countrymen had ample reason not to be ignorant of it: it could not be tarnished by anything that fell from his mouth, and I was not then in a situation in which an honourable man would permit himself such observations. That the calumnies it might be the interest of my enemies to circulate, would yield under the manifestation of truth, which could not long be concealed; in the mean time I was perfectly indifferent to them whilst I retained an approving conscience, as they would not be believed by those whose good opinion I valued. He remarked, that the mere approbation of my conscience was not enough; to which I replied, it was quite sufficient for an honest man. He attempted to wrest from me some declaration touching the nature of my orders, and asked me where they were. I told him I would give him no account of them, farther than that they had been destroyed, as my duty dictated. He insinuated a pretended doubt of my being an Englishman, or a British officer.

"Ridiculing this folly, I declared I was born in Ireland, and showed him my uniform: but he remarked, that was no proof of my being a British officer, for the brigands I had brought from England had uniforms. I replied, that I had no connexion with brigands, and that my title to the uniform I wore was derived from the commission in my pocket. He now attempted to pass some compliments on my personal character, but glancing, at the same time, some unjust censure on the national character. I rejected with disdain all praise that was offered at the expense of my country, whose reputation, I affirmed, was far superior to that of his country, for enlightened humanity. He appeared to regret the indecorum of his conduct, and begged this altercation might cease, on perceiving that it tended to his discomfiture, instead of humiliating or disconcerting me, as he intended. I readily agreed, reminding him, however, that it did not originate with me, and that I had been reduced to the necessity of repelling an indecent attack. Foiled in all his attempts to throw me off my guard, he at length suddenly said, with great affected emphasis, '*Tenez, Monsieur Wright; si j'étois à votre place, je montrerois encore plus de caractère que vous n'en montrez même, car je dirois, oui, c'est moi, qui les ai debarques:*' to which I replied, calmly, '*Ce n'est pas de son ennemi qu'un officier Anglais doit recevoir des leçons sur ses devoirs.*'" [ED. "You see, Mr. Wright, if I were in your place, I would show more character than you are showing yourself, for I would say, 'Yes, it is I who landed them',," to which I replied calmly, "An English officer does not receive lessons in duty from his enemy."]

Captain Wright was then summoned to appear as a witness against certain persons accused.

"In a few days after, I was brought down from an upper turret to a better apartment, and my servant was permitted to attend me. On the first day of the trial I was taken to the *guichet*, where a messenger was waiting with a gendarme to conduct me before the court, in conformity with the summons I had rejected. I repeated my verbal protest, exposed my reasons, asserted my rights, denied the competency of the court, claimed the law of nations and customs of war, and refused to accompany them. The messenger then told me he had orders to use no violence, and to treat me with respect, and begged me to address my protest in writing to the president. This I refused, upon the ground of having nothing to do with the court or the president, either immediately or remotely; assuring him, that neither violence nor civility should induce me to do a voluntary act of the nature of that required. Upon this he left me, to make his report; but returning some time after, accompanied by an officer and guard, he announced his having positive orders to take me before the court by force, if it was not to be accomplished by gentle means. The officer made the same declaration, entreated me not to place him under the necessity of recurring to violence, which he wished to avoid, and pointed out how ineffectual the resistance of one unarmed man must be against his guard. Having formally repeated by protest against this violation of the law of nations, and feeling that I had done my duty to my king and country, to the utmost of my power sustained my honour, and satisfied my conscience as a private man, I declared that, under compulsion of superior force, my appearance before the court must be quite involuntary, and that nothing should compel me to give any evidence whatsoever. I was then conducted to the court, and after hearing the act of accusation read, which occupied the whole sitting, I was remanded to my secret confinement, without having been examined; notice being given me, that on a future day I must re-appear, to undergo an examination. In the mean time, my officers, including two very young midshipmen, after having been threatened with torture, I believe at Real's police-office, as will appear by Lieutenant Wallis's letter, were brought to the Temple, and put under secret and solitary confinement, and were again examined by the keeper's son, who took a minute of their answers. In a week after my first appearance at the criminal court, I was again forced to appear, as had been announced to me, after formally protesting nearly in the same manner I had done before.

"I was for some time left in an antechamber, where the witnesses were collected: these, being for the most part what are technically denominated *témoins forcés*, [ED. forced witnesses] may be considered as such in the most literal acceptation of the phrase, for they were describing to each other the different kinds of torture that had been applied to them to extort confessions contrary to the truth, and against their consciences, for the purpose of making the public believe in a plot of assassination, of which the non-existence cannot perhaps be better proved, than by the circumstance of the government having totally omitted that charge in the official indictment, causing it to be published throughout the provinces, and using it in all the preliminary proceedings, as an engine of the inquisition, to intimidate the weak and unwary, and attach some popularity to measures that were everywhere reprobated. Some of these poor people had their thumbs screwed together by the cock of a musket, operating as a vice, while gunpowder was placed upon their nails and fired; others had burning coals, or hot embers, applied to the soles of their feet; the most shameful violence had been used to others; all had been threatened to be shot; the houses of many had been rifled, their furniture destroyed in search of written evidence, and their families put to the rout. All these atrocious acts the government agents were charged with in my presence, and in that of fifty soldiers, some of whom, having been actors in the inhuman outrages, denied a part, although much the gravest part was still re-asserted, and remained undisputed; and, from what I and my officers have experienced, there remains not the least doubt in my mind of the facts maintained. On leading me into court, the messenger informed me that I should be tried for my life, with the other prisoners, if I should refuse to answer the questions to be put to me, or to confirm my examination before Judge Thuriot: to this I replied: *"Soyez persuadé que je n'en ferai rien."* [ED. "Be assured that I shall do nothing of this."] By this menace, I first discovered the use intended to be made of the written interrogation I had signed; and the comfort I immediately felt reflecting upon the conduct I had prescribed to myself in the earliest stage of this painful and delicate business, and which had strictly regulated all I had said and signed, tended greatly to support and fortify my mind under a spectacle as novel to me as it was imposing in itself; forced under implied delinquency into the presence, as it were, of a whole nation, nay, even of Europe; my name artfully and most unjustly connected with pretended plots of assassination; opposed as a witness against forty unfortunate men arraigned for their lives; the character of my country manifestly the primary object of the enemy's attack; and not a little dependent upon the conduct I should hold, and the issue of the trial.

"It being observed that I walked lame as I was led into court, a chair was offered to me. Seating myself perfectly at my ease, with my leg in a resting posture across the opposite knee, I employed my eyes, previous to the examination, all round the hall, examining its structure, ornaments, and audience. The president, calling me by name, enjoined me, in a certain formula, to answer all the questions that would be asked me, without partiality, hatred, or fear. I replied, in French, that I had to observe, in the first place, that military men knew no fear; that I was a British prisoner of war; that I had surrendered by capitulation, after an action with a very superior force; that knowing my duty to my king and to my country, whom I loved, and to whose service I had devoted myself from my youth, and owing no account of my public services to any authority but my own government, I would not answer any one of the questions that might be put to me; that I claimed from him the law of nations, and the customs of war among civilised nations, those laws and customs which I had always extended to the numerous Frenchmen who had fallen within my power. The approbation, and the cries of silence from the vergers of the court, alternately interrupting me, I several times suspended my speech until silence was restored, and resumed it always where I had left off, in order that the public might hear the whole of what I had to say, and to defeat the trick that I observed was about to be practised, to permit me to say only what might answer the enemy's purpose. After this, the interrogations I had undergone before Thuriot were ordered to be read: the secretary had not finished the preamble, when I interrupted him, by saying, I had a preliminary observation to make: the president granted me *la parole*, and I seized the opportunity of declaring aloud, that those writings were incorrect, as, amongst other omissions, they did not contain the threat to send me before a military commission, to be instantly shot as a spy, if I did not betray my government, and dishonour myself. The rage and agitation of Thuriot at this moment became extremely remarkable to everybody; he rose, and addressed the president with great gesticulation, interrupting me; I still insisting, and succeeding to express myself loud enough to be heard by the whole audience, notwithstanding the reading which at times continued, and at others was suspended, until Thuriot's continued instances with the president induced the latter to call aloud iterately and precipitately, '*Faites retirer les témoins.*' [ED. 'Have the witnesses removed.'] During some of the interruptions, the secretary took a share in the debate, by telling me, first, that what I insisted on would occur in the course of the reading; but being contradicted by me, he then said it was in the second interrogation, which he would at length read; this provoked me to turn round and tell him, sternly and loudly, that he himself knew it was not in either, for he had written them both. The witnesses being ordered to withdraw, I descended two or three steps from my seat, then turned round, bowed to the man who had the civility to offer me a chair, then saluted the prisoners all round, and retired, bowing to the counsel and to the audience as I passed, without once turning towards the court. I have endeavoured to give an exact picture of this proceeding, to show how little the ends of substantial justice were the object in view; and how exactly it resembled a *pièce de thèâtre*, [ED. theatre play] where *les convenances* [ED. the proprieties] had been the chief object in contemplation, to deceive the public, and give a false colour to the scenery, that it would not naturally bear. I believe no European court of justice ever exhibited a scene of such base, criminal, and indecent artifice. I was remanded to my secret prison. There is reason to believe that my enemies regret ever having brought me into it. I have since told some of their agents that there was no little *maladresse* [ED. clumsiness] in letting me into their secrets behind the scenes, where I contemplated all the traps and wires that set their puppets in motion: some have frankly acknowledged the fact, whilst others have almost blushed in silence; but they are a very unblushing tribe. It is impossible for me to feel towards such people any other sentiment than the most sovereign contempt; and after the base and ungenerous falsehoods they have published against my reputation, for public purposes, knowing them at the same time to be falsehoods, I must, at the expense of every private and personal consideration, manifest that sentiment on every occasion, by all the dignified means in my power.

"I find I have omitted to state, that the former keeper of the Temple, his wife, the present keeper, the emigrant before mentioned, as well as the suborned witnesses and others, were called upon again in court to recognise and to be recognised by me: they gave similar evidence to that they had previously given, but I refused to answer either negatively or affirmatively, when asked if I knew them.

"It is manifest that the enemy at first meant to make me the victim of my devotion to my country; but finding that the engine of his inquisition had failed to produce the materials he sought for, to give a colour of justice to so flagrant a violation of the law of nations, and apprehensive, perhaps, of the application of the law of retaliation to some of the present prisoners in England, he laid aside this intention, though he still hoped to wrest from me declarations that, being artfully woven into the plot of assassination conjured up in Paris, might be shown to the world as presumptive proof that it had originated with the British government, as a British officer would appear to have been employed to land in France the persons to whom the execution of it was assigned by the French government. He seems also to have expected some avowal that he might strain into an unnatural form, in some degree to justify the destruction of men as respectable for their public character as they were for their talents and energy, whose influence he was jealous of, as capable of thwarting his ambition, and of opposing his usurpation. Another desire, not less near his heart, was to hold up to Europe an ignoble example of disloyalty and pusillanimity in the conduct of a British officer, yielding under the terror of his brutality, to support the calumnies he daily causes to be published against the national character of England, and the reputation of its incomparable navy.

"In a conversation I had with a Colonel Curts, he (Curts) speaking of the conduct of the war in Egypt and in Syria, glanced a little censure at my friend Sir Sidney Smith (for whom, however, he professed profound respect) for joining the Turks at St. Jean d'Acre, when Buonaparte's army was advancing against that place. I observed, that it was quite legitimate to support our ally, and very natural to Englishmen to follow their enemy wherever he led them; that it would be very fair to ask what business had a French army making war in a neutral country, without permission of the sovereign: and I took occasion to tell him, that he had better not go too deep into that subject, for he was speaking of a man who was perfectly acquainted with all that had passed in Syria: he ventured to ask me what? I cited Buonaparte's *ordre du jour* to his army, accusing Sir Sidney Smith of having sent to Constantinople for ships infected with the plague, for the premeditated purpose of destroying the French prisoners he had captured, although he was actually sending them to France most humanely, at great expense, accompanied by his own officers. Colonel Curts acknowledging the truth of this, I immediately observed, 'I suppose he will not think proper to retract this calumny.' He then attempted to retort some ridiculous charges against Sir Sidney Smith, which induced me to say, I was ready to avow and take upon myself every act of Sir Sidney's. Here this conversation ended, and considering the situation I am in, and the person I have to deal with, it will perhaps be thought that I went quite far enough; but I had in the rear of this fact such a *corps de reserve* as would have petrified him where he stood, if he had given me any very strong reason for bringing it forward. He said he had no doubt the minister of war would, from his report, make such a representation to the emperor as would operate a change in my favour. It was at this period of our conversation that I told him I would receive no favour or pardon, *je ne veux pas de grace, plûtot la mort sur le champ*; [ED. I want no mercy—rather death in the field;] and I discovered that he wished to know that very circumstance. He professed, upon introducing himself to me, to have a mission of delicacy; and I will say that he did not depart from it; but I entered into all the reasons I had for reprobating the conduct which had been held to me. These are the most essential circumstances that have presented themselves to my recollection.

"I have omitted to mention a circumstance or two, which will strongly characterise the régime these barbarians kept me very long under. I requested permission to have a flute for my amusement, which was positively refused: but during the time my officers were here, I procured one clandestinely, which has not been taken from me. I believe I mentioned (to you) verbally, that for ten months I was not permitted to obtain books for my amusement; on requesting that permission, through Fauconnier, a good many months ago, he told me I had nearly everything I could want; and casting his eyes on a few books my officers had left me, he replied, that I had already more than I could read. On another occasion, he told me, that they had a right to treat their prisoners of war as they pleased: this is the very answer made to Csesar by Arioviste, king of the savage Celts, during the war in Gaul; and it is not, by many, the first proof I have had, that the present rulers of this unfortunate country derive their principles from the barbarians. I practise patience, and the burthen of my song is, *dulce et decorum est pro patriâ mori.* [Ed.: It is sweet and honorable to die for the fatherland.]

"Confining myself to the more important facts, as much as possible, I have omitted a multitude of minor, though not less characteristic circumstances, in order to avoid trivial details, which, though not destitute of their peculiar interest, derive all that I attach to them from the extraordinary conduct they contribute to elucidate. I have purposely forborne to scatter flowers as I went, to embellish the tedious path; and preferring the opinion that will result from the operation of an unbiassed judgment, I have avoided any attempt to excite an interest by an appeal to the feelings.

"I have now to declare, that perfectly resigned as I am to my fate, I am able to support the worst a barbarous enemy can farther intend against me; that the character of my country, and the reputation of the navy, are the dearest considerations to me, and that in no possible circumstances will I ever lose sight of them, but make my death, should I die in the hands of the enemy, as disgraceful to him as it will be creditable to my country; and the history of that country will afford me a thousand examples to imitate, from the catalogue of British martyrs, and that the only circumstance that could give me pain, would be to see my government, yielding to the unjust pretensions of the enemy, make any undue sacrifice on my account."

This concludes Captain Wright's own account of his imprisonment, and the persecutions to which he was subjected. All that remains to be gathered concerning his fate must be derived from the French authorities.

[Office-copy.]

Procés-verbal, ascertaining the suicide of the individual
named John Wesley Wrigth, * prisoner at the Temple
house of arrest.

---

* This is the way in which they invariably spell his name.

In the year XIV, and on the fourth Brumaire, at ten o'clock of the morning, at our office, and before us, Pierre Dusser, commissary of police of Paris, Temple division, hath appeared the Sieur Louis Francois Fauconnier, concierge of the Temple house of arrest, and living at the same; who hath declared unto us, that Franois Savart, guardian of the said house, having entered the same this morning as usual, to visit the prisoners, and having reached the chamber occupied by John Wesley Wrigth, he found him covered with blood, and lying in his bed in a state of immobility, which should make it presumable that he died by effect of suicide; that in consequence, our attendance upon the spot was required, in order to proceed conformably to law, the same being duly recorded by our joint signatures.

We, the before-named commissary of police, in deference to the requisition hereinbefore stated, therefore personally went to the said house of arrest, and there found at the lodge the following gentlemen: Edme Francois Soupé, surgeon of the prison; Auguste Juste Ravier, captain of gendarmerie belonging to the department of the Seine; Louis Réne Pousignon, quartermaster of the select gendarmerie, and the before-named Mr. Fauconnier: all of whom immediately attended us into the building denominated the little Temple, contiguous to the Tower, where, having ascended into the second story, and entered a chamber which was opened by the before-named Mr. Pousignon, we there found, lying on a bed, a corpse of the male sex, appearing aged between forty and forty-four years, with brown hair and eyebrows, high forehead, gray eyes, nose well proportioned, mouth the same, chin projecting, visage oval, stature about one metre sixty-six centi-metres, which Mr. Fauconnier told us was that of the individual named John Wesley Wrigth, English captain, native of Cork in Ireland, and prisoner in this house since the 30th Floreal XII; which corpse had the throat cut, and held a razor shut in the right hand.

We then proceeded to take the evidence as here follows, in order to define, if possible, what are the motives which can have determined this individual to inflict death upon himself; viz.

Mr. Fauconnier declared, that yesterday at noon he saw the said J. W. Wrigth, to whom he carried the "Moniteur;"that he found him well and calm; that two hours afterwards, Savart, the guardian, carried in dinner, and found him in the same state; and that finally this morning the last-named person came to apprize him (Fauconnier) of the event which has occasioned this our attendance on the spot; and this he declares to be all that he knows, and here signs with his hand accordingly, &c.

Franois Savart, guardian of the Temple, declares, that yesterday, at two o'clock in the afternoon, he carried in dinner to the said J. W. Wrigth, whose corpse is lying on the bed in the room where we now are; that that person spoke to him in a customary way, and he did not appear at all wrong-headed; that this morning at eight o'clock he came to bring him a roll for break fast, and having opened the window shutters, he cast his eyes on the bed, and there saw, with astonishment, the same individual covered with blood, and in a motionless state, which caused him to presume he was dead; that he directly re-shut the room-door, and went to make report of this event to Mr. Fauconnier, the steward; which testimony he here signs, &c.

We next called on Mr. Soupé, the surgeon, to examine the body, and to explain the causes of death, who, in compliance therewith, declares as follows: "That on examining the corpse, he observes a transversal wound situated in the anterior and superior part of the throat, above the bone termed juxoid, in length about eighteen centimetres, penetrating unto the cervical vertebra; which wound appears to have been effected by an edged instrument, such as a razor, which in its course has cut the skin, the muscles, the tracheal artery, the oesophagus, and the sanguineous vessels of that part, whence has ensued a considerable effusion of blood, and the prompt death of the said Wrigth." Which declaration the deponent hath signed, &c.

Here follows an inventory of his effects.

We, commissary of police above named, seeing that, by the preceding declarations, and surgical report of the state of the corpse, and the razor found in the right hand, it appears demonstrated that the said Wrigth hath committed suicide with that instrument, and that the cause which prompted him unto such act was his reading the "Moniteur"of the third of this present month, which may have unduly exalted his imagination, and, in his condition of a stranger, led him to that act of de"spair, therefore find that there is no cause for more ample inquiry, and close the present inquest on the said day, month, year, and hour of one in the afternoon; and the said Sieurs Ravier, Pousignon, Fauconnier, and Savart, sign these presents with us, &c.

Extract from the Register of Commitments to the
Temple House of Arrest, deposited in the Archives of
the Prefecture of Police.

It appears in fol. 190 of the 4th register from the 3rd to the 4th Brumaire of the year XIV, that the Sieur John Wesley Wrigth, English captain, who entered this house by order of Monsieur Réal, counsellor of state, dated 30th Floreal, year XII, committed suicide in his chamber in the night of the 3rd Brumaire of the year XIV, by cutting his own throat with his razor; this suicide was ascertained on the morning of the 4th of the said month, by Messieurs Dusser, commissary of police of the Temple division, and Soupé, health-officer of the Temple house of arrest, according to the *procés-verbal* drawn up to such effect, which instrument bears date the above-said 4th day of the present month: he was interred the 6th day of the said month, as is ascertained by the register of the municipality of the 6th ward.

< Signed > PINAULT, the elder, clerk of the (Temple) lodge, and FAUCONNIER, keeper.

This extract delivered in conformity, the 30th April, 1816.

PORTIS,
Secretary-general.

Certified in conformity to the register of commitments,

LEMAITRE,
(L.S.) Keeper of the Archives and Depositaries.

Sixième Arrondissement, (Temple.)

Nos. des Inhumations.	Nos. du Reg.tre Municipal.	Dates de L'inhumation.	Noms et prénoms.	Ages.
1614	99	6 Brumaire an XIII. ou 9bre 1805.	WRIGTH, JOHN WESLEY	36
	inhumé	au Cimetière	de L'Est ou Pere La-Chaise.	

Copied from the public register of the above-named burying-ground, February, 1816, by the guardian; the same then on duty, and at the burial. N.B. In my presence and in the presence of Captain Arabin.

Villiers Cotterets, Jan. 23, 1816

Sir, Perhaps you will recollect that I forwarded to Vienna some particulars concerning the death of Captain With: but this packet seems to have had the lot of so many others, and did not reach its destination.

When I was quitting Paris, I called to present my compliments; and to leave you the address of Christopher, formerly turnkey at the tower of the Temple, as also your attendant at the period when you was shut up therein: not having been able to meet with him, to procure more ample details by word of mouth, I thought you might be glad to interrogate him yourself. Since my arrival at Villiers-Cotterets, not having received any answer to the letters which I took the liberty of addressing you, I know not whether you have seen this man.

Painfully affected by the details which Christopher gave me, my memory has faithfully collected and preserved them.

You know already, Sir, that Captain W. was condemned to seclusion until the return of peace, by the same tribunal which condemned to death George Cadoudal, Sac. Messrs. De Polignac (Julius and Armand) partook of the same lot as your friend, who was placed under secret custody in the same chamber which he occupied during his first captivity (1797.) As Messrs. De Polignac occupied your lodging, you must know how they could correspond with your friend . . . they found means to convey the instruments necessary for his escape. Christopher was informed of this project by the captain himself, who (he says) had much confidence in, and conversed often with him (Christopher) through the door. Mr. De Bourdillac, an emigrant condemned to be shot, and a Mr. De — —, were also in the secret; all went on well; the captain was going to be free; when one morning the police came, made a search, and found upon your friend cords, files, in short, everything that led to the conviction of a meditated escape: the whole was carried off, and even the money that was in his table-drawer, all in napoleons of forty fr. Our heroes, however, did not lose courage: they formed a new plan, which was about to be effectuated, when Christopher, going one morning to do the needful in the captain's chamber, was astonished to find him still in bed: he approached, and became seized with fright on seeing him pale as death: he drew the coverlid a little aside, and recoiled with horror at perceiving blood! He hastened down to Fauconnier, the concierge, and said to him: "Come up quick to Mr. With, I believe they have done the same to him as to Pichegru." Fauconnier treated him like an idiot, ordered him to hold his tongue, and walked quietly up, followed by a turnkey and by Christopher. He ordered him to uncover the bed: the captain was found lying at length; in the right hand he held a razor, pressed in such a way against his thigh, that there was an opening, but no blood. The concierge Fauconnier ordered Christopher to raise up the body; but when he moved it, he thought the head was going to detach itself from the trunk, having the neck cut unto the bone. (These are the expressions of Christopher.) Which, when the turnkey saw, he melted in tears, and let some expressions escape which signified that it was not Mr. With who had thus put an end to himself. The concierge did not call in any medical man; but drew up a minute of the circumstance, and had Messrs. De Polignac, and two other prisoners, neighbours of the deceased, called; who declared that they heard this officer play on the flute at one o'clock in the morning, and as to the rest, they did not hear any extraordinary movement in his chamber: they signed the minute; and Christopher with his wife were charged to bury the corpse, which was interred without noise, or any other forms. Messrs. De Polignac were afterwards removed to the dungeon of Vincennes, where the brother last mentioned (Armand) remained eleven years, and did not come out until the king's arrival: Mr. De Bourdillac, on the contrary, was set at liberty almost on the spot, and sent back to his own country. This man, who gave himself out for a nobleman,, was extremely intimate with the concierge; and every evening, after the general shutting up of the prisoners, he used to come down by stealth, and spent long evenings with him: such was their familiarity, that they thee'd and thou'd each other. Fauconnier had always been employed by the police during the revolution: he was Mr. B.'s successor at the tower of the Temple; and in F.'s time, Pichegru, many other prisoners, (whose names I cannot recall to mind,) and lastly, your worthy friend, died assassinated. The turnkey who evinced such sensibility was put in arrest, taken to La Force, where he remained a month, and was at length turned out of his place. Christopher told me he believed that the man had died of want: as to himself, he obtained that unfortunate man's place at the solicitation of Mr. De Bourdillac. But to return: Christopher was ordered to wash well away the blood which had flowed abundantly; to efface every trace of it under the bed; to keep the most profound secrecy as to the details; and simply to say, that the prisoner had cut his own throat with his razor; an article, it is to be observed, that he ought not even to have been possessed of, because no edged instruments are allowed to a prisoner when under the secret regimen. I learned this frightful event at the Magdelonettes, where I was detained: but I never, for a single instant, believed that this prisoner had committed suicide.

I believe, Sir, I have not omitted anything of this afflicting detail. Nevertheless, if you choose to see Christopher, he is a hackney coachman, and lives *rue des Vertus*, No. 6.

I have the honour to be, &c.

B.

Sir Sidney Smith employed emissaries, and received from them several communications very much resembling in substance the one that we have just quoted. These documents, that the friendship of Sir Sidney and the activity of his agents procured, were both numerous and voluminous; but they all appear to strain to work out the preconceived opinion of assassination. On the other side, let us see what Fauconnier, the gaoler of the Temple, himself says upon this transaction.

Were the prisoners who were at the Temple at that time to be questioned, not one of them would say that he suspects the captain to have been assassinated; for what other term can be given to such a death?

All knew it as soon as I did, and witnessed the arrival of the commissary to verify the death, but none of them had the idea that Buonaparte had ordered the captain's throat to be cut. If he had wished to get rid of the captain, which could be of little consequence to him, he could have had him transferred, with his unfortunate companions, as a prisoner of war, and very easily had him poisoned by the way. At this time the trial of Georges was ended, and the captain was detained as having escaped from the Temple in Floreal VI.

I know, for I was present, when the captain held a very animated conversation with the Duke of Rovigo (Savary). I have learned since that this conversation affected the captain very much, as when the Duke, with General Desaix, was on board the Tigre, commanded by Milord Sidney Schmit, on an affair of parley, Captain Reit behaved to him with the greatest attention and respect.

Two days before the unfortunate event, Mr. Paques, inspector-general to the ministry of police, came to visit the captain's chamber, and there found concealed a rope-ladder, and other implements which had been procured for him, to attempt an escape.

I am persuaded that this search was not made but on the information of some prisoner, who wished to ingratiate himself with the ministry.

Thus there is no doubt, that—1st, The reading the "Moniteur "announcing the victory at Ulm: 2dly, The effect of the very animated, and even, on the part of the captain, contemptuous conversation with the Duke of Rovigo: 3dly, The search of the inspector-general, Paques, in the captain's chamber, and discovery of the rope-ladder and other instruments proper for an escape, and which were taken away, and shown to the ministry: and, 4thly, The inward conviction of the captain, that seeing he was not treated as a prisoner of war, (although he received the allowance as such, but as a prisoner re-imprisoned, having previously escaped,) his detention would be very long—were the real motives of the captain to his desperate resolution not to endure existence under so much anxiety.

Here is the whole truth!

Now comes a prisoner, at the end of ten or twelve years, who lodged in a room beneath the captain's, to give an account tending to accredit, and even to persuade us, that Buonaparte, through the medium of the Duke of Rovigo, has had the captain assassinated in his chamber during the night; and insinuates that at that time there were some masons employed at the Temple, and that one of them, that is to say, the foreman, having been seduced and gained over by the Duke of Rovigo, had committed the murder to satisfy the vengeance of a cruel Corsican.

The prisoner, to support his story, talks of a noise that he heard over his head, and of workmen who did not work the next day, because the overseer, the man who, according to him, had given the fatal blow, not having returned, the workmen could not work for want of a master.

According to this version, which is not proved, we must answer, and that it is very easy to do, if we may be heard without prejudice.

The thing is impossible, unless, in regard to this assassination, (for what other term can we apply to this murder?) we can believe that it was

Savard who committed it. But we are well convinced that that is false—we must then conclude that the captain, alone, has voluntarily committed suicide.

Savard, only, had the keys of the captain's chamber, and he alone attended him.

Let us come to the proofs of the impossibility of the prisoner's story.

The prisoner who, unfortunately for him, was then very poor, and had, moreover, a wife who had been recently brought to bed, comes, after a lapse of time, to give us a new edition of this in his own way, probably to extract some benefit; I know not whether he is now rich or at ease, but at that time he lived on the bounty of his comrades in misfortune, and by the labour of his hands as a tailor. His wife and the infant she suckled came every day to share his dinner. The Abbé Alary was the prisoner who assisted them most. If the fact had existed, he would have spoken of it to his wife, she would have broached it in Paris, and this anecdote would have soon been well known.

But let us resume. All the prisoners know what strict attention was paid to the admission of the workmen at the Temple. No workmen could enter the court, nor go to work in whatever place, without being attended by a keeper, and especially if his business was in the interior of the tower. No workman could go out of the prison who was not attended by the same keeper, who was continually to watch him, in order that this work-man should have no communication with the prisoners, by stealth. The two keepers, also, who had the charge of opening the three gates, the two wickets of entry, would not open them to workmen who were not accompanied by the attendant keeper, for fear of surprise, and if they were many, they went out together, and were counted.

The admiral knows the captain's chamber perfectly well, as it was the same that he himself occupied at the time of his detention in the Temple.

In the part forming the antechamber, there is a little nook, which would hold a bed; this recess received its light from a little window that looked into a side-room, which was occupied by the reverend father, Pi-cot De Clos-Rivierre, an old Jesuit, and was then shut off by a door. It is in this recess, the prisoner asserts, that the assassin must have concealed himself. The captain being *au secret*, his door was fastened both with the key and with a padlock. Every day, at ten in the evening, the keepers made their last visit; counting the prisoners, and locking up all the rooms. Thus Savard would fasten that of Father Picot, then that upon the landing-place fronting the staircase—that of the captain being always shut, on account of his "secret." The door of the recess, whither the assassin would have retreated, must have been also shut; but admitting that it was not, the assassin would still find himself shut in between three doors—1st, that of the captain; 2nd, that of Father Picot; 3rd, that of the staircase. Besides, at the bottom of the stair, which was dark, there was a door fastened outside with a very heavy key. This door opened upon the great staircase of the tower, which was itself shut in by a strong door, through which led to the great gate of the tower, that opened into the court, and was fastened on the inside.

Now, how could this assassin open and shut all these doors, and avoid the sight of everybody? How could the assassin clandestinely open the captain's chamber, without making a noise? How could he, without light, and without using very great force, seize and throw down the captain, who was a vigorous and resolute man? How, and by what charm, could he quietly lay him on his bed, and upon his pillow, and, without making an alarming noise, kill him like a sheep? And with what? With his own razor!

According to the prisoner's account, he heard a noise; this noise, which must have been extremely loud, would have been heard also by the prisoners lodged above, and by Father Picot De Clos-Rivierre, (who lay on the same floor, and who rose regularly every day at four o'clock in the morning;) and by the sentinel placed under his windows; yet nobody but he heard anything! If there was any noise, the captain defended himself, and he was very able to defend himself, and would not suffer himself to be stretched like a sheep upon his bed, and timidly or cowardly present his neck to the assassin. There would have been scuffling in the room, blows given, blows returned: at length, if the assassin was the strongest, he must have thrown him down, cut his throat, and then placed him upon his bed, and upon his pillow, as he was found. But the boards, and all around his bed, would have been sprinkled, and even flooded, with the blood of the victim. Well! there was no blood but upon his bed and his pillow, where he was seen as he had fallen, after he had cut his throat,

If, without making a noise, and without waking the captain, the assassin was able to introduce himself and strike his blow, they could then have heard no noise. But he had then to seek for the captain's razor, for it was with his razor that he cut his throat. Then he must have cut straight from right to left, for the assassin could not have placed himself at the bedside in the recess, so as to cut from left to right, as the wound was made, and with a single stroke, as has been proved. Now, let us suppose, (as all suppositions are arbitrary,) that the assassin was able to effect his purpose without noise; the monster must quit the Temple, he must refasten the captain's door with the key and the padlock—he must open and shut the door on the landing-place, and all this without a light—he must open and shut the door at the bottom of the dark staircase; but this door would not open and shut on the inner side: he would have passed the door of the prisoner, who, being awaked by the noise that he said he heard, would have given notice to the sentinel. Again, he must open and shut the door at the bottom of the staircase of the tower, which only opens and shuts on the outside: then how could he procure the key to open the great gate of the tower? That key was always shut up in the turnkey's room. How could he avoid the sight of the sentinel who was placed opposite? How could he pass the guard-house, to present himself at the wicket, where the turnkeys would have asked him how and why he was in the tower at that time? Besides, the two great dogs who watch around the tower would have strangled him. This man did, therefore, pass through the keyhole, or, as a bird, fly over the walls! In the morning, the turnkeys opened the doors, visited the prisoners as usual, and it was at this time that Savard took the two keys of the captain's chamber, and of the door of the entry on the landing-place, and, after opening them, perceived, on entering, the tragical end of the captain, and, after having shut the door, came to inform me of it.

There is much more to the same effect in this document, which appears to have been addressed to Sir Sidney Smith, and it concludes thus

Captain Reit voluntarily killed himself.

This is my opinion, and I sign it.

FAUCONNIER,

Cy-devant Concierge

of the Temple.

In opposition to this, we must cite a portion of one more letter addressed to the indefatigable Sir Sidney. It is from the Abbé Alary, and, from the sacred character of the writer, should be received, if not with unlimited confidence, certainly with respect.

Although in relating to you the sad and deplorable death of our common friend, my heart is wounded afresh, I shall proceed to acquit myself of this painful duty. I shall not remark or dwell upon that which is already known to you, I mean the personal hatred Napoleon bore him, after you had withdrawn together from revolutionary tyranny, by escaping from the Temple, and especially after you had dimmed his star, and effectually repulsed him at St. John d'Acre. He accused him of having landed people in France, with an intention to attempt his life. Thus prejudiced, he poured upon him the whole weight of that resentment which his rage suggested against the English government and people. Involved in the criminal process, called "The Grand Conspiracy;"interrogated by wicked and corrupt judges urged to effect his destruction; it would have been promptly and openly effected, if the satellites of the more infamous butcher had not feared that your government would have avenged the law of nations so cruelly outraged. His death was from that time determined on; but they still vacillated on the means to be adopted. The firmness of his answers; his energy; a soul tempered in the school of adversity; the little hope of bending so firm a character, suspended their criminal audacity. But there were other motives for despatching a man whom they feared. Before the infamous execution of Georges Cadoual and his co-accused, these unhappy victims to the fury of a villain and his base instruments had permission to communicate with each other, and to take the air for a few hours in the day; but our friend was never allowed to participate in this act of humanity; he remained to the last moment of his life immured in his secret cell the parallel made by the people of the firmness of your countryman, was singularly contrasted with the weakness of certain of our own implicated in that affair, who had not, and have not, preserved for themselves more than a name without character, and a show of firmness, which never extended beyond their resistance to the will and orders of the king. A number of *détenus*, victims of the tyranny of the modern Attila, were witness to a controversy which captain Wright had with Savary, then aide-de-camp to Buonaparte, who came to offer him, in the name of his master, his restoration to liberty, if he would confess that he had orders from the English government to land in France those whom they termed Georges' band, and whom the Royalists (with some few exceptions) regarded as brave and honourable gentlemen. Our friend, indignant at a proposition which clashed with that high sense of honour by which his actions were invariably directed, answered him loud enough to be heard by those without "Tell your master, Savary, that I had you on board ship in Egypt that I did you the honour to admit you to the same table, and was far from imagining then that you could ever allow yourself to make a base proposal to a man who has the honour of being a captain in the navy of his Britannic Majesty. Had you any native military spirit in you, you would know that the sentiments professed by a soldier restrain him from making or accepting a dishonourable proposal, that must stamp an indelible stigma both on those who make it, and on those who listen to it without indignation." This animated conversation was heard by the *détenus* personalities were not spared—Savary, ashamed, withdrew—and our friend, from that day, was treated with increased rigour.

Until then I respected him, to admiration, but without knowing him intimately, not having communicated but by some marked salutations. About this time there left the Temple a certain Scotchman named Smith, inventor of some filtering machines, a sensible man, whose education had been neglected in his youth. This Smith was honest, and extremely devout; our friend was more particularly attached to him, after having experienced the ingratitude of those to whom he had rendered essential services.

*****

It was by the mediation of this Smith that our intimacy commenced. He had introduced me to the captain as a man the most firm and constant, as well as most capable of favouring and aiding his escape, (in the critical circumstances in which we were,) of which he always entertained a hope.

We lived in this intimate connexion as long as he existed, solacing our troubles in the bosom of friendship, reserving nothing secret from each other: I devoted to him every minute in which we could with any degree of safety converse viva voce, but much oftener by writing. Every evening, while our companions in misfortune were engaged at cards, or in their other amusements, I communicated to him the public news, and especially the substance of the private information which we had learned from friends who, with permission of the minister of police, came to visit us at the lodge.

You, no doubt, recollect certain boastings of Buonaparte, of flat-bottomed boats which he had built with so much ostentation, and in such numbers, for his pretended descent and invasion of England, You know that there had appeared in the newspapers of the day, an article, "inviting him to this glorious expedition without delay, as, in a short time, he would be otherwise occupied,"—alluding to the coalition, of which England was the soul. You recollect the activity of Buonaparte, and the unforeseen imbecility of the Austrians, frustrating the effects of the alliance, by suffering themselves to be beaten at Memingen and Ulm, before the allies could succour them. It is to be observed, that at the period of the rupture, several persons attached to the suite of the ambassador, Mr. De Cobenzl, were arrested at Paris. Among others, a Mr. Müller, a captain of cavalry in the Austrian army, and a French emigrant of the environs of Strasbourg. My friend having previously served in the corps of the Chevaliers de la Couronne, army of Condé, of which I was chaplain at headquarters, and having met in this place of misery, our friendship was renewed in a stricter union. He was soon informed of my intimacy with the captain, charged me with compliments which I reciprocally rendered, and they soon found means of conversing by a telegraph of communication, which was the more easily effected, as Mr. Müller was lodged over the wicket, and our friend in the chamber of the Little Temple opposite; the chamber which you had yourself occupied; and I was the interpreter of any part of their mute conversation which was not quite intelligible.

After some time, we perceived, and especially after the interview with the infamous Savary, that there was no hope of our friend being restored to his liberty. It was then that he resolved to acquire once more by stratagem, what he could not obtain from the justice of his tyrants. To procure the means, I engaged Mr. Müller to lend him twenty-five louis, which I sent him by Messrs. Poupard and Mingo: he was ignorant from whence the money came; but, thinking it sent on my part, and aware of my straitened circumstances, from a sense of delicacy he refused it; nor could I overcome his repugnance, but by assuring him that Mr. M., who had lent him the money, was beyond the want of it: in a few days after, upon certain suspicions of the commissaries of police, they came to his chamber, plundered him of his little property, and left him scarcely provided with the necessary articles of use. He was sensibly affected by this new outrage; fearing the necessity of addressing or supplicating the satellites of this horrible government, to obtain the means of subsistence. To tranquillise him, and that my eloquence and friendship might produce in his soul the effect I intended, I replaced, myself, the twenty-five louis lent by Mr. M., which had been taken from him. Mr. Poupard, who lodged directly under him, put them in a purse attached to the end of a string, which served to convey our daily correspondence.

In the evening of the next day he insisted on my taking two bills of exchange to insure our reimbursement, and gave me, at the same time, a voluminous letter in an envelope for a beloved sister that he had, of whom he often talked, as also of you, admiral.

I sent the bills and the letter to Madame la Marquise de L'Affalcique, (by birth Baroness de Mallecamp,) who knowing at that time Mr. Müller to be under rigorous arrest in his chamber, and knowing that they had rummaged many *détenus* in the interior of the Temple, as suspected of friendship and connivance, and dreading a domiciliary visit, burned the letter and bills, that she might not endanger herself by their being found in her possession.

In the meanwhile, the various events passing on the theatre of the world, interested and agitated us we wished to be actors in the scene, and were plunged into dungeons; when, suddenly, Buonaparte raised his camp at Boulogne, and marched with a brilliant army into Germany. We followed its movements, and took a lively interest in them. Of the Austrian army opposed to it we were apprehensive, but we hoped that, corrected by their former disasters and even faults, they would not expose themselves without being supported by the Russians, their powerful auxiliaries. I confess that the taking of Ulm, Memingen, Augsbourg, and the defeat of that army before its junction with the Russian army, disconcerted us a moment; but if the French government took care to inform us of that defeat on the other side, we lost no time in procuring information of the defeat off Trafalgar, which took place on the same day as the capture of Ulm. The total annihilation of that combined naval armament, and the consequence of capturing nearly all the French and Spanish ships which had not been sunk, made our hopes preponderate against our fears.

He, indeed, could not restrain the enthusiasm inspired by the news, but that it was heard without doors, and our gaolers perceived it. He had even the imprudence to hum some couplets which he had just composed in honour of Lord Nelson, and of gratifying with them some *détenus*, who, more fortunate than himself, walked in the court, while he had been constantly, and was still, a close and secret prisoner.

That same evening we continued our correspondence by writing. The medley billets which he addressed to me, in answer to details which I had given him, were pleasing, without any tincture of melancholy; alluding to an event which had happened that evening, an event which might have caused us to be shot, if I had not boldly prevented its coming to the knowledge of our executioners—it was this: I had addressed to him an account much less favourable than that which they had sent us upon the success of Buonaparte in Germany. This account diminished astonishingly the glory of the little man, miscalled great; it turned him into ridicule, which neither he nor his adherents could ever pardon. It was Poupard who customarily transmitted the correspondence, while I mounted guard, to prevent suspicion or surprise. I had but seldom acted as the messenger, and being less accustomed to it, I was consequently less dexterous. I gave notice, as usual, by striking two blows with the broom handle. He opened his casement window, dropped the string, at the end of which was the bag, and in it I put the despatch, pulled the string, which I immediately abandoned: it was also abandoned by our friend, and fell into the court at the moment when they were coming to shut our doors. I attempted a scheme, which succeeded: I said I was unwell, and without water, and requested they would open the door, and allow me to go and draw some. It was granted: at the instant that I cast the bucket into the well, I hastened under the window, and feeling about, happily found the bag and its contents, with which I immediately remounted and conveyed to him.

I was far (and I have no doubt he was the same) from foreseeing the sad event of the night; as no preliminary conversation no presentiment had occurred to give any reason to presume it.

His custom was, to rise with the day; his windows opened, we gave and received the customary mute salute. I descended to give it: what was my astonishment! his windows quite shut! I ran and applied to Mr. de Vaudricourt—to the good Vaudricourt, also his friend—sub-inspector of military reviews—one of those in whom he had the most confidence, and confidence well merited. He was as much surprised and alarmed as I, and added, what increased my apprehensions, that they had not been open all the morning; we suspected illness or indisposition. I went to inquire of those who occupied the apartment under him, who were also ignorant of his fate; but said they had heard some noise in his chamber during the night, as well as Messrs. Mingo and Poupard; but my fears were increased by the apostrophe addressed to them by the old Abbé, Mr. Bassinet, who lodged with them, saying, that they slept the whole night like marmots, but that he, an old man of eighty, had not been able to shut his eyes since an hour after midnight, so great had been the noise that had awoke him in the captain's apartment.

I related this discourse to Mr. de Vaudricourt; we went out, and walked to and fro much agitated, seeing the turnkeys sad and cast down. Mr. de V. called to one of them named Savard, and asked him "if Captain Wright was indisposed? He wished to go up to see him," The man, as he walked on, petrified with fright, said, "Well, they will not accuse me of having assassinated him." Judge of our painful astonishment we were soon after but too fully convinced that he was no longer in this world. Passing and repassing, we saw parties of the police successively arrive to ascertain this strange event—they unfold paper, &c. Whether from indignation, or curiosity to know what had happened to my worthy friend, I went up, came down again, passed and repassed before the door without daring to enter: but the door being a little open, I was perceived by a secretary of the police office, I believe his name was Pacq: he invited me to enter: I bowed, and casting a look at the bed, saw my friend lifeless—but yet apparently not bloody. I inquired of those who were in the room, of a prisoner of state named Joseph, a gentleman of Boulogne-sur-mer, and was told that he had cut his throat—that they had prepared a *procés-verbal*, and that I should go and sign. I again approached the bed—I saw the body as asleep; I raised the bed-clothes; uncovered him: saw his throat cut and bathed in his blood, still holding in his hand a razor shut. Filled with horror at the sight of this shocking spectacle, the blood froze in iny veins, I made a motion to retire, when I was opposed by the police, who told me I must sign the *procés-verbal*. This I refused, and without hesitation, indignantly replied, "that the man who cuts his own throat does not shut the razor for the use of another." Stricken with my observation, and knowing well the stubbornness of a character that never bent, they allowed me to withdraw without any further opposition, Here, sir, is what I know and have seen.

All the state prisoners, at that time confined in the Temple, believed with me that he was assassinated—it was the general report. These particulars are better known to me by reason of our intimate connexion, but the times and the tyranny of our Attila have not allowed me the opportunity of giving these details sooner. Having been exiled in Vivarias after my release from the Temple, I could not quit it without an express permission of the police. This rigid exile lasted until the return of the king. Forced a second time to expatriate myself for serving the cause of my king, and yielding to those sentiments which only loyalty induced, I followed him to Belgium, and had the honour of paying my respects to you at Brussels—you desired of me the relation which I now present you, a relation which, not being able to send you on your journey to Alost, as we agreed, I hesitated to send it you here, where Fouché was minister of the police, as I strongly suspected that man to have contributed to the assassination of our friend.

The truth still remains buried in a mystery that in all human probability never will be dispelled. We never can believe that Captain Wright slew himself. The refutation to the charge is in his own high and magnanimous character. He not only fought but suffered as a hero. He had not only the courage to act nobly, but to endure quietly. Moreover, he was eminently a good man—a man of principle: such a man could *not* be a suicide.

Was he the victim of a cowardly, detestable, and assassinating state policy? We think not. There were no adequate motives for it. It was too clumsily managed. Neither Buonaparte nor Fouché would have perpetrated an act so horrible so awkwardly. Where the evidence is so doubtful, let us not involve so many persons in the guilt of a base murder. How then did he meet a death evidently violent? There is no other solution to this very natural question than by supposing that he was sacrificed to private vengeance. This is our firm conviction.

All honour be to Sir Sidney Smith for the amiable zeal that he displayed in attempting to elucidate this dark crime. We esteem him for the steadiness of his friendship, we applaud him for his intelligence and activity in endeavouring to rescue his companion in arms and in captivity from the opprobrium of a suicide, and even love him for mingling so much of the good and brave man with the great. In spite of some few foibles, he is a glory to his country, and should that country ever cease to think so, her own glory is on the wane.

When he had done all that was possible to rescue Captain Wright's fame from a taint, he proceeded to erect a monument over his remains, which lie interred in the cemetery of Pére Le Chaise. The following is a description of it:

The upper part of the composition is of a pyramidal, or obelisk form, on the plane of which are the letters D. O. M.; and underneath an urn, in basso relievo, with two weeping figures on each side, with torches reversed, as on the point of extinction. The base has also a figure standing on each side, with torches reversed. The whole of the base, and the pedestal of the urn, are divided into six compartments, into which the inscription is distributed, as follows:

H. S. E.
IOANNES. WESLEY. WRIGHT.
ORTV. ANGLVS.
NAVIS. PRAEFECTVS. APVD. SVOS. EXTEROSQVE.
VIRTVTE. AC. PERITIA. CLARVS.
CVI. EARVM. RERVM.
QVE. AD. SVMMVM. GLORIAE. FASTIGIVM. PERDVCVNT.
NIHIL. PRAETER. OCCASIONEM. DEFVIT.
CLARVS. EDITVS. ATAVIS.
GENVS. FACTIS. ILLUSTRAVIT.

IN. CONSILIIS. CAPIENDIS. SOLERS.
IN. EXSEQVENDIS. STRENVVS. AC. FORTIS.

IN. REBVS. SECVNDIS. MODESTVS. IN. ADVERSIS. CONSTANS.
IN. DUBIIS. PRVDENS. ET. SAGAX.

REBVS. ALIQVAMDIV. FORTITER. AC. FELICITER. GESTIS. TAN-
DEM.
ADVERSIS. VENTIS. INTERCEPTVS.
ET. IN. LITVS. HOSTILE. DELATVS.
MOX. LUTETIAE. PARISIORVM.
IN. CARCERE. CVI. NOMEN. TEMPLVM.
NOCTVRNIS. CAEDIBUS. INFAMI.
CONCLVSVS. EST.
ET. DVRISSIMA. CVSTODIA. ADFLICTVS.
SED. INTER. VINCVLA.
ET. VINCVLIS. GRAVIORA.
ANIMI. FORTITVDO. ET. FIDELITAS. ERGA. PATRIAM.
VSQVE. INCONCVSSAE. PERMANSERVNT.
PAVLLO. POST. MANE. IN. LECTVLO. MORTVVS.
IVGVLO. PERFOSSO. REPERTVS.
PATRIAE. DEFLENDVS. DEO. VINDICANDVS. OBIIT.
V. KAL. NOVEMB. ANNO. SACRO. MDCCCV
AETATIS. SVAE. XXXVI.

GVLIELMVS. SIDNEY. SMYTHE.
VETERIS. AMICITIAE. MEMOR.
HOC. MARMOR.
PONENDVM. CVRAVIT.
ANNO. SACRO.

Edward Howard

MDCCCXVI.

[Editor's Translation]

HIS EXCELLENCY
JOHN WESLEY WRIGHT
ENGLISHMAN
COMMANDER OF A SHIP. FAMOUS AT HOME AND ABROAD
FOR BRAVERY AND SKILL.
TO WHOM OF ALL THOSE THINGS
THAT LEAD TO THE HIGHEST PEAK OF GLORY
NOTHING WAS LACKING EXCEPT OPPORTUNITY.
FAMOUS, NOBLE, HE MADE THE TRIBE
OF HIS ANCESTORS ILLUSTRIOUS.

SKILLED IN STRATEGY
VIGOUROUS AND BRAVE IN EXECUTION.

MODEST IN SUCCESS, STEADFAST IN ADVERSITY
PRUDENT AND WISE IN DOUBTFUL CIRCUMSTANCES.

FOR SOME TIME, HIS DEEDS WERE BRAVE AND SUCCESSFUL
BUT FINALLY, HE WAS CAUGHT UP BY UNFAVOURABLE WINDS
AND TOSSED UP ON A HOSTILE SHORE.
SOON HE WAS CONFINED AT LUTETIA OF THE PARISII
IN A PRISON CALLED THE TEMPLE.
INFAMOUSLY SEIZED AT NIGHT,
HE WAS SUBJECTED TO THE HARSHEST DURANCE
BUT IN CHAINS
AND WORSE THAN CHAINS
HIS STRENGTH OF SOUL AND LOYALTY TO HIS COUNTRY
REMAINED UNSHAKEN.
SOON THEREAFTER HE WAS FOUND IN BED, DEAD
WITH HIS THROAT CUT.
HE DIED MOURNED BY HIS COUNTRY AND AVENGED BY GOD.

27TH OF OCTOBER IN THE YEAR OF OUR LORD 1805
AT THE AGE OF 36.

WILLIAM SIDNEY SMITH
MINDFUL OF OLD FRIENDSHIP
HAD THIS MARBLE MONUMENT ERECTED
IN THE YEAR OF OUR LORD
1816

CHAPTER XVI

SIR SIDNEY MADE A KNIGHT COMMANDER OF THE BATH • THE DUKE OF WELLINGTON INVESTS HIM • SIR SIDNEY'S SPEECH ON THE OCCASION • SIR SIDNEY'S REMONSTRANCE TO BONAPARTE.

TOWARDS the termination of this year, 1815, our officer was honoured, in a most particular manner, by his sovereign.

His grace the Duke of Wellington having received the gracious commands of his royal highness the Prince Regent of the United Kingdoms, through his royal highness the Duke of York, grand-master of the most honourable order of the. Bath, to invest Vice-Admiral Sir William Sidney Smith, knight-commander-grand-cross of the royal military order of the sword, with the insignia of commander of the aforesaid, his grace fixed on the 29th of December for the performance of the ceremony, which took place accordingly at the Palace Elisée-Bourbon, the knights-grand-crosses, knights-commanders, and companions being present, as also his grace the Duke of Richmond and the Right Honourable the Earl of Hardwick, both knights of the most noble order of the garter.

At six o'clock the commander elect arrived at the palace, and being conducted and supported into the presence of the noble duke representing the sovereign on the occasion, by the two junior grand-crosses Sir James Kempt and Sir Henry Colville; after the usual reverences in advancing, (the commander elect being already a knight, the usual ceremony of dubbing him as such was formally dispensed with,) his grace proceeded, according to the order of his royal highness the grand-master, which he first read, and invested the commander with the insignia of the order: after which his grace embraced Sir Sidney Smith twice most cordially, with every demonstration of the feelings of esteem and regard, feelings which the knights, grand-crosses, and commanders, many of whom had served in Egypt as his juniors in rank, also testified; and it certainly may be said to be a proud day for England when such a scene took place in the evacuated palace of Buonaparte, between these two British officers of the two services, one of whom first checked, and the other of whom finally closed, the career of that ambitious chieftain.

The banquet being announced, his grace desired his excellency the British ambassador, Sir Charles Stuart, G.C.B., to conduct the new knight commander to the hall of the same, where the members of the order, including some foreigners of distinction, amongst whom were Don Michael Alava, General Muffling, and Count Demetrius Valsamachi, a nobleman of the Ionian Islands, were entertained most sumptuously in the usual style of the duke's elegant hospitality.

After the health of the King and Prince Regent had been drunk, the duke gave the health of "Sir Sidney Smith:" the company hereupon rose, and followed his grace's example in greeting the new commander with the most cordial acclamations. When silence was restored, Sir Sidney Smith rose, and addressed the company nearly as follows:

"My Lords, noble Knights, Grand Crosses, Commanders, and Companions! I should not do justice to my feelings, were I not to endeavour to express them in returning you my thanks for the honour you have done me by this reception: at the same time, I feel I cannot do justice to them by any mode of expression I can make use of.

"The language of *compliment* must die on the lips of any man in the presence of the Duke of Wellington; first, from the inadequacy of all language to express what every man must feel when speaking of such a highly distinguished chief; next, from the recollection of the noble simplicity of his character which disdains it. It will, I trust, be readily believed, that I must be most truly gratified to be invested by a knight of such high renown and glorious achievements; and the more so in this *particular place*, and in an assembly of so many illustrious and highly-distinguished knights-commanders and companions. A combination of circumstances, which could only happen in the present times, and are mainly owing to the successful result of the battle of Waterloo. Noble and illustrious knights, I beg you to accept the expression of my humble thanks for the honour you have done me."

The Duke of Wellington having acceded to Sir Sidney Smith's request to be allowed to propose a toast to the company, he proceeded to say: "I beg leave to call to remembrance that this day (the 29th of December) is the anniversary of a re-union of illustrious knights of various orders, which took place at Vienna, where many sovereigns were present, and when the toast I shall have the honour to propose to you was drunk by them with a manifestation of their conviction, that the object of it intimately concerned knighthood as such, in all nations. I beg leave to propose the health and deliverance of the *white Slaves in the Barbary States*."

The toast was received with the most marked approbation, and drunk with the usual demonstrations thereof, by three times three regular and hearty cheers, when the company adjourned to the ball-room, preceded, on the indication of the Duke of Wellington, by the new knight-commander, supported by his Britannic Majesty's ambassador, in the same order as on entrance, where a brilliant assembly of ladies, English, French, Spanish, Russian, &c. &c., continued to increase till a late hour; his Royal Highness the Duke of Berry, the French, and the foreign ministers, were also present, and all joined in cordial congratulations of, and compliments to, the cosmopolite chieftain, president of the knights liberators of the white slaves in Africa; who, we observed, was decorated with the various orders of the nations he has contributed by his endeavours to release from the yoke of the former inhabitant of the palace where this extraordinary assembly was held; then a prisoner on the top of a rock in the Southern Atlantic. These circumstances reminded the Parisians of the prophetic inscriptions left by Sidney Smith on the window shutter of the Temple prison, when he escaped, of which many copies were taken and are now again in circulation, and read with great interest since the accomplishment has taken place: we have been favoured with a translation, of which we give our readers a copy, the original having been in French, and respected by various successive guardians of the tower, till the Prince de Rohan, afterwards Duke de Rohan, subsequently a prisoner in that tower, removed it for its preservation, and we are assured he now possesses it.

SIDNEY SMITH TO BUONAPARTE

Fortune's wheel makes strange revolutions it must be confessed; but for the term revolution to be applicable, the term should be a complete one, for a half turn is not a revolution; (see the Dictionary of the Academy;) you are at present as high as you can mount. Well! I don't envy you your fortunate situation, for I am better off than you; I am as low in the career of ambition as a man can descend; so that let fortune turn her wheel ever so little, and as she is capricious, turn it she will, I must necessarily mount, and you as necessarily must descend. I do not make this remark to you to cause you any chagrin; on the contrary, with the intent to bring you the same consolation I have at present, when you shall arrive at the same point where I am; yes! the same point; you will inhabit this prison, why not as well as I? I did not think of such a thing any more than you do at present, before I found myself brought hither. In party wars 'tis a crime in the eyes of opponents for a man to do his duty well; you do yours now, and consequently you by so much irritate your enemies; you will answer me.

'I fear not their combined hatred, the voice of the people is declared for me, I serve them well:' that is all very good talking; sleep in quiet, you'll very soon learn what one gains by serving such a master, whose inconstancy will perhaps punish you *for all the good* you do him. 'Whoever' (says an ancient author, Pausanias Atticus) 'puts his entire confidence in public favour, never passes his life without pain and trouble, and seldom comes to a good end.'

Finis coronat opus.
[Ed. The end crowns the work]

In fact, I need not prove to you that you will come here and read these lines, because here you must be to read them. You will certainly have this chamber, because it is the best, and the keeper, who is a very civil good sort of man will, of course, treat you as well as he does me.'

N. B. These lines having appeared in the Parisian papers in 1799, and having been put into Buonaparte's hands at Cairo, on his return from his unsuccessful Syrian expedition, where he was foiled and worsted by the writer of them, he exclaimed, '*It is very extraordinary;*' and on his return to Paris, fearing the accomplishment of the remainder of the prediction, after having procured through Regnauld de St. Jean d'Angely the sight of a copy in the hands of Baruel Beauvert, he forthwith ordered the building to be levelled to the ground.

After this display of his country's gratitude to Sir Sidney Smith, which became so much the more enhanced, as it may be said to have taken place almost in the presence of so many sovereigns, Sir Sidney had little else to do but to enjoy his richly-merited rewards, the universal admiration, and the approbation of his own mind, ever active in doing good, not only for his country, but for the whole human race.

He prosecuted with ardour his plans for the abolition of white slavery even after the destruction of the pirates' nest in Algiers.

We do not think that his noble intention was patronised so much as it deserved at the time. But there seems to have been a ruling Providence in this apparently mortifying result. Had Sir Sidney Smith's propositions been carried fully into effect, the Algerine insolence and rapacity would have been repressed, but we do not think that these barbarians would ever have been wholly reclaimed from their piratical tendencies.

Their measure of iniquity became full and intolerable, and they are now obliterated totally from the very maps, and exist only in history.

CHAPTER XVII

SIR SIDNEY'S EXERTIONS IN FAVOUR OF THE WHITE SLAVES • LETTERS
FROM THE VARIOUS MINISTERS OF THE EUROPEAN POWERS ON THE
SUBJECT • ALSO FROM THE CONSULS AT TRIPOLI • SIR SIDNEY MADE
ADMIRAL • A BRIEF SKETCH OF HIS CHARACTER.

DURING all these proceedings, Sir Sidney Smith was actively engaged in
bringing his plans to maturity for the promotion of his new order of
knighthood, and from time to time produced and published papers in
relation to it. To give the reader all these documents, would only need-
lessly swell out these volumes; and our omitting to do so is the more war-
rantable, as public events outstripped the exertions of Sir Sidney in making war against, if not in extirpating, the pirates.

They, in the first instance, received chastisement from the Americans, and afterwards Lord Exmouth gave the Dey of Algiers a lesson so
severe, that if the Algerines had only possessed but a small portion of the
common sense allotted to humanity in general, their beautiful country
would not now have been a French colony.

But a few of these documents we feel bound to give, as they evince
the ardour and intelligence with which our hero prosecuted his designs,
and besides, are very favourable specimens of his style of composition.
But, in the first place, we shall give a few specimens of the manner in
which Sir Sidney's philanthropic design was viewed by various persons
high in office.

*Letter from the Count de Vallaise, Minister of his
Majesty the King of Sardinia, to Vice-Admiral
Sir Sidney Smith.*

Turin, October 5, 1814

Sir! Admiral! I am charged by his majesty the King, my
august master, to express to your excellency the satisfaction
which your letter, transmitted to him by the Baron de la Cainéa,

afforded his majesty, and the gratitude with which he received the congratulations that you were pleased to offer him on the occasion of his return to his dominions on the continent.

The principles which influence your excellency in favour of the miserable victims of the negro slave-trade, are too conformable to the religion and sentiments which he professes, not to make him desirous to see your enterprises crowned with the success which they merit, and not to feel most happy if he can contribute to the result which you have in view, and in which all hearts, susceptible of the feelings of charity and compassion, concur with you in devoutly wishing.

The countless exploits by which Great Britain has rendered herself illustrious, and which will make the end of the eighteenth century, and the beginning of the nineteenth, as brilliant as it is honourable to her, are, in the estimation of the true friends of humanity, a title much less glorious to her than that of the abolition of the slave-trade, for which she has openly recognised one of the most consolatory precepts of the Christian religion—that which renders all men as so many brothers.

His majesty, therefore, charges his plenipotentiaries at Vienna to enter fully into these same views, whether for the abolition of the slave-trade, or for the suppression of the piracies of the Barbaric States, and commands me to make known to them your excellency's propositions, and his majesty's intentions thereon.

I congratulate myself, sir, admiral, on the opportunity which the execution of my sovereign's commands affords me, of offering to you the assurance of the very distinguished consideration with which I have the honour to be, sir, admiral, &c. &c. &c.

The Count de Vallaise

Extract from a Letter of his Excellency the Chevalier
M. the Marquis de Riviére, his most Christian Majesty's
Ambassador at the Sublime Ottoman Porte,
to Sir Sidney Smith, Knight Grand-Cross of several Orders.

Epernay, September 16, 1814

Most trusty Knight, This letter will be forwarded to you by M. the Prince of Benevento, who, ever since my arrival, has employed his kind offices in my behalf in the most generous manner. The King has had the condescension to approve of the choice which he was pleased to present to him, and I am appointed ambassador to the Sublime Porte—an event which will a little derange our correspondence: but, as I have spoken to the prince of your philanthropic and noble ideas relative to the Barbaric States, he knows that you are in this matter the advocate of the

Christian, as you are of the negro slaves; he will converse with you on the subject, and has promised to cause instructions to be transmitted to me, in the event of my being wanted, previously to my departure for Constantinople...

The conferences which you will have with the prince, who well knows that your plan embraces objects of incalculable interest to the morality of the whole world, may be the means of retarding or accelerating my departure. I shall expect to hear from you, and to receive his orders, before I set out for Toulon.

Letter of Prince Talleyrand to Sir Sidney Smith.

Vienna, Dec. 24, 1815

I have read the letter which the Right Hon. Sir Sidney Smith has been pleased to send me for M. de Riviére: it shall be forwarded this day. I have recognised in it all the humane views which characterise Sir Sidney Smith, and which render him one of the most praiseworthy men of his time.

Extract of a Letter from the Marquis de Riviére to Sir Sidney Smith, Paris, November 3, 1814

The prince appears to have imbibed your humane and noble sentiments. The evil is great; the remedy ought to be prompt and efficacious. I have collected what several consuls of respectability had told me. I sent the note to the prince, agreeably to your desire. It should seem that everything is at a stand at the idea of three viceroyships, (pachalics,) but the pashas sent by the Porte will soon shake off the yoke...

The Porte could not alone, I fear, change the government of the three Barbaric powers, if the allied fleets should not second her efforts. I have not been to see you at Vienna, awaiting my instructions on this subject, and intending to proceed by sea...

...I wait here for the decision of Prince Talleyrand. If the Turks are convinced that we are influenced by honourable and generous motives, without wishing to diminish their power, but, on the contrary, to consolidate it, they will, I think, exert themselves with good faith. We ought upon this subject, my dear knight, to speak with an open heart, without any political reservation; the interests of humanity, of Christianity, to which we would give freedom, ought alone to influence our conduct, and the shackles of traffic ought to disappear...

Extract of a Letter from M. the Chevalier de Revel, Governor of Genoa, to Sir Sidney Smith, dated

Turin, November 9, 1814

...Compassion for the blacks is worthy of praise; but there are other men, my dear admiral, who claim it against Africans more barbarous than the Europeans who carry on traffic in the former. Your stations in the Mediterranean have afforded you an opportunity of knowing the miseries of the Christian slaves in Barbary. If the commercial interests of England be against it, the sentiments of the nation, and the conduct of the parliament, with respect to the blacks, do not leave any room to apprehend that they can form an obstacle to a measure which humanity and religion, as well as the knowledge and civilisation of the times demand. These principles impose upon the grand powers the duty of suppressing those infamous piracies; but I presume to affirm, that upon Great Britain, who has pledged herself, who has contracted the honourable and holy engagement, by occupying Malta, once the bulwark of Christendom, the obligation strictly devolves. The squadrons of the order protected the navigation and the coasts of those nations which could not purchase peace from the Barbaric powers. Is not England charged with this protection? As to her ability to do so there can be no doubt. Her interposition has recently secured Portugal, Spain, and Sicily from the attacks of those atrocious pirates: Italy now implores the same boon.

During maritime wars, France having occasion for the navigation of the Italians, drives the corsairs from their shores; she recalls them on the arrival of peace, for the purpose of entering herself into possession of the coasting trade—an occurrence which has taken place at the present as in former times. Those robbers have again made their appearance off the coasts of Italy, and very recently carried off some hapless cultivators between Nice and the Var.

I am persuaded that this cause, which so forcibly appeals to the humanity and glory of England, responsible for everything that is done on the seas, and still more particularly in this case, will excite your generous enthusiasm, and that you will be of opinion that, if England insists upon the other powers conforming to her principles with respect to the blacks, she will feel herself obliged to take upon herself the noble functions of the order of Malta, with the efficacy of her power.

Letter from the First Minister of his Majesty
the Emperor of Austria

Vienna, December 17, 1814

The Prince of Metternich has received the note which Sir Sidney Smith, admiral of his Britannic majesty, has done him the honour to address to him, on the 13th of this month, and the documents which he has been so obliging as to communicate to him: he has that of returning the subjoined, after having examined them; and reserves himself for a conference on the subject at the first opportunity.

The Prince of Metternich has the honour to renew to Sir Sidney Smith the assurance of his distinguished consideration.

Letter from Prince Louis Lichtenstein.

Vienna, January 30, 1815

The undersigned has the honour of recommending the petition of Captain Felsch to M. the Admiral Sir Sidney Smith, praying that his excellency would have the kindness to contribute to the liberation of his brother.

Captain Felsch's Petition

Vienna, January 10, 1815

My brother, Francis Felsch, who is at this instant groaning under slavery at Algiers, in Africa, was enlisted in 1798, if my memory serves me correctly, as a drummer in the Huff regiment, now Archduke Louis', No. 8. According to a letter (which I still have) from the said regiment, he was made prisoner on the 10th of April, 1800, on the summit of Mount Sette-Pannj, in Italy, and was compelled, although quite a youth, to enter into the French Polish legion; he went afterwards into Spain, where he was forced, by hunger, to enlist, which is proved by a letter from Barcelona, under date the 27th of February, 1803, confirming that he was a sub-officer in the King's guard. I have not the least information of the manner in which he fell into the unfortunate and lamentable situation he now is, inasmuch as he does not give any explanation whatever on the subject in his letter, dated Algier, August 1, 1814.

The voice of humanity, no less than fraternal affection, enjoins me to attempt every expedient to restore this wretched young man to liberty, or at least to alleviate his afflictions, which are grievous.

Not being, by any means, in circumstances to pay a heavy ransom, I rely wholly upon the protection of the government, my brother being an Austrian subject, and the son of an Austrian soldier: the claim is weak he has another he is a man I, therefore, appeal to humanity on his behalf.

The following letter to the first minister of his majesty the King of Sardinia is from the pen of Sir Sidney Smith:

Vienna, January 10, 1815

Sir, I beg leave to submit to your excellency, for the information of his majesty the King of Sardinia, a statement of the measures which I have taken, and of their progress towards the object so anxiously desired the liberation of the Christian slaves in Barbary, and the cessation of the depredations and outrages against Europe, which continue to increase the number of those unfortunate and innocent victims.

1st. I have despatched couriers with instructions to my confidential agents and correspondents, in Asia as well as in Africa, to influence the native princes, who are equally aggrieved with the Europeans by those exotic robbers, and to engage them, in defending themselves against aggression, to occupy a greater portion of their forces.

2nd. I have engaged the august sovereigns, and the illustrious personages, royal and noble, assembled in this capital at the Congress, to establish, in their capacity of *Christian knights*, a charitable fund for the support of the religious establishments in the Holy Land, through whose medium succour and consolation may be administered unto those hapless captives who toil in chains, under a scorching sun, and under the blows of their fanatical and inexorable taskmasters; scarcely fed sufficiently to sustain nature, having only rations of bad bread, rice, and oil, five days out of the seven they work like beasts of burthen; and the Fridays and Sundays subsisting on the charity of the European consuls, on that of good *Mussulmans* who *profess* and *practise* hospitality in obedience to their law, and on that of the *Jewish* merchants. This state of things being a reproach to all Europe, professing, as she does, the *Christian* religion, one of the fundamental principles of which is *charity*, has been taken into serious consideration by a convention of knights, imperial, royal, noble, and illustrious, composed of all the nations, and of all the orders of knighthood, and which was holden at the Augarten, in a house appertaining to his imperial and royal majesty the Emperor of Austria, having for its purpose the formation of a fund as above mentioned, whose object interests religion, humanity, and the honour of Christendom. These principles having been formally set forth and recognised in the invitations given by the knights to each other, to their friends and their families, and signed with their illustrious names, I have the satisfaction of being enabled to acquaint your excellency, that in conformity with the noble example of the august sovereign, a subscription has been opened, and goes on increasing; the sum already in the chest, under the charge of Messrs. Fries and Co., and which will be distributed under the inspection of the ministers plenipotentiary of the sovereigns at war with the Barbaric States, being already sufficiently considerable to defray the disbursements that

have been made, and to afford *instant* relief to the wretched sufferers, awaiting an ulterior measure for their deliverance—for
putting an end for ever to the depredations whereby their number is daily augmented. In order to strike at the root of the evil,
possessing some influence among the counsellors of the divan at
Constantinople, I conceive that I *have the power*, and consequently *ought to have the inclination,* to employ it to induce the
Ottoman Sultan to contribute his assistance for the repression of
atrocities which commit him in the face of all Europe, and disgrace him in the eyes of his own subjects, rebellious and disobe-
dient under the *fermans* inculcating *peace* with the European
powers in amity with him. Being well acquainted with the tone
and temper of the Sublime Porte, I know what personages to apply to, and the language to put into the mouths of my correspondents, without offending the self-love of the haughty; on the contrary, I have been anxious to dispose them to save appearances,
by anticipating the wishes of the Powers, before they should be
urged by remonstrances, threats, or reprisals. I have now the
gratification to announce to your excellency a preliminary success, which will be complete, if it be followed up and supported
in the manner which I have intimated to Prince Talleyrand, who
evinced his approbation of my suggestions, by transmitting them
to the Marquis de Riviére, ambassador of his most Christian
Majesty at the Ottoman Porte. I am ignorant of the relations subsisting between the Crown of Sardinia and the Sublime Porte;
but if they be not direct, they may be carried on through the medium of an ambassador from a friendly power, preparatory to a
formal embassy, which the annexation of Genoa, and the change
in the flag of the King, render indispensably necessary. The combination of the maritime forces of the two countries against the
enemies that act hostilely against the subjects of the two, might
result from it, and I offer myself to facilitate that object, as well
as to arrange the application in a proper manner to bring the
barbarians in Africa to reason, and deprive them for ever of the
means of annoyance; provided it be desired and demanded by
my government in an official and formal manner; without which
I must confine myself to friendly invitations addressed to my fellow *knights*, who have taken the same oath with myself, and have
it likewise in their memory and in conscience; and to the pointing out the mode of administering the charitable contributions
for supporting the existence of the miserable slaves in Africa, for
procuring their liberation, and for preventing an increase of their
number. It is only under this relationship that I can request your
excellency to have the kindness to lay this exposition under the
eyes of the King, as a *good knight*, as also the contents of the extract from the subjoined communication of one of my correspondents at Constantinople, and of the comments which I felt it my

duty to address to Prince Talleyrand, on forwarding it to that minister.

I have the honour to be, with perfect consideration, your excellency's faithful and devoted servant,

W. SIDNEY SMITH

Knight of the Military Order of the Bath,
and Grand Cross of other Orders,
President of the Philanthropic Association
of Knights at Vienna.

Afterwards Sir Sidney addressed the following circular to the:

*Consuls of the Nations at peace with the Barbaric
Regencies, resident at those Regencies respectively*

Vienna, January 20, 1815

Gentlemen, In order to give full and entire effect unto the benevolent intentions of the imperial, royal, noble, and illustrious knights of all the nations and orders assembled in this capital, and who have, at my suggestion, in compliance with the earnest request of the brethren of the religious orders in the Holy Land, formed the basis of a charitable fund, the immediate object of which is to comfort, relieve, and emancipate the unfortunate slaves in Barbary, I have to request and enjoin you, in my quality of president of the charitable society, to take the trouble of administering and applying that part of the sum subscribed which shall be destined and granted, in the proportion which the Christian slaves in the state where you reside, bears to the aggregate number in Barbary, according to your knowledge of their necessities, and at your own discretion—begging of you to inform me of the exact amount of the said proportional number, and to render me an account of the application of this sum for the satisfaction of the charitable contributors—informing me likewise of the sum which will be requisite to establish an hospital upon a suitable footing for the sick, and to provide them with subsistence on the sabbath-days, days on which I understand the government withholds their ordinary rations, not requiring their labour upon public works, but on those days they are, in order to live, reduced to the necessity of working for private persons, contrary to the precepts of their religion contained in the decalogue.

I also entreat you, gentlemen, to apprise me of every thing that can be useful for me to know, in order that I may be enabled to point out the application of the sum which shall be remitted for effecting the deliverance of those unhappy sufferers, and to prevent the increase of their number by a general measure, which all Europe is inclined to adopt, in order to abolish for ever that shameful traffic in slaves, both *white* and *black*, carried on in the *north* of Africa as well as in the *west*, to the prejudice of the productive industry of the natives of the respective countries; internal and external tranquillity, and legitimate trade, being the probable effects of a better order of things.

Your enlightened experience will doubtless suggest the necessity of avoiding the slightest intimation of an intention to ransom those hapless and innocent victims; an intimation which could not fail to excite the cupidity of their owners, or to stimulate the avidity of the corsairs in pursuit of their prey, with a view of making their captives an object of traffic, without, however, your discouraging the hope of reward for the preservation of the life, the health, and the property of the Europeans who may fall into their hands; exciting also in the minds of the rulers, without irritating them by menaces, the idea that the powers will no longer be tributary, as may be said, to governments which are not powers having a right to declare war against nations in amity with the Sublime Ottoman Porte, and with the Sultan, their lawful sovereign, who, being himself at peace with all Europe, will no longer tolerate acts of violence which might commit him, and destroy the harmony so happily existing between the Sultan and his neighbours.

I leave it to your wisdom to weigh these matters, and to use arguments calculated to make them be duly appreciated by the enlightened and just Mussulmans, avoiding every expression or act that can have a tendency to aggravate an evil which it so highly imports religion, humanity, and the honour of Christendom, rather to see diminished, and ultimately extinguished.

The state of the charitable fund, and the confidence which the subscribers repose in me, put me in a situation and empower me to refer you to the foregoing exposition, and to empower you to draw, to that effect, bills of exchange signed by three of you gentlemen consuls, on Messrs. Gaulis, brothers, at Genoa, by the earliest opportunity, for the sum of two thousand ducats, that shall be remitted to them by Messrs. Fries and Co.; which sum you will be pleased to employ agreeably to the charitable and beneficent intentions of the contributors, rendering to me an account of the application of the sum, and of your further wants, for their information and satisfaction; addressing your letters for me at this house in Vienna, by the way of Sicily, and per duplicate through the medium of Messrs. Gaulis, Genoa.

I have the honour to be, gentlemen consuls, your faithful and devoted servant,

W. SIDNEY SMITH,
President of the Society of Knights
Liberators of the White Slaves

in Africa.

This produced the following answer from the:

Consuls resident with the Basha and Regency of Tripoli,
in the West, to the above Circular Letter.

Tripoli, July 24, 1815

Sir, We have received the letter which you did us the honour to write to us on the 20th of January, and we hasten to present to you the most sincere assurance of the enthusiasm with which we unite our sentiments to all those which have given birth to the beautiful institution with which you have made us acquainted. Humanity is its basis, and posterity will preserve the remembrance of it, as a monument of grandeur and beneficence.

It is not only the glory of this sublunary world; it is the imperishable glory of the elect which awaits those nations and the individuals who shall have the honour in concurring towards the success of this noble enterprise.

To you, sir, it is, that the unalterable homage of our gratitude ought to be addressed. When the interests of humanity occupy so large a place in the soul of a hero, 'tis then the heroic character becomes complete, and that the whole world offers to him its unreserved admiration.

We have acted with prudence and circumspection in the communication which we have made to his highness the Basha, and it is with heartfelt satisfaction that we have the pleasure of informing you, that it was received by him in the most favourable manner; that the Basha, of his own motion, participates in almost all your wishes, and enters in all respects into the views of the institution; and, finally, to give a proof of his friendly disposition towards the Christian world, he will diminish the price for the ransom of the slaves, whose redemption shall be consequent upon this institution.

We have the honour of proposing to you a code of laws and regulations, to which we annex an estimate of the expenses, which we think worthy of your approbation.

In our function of agents for such an institution, we shall consider as a sacred duty the rendering ourselves worthy of the confidence with which we are honoured, and to merit in every respect the founder's approbation.

We have the honour to be, with the best consideration, your excellency's most obedient and faithful servants,

H. WARRINGTON,
British Consul-General.

P. N. BURSTROM,

Swedish Consul.

R. B. JONES,
Consul-Gen, for the U. S.

Deliberations of the Consuls residentiary at Tripoli

At a meeting of the consuls at Tripoli, having for its object to take into consideration the contents of a letter addressed by Sir W. Sidney Smith, president of a noble and benevolent institution, consecrated to the relief of all the Christian slaves who are, in the territory of the regency of Tripoli, and to the amelioration of their condition.

After having minutely considered the details, the motives, and objects of this institution, as they are severally set forth in the above-mentioned letter, we, (the undersigned,) wishing to draw up, with the greatest care, a code of laws and regulations which may fulfil in every particular the permanent intentions of that society, and to prevent, by all the means in our power, even the possibility of abuse in the application of the funds which shall be destined for the relief of humanity the most noble attribute of Christianity have unanimously adopted the following regulations, which we submit, with deference and respect, to Sir W. Sidney Smith:

Art. 1 . It is absolutely necessary to establish an hospital, the first expense of which will be, in Spanish dollars ... 1,500

2. The number of sick slaves may be estimated at an average of fifty per day, throughout the year, which, at the rate of eighteen buchamsiers each, will amount to ... 4,160

3. Fifty beds, with the furniture, would cost ... 500

4. The attendance of an expert surgeon ... 600

5. A comptroller of expenses ... 200

6. Two infirmary nurses ... 100

7. The society taking upon itself the purchase of medicines, and sending them to Tripoli, they would cost ... 1,000

8. The mean number of Christian slaves at Tripoli is about four hundred, for the clothing of each, viz. cap, jacket, pantaloons, shirt, handkerchief, and shoes, at the rate of six dollars each ... 2,400

9. To provide each of these four hundred slaves with a good dinner every Sunday, at twelve buchamsiers a head, would come to ... 3,122

10. Supposing this regency to make one hundred and fifty slaves a year, we propose to redeem fifty annually; this benefit is not confined solely in restoring those captives to their country and their families, but the prospect of a period that would not exceed three years, would likewise mitigate the sufferings and horrors of bondage. The Basha would grant, gratuitously, every slave a guarantee against any future captivity fifty ransoms, at three hundred dollars   15,000

11. Necessary charges for the keeping of the registers, and making out the accounts for the examination of the committee   300

Dollars   28,824

12. A committee composed of three consuls shall be formed for carrying this plan into effect; they shall have the direction, and even make themselves responsible for the same.

13. Their powers shall continue for two years, at the expiration of which, or in case of a vacancy, the consuls and agents of other nations shall cause them to be succeeded by competent persons, (the same being eligible,) in such a manner that the committee shall always consist, at least, of two.

14. Monthly statements of the situation of every part of this administration shall be transmitted to the president, Sir W. Sidney Smith.

15. The majority of the committee (two) shall be decisive and obligatory on the third member, upon every matter under deliberation.

(L. S,) H. WARRINGTON,
British Consul-General.

(L. S.) P. N. BURSTROM,
Swedish Consul.

(L. S.) R. B. JONES,
Consul-General U. S.

These views of the consuls seem just, moderate, and practicable. However, a separate treaty of peace, signed in December, 1815, between the United States and the Dey of Algiers, gave a severe blow to Sir Sidney Smith's organisation, as it, though humbling the power of the Dey, taught him to look forwards for compensation from more piracies, and other powers, each to take care of themselves, separately.

Notwithstanding all Sir Sidney's well-planned schemes, and his indefatigable exertions, the operations of this society of philanthropic knights never obtained any great weight, or produced any very remarkable results; and Lord Exmouth's chastisement of the Dey of Algiers seemed to have paralysed their energies to a state that bordered upon inanition. Thus things remained until the plan gradually faded away from the public attention.

We shall not, therefore, follow Sir Sidney Smith farther through all his miscellaneous labours on this subject. Sufficient has been adduced to show his manner of operations, and the diplomatic and skilful mode in which he managed his correspondence.

We have now but little more to record. The years of his life that he passed, cherished and honoured in the bosom of his family, will afford ample materials to his private biographer, with which to erect an enduring monument to his household virtues.

On the 19th of July, 1821, he obtained the rank of full admiral, and very long may he live in health, and surrounded by what makes man most happy, to enjoy his well-earned honours.

We saw the veteran hero on the day of the coronation of our present most gracious sovereign, and though he walked a little lamely from the effects of his former wounds, he appeared otherwise in excellent health, and still to possess the stamina of a dozen more naval victories.

It is a most delicate and a very embarrassing office to make personal comments upon characters still in existence. Whatever may be a man's avowed contempt for commendation, however refined may be the quality, and however vast the quantity tendered to him, the chances are many that something in the panegyric will displease, that some much-cherished trait will be omitted, and some quality, of which the possessor is secretly proud, will not be sufficiently dwelt upon. When a person, or, at least, an ordinary one, forms an estimate of his own merits, (and who is there that does not?) he will find praise too often take a wrong direction, and, in whatever direction it may take, he will deem it fall short of the mark.

But when duty demands the language of censure to be used, how shall the writer escape the reprehension of the living subject of his remarks? Truly, it is much more pleasant to write characters of the dead; but, as we fervently hope that these means of lightening a biographer's task may be long before they exist in respect to Sir Sidney Smith, we must perform our invidious duty in the best manner that we are able, and in no invidious spirit.

Man, either in private or public life, lives not for himself only In the social circle of his acquaintance, his acts will be commented upon, his manners criticised, and his motives arraigned. And this is right. It is a healthful check upon his own character. In whatever circle, whether great or small, in which influence is exerted, that influence should never be permitted to travel beyond the control of opinion. It is the only power that society possesses for the preservation of all the nicer and more refined moralities, for the sustaining of honourable feelings, and the expanding the graces and elegancies of life. Since people will talk of us, a plain obligation lies before us to give them the opportunity of only talking well.

If these observations have force on private individuals, how much more applicable are they to one who challenges the observations of his fellow men, by acting before them great and conspicuous parts. If any actor comes forward to play an important *rôle*, and he shrinks from or rebels against criticism, it is morally certain that he has undertaken that which he cannot worthily perform, and that he should give place to better men.

Of Sir Sidney Smith's private life, let those, and they are many, who have been made happy with his social virtues, and have rejoiced in his household amiabilities, speak. The voice of the friend, the relation, and the guest, will not be silent. It is our province to judge of his public conduct by his public acts.

Of his personal appearance we have thrice spoken, as it manifested itself at three different epochs of his life. It will be sufficient here to repeat, that he has been very happy in this respect.

He possesses a mind fertile in resources, and an intuitive power to meet contingencies, however sudden and appalling, with the rapidity of lightning, and the certainty of mathematical calculation. This is an invaluable faculty in a commander, and no commander possesses it in a more eminent degree than Sir Sidney. He is not only constitutionally active, but restless, though sufficiently cautious and deliberate in working out the promptings of his enterprising nature. Eager for the excitement of action, whenever the danger of battle has commenced, and the roar of war is up, he evinces a presence of mind and a coolness that look very like enjoyment, and if it be so, may God forgive him for it. He is the very chief under whom men wish to fight; for they feel assured that they are fighting to good purpose, and that, whatever may be their individual fate, the general success is certain. It is a sustaining thought, in the hurry and tumult of mortal strife, to know that you have only to do bravely, for there is one directing your energies who is thinking coolly.

The powers of Sir Sidney's mind have been advantaged only by the desultory sort of discipline incidental to a stirring life. Men have educated him more than books, action more than study. Yet books have not been disregarded, nor study neglected. Consequently, he is more useful than profound, his views more clear than far-sighted, his understanding more expansive than deep. He is not free from bigotry, but it is the high-toned bigotry of lofty and elevating prejudices, the pride which belongs to a refined state of feudalism, that manifests itself in the grand exaggerations of chivalry. We believe, in our hearts, that he loves the masses of mankind, but we think that he is too anxious for the privileges of the classes, and would not be over much rejoiced to see so much good and happiness be the lot for the undistinguished whole, that it would leave no room for distinction to the glorious few. Perhaps, with all his philanthropy, he would not welcome the time when there would be no further need of great generals and ducal Wellingtons r of conquering admirals arid star-decorated Sir Sidney Smiths. In a man trained to animating danger and victorious strife, this can neither be imputed to him as a fault, nor even a failing. Such self-abnegation belongs only to perfection higher yet than any admiral or general attained—that of the humble Christian philosopher. It is only he who feels how sinful is the price of glory, when it is paid for in blood—blood in quantities so greatly horrible!

It is impossible to compare Sir Sidney Smith's professional abilities with those of any other naval commander. He was, in many essentials, utterly unlike those who achieved for England her proudest naval victories. He would have dared more, and probably have done more—yet, we think, have risked too much. After all, so much, in a naval combat, depends upon accident, that success more often attends upon too much than upon too little risk. Still, had Sir Sidney attained any great naval command, there was danger of his not being able to resist the fascinations of the splendid, the magnificent, and the chivalrous, both in treaty and in fight, to the neglect of the stern, the hard, and the usefully successful. Even in his limited commands, refined notions of honour have saved the enemy from destructive broadsides that could have been poured in at an advantage, and which few, besides himself, would have deemed unfair.

In all relations of life, he was always esteemed just, charitable, and more than safely generous. He is not deficient in a certain conversational species of eloquence, and displays much facility in composition. As a friend, or as an enemy, there are but few living who could excel him—for if a man must have an enemy, a more candid or a more generous one never existed.

Now to the graver consideration of his faults—they are mostly those of the sanguine temperament, and are but a little worse than virtues exaggerated into failings. Shall we be thought severe when we say that a pride to which he is justly entitled was sometimes sublimated into vanity—that his greediness for glory compelled him to attempt to gather it in fields where he ought not to have been found? This zeal led him into interferences that were inimical to his own interests, and thus, through his eagerness to do too much, his country suffered from his being permitted to do nothing.

This desire of being continually seen under a triumphal arch induced him, at one time, to affect a little singularity of dress, and has, at all times, attracted about him a crowd of flatterers, a train that is always attendant upon the eminent. After all, they are but the gilded settings of a glorious portrait.

Than Sir Sidney Smith, no one ever inscribed on the pages of history, and even of romance, more emphatically deserved the title of hero. That he had not the requisites to become a truly "great man," we will not say, for he was denied the opportunity.

APPENDIX CONTAINING
ANECDOTES AND OFFICIAL DOCUMENTS

IN the pages that the reader has hitherto perused, we have given a continuous narrative of the public life of Sir William Sidney Smith; but, in the occurrences of a career so extremely active, a career in which almost every day had its exciting adventure, much that was not essential to the totality of these memoirs was necessarily omitted. But, as there were very many facts collateral to the main action of the biography, and several circumstances explanatory of our hero's character, as bearing with strength upon many of his adventures, we have thrown these together in the form of an appendix, which appendix we have also made the vehicle of laying before the public a few of the anecdotes that have been assigned to one of the most anecdotal characters that ever existed. Some of these *histori- ettes* we ourselves hold to be apocryphal, but a man's bias and the calibre of his mind may be as well, and, in some cases, better estimated by the stories that the world fastens upon him, than by the relation of isolated facts in which he was actually concerned, or by deeds that he really performed.

This appendix will also give us the opportunity of explaining ourselves on a few subjects, on which, in our previous text, we may have been misunderstood, and also of correcting one or two errors into which we have been inadvertently led, by incorrect information, in the early pages of the work, and which pages were unfortunately printed off before the inaccuracies were discovered.

PUBLIC TRIBUTES TO SIR SIDNEY SMITH

These we have, generally speaking, noticed as they occurred in the order of time of these memoirs. They are numerous, and we know that those who have perused this work will acknowledge that they are no more than just.

For our own part, we do not think that they have been adequate either to his acknowledged services, or to his great merits, for, had they been anything like an equivalent to his capacity and talent, he would have been the most panegyrised person, with but few exceptions, of the times in which he acted.

With the exception of the period of his early career, he has always had to struggle against some sinister, secret, and powerful interest. He was not strong enough to overawe opposition, though his strength was sufficient to make that opposition a concealed, therefore, too often, a more prejudicial one. He was more solicitous to conquer admiration than to disarm enemies. From the object in view—and that object was always a worthy, and sometimes a vast one—he was seldom or never deterred by considerations of worldly, much less of self-interested prospects. He was just the man to subdue the enemies of his country, and by his uncompromising character to increase his own. Thus, so few friends had he in the House of Lords, that when the thanks of that assembly were voted to General Hutchinson, Lord Keith, and others, and William the Fourth, then Duke of Clarence, wished to particularise Sir Sidney Smith for his various and eminent services on that occasion, it was opposed by the ministers and others on several frivolous grounds, and thus his royal highness was induced to consent to withdraw his motion. This occurred on the 21st of March, 1801.

But there were other and more generous feelings entertained and cherished in those quarters where political intrigue was, as yet, unknown, and where merit still kindled the enthusiasm of sympathy in minds that, possessing high qualities, knew the value of, and venerated those that possessed them. At the early age of nineteen, Reginald Heber, the future Bishop of Calcutta, the admired author, and the all but idolised spiritual pastor, thus expresses himself on the occasion of Sir Sidney Smith's victory at Acre, in the poem that obtained the prize at Oxford.

> Ye sainted spirits of the warrior dead,
> Whose giant force Britannia's armies led!
> Whose bickering falchions, foremost in the fight,
> Still pour'd confusion on the Soldan's might;
> Lords of the biting axe and beamy spear,
> Wide conquering Edward, lion Richard, hear!
> At Albion's call your crested pride resume,
> And burst the marble slumbers of the tomb.
> Your sons behold! in arms, in heart the same,
> Still press the footsteps of parental fame,
> To Salem still their generous aid supply,
> And pluck the palm of Syrian chivalry.
> When he, from towery Malta's yielding isle,
> And the green waters of reluctant Nile,
> Th' apostate chief, from Misraim's subject shore,

To Acre's walls his trophied banners bore;
Where the pale desert mark'd his proud array,
And Desolation hoped an ampler sway;
What hero, then, triumphant Gaul dismay'd?
What arm repell'd the victor renegade?
Britannia's champion! bath'd in hostile blood,
High on the breach the dauntless SEAMAN stood.
Admiring Asia saw the unequal fight,
E'en the pale crescent bless'd the Christian's might.
O day of death! O thirst beyond control,
Of crimes and conquest in th' invader's soul!
The slain, yet warm, by social footsteps trod,
O'er the red moat supplied a ghastly road;
O'er the red moat our conquering thunders flew,
And loftier still the grisly rampier grew,
While proudly gleam'd above the rescued tower
The wavy cross that mark'd Britannia's power.

This is an extract from a very beautiful and well sustained poem, elaborately finished, and almost first-rate. The poem itself does not certainly evince any very lofty or very romantic flight, but it is eloquent, solemn, and holy; and will well repay any one, who, not yet having perused it, may attentively read the whole. We have no hesitation in saying, that had the bishop, who died so unfortunately and prematurely in the East, staid quietly in the

West, and cultivated the Epic muse, there are no degrees of excellence to which he might not reasonably have aspired.

We now proceed to give another poem in honour of Sir Sidney Smith, of a much less ambitious character, and, truly, of much inferior merit. It is from the pen of Dr. Houlston.

1.
Says Fame, t'other day, to the Genius of Song,
A favourite of mine you've neglected too long;
He's a sound bit of oak, a son of the wave,
The scourge of proud France, Sir Sidney the brave.
    Whose wreath from his country, the hero's
        bright crown,
    The grand Sultan decks with the gem
        of renown.
2.
"Madame Fame,"cries the Genius, "no bard in my train
Of Sir Sidney's desert can equal the strain;
Buonaparte alone can but sing his merit,
His laurels and glory, his valour and spirit.
    Whose wreath," &c.
3.
Neptune swore it was true, for so active was he,

That he never can rest with Sir Sidney at sea;
As some feat or other he's always performing,
Either burning or sinking, capt'ring or storming.
Whose wreath, &c.

4.

"Master Neptune," said Mars, "I claim, as my son,
A share of the glory Sir Sidney has won;
Though a brave British tar, as a soldier he'll fight,
All Egypt resounds from morning till night.
Whose wreath," &c.

5.

Since Fame and their godships thus jointly agree
Sir Sidney's a hero on land or at sea,
With justice, brave Turks, from so bright an example,
Proclaim him "The wonderful Knight of the Temple."
Whose wreath, &c.

6.

While George of Old England, and Selim the Great,
Hold firm the alliance 'gainst Gaul's hydra state,
The Lion and Crescent triumphant shall reign,
And Sir Sidney do honour to both o'er the main.
Whose wreath, &c.

And now we proceed to give the best genealogical account of Sir Sidney's family with which we have met. It is an extract from the "Gentleman's Magazine." In a former part of the work we stated a report, upon what we held to be the best authority, that John Spencer Smith, Esq., our plenipotentiary at Constantinople, had intermarried with a Turkish lady of high rank. That error is here corrected.

PEDIGREE OF ADMIRAL SIR SIDNEY SMITH, K.C.B.

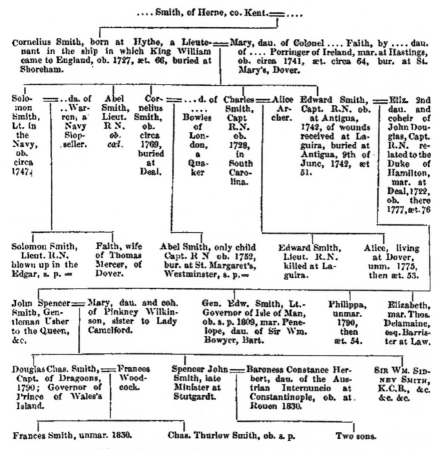

.... Smith, of Herne, co. Kent.══ ....

Cornelius Smith, born at Hythe, a Lieutenant in the ship in which King William came to England, ob. 1727, æt. 66, buried at Shoreham. ══ Mary, dau. of Colonel .... Faith, by .... dau. of .... Porringer of Ireland, mar. at Hastings, ob. circa 1741, æt. circa 64, bur. at St. Mary's, Dover.

| Solomon Smith, Lt. in the Navy, ob. circa 1747. ══ ..da. of ..Warren; a Navy Slop-seller. | Abel Smith, Lieut. R N. ob. cœl. | Cornelius Smith, ob. circa 1769, buried at Deal. ══ ... d. of .... Bowles of London, a Quaker | Charles Smith, Capt R.N. ob. 1728, in South Carolina. ══ Alice Archer. | Edward Smith, Capt. R.N. ob. at Antigua, 1742, of wounds received at Laguira, buried at Antigua, 9th of June, 1742, æt 51. | ══ Eliz. 2nd dau. and coheir of John Douglas, Capt. R.N. related to the Duke of Hamilton, mar. at Deal, 1722, ob. there 1777, æt. 76 |

Solomon Smith, Lieut. R.N. blown up in the Edgar, s. p. ══

Faith, wife of Thomas Mercer, of Dover.

Abel Smith, only child Capt. R N ob. 1752, bur. at St. Margaret's, Westminster, s. p. ══

Edward Smith, Lieut. R.N. killed at Laguira.

Alice, living at Dover, unm. 1775, then æt. 53.

John Spencer Smith, Gentleman Usher to the Queen, &c. ══ Mary, dau. and coh. of Pinkney Wilkinson, sister to Lady Camelford.

Gen. Edw. Smith, Lt.-Governor of Isle of Man, ob. s. p. 1809, mar. Penelope, dau. of Sir Wm. Bowyer, Bart.

Philippa, unmar. 1790, then æt. 54.

Elizabeth, mar. Thos. Delamaine, esq. Barrister at Law.

Douglas Chas. Smith, Capt. of Dragoons, 1790; Governor of Prince of Wales's Island. ══ Frances Woodcock.

Spencer John Smith, late Minister at Stutgardt. ══ Baroness Constance Herbert, dau. of the Austrian Internuncio at Constantinople, ob. at Rouen 1830.

SIR WM. SIDNEY SMITH, K.C.B., &c. &c. &c.

Frances Smith, unmar. 1830.

Chas. Thurlow Smith, ob. s. p.

Two sons.

Arms granted to Sir Sidney Smith in 1803.—Azure, on a chevron engrailed between three lions passant guardant Or, a wreath of laurel Proper, between two crosses Calvary Sable, with a Chief of Augmentation.—Crest, a leopard's head Proper, gorged with a plain collar, therefrom a line reflected, issuant out of an eastern Crown Or; with a Crest of Augmentation.

SIR SIDNEY SMITH'S COAT OF ARMS AND CREST

Arms granted to Sir Sidney Smith in 1803 Azure, on a chevron engrailed between three lions passant guardant Or, a wreath of laurel Proper, between two crosses Calvary Sable, with a Chief of Augmentation. Crest, a leopard's head Proper, gorged with a plain collar, therefrom a line reflected, issuant out of an eastern Crown Or; with a Crest of Augmentation.

The Arms of the Smythes of Corsham were, Azure, an escutcheon Argent, within, six lions rampant, Or; and were allowed to the younger branches at the Herald's Visitation of Wiltshire in 1623, upon the production of an ancient seal, then, it is said in the Visitation, two hundred years old.* Customer Smythe, however, obtained two grants of arms to himself and his descendants, differenced from the old coat; the first grant being per pale Or and Azure, a chevron between three lions passant guardant counterchanged: and the second grant, from Clarencieux Cooke, in 1588, was the coat and crest now used by his noble descendants; namely, Azure, a chevron engrailed between three lions passant guardant Or. Crest— An Ounce's head erased Argent, Pelletee, and gorged with a collar Sable, edged Or, charged with three Pallets, and chained Or— The arms and crest of Sir Sidney Smith, however they may be described in the instrument, are in fact a new grant, and were founded upon the coat allowed to Customer Smythe in 1588, from the idea that he was descended from that person, though the pedigree could not be deduced; a common practice where a connexion between a grantee arid a family entitled to Arms is presumed to exist. But an heraldic eye will at once discover, by the chevron being charged with 'a wreath of laurel Proper, between two crosses Calvary Sable,' and by the crest being 'a leopard's head Proper, gorged with a plain collar, therefrom a line reflexed' that the Arms and Crest of Sir Sidney Smith are totally distinct from those of the Viscounts Strangford.

SIR SIDNEY SMITH'S CAPTURE AT HAVRE

We now present to our readers the detailed account of the capture of Sir Sidney Smith, at Havre, by his secretary, friend, and fellow prisoner, the unfortunate Captain Wright. We have before stated, that many were the absurd rumours respecting the apparently rash act that led to this celebrated captivity. At this time, Captain Wright was only a midshipman, but a very matured one.

"Having anchored, on the morning of the 17th of April, in the outer road of Havre de Grace, with the Diamond alone, we discovered at anchor, in the inner road, an armed lugger. A project was immediately conceived of boarding her in the night by means of our boats. In justice to the merit, and indeed necessity of this project, in a national point of view, it is necessary to inform you, that this was the only remaining vessel which continued to annoy the English trade within the limits of our squadron. She had been recently equipped at Havre; carried ten three pounders and forty-five men; was commanded by a bold, enterprising man, with a private commission, and sailed so well in light winds, as to have more than once eluded the pursuit of our frigate, when returning from the English coast. Her first depredations on our trade were of a magnitude to warrant the risk of a small sacrifice in her capture; and Sir Sidney had established it as a point of honour in his squadron, that an enemy's vessel within the limits of his command should not even pass from port to port.

---

* This coat produced in an old seal, to be the right coat of this family, and is said to be two hundred years old.

"The force employed in our enterprise consisted of the launch, armed with an eighteen-pounder carronade and muskets, four other boats with muskets, including an armed wherry, in which Sir Sidney commanded in person, and carrying in all fifty-two persons; viz. nine officers, six of whom were from twelve to sixteen years of age, three servants, and forty seamen. We were all volunteers; were disposed to surmount all obstacles that should oppose our purpose; not a breath of air not a ripple on the water: the oars were muffled, and everything promised the happiest success. We quitted the ship about ten o'clock, preceded by Sir Sidney Smith in his wherry. Arrived within sight of the Vengeur, we lay upon oars to reconnoitre her position, and to receive definite orders. This done, we took a broad sheer between her and the shore, in order to assume the appearance of fishing-boats coming out of harbour, and thereby protract the moment of alarm: in this we succeeded beyond expectation, and afterwards rowed directly towards her, reserving our fire till she should commence the action. This happened after hailing us within about half-pistol shot; the boats returned it in an instant, and within less than ten minutes we had got possession of the vessel.

"It was now that we first discovered our difficulties. The enemy had very wisely cut their cable during the action; the vessel had therefore been drifting towards the shore all this time. On perceiving it, we sought in vain for a second anchor heavy enough to hold her against the strength of a very rapid tide that rushed into the Seine. All the boats were sent ahead to tow, and every sail was set; but it was all in vain. After all these fruitless efforts, we tried the effect of a small sledge, without hope of its holding. The vessel dragged it a long way, and at length brought up.

"Here, therefore, we lay, anxiously expecting daylight, to discover the extent of the evil we had to encounter, or for a propitious breeze to assist our escape. Daylight at length appeared, and terminated our suspense. Our position was in the last degree critical: we were half a league higher up the river than Havre, the town and harbour of which was now in motion, in hostile preparation. Nothing remained for us but to make every possible preparation on our parts for a desperate and unequal conflict. The vessel, however, was destitute of every material article of defence, such as grapeshot and match. There was not a single round of the former, and the latter was so bad that it would never fire upon the first application. It was resolved, however, to fight as long as the lugger could swim, in the expectation that, by protracting our surrender, a prosperous wind might deliver us, even in the last extremity.

"All Havre was now in motion to attack us—some shot had reached us whilst we were in the act of discharging our prisoners, and sending them on their parole to Honfleur; for, with his usual humanity, Sir Sidney Smith proposed to send them away, clear from the dangers of a battle in which they could not co-operate. They received his kindness with gratitude.

"The attack now commenced. We got under weigh to attack a large lugger which was advancing, whilst the boats were detached to rake her with grapeshot and musketry. The result was that she sheered off. We had not, however, escaped clear; her grape and musketry had considerably disabled our rigging, and wounded some of our best men: your young friend Charles B. was among the number. This action was scarcely over, when we were surrounded on all sides by a variety of small craft, crowded with troops; and another action immediately commenced, more desperate and more unequal than the former. Sir Sidney ordered all the muskets to be collected and loaded, and made such a distribution of them, that each man was enabled to fire several rounds without the necessity of reloading; the midshipmen reloaded them as fast as they were discharged. In this manner, an incessant fire was kept up for some time. No breeze, however, appeared, and resistance was evidently in vain, as the country was assembling. In a word, we were compelled to surrender."

THE BURNING OF THE FLOTILLA OFF BOULOGNE

We omitted to state, that whilst Sir Sidney had the command of the Antelope off Boulogne, he made an attempt to burn the flotilla in that harbour.

One very dark night, two long galleys, with some other boats, stoutly manned by a number of volunteers from the squadron, entered the harbour unperceived, and had set two of those fire machines, called carcases, adrift, which floated in with the tide, among the shipping. These were filled with large quantities of combustible matters, and were to explode at a given time, (fifteen minutes.) In this they succeeded, but, from the powder being too weak, or from some other unknown cause, they had not the desired effect, although a very considerable conflagration ensued.

The men in the boats were unfortunately discovered, at the same moment, by the soldiers at the batteries, who immediately commenced a heavy fire of musketry upon them. The shot flew about like hail, and a great quantity went through the boats, and one or two men were killed, and a few wounded, whilst the rest escaped unhurt. This attempt was looked upon merely as an experiment, and we are unpatriotic enough to express our pleasure that it did not succeed.

Every friend to humanity should rejoice in failures of this description of warfare. It is riot conducted upon just principles. When a town is besieged, there must always be some previous notice given from the very nature of the warfare, so that non-belligerents of all sorts have time to provide for their safety; at all events, they are not taken by surprise, and can always expostulate with the military defenders of the place, as to the policy of jeopardising their lives by a resistance. But when a fireship is sent into a harbour at the dead of night, women, children, and non-combatants of all descriptions are ruthlessly exposed to lacerating and dreadful deaths, without their having any opportunity or option given either of retreat or surrender; it is, therefore, an assassination. Should these wholesale private murders succeed, retaliation always follows, and each retaliation is more dreadful than the one to which it gave rise; thus generous courage becomes barbarised, and seamen and soldiers are made so many midnight and plotting fiends, rather than brave and avowed assailants.

ANNECDOTE: SMITH AND THE PROPHECY

We shall begin our division of anecdotes by one confessedly spurious. Though a lie, from beginning to end, it is yet the father of a son, not only true, but true by Sir Sidney Smith's own attestation, and authenticated by his signature. Thus says the mendacious father of the veracious offspring.

In Cave's "Northern Summer." there are published, among the anecdotes of Captain Elphinstone, the following relating to Sir Sidney:

"Being sent, some years since, on shore on the Irish coast, with a brother officer, who is now holding a deservedly high situation in the naval service, to look for some deserters from their ship, after a long, fatiguing, and fruitless search, they halted at a little inn to refresh themselves. Having done so, Sir Sidney suddenly became silent, and seemed lost in meditation.

"'My dirk for your thoughts,' exclaimed his friend, gently tapping him on the shoulder. 'What project, Sidney, has got possession of you now?'

"'My good fellow' replied the young warrior, his expressive countenance brightening as he spoke, 'you will, no doubt, suppose me a little disordered in my mind; but I have been thinking that before twelve years shall have rolled over my head, I shall make the British arms triumphant in the Holy Land.'

"We need not knock at the cabinet-door of St. Cloud to know how splendidly this prediction was verified."

Thus far the anecdote-monger; now for Sidney himself. Upon being questioned as to the authenticity of this juvenile prophecy, so boldly attributed to him, with his usual promptitude, he answered by writing on the margin of the book:

"December 29th, 1805. S. S. was never in Ireland in his life. The author has recorded the waking-dream of some other person, not of

W. SIDNEY SMITH."

SIDNEY SMITH DESCRIPTIONS

There are no positions in which a man of honour may be seen in which Sir Sidney Smith does not excel. He is as amusing at the convivial board, as he is great in danger and heroic in battle. His social qualities are of the very highest order. Gentlemanly, yet frank; straightforward, yet urbane, blending in his diction and manner suavity with energy, his conversation is a mental treat of the most refined description. He speaks only to please. No man can better relate a story, and few have so many to relate. He is an inexhaustible mine of anecdote, a mine, in which all the ore is of the most intrinsic quality.

His ubiquitous travels, his many adventures by flood and field, and his strong discriminating mind, have supplied him with a fund of anecdote, that we fervently hope will not, for the want of a chronicler, be lost to posterity. We have endeavoured to collect a few of these from creditable oral testimony, and from those on record dispersed in several publications.

He is thus described by one, who is, at the time of publishing these memoirs, personally acquainted with him. The extract is from that valuable periodical, the "United Service Journal."

"He is a man remarkably polished and refined, but his politeness is more that of the heart than the studied air of the man of the world. He is generous to a fault, and one who practises that generosity with elegance and grace, considering, no doubt, the manner in which an obligation is conferred, as equally essential, in some instances, as the gift itself. His heart, indeed, is the source of all good and elevated actions, and his conduct, on many occasions, has reminded me of that beautiful saying of the moralist, ' I desire to be happy, but I live in society with other men who also desire to be happy; let us then endeavour to discover the means by which I can augment my own happiness, whilst I add to, or, at least, do not diminish, that of others.' He is, besides, one of those happy people on whom nature or philosophy, or rather both, have fixed their throne, and banished care and disappointment from their peaceful territory."

His friend proceeds to state, "His presence is esteemed an honour in every society; and his amiable and entertaining manners are a charm in every company. I need scarcely add, that his intellectual acquirements are of the highest order. The easy and scientific manner in which he discusses the most difficult and abstruse topics, at interviews with those to whom such subjects are interesting, stamps at once the man of genius, and adds additional lustre to the exalted character of the hero of Acre."

SIR SIDNEY SMITH AND SLAVERY

Sir Sidney Smith was ever actuated by the most liberal and far-seeing views. Where was the great accumulation of misery, there was his gallant and gentle heart. Slavery in all its forms was ever his detestation, and he devoted his time, his energies, and too much of his not over abundant, means, to alleviate, if he could not suppress it. The slavery of the white population by the Mahometans was always a source to him of great grief and anxiety, and his efforts were strenuous and unremitting in opposing it to the extent of his means. To abolish this terrible traffic in white and European slaves, as we have before stated, he endeavoured to form a society, and to further the object by subscription. Although large sums were collected, to which he added far more than could have been expected from the most profuse liberality, it was abandoned, as being wholly inadequate to work out the ends proposed. On this subject Sir Sidney received the following letter from the late Duke of Gloucester:

Dear Sir Sidney Smith, In looking over my papers this day, I was much shocked to find a letter of yours so long unanswered: having had the pleasure of receiving it at a moment when my time was entirely taken up, and when each day's post brought me a great number of letters, I mislaid it, and did not, till this morning, put my hand upon it. I now seize the earliest opportunity to return you my thanks for your obliging congratulation upon my marriage, in which the Duchess desires to unite with me; and I must request of you to express to Lady Sidney Smith, and all her fair daughters, my sense of the interest they are so good as to take in an event that has confirmed my happiness. I have now to congratulate you on the success of the attack upon Algiers. This brilliant event reflects great credit upon Lord Exmouth, who appears to have concluded the operation with much skill and decision, and adds fresh lustre to our tars, who have indeed acted upon this occasion like themselves. In my last letter I entered fully into the subject of that terrible system of white slavery, and stated to you my sentiments respecting the mode of putting an end to it. I will, therefore, now merely express my hope that your health is perfectly good, and renew to you the assurance of the great regard with which I am,

Dear Sir Sidney,

Very sincerely yours,

WILLIAM FREDERICK

These are the sentiments alluded to:

I most highly appreciate the noble motives that instigated you to the undertaking motives worthy of yourself and most anxiously wish to see this detestable traffic in white slaves put an end to, an object which every Briton cannot fail to have at heart. Yet I do not conceive that by private subscription it can ever be accomplished, and I am clearly of opinion that it can solely be done by the powers of Europe determining, by force of arms, to stop this disgraceful and abominable trade. In such a way this very desirable object may be attained, and I should be happy to see you in command of a squadron for that purpose.

SIR SIDNEY'S CONFINEMENT IN THE TEMPLE

We have before dwelt upon that paragon of gaolers, M. Lesne, who was, in his way, nearly, if not quite, as chivalrous as Sir Sidney himself. In those rambles together on the Boulevards, in which there was so much mutual confidence displayed, the captive and the keeper often changed offices, the noble prisoner taking under his charge the elevated gaoler. This latter excellent soul would often, in these amiable perambulations, indulge in so many *bons coups de vin*, that not only care, but even assistance, was necessary to convey him back to the Temple; and so strange did this travestie seem, that more than once he was actually refused re-admittance into his prison, with his drunken keeper, by the guard on duty.

The room allotted to Sir Sidney in the Temple was the same which the unfortunate King Louis XVI occupied in the interval between his removal from the palace of his ancestors to the scaffold. It was an apartment that could boast of but few of the comforts so much prized by an Englishman, and had that intolerable nuisance, a smoky chimney; and the gaoler would point out the very spot where the king would throw himself upon the floor on a mattress, in order to escape, in some degree, from the clouds of smoke that filled the room, and in this humiliating condition his Queen and the Princess Elizabeth would kneel by his side, and occupy themselves in repairing his clothes.

We give the following anecdote upon the faith of the gentleman who furnished it to the "United Service Journal." We do not much admire the spirit of irritation that it evinces against Buonaparte; and, as to its accuracy, the reader must pass his own judgment upon it.

"Sir Sidney, more happy than the monarch of whom we have been speaking, used to go and sit by the gaoler's fire whenever the wind was so high as to render it absolutely impossible to have one in his own room. One day, as he sat, as usual, with this prince of gaolers, of whose ready disposition to serve him to the utmost of his ability he was well assured, he abruptly asked him if he could get a letter, which he was about to write, forwarded to Napoleon?

"'What! seriously?'

"'Yes, seriously,' replied Sir Sidney.

"'But I must first know your designs. What are they?'

"Sir Sidney told him.

"'Well, then, rely on my zeal. Parbleu! I will deliver it myself. There, Sir Sidney—that's all that I have to say to you.'

"'It is really involving you in trouble" said Sir Sidney, fearing the good fellow might compromise himself, and, perhaps, lose his situation by doing so.

"'Not at all' said he. 'I have made up my mind. I will place it in his own hands. My life upon it!'

"Sir Sidney, therefore, wrote the letter, which contained a respectful, but spirited and energetic remonstrance against the arbitrary and severe measures that had been resorted to in his particular case, and requested, not as a favour, but as a matter of right, that he might thenceforth be treated in the same manner, and be allowed the same privileges, in every respect, as the other prisoners of war; and concluded by requesting of Napoleon the favour of an early, and, he trusted, a satisfactory answer.

"Furnished with his credentials, off trudged the old gaoler to the house of Napoleon, resolved, in his own mind, to add all the weight he could to the request that the letter contained, by speaking boldly in favour of his prisoner. But Buonaparte, who was vexed to the soul by the recent destruction of the fleet at Toulon, entertained a bitter animosity towards Sir Sidney; and the great man took no care to conceal it; but, on the contrary, availed himself of such an opportunity to show the spirit that actuated him, to offer insult when it could not be resented.

"When the gaoler returned from his embassy to the general, and entered the room where Sir Sidney sat, he threw himself moodily in the chair on the opposite side of the fireplace, and began poking the fire with a thoughtful and gloomy countenance, and seemed to be seriously engaged in a service which was not required of him, that of raking out the fire, which he would not have failed to have done, had not Sir Sidney put a stop to his ill-timed zeal, by asking him 'to report progress'

"At length, after sundry strange noises proceeding from his thorax, and a pish! and a bah! and a toss of his head, he thrust his hands into his pockets, and stretching out his legs at their full length, he looked Sir Sidney in the face for the first time, and said, 'Such language makes me mad!'

"'What reception did he give you? Have you seen Buonaparte?'

"'I have' replied the old fellow, ' and his discourse has made my head ache.'

"'Well, never mind; let us hear all about it.'

"'His language has irritated me—made me mad.'

"'Pshaw! don't repeat; you've said that before. What did he say about me?'

"'He said that you might stay here till you rotted;' passing his hand over his face to conceal his emotion.

"'And was he angry with you?'

"'Why, he told me not to shove in my nose where I had no business.'

"In short, the old gaoler met Buonaparte on the staircase, and delivered Sir Sidney's letter into his own hands, which Napoleon perused on the spot, and flew into a passion with the gaoler for bringing it.

"His insolent reply, which was not confined to the words used by the gaoler, had no other effect at the time than to cause him to be heartily censured for it by his personal friends and adherents; and Sir Sidney took no further notice of him and his message."

We have abridged this anecdote considerably; and here we would willingly pause, as we think what follows does not redound so much to the credit of our hero, as his enthusiastic admirer, the relater of this anecdote, appears to think. We will give it, however, and give it also all the benefit of our doubts.

"Until an opportunity afterwards presented itself, when no longer a prisoner, but a triumphant conqueror, face to face with his haughty foe at the siege of Acre, opposing his further advance into Egypt, mowing down his columns and battalions that mounted the breach in quick succession to seize upon the golden key (why golden?) to the treasures of the East, and completely *upsetting* all his plans and projects for the conquest of India, the hero of Acre, exulting with honest pride at the success of his arms, and at having shown Napoleon that he had found his match for once, was also resolved to *square yards* with him for his former behaviour; and after a most signal defeat, and when he must have seen that he would be compelled to raise the siege, and was deeply mortified, peevish, and out of temper with himself, and with every one else, a letter was conveyed to him by one of his own soldiers who had been taken prisoner, and who had been set at liberty for the purpose, from his old correspondent and victorious enemy, Sir Sidney Smith, written in a style of exquisite good-humoured irony, perfectly free from recrimination, but well calculated, as was the message which accompanied it, to humble him, and render him ridiculous to all around him. And he was heartily laughed at by his friends; some of whom Junot among the number, as I have said before were highly indignant at his conduct upon the occasion recorded above, and told him that Sir Sidney had taken an admirable occasion to be revenged, which they could not but foresee would be attended with fatal consequences to their expedition; and so it turned out, for his failure at Acre was followed by a train of disasters, the abandonment of his enterprise, and, finally, his expulsion from Egypt."

This last extract we have copied *verbatim*. As this anecdote purports to have been derived from Sir Sidney Smith personally, it acquires an importance not due to it intrinsically. Can this be another version of the story of the solicited duel with Buonaparte? Surely there must be some mistake, either with the author or the repeater of this ill-disguised gasconade.

BUONAPARTE ON SIR SIDNEY SMITH

Let us put in contrast some few words that Buonaparte used, speaking of Sir Sidney Smith's conduct in Egypt.

"Sir Sidney Smith is a brave officer. He displayed great ability in the treaty for the evacuation of Egypt by the French. He took advantage of the discontent which he found to prevail among the French troops at being so long away from France, and at other circumstances. He also showed great humanity and honour in all his proceedings towards the French who fell into his hands."

We fear that Sir Sidney Smith may have occasion fully to appreciate the Spanish proverb "God preserve me from my friends!"

OFFICIAL
AND
AUTHENTIC DOCUMENTS

SMITH'S RECONNAISSANCE OF BREST

IN the early part of the work we mentioned Sir Sidney's intrepidity and aptitude for a particular and delicate service, in his reconnaissance of Brest harbour. The following is his account of the matter.

Diamond, at Sea, Jan. 4, 1795

Sir, In pursuance of your orders, I this morning looked into the port of Brest, in this ship, in order to verify the intelligence of the enemy's fleet being at sea.,

I went round the west point of Ushant yesterday, and the wind being easterly, I was obliged to work to windward between the shoals off Point St. Matthew and the rocks to the southward, in order to come near enough to look into the road. We observed a large ship under French colours working in a-head. She took no notice of us, probably supposing that we were of her own nation, from our making so free with the coast. I hoisted French colours, having previously disguised the figure of the ship, in order to favour such a deception. The tide of ebb coming strong out of the harbour, the enemy's ship anchored; and I accordingly anchored astern of her at sunset: I was in hopes, that when the flood made again, she would have weighed, and have proceeded up the passage, that we might have done the same, without approaching her so near as to risk detection, and the consequent frustration of our object; but she continued to lie fast: and I was obliged either to relinquish the going close enough to the harbour to make my observations, or to alarm the coast by attacking her, or else to pass her silently, and thereby leave her in the channel of my retreat. I considered the occasion of my being detached from the squadron as an object of sufficient national importance to justify all risks, and accordingly weighed and passed her sufficiently near to observe, by the light of the moon, that she was a line-of-battle ship. As we proceeded, we saw two other ships at anchor, one of which was evidently a frigate. Not being satisfied that I should, from my then position, be able to discern the anchorage plainly when the day broke, I was obliged to go between those ships and the Toulinguet rocks, observing the precaution, in passing, to give all orders in a low tone of voice, that the enemy might not hear us speak English. They took no notice of us; and by daylight this morning I had attained a position from whence I could discern the usual anchorage of Brest sufficiently distinct to ascertain that there are no men of war in the road, (the basin is not discoverable from without the forts.) I observed the wreck of a large ship on Mingan rock. It now became necessary to make the best of my way out of the passage. Accordingly, I altered my course for that purpose, taking a direction to repass the line-of-battle ship. A corvette, which was steering out in a parallel direction to us, was the first who took the alarm at this change of movement. She brought-to, making signals which communicated the alarm to the other two ships; these both hoisted their topsail-yards immediately, and began getting under sail: my situation now became critical. I saw by the course the line-of-battle ship had taken to cut me off in my passage between her and the rocks, that I could not effectuate it; and there seemed to remain no alternative but to remove their alarm by a conduct that should bespeak ourselves unconcerned. Therefore repeating such of the signals as I could, I steered down directly within hail of this ship, which lay in my way between Basse-Buzec and the Trepieds. I could, by this time, perceive she was a disabled ship, with jury-masts, pumping from leaks, and that some of her upper-deck ports were without their guns. To avoid being questioned in any embarrassing way, I began the conversation in French with the captain, who was in the stern-gallery, accounting for my change of course by saying I observed his disabled state, and came down to him to learn if I could render any assistance. He answered, thanking me for the offer, saying he had men enough; which indeed I could plainly perceive, as they were crowded on the gunwale and quarter. Looking at this ship, I could not but form speculations, from her crippled state, that I should be able to preserve my position under her stern, so as to rake her repeatedly; thus beginning an action with such advantage as would be sufficient to ensure us a favourable issue: my guns were ready pointed; but I then reflected that it was worse than useless to fire, since I could not hope to secure the prize, and carry her off from the two other ships; and as the execution of the service I was sent upon might be rendered abortive by the unfavourable result of so unequal a contest as fighting all three together in a frigate, the utmost that I then could do would be to give her a most destructive raking fire, and sail away: this my men were ready and eager for; but I overruled the idea: considering the shocking carnage from our double-loaded guns enfilading a crowded ship, within half-pistol shot; and considering it unmanly, as well as treacherous, to make such wanton havoc while speaking in friendly terms, and proffering assistance. I believed that my country would readily relinquish a trifling degree of benefit to be purchased at the expense of humanity and of national character; and I hope that for these reasons I shall stand justified in not having made use of the accidental advantage in my power for the moment. We parted, after some conversation, with mutual compliments, the French captain telling me his ship's name was Le Caton; and I, in answer to his *quaere*, named mine as one of the Norway squadron, which it was not likely he would know by sight. The other ships, seeing that we were spoken by the Caton, discontinued the pursuit, and we passed the rocks unmolested. I am, &c.

W. SIDNEY SMITH

Captain Sir J. B. Warren

SMITH'S TREATMENT DURING HIS IMPRISONMENT

One of the motives assigned by the French directory for their harshness to Sir Sidney Smith and his secretary, Mr. Wright, was a charge contained in an act of accusation against them, signed Barras, of having made an incendiary attempt on the town and fort of Havre de Grace. On this accusation, Mr. Wright was subjected to a long and severe interrogation by the Juge de Paix de la Place Vendome. He was asked if their only intention was against the lugger that they attacked? If Sir Sidney never disguised himself? If they did not mean, clandestinely, to burn the arsenal and town? If Sir Sidney did not wish to corrupt a certain Frenchman? If their frigate had not attempted to burn French vessels afloat and building, by means of catamarans? If they had not landed rebels on the coasts of Britanny and Normandy? If they had not landed arms and ammunition? If Sir Sidney wrote his own French letters? Whether he did not know several royalist generals? And many other questions equally irrelevant and impertinent, as being put to a prisoner of war. All these were answered with spirit, judgment, and discrimination.

The incarceration was, as we have before related, very rigorous. The following document from the pen of Sir Sidney Smith, claiming the rights of a prisoner of war, is a fair specimen of his proficiency in the French language.

> *Le Commodore Anglais Sidney Smith, au Général*
> *Pichegru, Président du Conseil des Cinq-Cents.*

> *À la Tour du Temple, le 8 Juin, 1797.*

> *Citoyen Président,—Quand j'apprends, au fond de ma prison, que Pichegru est porté au fauteuil d'un des conseils de la nation, et Barbé-Marbois à celui de l'autre, je respire; parce que cet hommage rendu à la vertu, à la probité et aux talens, offrant la preuve que la majorité de vos collègues vous ressemble, offre en même temps l'espérance que la modération et l'humanité régneront en France, et rétabliront l'harmonie entre nos deux nations, qui sont faites pour s'entre-estimer, et qui ne sont pas plus ennemies au fond pour être rivales.*

> *Je me rappelle que la non-exécution du décret de mort rendu contre les prisonniers de guerre Anglais est due en partie à votre fermeté et à votre humanité: vous avez sauvé votre nation de cette tache de barbarie; il vous reste encore à effacer celle d'un manque de générosité dans un temps où on en fait profession.*

> *Je suis prisonnier de guerre: je n'ai rendu mes armes qu'après une résistance opiniâtre, que l'honneur et l'espérance de me tirer d'affaire me commandèrent. On a prétendu me chicaner sur la foiblesse de mon détachement, qui osa mesurer ses forces pendant trois quarts -d'heure contre celles qui nous en-*

touroient. On m'a incarcéré comme un criminel, et j'ai souffert toute la rigueur d'un emprisonnement solitaire depuis treize mois. J'ai réitéré mes réclamations au ministre de la marine, comme ayant été pris sur mer; mais il n'a pas daigné me répondre. J'ai envoyé on exposé de ma situation au directoire exécutif sans aucun fruit. Apres sept mois de détention, le ministre de la justice m'a envoyé un juge de paix, qui m'a interrogé sur une inculpation vague d'avoir fait quelque chose contre le droit des gens. J'auroîs pu me dispenser de répondre a des questions sur mon service de deux ans antérieur à ma capture. J'ai cru pourtant devoir détromper le gouvernement, qui paroissoit avoir été induit en erreur sur mon compte. Le juge de paix, évidemment convaincu qu'on avoit été trompé par des rapports exagérés, et frappé lui-même de l'absurdité de poursuivre un officier pour des faits ordinaires de guerre, me promit formellement, sinon ma liberté, au moins un adoucissement à la rigueur de ma détention ; mais six mois se sont écoulés depuis, et je n'ai plus entendu parler de lui : j'ai cru devoir attendre que le gouvernement prit d'autres renseignemens, s'il croyoit en avoir besoin ; et ce n'est qu'a l'ani-versaire de ma captivité que j'ai écrit de nouveau au directoire la réclamation dont une copie est ci-jointe. Je n'ai pas eu de réponse sur le fond de ma réclamation. Je dois pourtant dire que, sur la représentation que je fis de l'inconvenance qu'il y avoit d'assimiler un assassin à un prisonnier de guerre, on a transféré Poule dans une autre prison, vu mon refus d'admettre l'excuse qu'où me fit de son délit de lèse-nation, le double crime ne pouvant que me répugner davantage. Je dois aussi témoigner ma reconnaissance au ministre de la guerre, qui a eu l'humanité de me rendre une visite, et de m'adresser des paroles de consolation en me tranquillisant sur l'idée que je m'étois formée qu'on avoit encore des impressions défavorables à ma réputation.

L'accusation, mise en avant par le juge de paix, fut que j'étois ennemi de la république. Vous savez, général, que le mot d'ennemi a une signification purement technique entre militaires, sans le moindre caractère de haine. Vous admettrez ce principe sans difficulté ; et il en résulte que je ne dois pas être persécuté pour le mal que j'ai pu vous avoir fait, étant armé en guerre contre vous.

J'espère que le conseil daignera trouver bon que je ne m'adresse pas à lui avec le ton d'un suppliant. Accoutumé par mon éducation Anglaise à ne respecter le pouvoir que pour le bien qu'il fait, et à ne pas redouter le mal qu'il peut prétendre me faire, je crois devoir me borner à l'instruire de ma position : d'ailleurs, ce seroit faire injure au conseil que de solliciter sa justice et son humanité comme une grâce, en paroissant douter de son empressement à les déployer. Non !—malgré tout ce que *j'ai souffert, je n'ai nul doute sur la générosité Française ; je me plains seulement qu'elle n'ait pas son libre cours. Les portes de ma prison sont formées pour ceux ' qui, ayant été mes prisonniers en Angleterre, s'empresse-roient (je ne doute pas) à m'apporter, aujourd'hui que j'en ai besoin, à mon tour, les mêmes consolations que je leur ai offertes alors. Je crains que cet example de rigueur ne passe en usage entre nos deux nations par des représailles ; j'ai fait mon possible pour l'empêcher, afin que les petites passions ne viennent pas troubler les passions nobles qui doivent animer les militaires de tous les pays. J'ai le bonheur de savoir que j'ai réussi jusqu'ici; mais je crains de ne pas avoir le succès désiré jusqu'à la fin sans votre aide ; vous en jugerez par les pièces ci-jointes, que je prends la liberté de déposer sur votre bureau : vous y verrez qu'il y a plus de huit mois que l'échange des prisonniers est arrêté par le refus de me délivrer : ainsi, en vous rappelant mes malheurs, je vous rappelle ceux de dix mille Français. C'est votre influence que je demande plutôt qu'un acte en corps, à moins que vous ne veuillez décider la question de savoir si le ministre de la justice a le droit de mettre un étranger sous des lois qu'il ne connoît pas, et en même temps d'en violer tous les principes en prolongeant la durée du secret qui le prive de tout conseil et de moyens de défense. Au reste, je respecte trop le principe de la démarcation des pouvoirs pour ne pas reconnoître que, comme prisonnier de guerre, je suis entièrement à la disposition du pouvoir exécutif; mais il est sans doute trop occupé de grandes affaires pour penser à un individu.*

Je vous prie, citoyen président, d'être persuadé que je suis pénétré de respect pour les autorités, en vous offrant les hommages dus à la place distinguée que vous occupez; je vous prie d'être assuré de ma vénération pour l'auguste fonction de représentant du peuple Français, et d'accepter le témoignage de mon estime pour vous personnellement.

Votre prisonnier,

(Signé) W. Sidney Smith.

[Editor's Translation]

The English Commodore Sidney Smith, to
General Pichegru, President of the Council of Five Hundred

At the Temple Tower, June 8, 1797

Citizen President, — When I learned, from the depth of my prison, that Pichegru has been elected chair of one of the national councils and Barbe-Marbois of the other, I breathed more easily, because this recognition of virtue, honesty and talent, offering proof that most of your colleagues are like you, offers at the same time the hope that moderation and humanity will reign in France and re-establish harmony between our two nations, which were made to hold each other in high regard and are not, at bottom, enemies just because they are rivals.

I remember that the non-execution of the death sentence handed down against the English prisoners of war is due in part to your firmness and your humanity; you have saved your nation from the stain of barbarity. It only remains for you to expunge the stain of a lack of generosity in a time when it is spoken much of.

I am a prisoner of war; I only surrendered my weapons after stubborn resistance, imposed upon me by my honour and the hope of finding a way out. I was harassed because of the weakness of my detachment that dared to match forces for three quarters of an hour with those who surrounded us. I was imprisoned like a criminal and suffered all the hardships of solitary confinement for thirteen months. I repeated my complaints to the Minister of the Marine, since I was taken at sea, but he did not deign to reply. I sent a description of my situation to the executive director, but it was fruitless. After seven months of imprisonment, the Minister of Justice sent me a magistrate who interrogated me on a vague accusation of having done something against human rights. I could have refrained from answering questions about my service during the two years before my capture. But I thought I should enlighten the government, which seemed to have been led into error about me. The magistrate, apparently convinced that he had been deceived by exaggerated accounts, and himself struck by the absurdity of prosecuting an officer for ordinary acts of war, promised me formally if not my liberty, at least a softening of the severity of my imprisonment, but six months have gone by since then and I haven't heard another word about him. I thought I should wait until the government acquired other information, if it was considered necessary, and it was only on the anniversary of my captivity that I once more sent the Directoire my appeal, a copy of which is appended here. I have not had an answer to the basis of my appeal. Still, I must say that because of what I said about the impropriety of comparing a prisoner of war to an assassin, Poule was transferred to another prison, seeing that I refused to accept the excuse made to me for his crime of offence to the nation, a double crime which could only disgust me more. I must also state my gratitude to the Minister of War who was humane enough to visit me and to speak words of consolation, reassuring me about my conviction that people still had an unfavourable impression of my reputation.

The accusation, advanced by the magistrate, painted me an enemy of the Republic. You know, General, that the word enemy has a purely technical significance among military men, without the least tinge of hatred. It will not be difficult for you to accept this principle and consequently, I should not be persecuted for the harm I could have done you if I was armed and at war against you.

I hope that the Council will see fit to approve the fact that I do not address it with the tone of a supplicant. Accustomed as I am by my English education to respect power only for the good that it does, and not to fear the evil that it wishes to do me, I believe I should limit myself to informing the Council of my position. What is more, it would be an offence to beg for its justice and humanity as a favour, which seems to doubt its eagerness to grant them. No! In spite of everything I have suffered, I have no doubt about French generosity; I am only complaining about the fact that it is not running its course freely. The doors of my prison are formed for those who, having been my prisoners in England would hasten (I have no doubt) to bring me today, when I have need of them in my turn, the same consolations that I offered them then. I am afraid that this example of sternness pass into custom between our two nations in the form of reprisals; I have done all I could to prevent it, so that petty passions do not come to cloud the noble passions that should move the hearts of military men in all lands. I have the good fortune of knowing that I have succeeded up to now, but I fear that I will not have the desired success to the end without your help; you will judge from the documents attached to this letter which I take the liberty of placing on your desk. You will see there that more than eight months have passed since the exchange of prisoners was halted by the refusal to turn me over. Thus, in recalling my misfortunes to you, I remind you of the misfortunes of ten thousand Frenchmen. (It is your influence I am asking for, rather than a physical act, unless you do not wish to decide that question of knowing whether the Minister of Justice has the right to subject a foreigner to laws he does not know and at the same time to violate all their principles by prolonging the duration of the secrecy that deprives him of all advice or means of defending himself. As for the rest, I have too much respect for the principle of division of powers not to acknowledge that as a prisoner of war, I am entirely at the mercy of the executive power, but that it is doubtless too taken up with great affairs to think of an individual.

I entreat you, Citizen President, to be persuaded that I am full of respect for the authorities, offering you the homage due to the august position you hold. I beg you to be assured of my veneration for the august function of the representative of the French people and to accept the witness of my esteem for you personally.

Your prisoner,

(Signed) W. SIDNEY SMITH

Enclosure.

À la Tour du Temple, le 18 Avril, 1797.

Citoyens Directeurs,—Aujourd'hui il y a eu un an le sort d'un combat me jeta entre les mains d'un ennemi que je croyois alors aussi généreux qu'il prétendoit l'être. Apres les témoignages de considération dont me comblèrent mes vainqueurs, et la promesse qu'ils me rirent de me rendre mon epée selon l'usage, je ne m'at-tendois pas à être traduit de prison en prison comme un criminel, et emprisonné d'une manière plus rigoureuse que les condamnés mêmes : je ne m'attendois pas, sans doute, à être mis dans la même enceinte et sous le même régime du secret que les assassins Migelli et Poule. L'interrogatoire que j'ai subi doit avoir prouvé au directoire que je n'ai fait que ce qu'il ordonne tous le jours, louant ses officiers, comme de raison, pour leurs succès du même genre. D'après cette considération, j'espère que vous jugerez une année de détention être une peine suffisante pour un délit si commun que celui de bien faire son devoir; je vous prie en conséquence, citoyens directeurs, de vouloir bien donner des ordres pour lever le secret rigoureux sous lequel je suis renfermé, afin que, si ma captivité doit être prolongée encore, ma détention n'ait plus le caractère d'une peine afflictive et infamante.

Salut et respect,

(Signé) W. Sidney Smith.

Au moment même que j'écris, mes gardiens m'annoncent l'arrivée d'un courrier pour ouvrir les négociations pour la paix; je crois donc devoir me borner à vous soumettre pour ne pas mettre en avant des expressions de l'indignation que ressentoit mon gouvernement, lors du mauvais succès de l'application que fit Lord Malmes-bury en ma faveur, dans un tems où on se rapproche de nouveau.

Je serois bien coupable si je ne sacrifiois pas toute considération personnelle à l'intérêt général de l'humanité, qui va reprendre son empire sur tous les cœurs, au moins il faut l'espérer.

[Editor's Translation]

At the Temple Tower, April 18, 1797

Citizens Directors, — Today it is one year since chance threw me into the hands of an enemy whom, at the time, I considered to be as generous as he claimed to be. After the signs of consideration showered on me by my conquerors and the promise they made me to return my sword, as is the custom, I did not expect to be moved from prison to prison like a criminal or to be imprisoned more harshly than even those condemned to death. I surely did not expect to be placed in the same stronghold and under the same regimen of secrecy as the assassins Migelli and Poule. The interrogation I underwent should have proved to the Directoire that I did nothing but what they order every day, praising their officers, and rightly so, for their successes of the same kind. Keeping this in mind, I hope that you will find a year of imprisonment a sufficient penalty for a crime so common as doing one's duty well. As a result, Citizens Directors, I ask you to give orders to lift the rigourous secrecy under which I am imprisoned, so that, if my captivity is to be prolonged, this punishment of detention no longer bears the character of affliction and infamy.

Salutations and respect,

(Signed) W. SIDNEY SMITH

At the moment at which I write, my guards inform me of the arrival of a courier to open peace negotiations. Therefore I think I ought to refrain from emphasizing expressions of the indignation felt by my government at the failure of Lord Malmesbury's request in my favour at a time when we are once more coming to a rapprochement.

I would be very guilty if I did not set aside all personal considerations in the broader interest of humanity that will resume its hold over all hearts, or at least we must hope so.

Traduction d'une Lettre du tres-honorable Lord Malmesbury à Sir Sidney Smith.

Paris, 27 Octobre, 1796.

Mon chèr Monsieur,—Vous pouvez être assuré que j'entre bien sensiblement dans votre situation, et que je ne négligerai rien de ce qui pourra dépendre de moi, soit comme homme public ou homme privé, pour vous faire obtenir les adoucissemens toujours accordés aux officiers de votre grade, et auxquels vous avez tant de titres: les lettres ci-jointes vous offriront, j'espère, quelque consolation, et je peux ajouter que votre situation et vos services ne sont pas oubliés en Angleterre.

J'espère bientôt être à même de vous donner de meilleure information; au moins, aucune application envers ce gouvernement ne sera négligée de ma part.

Je suis, mon cher Monsieur, avec grande estime et considération, votre fidèle serviteur,

(Signé) Malmesbury.

Nota. Cette lettre n'a eu d'autre suite qu'un redoublement de rigueur : la consigne qui m'interdit d'échanger une parole avec qui que ce soit pendant ma triste promenade dans la cour de la prison existe encore aujourd'hui, et est rigidement exécutée. Non seulement Lord Malmesbury n'a pas pu obtenir la permission de me voir, maïs le commissaire de S. M. Britannique pour l'échange des prisonniers a été refusé de même, quoiqu'ayant des rapports plus directs avec moi comme prisonnier de guerre.

Salut et respect,

(Signed) W. Sidney Smith.

[Editor's Translation]

Translation of a letter from the Right Honorable Lord Malmesbury to Sir Sidney Smith.

Paris, October 27, 1796

Dear Sir, — Be assured that I feel your situation most deeply and that I will overlook nothing in my power, either as a public or a private man, to obtain for you the leniencies always granted to officers of your rank and to which you are so richly entitled: the enclosed letters will, I hope, provide you with some consolation, and I might add that your situation and your service have not been forgotten in England.

I hope that I will soon be able to give you better information. At least, no representations made to this government will be neglected on my part.

I am, dear sir, with great esteem and consideration, your faithful servant,

(Signed) MALMESBURY

Note: This letter had no effect but a redoubling of severity. The order that forbade me to exchange a single word with anyone during my mournful walks in the prison courtyard still stands today and is rigourously enforced. Not only did Lord Malmesbury fail to obtain permission to see me, but the commissioner of H.M. Britannica for the exchange of prisoners was refused in the same way, although being more directly concerned with me as a prisoner of war.

Salutations and respect,

(Signed) W. SIDNEY SMITH

The publication of these documents produced the following comments in the French public journals of the day.

The "Postilion de Palais" observes: "Commodore Sidney Smith, detained in the Temple, these thirteen months, a most rigorous and solitary prisoner, has just addressed a letter to General Pichegru, which has been published. We shall neither discuss the right of the persons violated, nor the motives of this violation."

"An English personage of distinction," says "Le Grondeur," of the 21st of June, 1797, "detained for these thirteen months in the tower of the Temple, first addressed himself to the directory, and then to the legislative body, through the intervention of Pichegru, in order to be exchanged.

"It appears that, hitherto, they have paid but little attention to his solicitations. He is reproached, they say, with the obstinate defence that he dared to make against the superior force that surrounded him last year, when he was taken in the very mouth of the Seine, between Havre and Harfleur. In England, he would have been punished for lack of bravery; in France, he is punished for being too brave."

"L'Europe Politique et Littéraire" remarks, that "Some papers have published the following letter from Commodore Smith, an English prisoner, detained under the most rigorous solitary confinement. It is the duty of 'L'Europe Politique' to denounce to the public opinion the crime of the violation of the rights of the people towards a brave officer, against whom, if we may judge by his letter, there can be no other reproach made than that of fighting courageously against enemies who know not how to honour courage.

"Are they the sovereign people, and a sovereign people well instructed in personal rights, whose minister of justice causes a prisoner to be interrogated by a justice of peace, (juge de paix,) who gravely asks him if 'he be an enemy to the republic?'

"Are they not a careless sovereign people who suffer, without complaint, ten thousand soldiers (sovereigns as well as themselves) to remain in captivity, because the minister of justice keeps in solitary confinement one single enemy who is not even a sovereign?"And much more, in the same biting style of reproach.

"The liberty of La Fayette has been demanded of the emperor. A peace is being negociated with England, yet, by one of those contradictions to which our country is too much familiarised, Commodore Smith is still imprisoned in the Temple. All the demands of justice have, hitherto, been in vain. It is a part of the laws of honour to soften the rigours of war. Among belligerent states, a reciprocity of advances ought to distinguish civilised from barbarous nations. Why, then, has the directory no regard for those laws which console humanity in the absence of peace? They talk incessantly of the dangers of reaction, but ought they not also to fear those of reprisals? Commodore Smith is useless to France, and the seamen that can be exchanged for him are very necessary to us. The government ought to think only of increasing the number of its defenders, but it only increases the number of its victims: Robespierre, in the drunkenness of his tyranny, had put without the pale of the law all English prisoners. Is it wise now to renew the atrocities of Robespierre? I know not if, with such measures, peace is sincerely desired, but I know well that this precious gift of heaven will not be found in the Tub of Regulus." Thus observes the "Quotidienne," alluding to the Carthaginians when they tortured the Roman general.

"L'Invariable," of the 28th of June, remarks, "There have just arrived at Saint Servan, from an English packet-boat, a great quantity of our prisoners, who have informed us that several ships are going to land others in the different French ports. These are happy omens of peace. Why, then, does the government here, under its very eyes, notwithstanding the loud expression of public opinion, still persevere in keeping in the Temple, Englishmen, that it holds not as common prisoners, but as hostages, of whose escape it is afraid?"

All these appeals to the public were useless; peace did not ensue, and the distinguished prisoner was not liberated. But Sir Sidney had his amusements in a correspondence with his friends, among whom is to be distinguished the late eminent physician, Sir Gilbert Blane. The doctor is eminently philosophical in his correspondence, and recommends his friend to read Sully, Vertot, Marmontel, to take salts, write his own life, and study chemistry—occupations enough to dispel ennui, or to procure it. It is well to have judicious friends.

We transcribe another letter of Sir Sidney's in the French language. It will explain itself.

À la Tour du Temple, 3 Octobre, 1797.

Monsieur,—Jusqu'ici j'ai reçu la visite d'un adjutant-général de tems en teins pour recevoir mes réclamations. J'ai été sensible à cette marque d'attention que me prouvoit que je n'étois pas entièrement délaissée par mes confrères les militaires, entre les mains de guichetiers du pouvoir civil, avec lesquels je ne croyois jamais avoir à faire comme prisonnier de guerre. Les visites de cet officier sont discontinuées, et il m'a fait savoir qu'il a cessé ses fonctions. Je prends la liberté en conséquence» monsieur, de vous prier de nommer un autre officier pour remplacer l'Adjudant-General Hocherot dans ce service auprès de moi. Vous devez sentir, monsieur, qu'il ne peut qu'être une grande satisfaction à un prisonnier, détenu depuis si long-temps dans la plus rigoureuse solitude, de voir entrer chez lui une figure humaine, et surtout un militaire muni d'autorité de recevoir et de faire droit, sur le champ, à ses réclamations. Si cette considération n'est pas de poids auprès de vous, vous admettrez, monsieur, que votre honneur national l'exige ; puisque ce fait de l'emprisonnement d'un officier de grade supérieur, pris par le sort d'un combat, appartient à l'histoire de votre nation soi-disant généreuse, et il vous importe qu'il n'y soit pas mis "plus de rigueur que celle qui seroit nécessaire pour s'assurer de la personne d'un prisonnier ; ce qui est sévèrement réprimé" par les loix fondamentales de l'état Le passé vous ne pouvez ni remédier, ni effacer de vos annales, pas plus que la Russie ni l'Autriche ne peuvent déchirer les pages de leur histoire qui regardent Kosciusko et La Fayette: mais l'avenir est entre vos mains, quant au sort de celui qui a l'honneur de se souscrire,

Monsieur,

Avec considération et respect,

Votre serviteur très humble,

(Signé) W. Sidney Smith.

P. S. Je désire que cette réclamation soit considérée comme ayant rapport à l'autre officier Anglais, M. John Westley Wright, prisonnier de guerre, détenu dans la même tour, mais séparé de moi. Il est également en droit d'attendre les égards d'usage entre nos nations respectives.

[Editor's Translation]

At the Temple Tower, October 3, 1797

Sir, up to now I have been visited by an adjutant general from time to time who received my appeals. I was grateful for this mark of attention that proved to me that I had not been entirely abandoned by my fellow military men into the hands of civilian clerks, with whom I had never thought to have business as a prisoner of war. The visits of this officer have been discontinued, and he has let me know that he has ended his functions. As a result, I take the liberty, sir, of asking you to name another officer to replace Adjutant General Hocherot in this service to me. You must understand, sir, that it can only be a great satisfaction for a prisoner, detained for so long in the strictest solitude, to see a human figure come in to him, and especially a soldier with the authority to receive his appeal and act on it immediately. If this idea carries no weight with you, you will admit, sir, that your national felicity demands it, since this fact of the imprisonment of an officer of high rank, taken by chance of combat, is part of the history of your reputedly generous nation, and it is your duty to see that it is not done with "more strictness than necessary to secure the person of the prisoner, which is severely condemned" by the fundamental law of the state. You can neither correct nor erase the past from your annals, no more than Russia or Austria can tear from their history the pages regarding Kosciusko and La Fayette, but the future is in your hands, as to the fate of him who has the honour of signing himself,

Sir, with consideration and respect,
Your very humble servant,
(Signed) W. SIDNEY SMITH

P.S. I wish this appeal to be considered as including the other English officer, Mr. John Wesley Wright, prisoner of war, held in the same tower but separately from me. He also has the right to expect the consideration customary between our two nations.

It had the effect of his being again considered a prisoner of war. As the probability of his exchange increased, he thus addressed the minister of the marine:

À la Tour du Temple, 5 Octobre, 1797.

Monsieur,—Je viens de recevoir à l'instant une lettre de Mons. Swinburne, Commissaire de S. M. Britannique pour l'échange des prisonniers de guerre, datée du 6 du mois passé. Comme cette lettre annonce la probabilité de mon prochain échange, je ne vous aurois pas donné la peine de lire mes dernières réclamations, si je l'avois reçue plutôt ; et je vous prie de les regarder comme non avenues.

Le préposé à la garde du Temple m'a fait part d'une lettre officielle (qui accompagnoit celle dont il est question ci-dessus) de la part de la commission des échanges, dans laquelle il lui est annoncé que je dépends désormais de votre ministère, ce qui me donne la plus grande satisfaction, et c'est avec confiance que je m'adresse à vous pour obtenir de l'adoucissement à la rigueur de ma détention ; me croyant en droit d'attendre de vous, monsieur, les égards d'usage entre nos nations respectives envers les officiers de mon grade prisonniers de guerre, et que je me suis toujours fait un plaisir de témoigner à tous ceux qui ont été entre mes mains.

Je prends la liberté de renouveller ma démande (d'après le changement annoncé) que mon domestique, John Phillips, soit réuni à moi. Il est à Françiade, sous la surveillance du Citoyen Collinet, économe de la maison de santé de cet endroit.

Si vous voulez avoir la bonté, monsieur, de m'envoyer un officier de votre part muni d'autorité de donner des ordres au concierge, il verroit lui-même la justice des réclamations qui j'ai à faire, et je suis sûr qu'il y feroit droit sur cette évidence.

Je suis, Monsieur,
Avec considération et respect,
Votre très humble serviteur,
W. Sidney Smith.
Prisonnier de Guerre Anglais.

A Mons. le Ministre de la Marine et des Colonies, à Paris.

[Editor's Translation]

At the Temple Tower, October 5, 1797

Sir, — I have just now received a letter from Mr. Swinburne, Commissioner of His Britannic Majesty for the exchange of prisoners of war, dated the 6th of last month. Since this letter announces the probability of my coming exchange, I would not have subjected you to the trouble of reading my last appeal if I had received it earlier and I request that you consider it as not having been received.

The captain of the Temple guard has told me about an official letter (accompanying the letter described above) from the Commission for Exchanges, in which he is informed that I am from now on the concern of your Ministry, which gives me the greatest satisfaction, and it is with confidence that I address you to obtain a softening of my rigourous detention, believing that I have the right to expect from you, sir, the consideration, customary between our respective nations, toward officers of my rank who are prisoners of war and which I was always pleased to extend to all those who fell into my hands.

I take the liberty of repeating my request (on grounds of the announced change) that my servant, John Phillips, be returned to me. He is at Frangiade, under the supervision of Citizen Collinet, steward of the hospital of that town.

If you would be so kind, sir, as to send me an officer with the authority to give orders to the warden, he would see for himself the justice of the appeals I make, and I am sure that he would act rightly on this evidence.

I am, sir,
With consideration and respect
Your very humble servant
W. SIDNEY SMITH
English prisoner of war

To the Minister of the Marine
and the Colonies, at Paris.

Sir Sidney next addressed the minister of the interior, remonstrating on the severity of still treating him as a condemned criminal, after having been placed on the cartel of the exchange. The following is his letter.

À la Tour du Temple, Paris, le 9 Octobre, 1797.

Monsieur,—Depuis qu'on m'a annoncé que de dépendois entièrement du ministère de la marine, j'ai conçu l'espoir que je ne serais plus détenu avec une rigueur inouïe pour des condamnés, bien plus pour un prisonnier de guerre. Ma santé en souffre journellement de plus en plus, et je vous prie instamment de prendre ma position en considération, et de m'accorder des adoucissemens d'usage pour un officier et un homme d'honneur, sous telle surveillance qu'on jugera à-propos en attendant l'échange. ———Je dois aussi vous faire part, monsieur, de la position du seul de mes officiers que n'est pas échangé. Mes capteurs, lors de mon transferrement du Havre à Rouen, eurent la bonté de me permettre de choisir, pour m'accompagner, un officier parmi le brave détachement qui partageoit le sort du combat. Je choisis naturellement celui pour lequel j'avois le plus d'estime, et avec lequel j'étois le plus intimement lié, M. John Westley Wright, midshipman, fesant les fonctions de secrétaire. Cette distinction lui a valu une détention de dixhuit mois au secret, séparé de moi, excepté un intervalle de deux mois à l'Abbaye qu'on permit notre réunion. Il est difficile de concevoir d'où est parti le trait de malice qui ait pu induire le gouvernement à donner un pareil ordre, et il ne peut y avoir de raison pour que cela subsiste encore dès que nous sommes mis sur le cartel de l'échange.

Agréez Tas sur an ce du respect
Et de la considération avec lesquels je suis,
Monsieur,
Votre très humble serviteur,
W. Sidney Smith.

A Monsieur le Ministre
de l'Intérieur, à Paris.

P. S. En attendant votre décision ultérieure sur l'objet de ma démande, je vous prie, monsieur, d'autoriser le préposé à la garde du Temple de me permettre de continuer l'usage des bains, que le ministre de l'intérieur m'avoit accordé.

[Editor's Translation]

At the Temple Tower
Paris, 9 October 1797

Sir, — Since being informed that I am entirely dependent on the Ministry of the Marine, I have formed the hope that I would no longer be detained with a severity unheard of for those condemned to death, not to mention a prisoner of war. My health is suffering from this more and more every day and I pray that you take my situation into account at once and grant me the clemency customary for an officer and a man of honour, under the surveillance that seems appropriate, while waiting for the exchange. I must also inform you, sir, of the position of the only one of my officers who has not been exchanged. When I was transferred from Havre to Rouen, my captors were kind enough to let me choose as a companion an officer from among the brave detachment that shared the fate of the engagement. Naturally, I chose the one I esteemed most highly and with whom I was most closely connected, Mr. John Wesley Wright, midshipman, who acted as my secretary. This distinction earned him a secret confinement of eighteen months, separated from me, except for an interval of two months at the Abbey, during which we were allowed to be reunited. It is difficult to imagine the source of the stroke of malice that could have made the government give such an order, and there can be no reason why it should persist, now that we have been placed on the exchange agreement.

Receive the assurance of the respect
and consideration with which I am,
Sir,
your very humble servant
W. SIDNEY SMITH

To the Minister of
the Interior, at Paris

P.S. In awaiting your final decision regarding my appeal, I beg you, Sir, to authorise the Master of the Temple guard to allow me to continue using the baths that the Minister of the Interior had granted me.

The only real satisfaction this application produced was fine words. Thus writes Talleyrand, then minister for foreign affairs:

I have, sir, forwarded, with all the eagerness that you could wish, the letter that you addressed to me some days ago, the object of which was to have some tidings of your brother. Be assured, sir, that I shall not display less zeal than my predecessor, in endeavouring to alleviate your situation, in procuring you this kind of facility, as well as everything else which may depend on me. The French know how to respect misfortune. The opportunity of relieving it will always be dear to them.

The minister of the interior thus answers his application:

I find it but just, sir, that you should continue the use of those baths that may be necessary to your health, and I authorise citizen Lesne to procure for you, as respects this, all that may be needful for you.

As to your other demands, I cannot comply with them, and it will be useless to occupy the executive directory with them, which has done all in its power for you, in granting you the favour of being considered as a prisoner of war, and of being permitted again to see your country, as soon as your government shall have fulfilled the conditions of your exchange.

PLEVILLE LOPELEY

That there was some interest of immense power operating against our officer must be apparent, and will be made the more apparent by the following letter addressed to General Smith from Mr. Dundas, and forwarded by the former to Sir Sidney.

Walmer Castle, Tuesday Morning.

Mr. Dundas presents his compliments to General Smith, and returns him the last correspondence from Sir Sidney, which he has perused. Mr. Dundas is sorry to observe that the *arrêté* of the directory there alluded to, by which Sir Sidney is *susceptible of exchange*, stipulates that this exchange shall be granted in return for four thousand French seamen a condition so evidently inadmissible, that Mr. Dundas cannot entertain an expectation that the prospect of Sir Sidney's return to England is thereby improved.

Was the demand of the French directory a mockery, or was it only considered as a fair equivalent for our officer? If the latter, how could a greater eulogium be invented?

In the course of his captivity, Sir Sidney wrote the following letter to his mother:

Abbaye Prison, Paris, April 28, 1796

My dear Mother, I hope the French gazettes, copied into the English papers, will have announced my captivity to you ere this, and consequently relieved your mind from the anxiety you must have been under, lest something worse had befallen me. I am well in health, and all the better for having nothing to do or to think of; the only pain I experience is the recollection of what those must suffer who interest themselves in my fate, till they know my safety; and this is now diminished by the indulgence that is granted me of writing this letter. It will be no small consolation to you to know, that humanity is as much the characteristic of the present rulers in France, as cruelty was that of those they have supplanted.

Robespierre's system ended with him, and it is no longer a crime to be kind to the unfortunate. Urbanity of manners is by no means extinguished in Paris; this we daily experience, as far as our confined situation allows.

Believe me, my dear mother,

Your affectionate and dutiful son,

W. SIDNEY SMITH

Mrs. Smith, Catherine Place, Bath.

P. S. May 6. A delay in the departure of my letter enables me to add, that I experience some relaxation of the strictness of confinement; wood fires make the air of Paris clear and good: white bread is granted me to-day.

As all Sir Sidney's own correspondence must be highly valuable to the admirers of his character, we quote the following letter, for which, and for many others, with numerous facts and anecdotes, we are indebted to the Naval Chronicle.

Our hero thus writes to his brother at Constantinople, dated Tigre, Acre Bay, 29th April, 1799.

Though I don't choose to trust anything of consequence to a chance conveyance, I will not fail to take that chance for meeting your impatience to know our situation, grappled as we are with Buonaparte and his army. The fire never ceases on either side, except when we are both too tired to go on. His whole attention and ammunition are devoted unto the increasing of the breach made in the north-east angle of the town, on which he has thirty pieces of cannon playing, while we take those batteries and his trenches in flank with the ships and gunboats, causing his fire to slacken occasionally by well-placed shots: he sprang the mine (in which Wright was wounded) on the 25th; when instantly ladders were placed, and a party mounted to the assault: they were beaten back; and the occasion calling for me to risk the Tigre in the shoal water to the south of the town, I did not hesitate to do it. Our fire, such as Buonaparte, I am sure, never saw before, cleared his trenches, and reduced all to silence in a very few minutes: but this sort of general discharge cannot be repeated except on such critical occasions, as our ammunition begins to run low. Send us powder and shot by all means, and conveyances, and at any price, or we shall soon be on a par with the enemy in that respect; at present we are superior to him in everything but numbers. I cannot better describe the position of the enemy for these forty days past, than by telling you we throw stones at each other when flints fail and ammunition runs short. Morris, poor fellow! is killed. Janverin, who has a ball through the muscle under the right arm, is almost well. Wright is better, and in a fair way: he has two balls through the upper part of the right arm. I have sent him in the Alliance to Béruti, where, by-the-bye, the inhabitants receive our people with acclamations, as having saved the country hitherto, bringing water and refreshments miles down to our boats, in troops of hundreds, (nay, I may almost say thousands,) now that they are undeceived as to the French rumour of our being in league with them against Jezzar: no great proof of their own popularity. I have written to the princes of Mount Lebanon: the Porte should mark to them its confidence in our co-operation.

Yours affectionately,

W. S. S.

On this occasion, it is understood, that as Sir Sidney Smith was going over the ship's side to land and hasten to the breach, the first lieutenant and master of the Tigre chose that unseasonable moment to *serve* him with a written protest against "placing his majesty's ship in danger of being lost;" to which the saviour of Turkey calmly replied, "Gentlemen His majesty's ships are built on purpose to be placed in danger of being lost whenever his majesty's service requires it, and of that the commanding officer is the best judge."

JOHN SPENCER SMYTHE, (OR SMITH,) ESQ

This gentleman's service in the foreign line commenced as private secretary under Robert Listen, Esq., ambassador to the Othman Porte, in 1793. He succeeded that able and virtuous statesman in 1795, as *charge d'affaires*, and was appointed secretary of legation on the 1st of May, 1798, receiving the rank of minister plenipotentiary a few days afterwards, i. e. on the 4th. In the December following, Mr. Smythe negociated the first treaty of alliance that ever existed between Great Britain and Turkey; and signed it, conjointly with Sir Sidney Smith, on the 5th of January. He obtained the freedom of the Black Sea for the British flag in October, 1799. On the Earl of Elgin's being nominated ambassador extraordinary to carry out* the ratification of the treaty of alliance (just mentioned,) Mr. S. received the further honorary appointment of secretary to the embassy extraordinary. Being eventually superseded by the Earl of Elgin, he returned home from the Levant, on leave of absence, in 1801-2.

The following extract from Tweddell's Remains is not misplaced here:

The destruction of Pera by fire, on the 13th of March, 1799. On arrival of the intelligence of that desolating calamity, which left Mr. Smythe in a state of destitution so entire as even to be without a change of raiment, the Levant Company, with its accustomed liberality, voted and despatched to him the sum of one thousand pounds on the instant; judging, no doubt, or rather feeling, that, in such a distressing emergency, the maxim, *bis dat qui cito dat* [Ed. He gives twice, who gives promptly], was recommended by every principle of justice and humanity. It was understood that government, also, after a deliberation of about four years, made some further indemnification for the loss sustained, judging, it is likely, that the royal bounty would be more highly appreciated, from not having been issued with mercantile haste, but after a dignified expenditure of consideration and care. No pecuniary retribution, however, can compensate to a literary man the loss of scientific MSS. and the records of laborious research: these Mr. Smythe, by the advantage of a long residence in the East, and extended travels in European and Asiatic Turkey, had largely accumulated with the taste of a cultivated mind, and the knowledge of an Oriental scholar; these all perished in the flames of Pera, and society has to lament the irreparable loss of collections particularly valuable in the department of geography.

This letter from Sir Sidney to his brother, written during the height of the siege and defence, will be found most interesting:

Tigre, Acre, May 14, 1799

My dear Brother, Events succeed each other so fast here, that it is impossible for those who are employed in creating them to record them. Suffice it therefore to say, that the enemy has been repulsed in eleven different attempts to assault this place: that this day they are not in possession of Acre, although they have a lodgment in the north-east angle of the north-east tower, one half of which is theirs, and the other ours; while we also have possession of the two new English ravelins that flank the approach to this lodgment, and have raised batteries *within* the breach, which is wide enough for fifty men abreast! the fire from which completely cleared it the last assault, and besides increased the number of the dead in either ditch. Our labour is excessive; many of us (among whom is our anxious and zealous friend Phèlypeaux) have died of fatigue. I am but half dead; but Buonaparte brings fresh troops to the assault two or three times in the night, and we are thus obliged to be always under arms. He has lost the flower of his army in these desperate attempts to storm, (as appears by the certificates of former services, which we find in their pockets,) and eight generals.

A report is brought us by an Arab, that Buonaparte is wounded in the thigh, but I know not if it is true. Scarce a day but I lose somebody: how I have escaped hitherto, I know not, fired at and marked as I am from *within*, as well as from *without*. Still, however, we keep the bull pinned, and compare our breach to a mousetrap, in which any mouse, or number of mice, that come, are sure to be caught. We have now been near two months constantly under fire, and firing; our ammunition is consequently nearly expended, and, unfortunately, as we cannot be in two places at once, and Jezzar tells me, if I go, the place is gone, we cannot take care of the coast lower down than Mount Carmel, so that the French not only receive supplies from Alexandria, by way of Jaffa, but they have taken Abdulha Aga, and the bombardiers from Constantinople, and are actually throwing those Turkish shells at us. I sent the Theseus after three French frigates yesterday, off Caesarea, being just able to spare her for an interval; she got sight of them, and chased them, but her disablement from a sad accident obliged her to haul off: sixty odd shells blew up at three explosions, under the fore part of the poop, killed and wounded thirty-two men, including those who jumped overboard and were drowned; and, alas! amongst the former, we have to lament Captain Miller, my zealous and indefatigable supporter to the north, a station I have been obliged to take during his absence; and I now cannot chase these frigates without leaving the town to its fate. *Why have I not some efficient frigates?* Hassan Bey's two frigates are not effective; or, if effective as to crews, have been obliged to disembark their men to defend the breach in their turn. The Chiftlik men, who were unsteady the first day (and it must be owned they joined me at a time that we were under a fire that was enough to astonish young soldiers) have now recovered their credit. You must see, by my writing, that I am almost blind; what with the dust from the shells, hot sun, and much writing to keep things square here. I have two emissaries from the Druses and Christians of Mount Lebanon, who are come in consequence of my message to them to that effect; and they promise me, that all I required of them should be done against the enemy, now they see how powerful we are to protect them. Wright is at Bairuti, better.

I really have not time to write to my uncle; and I therefore mean to send him my journal materials open through your channel. Adieu!

W. SIDNEY SMITH.

BUONAPARTE IN EGYPT

The following translation of the proclamation issued by Buonaparte, in the Arabic language, on his landing in Egypt, will prove that he stopped at no lengths to gain his purpose:

*Alexandria, Messidor 13, Year VIth of the
Republic, One and Indivisible, the — —of
the Month of Muharrem, the Year of the Hegira, 1213*

BUONAPARTE, MEMBER OF THE NATIONAL INSTITUTE,
COMMANDER-IN-CHIEF.

In the name of God, gracious and merciful. There is no God but God; he has no Son or associate in his kingdom.

The present moment, which is destined for the punishment of the Beys, has been long anxiously expected. The Beys, coming from the mountains of Georgia and Caucasus, have desolated this beautiful country, long insulted and treated with contempt the French nation, and oppressed her merchants in various ways. Buonaparte, the general of the French Republic, according to the principles of liberty, is now arrived; and the Almighty, the Lord of both worlds, has sealed the destruction of the Beys.

Inhabitants of Egypt! When the Beys tell you the French are come to destroy your religion, believe them not; it is an absolute falsehood. Answer those deceivers, that they are only come to rescue the rights of the poor from the hands of their tyrants; and that the French adore the Supreme Being, and honour the Prophet and his holy Koran.

All men are equal in the eyes of God; understanding, ingenuity, and science, alone make a difference between them: as the Beys, therefore, do not possess any of these qualities, they cannot be worthy to govern the country.

Yet are they the only possessors of extensive tracts of land, beautiful female slaves, excellent horses, magnificent palaces? Have they then received an exclusive privilege from the Almighty? If so, let them produce it. But the Supreme Being, who is just and merciful towards all mankind, wills that, in future, none of the inhabitants of Egypt shall be prevented from attaining to the first employments and the highest honours. The administration, which shall be conducted by persons of intelligence, talent, and foresight, will be productive of happiness and security. The tyranny and avarice of the Beys have laid waste Egypt, which was formerly so populous and well cultivated.

The French are true Mussulmans. Not long since they marched to Rome, and overthrew the Pope, who excited the Christians against the professors of the Mohammedan religion. Afterwards they directed their course to Malta, and drove out the unbelievers, who imagined they were appointed by God to make war on the Mussulmans. The French have, at all times, been the true and sincere friends of the Ottoman emperors^ and the enemies of their enemies. May the empire of the Sultan therefore be eternal; but may the Beys of Egypt, our opposers, whose insatiable avarice has continually excited disobedience and insubordination, be trodden in the dust, and annihilated.

Our friendship shall be extended to those of the inhabitants of Egypt who shall join us, as also to those who shall remain in their dwellings, and observe a strict neutrality; and when they have seen our conduct with their own eyes, hasten to submit to us; but the dreadful punishment of death awaits those who shall take up arms for the Beys, and against us. For them there shall be no deliverance, nor shall any trace of them remain.

Art. 1. All places which shall be three leagues distant from the route of the French army, shall send one of their principal inhabitants to the French general, to declare that they submit, and will hoist the French flag which is blue, white, and red.

Art. 2. Every village which shall oppose the French army shall be burned to the ground.

Art. 3. Every village which shall submit to the French shall hoist the French flag, and that of the Sublime Porte, their ally, whose duration be eternal.

Art. 4. The chiefs and principal persons of each town and village shall seal up the houses and effects of the Beys, and take care that not the smallest article shall be lost.

Art. 5. The Shekhs, Cadis, and Imams shall continue to exercise their respective functions, and put up their prayers and perform the exercise of religious worship in the mosques and houses of prayer. All the inhabitants of Egypt shall offer up thanks to the Supreme Being, and put up public prayers for the destruction of the Beys.

May the Supreme God make the glory of the Sultan of the Ottomans eternal, pour forth his wrath on the Mamelouks, and render glorious the destiny of the Egyptian nation.

GENERAL BUONAPARTE TO THE INHABITANTS OF
CAIRO, FEB. 20.

Wicked men have succeeded in leading part of you astray; and they have perished. God has directed me to be merciful to the people; I have been irritated against you on account of your insurrection. I have deprived you for two months of your divan; but I restore it to you this day. Your good conduct has effaced the stain of your rebellion. Scheriffs, Ulemas, preachers at the mosques, make it known to the people, that those who may declare themselves my enemies, shall have no refuge either in this world or in the next! Can there exist any man so blind as not to see that destiny directs all my operations? Can any one be so incredulous as to make it a question of doubt, that everything in this vast universe is submissive to the empire of Fate?

Inform the people, that since the creation of the world it has been written, that after having destroyed the enemies of Islamism, and laid their crosses prostrate, I should come from the extremity of the West to fulfil the task which has been imposed upon me. Show to the people's conviction, that in the holy book of the Koran, and in more than twenty passages of it, what happens has been foreseen, and what will happen has been equally unfolded. Let those, then, who are prevented only by the fear of our arms from cursing us, change their sentiments; for, in addressing prayers to Heaven against us, they solicit their own condemnation. Let the true believers pray for the success of our arms. I might demand of each of you the causes of the secret sentiments of your hearts; for I know all, even what you have not revealed to any one. But the day will come, in which all the world shall clearly see that I am conducted by a being of superior order, and that every human effort cannot prevail against me. Happy those who shall sincerely be the first to range themselves on my side!

BUONAPARTE.

The following is the document alluded to in the former part of our narrative, by which Buonaparte officially made Sir Sidney Smith mad:

ORIENTAL ARMY
Camp before Acre, 28 Germinal:
Year VII. of the Republic.

The Adjutant-General Boyer, (representing the General-
in-Chief of the Staff of the Army,) to the Squadron-
Chief) Lambert, Commandant at Khaiffa.

Citizen Commandant, Annexed I remit unto you an order of the General-in-Chief, which you will please to cause to be executed punctually, viz. "The commandant of the English squadron cruising before Acre, having had the barbarity to cause to be embarked on board a ship or vessel at Constantinople, French prisoners, under the pretext of sending them back to Toulon, but solely to get rid of them by the way. Besides, this man being a sort of madman, you will make known to our commandant of the coast, that my intention is, that no communication be holden with the same. In consequence, flags of truce shall be sent back before they arrive within musket-shot of the shore. I order equally, that conformably to the present dispositions of the above order, (arrêté,) in case an English flag should present itself, there be delivered thereunto a copy of the order, which is not to be acted upon, except relatively to the present commander on the station.

BUONAPARTE."

A copy in conformity,

BOYER,

Adjutant-General.

Certified true and conformable to the original,

F. LAMBERT.

SIR SIDNEY SMITH AND THE TREATY OF EL-ARISCH

Sir Sidney Smith's right to be a party to the treaty of El-Arisch has been often questioned, not only in parliament, but elsewhere. The subjoined credential places the question of his right at rest for ever.

GEORGIUS R.

Georgius Tertius Dei gratia Magnae Britanniae Francise et Hiberniae Rex, fidei defensor, Dux Brunsvicensis et Luneburgensis, Sacri Romani Imperil ArchiThesaurarius et princeps elector, &c. Omnibus et singulis ad quos praesentes hae literae pervenerint, Salutem. Cum in praesenti rerum publicarum statu tarn nobis quam augustissimo et invictissimo principi Sultano Selim, Turcici regni dominatori potentissimo imperil Orientis monarcho, e re communi visum sit, tractatum inire quo amicitia inter nos firmetur et augeatur, atque mutuae securitati melius consulatur et provideatur; cumque ad hoc opus peragendum et ad exoptatum exitum perducendum opera uti duxerimus per quam fidelium et delectorum nobis Gulielmi Sidney Smith, regii militaris ordinis de ense equitis, et in exercitu regio nostro navali praefecti, ac etiam Johannis Spencer Smith armigeri, Ministri Plenipotentiarii nostri, partes hoc tempore apud aulam supradicti augustissimi et invictissimi principis Sultani Selim, sustinentis virorum probatae nobis fidei ac in rebus gerendis industriae solertiae et prudentiae. Sciatis igitur quod nos eosdem vel eorum quemvis quern ad aulam supradicti invictissimi principis adesse contigerit constituimus fecimus et ordinavimus, ac per praesentes constituimus facimus et ordinamus nostros veros certos et indubitatos commissaries procurators et plenipotentiaries, vel commissarium procuratorem et plenipotentiarium. Dantes et concedentes iisdem conjunctim vel eorum cuivis separatim quern scilicet ad aulam supradicti invictissimi principis adesse contigerit, omnem et omnimodam facultatem potestatem et auctoritatem pro nobis et nostro nomine cum ministro ministrisve ex parte supradicti augustissimi et invictissimi Sultani Selim plena itidem potestate munito vel munitis congrediendi et colloquendi ac de praedicti tractatus conditionibus tractandi et conveniendi eaque omniaque ita conventa et conclusa fuerint pro nobis et nostro nomine signandi, ac eadem mutuo extrabendi recipiendique reliquaque omnia ad opus supradictum debited exequendum factu necessaria praestandi perficiendique tarn amplis modo et forma ac nosmet ipsi si interessemus facere et praestare possemus spondentes et in verbo regio nostro promittentes nos, quaecunqua vi praesentium concludi et signari contigerint, rata grata et accepta omni meliori modo habituros; neque passuros unquam ut in toto vel in parte a quopiam violentur, aut ut illis in contrarium eatur. In quorum omnium majorem fidem ac robur praesentibus manu nostra regia signatis, magnum nostrum Magnae Britanniae sigillum apponi fecimus. Dabantur in palatio nostro divi Jacobi tricesimo die mensis Septembris Anno Domini 1798, regnique nostri tricesimo octavo.

L. S. Pendentis.

[Editor's Translation]

GEORGE R.

George the Third, by the grace of God King of Great Britain, France and Ireland, Defender of the Faith, Duke of Brunswick-Luneburg, Arch Treasurer of the Holy Roman Empire and Prince Elector, etc. To each and every one who may read these presents, Greetings. Since in the present state of our nations it seems both to us and to the most august and invincible prince Sultan Selim, king of the Turkish kingdom and most powerful monarch of the Orient, in our common interest to enter into an agreement by which our friendship would be confirmed and increased and our mutual security might be better discussed and provided for, we have designated, for the purpose of carrying out this work and arriving at the desired result, the effort of our faithful and beloved subjects William Sidney Smith, knight of the Royal Military Order of the Sword and commander of a ship in our royal military, and John Spencer Smith, man at arms, our Ministers Plenipotentiary at the court of the above-mentioned most august and invincible prince Sultan Selim, sustaining and supporting men of proven loyalty to us and skilled, prudent and industrious in the management of affairs.

Therefore let it be known that, whichever of them happens to be at the court of the above-mentioned invincible prince, we create, make and name and by the present document create, make and name our true, certain and indubitable proxy, agent and plenipotentiary or proxies, agents or plenipotentiaries. Giving and granting them together or singly what is naturally required in order to enter the court of the above-mentioned most august and invincible Sultan Selim and provided with every power and every kind of ability, power, and authority to [speak] in our name to a minister or ministers of the above-mentioned Sultan Selim and provided with the same power of debating and discussing and managing the conditions of the above-mentioned agreement and signing for us and in our name all the things that are so agreed upon and settled, and to call for and receive all the remaining things necessary to accomplish and provision the above-mentioned work in sufficiently broad scope, and if we ourselves are interested to undertake and accomplish an action, to promise with our royal word that by whatever force the present agreement may be concluded and signed, ratified and accepted, we will maintain it in the best way, nor will we ever suffer it to be violated in part or in whole or to be gainsaid by anyone. In token and confirmation of these things signed by our royal hand, we have caused the Great Seal of our Great Britain to be affixed.

Given in our palace of Saint James on the thirtieth day of September in the year of Our Lord 1798 and of our reign the thirty-eighth.

THE END

The Midshipman Prince

By Tom Grundner

ISBN: 978-1-934757-00-0
272 Pages - 6" X 9" Paperback

The first book in the Sir Sidney Smith nautical adventure series

How do you keep a prince alive when the combined forces of three nations (and a smattering of privateers) want him dead? Worse, how do you do it when his life is in the hands of a 17 year old lieutenant, an alcoholic college professor, and a woman who has fired more naval guns than either of them?

From the Battle of the Capes, which sealed the fate of Yorktown, to the Battle of the Saints, which shaped the fate of the Caribbean, *The Midshipman Prince* will take you on a wild ride through 18th Century nautical history.

Based on the life of Admiral Sir Sidney Smith (1764 - 1840)

www.FireshipPress.com

HMS Diamond

By Tom Grundner

ISBN: 978-1-934757-01-7
236 Pages - 6" X 9" Paperback

The Sir Sidney Smith
nautical adventure series continues

Sidney Smith, now "Sir Sidney," is reunited with his friends, Lucas Walker and Susan Whitney.

After surviving the horrors of the destruction of Toulon, Sir Sidney is given a critical assignment. British gold shipments are going missing. Even worse, the ships are literally disappearing in plain sight of their escorts and the vessels around them. The mystery must be solved if Britain is going to maintain its lines of credit and continue to finance the war. But to do that Sir Sidney must unravel a web of intrigue that leads all the way to the Board of Admiralty.

Based on the life of
Admiral Sir Sidney Smith (1764 - 1840)

www.FireshipPress.com

Printed in the United States
126714LV00003B/31/P

9 781934 757109